T0323653

New Models for Managing
Longevity Risk

New Models for Managing Longevity Risk

Public-Private Partnerships

Edited by

Olivia S. Mitchell

OXFORD

UNIVERSITY PRESS

OXFORD
UNIVERSITY PRESS

Great Clarendon Street, Oxford, OX2 6DP,
United Kingdom

Oxford University Press is a department of the University of Oxford.
It furthers the University's objective of excellence in research, scholarship,
and education by publishing worldwide. Oxford is a registered trade mark of
Oxford University Press in the UK and in certain other countries

© Pension Research Council, The Wharton School, The University of Pennsylvania 2022

The moral rights of the authors have been asserted

Impression: 1

Published in the United States of America by Oxford University Press
198 Madison Avenue, New York, NY 10016, United States of America

British Library Cataloguing in Publication Data
Data available

Library of Congress Control Number: 2021944221

ISBN 978–0–19–285980–8

DOI: 10.1093/oso/9780192859808.001.0001

Printed and bound in Great Britain by Clays Ltd, Elcograf S.p.A.

Links to third party websites are provided by Oxford in good faith and
for information only. Oxford disclaims any responsibility for the materials
contained in any third party website referenced in this work.

Preface

Notwithstanding the terrible price the world has paid in the Coronavirus pandemic, the fact remains that longevity at older ages is likely to continue to rise in the medium and longer term. This volume explores how the private and public sectors can collaborate via public-private partnerships (PPPs) to develop new mechanisms to reduce older people's risk of outliving their assets in later life. As we show in this volume, PPPs typically involve shared government financing alongside private-sector partner expertise, management responsibility, and accountability. In addition to offering empirical evidence on examples where this is working well, our contributors provide case studies, discuss survey results, and examine a variety of different financial and insurance products to better meet the needs of the aging population. The volume will be informative to researchers, plan sponsors, students, and policymakers seeking to enhance retirement plan offerings.

In preparing this book, many people and institutions played key roles. Surya Kolluri was instrumental in identifying many of the experts who furnished invaluable insights in the chapters that follow. We are grateful to our Advisory Board and Members of the Pension Research Council for their intellectual and research support. Additional support was provided by the Pension Research Council, the Boettner Center for Pensions and Retirement Research, and the Ralph H. Blanchard Memorial Endowment at the Wharton School of the University of Pennsylvania. We also are pleased to continue our association with Oxford University Press, which publishes our series on global retirement security. The manuscript was expertly prepared by Natalie Gerich Brabson and Sarah Kate Sanders.

Our work at the Pension Research Council and the Boettner Center for Pensions and Retirement Security of the Wharton School of the University of Pennsylvania has focused on aspects of pensions and retirement wellbeing for almost 70 years. This volume contributes to our ongoing goal to generate useful research on and engage debate around policy for retirement security.

Olivia S. Mitchell
Executive Director, Pension Research Council
Director, Boettner Center for Pensions and Retirement Research
The Wharton School, University of Pennsylvania

Contents

Part III. Implications for the Financial Sector and Policymakers

List of Figures

List of Tables

Notes on Contributors

Arielle Burstein is a Senior Business Change Advisor on the behavioral health team at CareMore, where she is responsible for program management and development. Her specialties are in retail, health, and personal finance. Previously she was an Associate Director with the Milken Institute Center for the Future of Aging, and she also worked at the Massachusetts Institute of Technology's AgeLab, a multidisciplinary research program. Her BA in International Relations and Hispanic Studies is from Wheaton College.

Adelina Comas-Herrera is co-lead of Strengthening Responses to Dementia in Developing Countries, as well as an Assistant Professorial Research Fellow at the Care Policy and Evaluation Centre, at the London School of Economics and Political Science. Her main research interests include economic aspects of care, treatment, and support of people with dementia, and long-term care financing, in the UK and globally. She serves as a consultant for the Inter-American Development Bank's aging and long-term care program, and she was a member of the World Health Organization Guideline Development Group developing risk reduction guidelines for cognitive decline and dementia. She received her BA and MS in Economics at Universitat Pompeu Fabra.

Jason Davis is a Senior Associate of Innovative Finance at the Milken Institute where he helps execute Financial Innovations Labs, intensive one-day workshops that address economic and social challenges. His work encompasses research, stakeholder outreach, Lab execution, and the preparation of subsequent Lab reports. Previously, Jason worked in the media field, holding positions at a variety of organizations in New York and Los Angeles. He is a graduate of Syracuse University and holds an MBA from Loyola Marymount University.

William J. Dionne is the Executive Director of the Carter Burden Network. He also serves on the Governor's Task Force on Aging of New York State, and he was appointed to the Governor's Advisory Committee on Aging. Previously, he served on the Board of the Park Slope Geriatric Day Center, one of the first social model adult day programs in NYC, and was its Executive Director. He is a member of the Older Adults and HIV Statewide Advisory Group, and he was awarded the José R. Sanchez Community Leadership

Award by the Metropolitan Hospital Center Community Advisory Board for his leadership benefiting the East Harlem community.

Tim Driver founded Age Friendly Ventures, the parent organization of Age Friendly Advisor, Mature Caregivers, and RetirementJobs.com. He also serves as a Director at The Age Friendly Foundation. Previously he served as a Board Member and SVP at Salary.com; was a group director in Personal Finance and Strategic Businesses units at AOL; and held a senior consulting role at Accenture. He served as Employment Committee Co-Chair for Massachusetts Governor Baker's Council to Address Aging, and was recognized by PBS Next Avenue as an Influencer in Aging. He earned his BA from Macalester College and MBA from Georgetown University.

Maria D. Fitzpatrick is an Associate Professor in the Department of Policy and Management, Director of the Cornell Institute for Public Affairs, Associate Director of Data for Evidence-Based Policy at the Bronfenbrenner Center for Translational Research, and Research Associate at the National Bureau of Economic Research. She received her BA in Economics from the University of North Carolina at Chapel Hill, and her MA and PhD in Economics from the University of Virginia.

Jonathan Barry Forman was the Kenneth E. McAfee Centennial Chair in Law at the University of Oklahoma, where he taught courses on tax and pension law. Previously he served as Professor in Residence for the Internal Revenue Service Office of Chief Counsel, and he was a member of the Board of Trustees of the Oklahoma Public Employees Retirement System. He was also active in the American Bar Association, the American College of Employee Benefits Counsel, the American College of Tax Counsel, the Association of American Law Professors, and the National Academy of Social Insurance. He received his BA from Northwestern University, his MA in Psychology from University of Iowa, his MA in Economics from George Washington University, and his JD from University of Michigan.

Richard K. Fullmer is the founder of Nuova Longevità Research, an independent consultancy that specializes in retirement and pension research, where he works on longevity risk, plan design, and investment strategy. His interests include topics pertaining to longevity and sustainability risk, portfolio decumulation, tontine finance, and mortality-pooled investment design. He serves on the *Journal of Retirement* Advisory Board, and he received the Edward D. Baker III Journal Research Award from the Investments and Wealth Institute. He received his BA from Washington State University and MS from Boston University.

Dozene Guishard is the Director of Health and Wellness Initiatives at Carter Burden Network and Co-Principal Investigator to an Administration for

Community Living-funded Nutritional Innovation project. She also serves as the Board Chair of Alzheimer's Association of the Hudson Valley, a member of Metropolitan Hospital Center New York Health + Hospitals Community Advisory Board, an advisor on the One City Health Strategic Advisory Workgroup, and a director on The Steve Fund Board. Previously she served as Executive Director of Westchester County Department of Senior Programs and Services' Livable Communities project; Project Manager for the New York State Office for the Aging's Living Well Chronic Disease Self-Management Program; Director of New York City Department of Health and Mental Hygiene's 10 Tuberculosis Control clinics; administrator at State University of New York at Downstate Medical Center and Harlem Hospital Center; and as Senior Business Management Specialist at TIAA Institute. She received her Bachelor's degree in Social Gerontology from the State University of New York at Buffalo, her Master's in Gerontological Administration from The New School, and her Doctorate in Education from St. John Fisher College.

Amanda Henshon is Executive Director of The Age Friendly Foundation. Previously, Henshon worked in corporate Law at Ropes & Gray LLP. She has served as Trustee of the Wellesley Free Libraries, including Board Chair; and spearheaded the creation of the Wellesley Free Library Foundation. Henshon holds a JD from Harvard Law School, a Masters in Political Science from Yale University, and a BA from Amherst College.

Nancy A. Hodgson is the Anthony Buividas Term Chair in Gerontology, Associate Professor in the Department of Biobehavioral Health, and Program Director of the Hillman Scholars Program in Nursing Innovation, all at the University of Pennsylvania. Her area of inquiry is biobehavioral research methods for older adults with dementia. She also serves as chair of the Clinical Management of Patients in Community-based Settings Study Section in the Center for Scientific Review of NIH; Academic Research Representative on the Pennsylvania Long-Term Care Council; Fellow in the American Academy of Nursing; and on the Gerontological Society of America. She received her MSN and PhD in Nursing from the University of Pennsylvania.

Wenliang Hou is a senior research advisor at the Center for Retirement Research at Boston College, where he conducts research on retirement saving, pension plans, annuities, and long-term care insurance. Previously, he worked in retirement planning and insurance pricing at MassMutual Financial Group in Hong Kong, and AIA Group Limited in Shanghai. He is also a CFA charterholder, an active member of CFA Society Boston's Financial Literacy Initiative, and an actuary (Associate of the Society of Actuaries) specialized in quantitative finance and investment. He earned his MS in actuarial science from the University of Nebraska-Lincoln, and he is completing his PhD in Economics at Boston College.

John Kiff is Senior Financial Sector Expert at the International Monetary Fund where he collaborated on the semi-annual Global Financial Stability Report. His interests focus on FinTech issues, over-the-counter derivatives, and pension risk transfer markets. Previously, at the Bank of Canada, he managed the funding and investment of the government's foreign exchange reserves including running its interest rate and currency swap book. He received his Bachelor's in Commerce at Carleton University.

Christopher Mayer is the Paul Milstein Professor of Real Estate and Professor of Finance at Columbia Business School, where he Co-Directs the Paul Milstein Center for Real Estate. His research explores topics in real estate and financial markets including housing cycles, mortgage markets, debt securitization, and commercial real estate valuation. Mayer is also a NBER Research Associate; Director of the National Reverse Mortgage Lenders Association; a member of the Academic Advisory Boards for Standard and Poor's and the Housing Policy Center at the Urban Institute; and CEO of Longbridge Financial, LLC, an innovative reverse mortgage company focused on delivering responsible home equity products to older Americans to help finance retirement. Previously he served as Senior Vice Dean at Columbia Business School; he also worked at The Wharton School, the University of Michigan, Harvard Business School, and the Federal Reserve Bank of Boston. He earned a BS in Math and Economics from the University of Rochester with highest honors, and his PhD is in Economics from MIT.

Kathleen McGarry is a Professor and Vice Chair in the Department of Economics at UCLA and a Research Associate at the NBER. Previously she taught economics at Dartmouth College and served as a Senior Economist at the Whitehouse Council of Economic Advisers. Her research focuses on the economics of aging, particularly the role of public and private transfers in affecting the well-being of the elderly, and the functioning of insurance markets catering to the elderly population. She received her BS in mathematics and MA and PhD in Economics from Stony Brook University.

Olivia S. Mitchell is the International Foundation of Employee Benefit Plans Professor, and Professor of Insurance/Risk Management and Business Economics/Policy; Executive Director of the Pension Research Council; and Director of the Boettner Center on Pensions and Retirement Research; all at The Wharton School of the University of Pennsylvania. Concurrently Dr. Mitchell is a Research Associate at the NBER; Independent Director on the Allspring Funds Boards; Co-Investigator for the Health and Retirement Study at the University of Michigan; and Executive Board Member for the Michigan Retirement Research Center. She also serves on the Academic Advisory Council for the Consumer Finance Institute at the Philadelphia Federal Reserve; the Advisory Committee of the HEC Montreal Retirement and Savings Institute; and the UNSW Centre for Pensions and Superannuation. She has also served as Vice President of the American Economic Association. She earned her MS and PhD degrees in Economics from the University of Wisconsin-Madison, and her BA in Economics from Harvard University.

Stephanie Moulton is an associate professor in the John Glenn College of Public Affairs at The Ohio State University, a faculty affiliate of the Center for Financial Security at the University of Wisconsin, and a visiting scholar at the Philadelphia Federal Reserve Bank. Her research focuses on household finances and debt, including the role of public policy in mortgage and credit outcomes for vulnerable populations. She is also the principal investigator on a multi-year analysis of reverse mortgage borrowers, funded by the MacArthur Foundation, the US Department of Housing & Urban Development, and the Social Security Administration. Moulton was a postdoctoral honoree at the Weimer School of Advanced Studies in Real Estate and Land Economics. She received her PhD from Indiana University.

Alicia H. Munnell is the Peter F. Drucker Professor of Management Sciences at Boston College's Carroll School of Management where she also serves as the Director of the Center for Retirement Research at Boston College. Previously she served as a member of the President's Council of Economic Advisers and Assistant Secretary of the Treasury for Economic Policy; she also worked at the Federal Reserve Bank of Boston as Senior Vice President and Director of Research. She is a member of the Board of The Century Foundation, the NBER, the Pension Research Council Advisory Board, and the Pension Rights Center. She earned her BA from Wellesley College, her MA from Boston University, and her PhD from Harvard University.

Caroline Servat is an Associate Director at the Milken Institute Center for the Future of Aging. Her work focuses on research, developing collaborative partnerships, and analyzing best practices for aging policy at the local and regional levels. Recently, she launched a new initiative, Age-Forward 2030, which engages cross-sectoral policymaking to help cities prepare for an older, increasingly diverse, and economically stratified population by integrating population aging into strategies for economic growth, inclusion, and resiliency. Her research explores the importance of public-private partnership models for housing and healthcare in community, the promise of coordinated care delivery models, and the impact of longevity on local workforce policy. She studied political science and theater at Bates College and completed her master's degree in public policy at the University of Southern California.

Nora Super is Senior Director of the Milken Institute Center for the Future of Aging, where she oversees aging-related initiatives. Previously she served as the Chief of Program and Services at the National Association of Area Agencies on Aging; she was also Executive Director of the White House Conference on Aging; and she served at the US Department of Health and Human Services, AARP, and Kaiser Permanente. She was named an Honoree for Outstanding Service to Medicare Beneficiaries by the Medicare Rights Center. She received her BA from Tulane University and MPA from George Washington University.

Abigail N. Walters is a Senior Research Associate at the Center for Retirement Research at Boston College. Previously she was a research assistant at the Department of Sociology at Simmons College, where she analyzed FDA regulations and women's medical devices. She earned her Masters of Public Policy and BA in Economics and Political Science from Simmons College.

Douglas A. Wolf is Professor of Public Administration and International Affairs and the Gerald B. Cramer Professor of Aging Studies at Syracuse University. He is a demographer, policy analyst, and gerontological investigator whose research addresses the economic, demographic, and social aspects of aging and long-term care. Previously he served as an economist in the Office of Income Security of Health, Education and Welfare (now DHHS), at the Urban Institute culminating in a position as Director of its Population Studies Center, and as Research Scholar affiliated with the Population Program of the International Institute for Applied Systems Analysis in Laxenburg, Austria. He is also a Fellow of the Gerontological Society of America. He received his PhD in Public Policy Analysis from the University of Pennsylvania.

Chapter 1

Introduction: New Models for Managing Longevity Risk

Public-Private Partnerships

Olivia S. Mitchell

There are now half a million centenarians in the world, and their number is projected to grow eightfold by 2050 (Stepler 2016). Inevitably, longer human lifespans, especially at older ages, are reshaping how we must think about work, planning, saving, investing, insuring, and financing our livelihoods in retirement. This volume offers a perspective on how public-private partnerships (PPPs) can play an important role in enhancing retirement security.

Such partnerships generally involve a governmental organization collaborating with private sector firms to provide needed goods and services, in ways that neither party could likely achieve on its own. Typically, PPPs involve government financing, while the private sector partner provides expertise, management responsibility, and accountability.[1] This book captures perspectives from experts in the field to explore how governments and the private sector can be tapped to provide and enhance retirement security along several dimensions. In addition to empirical evidence, our contributors detail case studies, discuss survey results, and examine a variety of different financial and insurance products to better meet the needs of the aging population.

Several key themes emerge from the research reported in this volume, as follows:

(1) Longevity may be a difficult concept for many people to understand. Empirically, however, peoples' expectations about their chances of survival generally agree with data on the factors predictive of longer lifetimes. Nevertheless, people confront much uncertainty about how likely they are to become disabled in old age, which can threaten financial security if assets are required to pay for long-term care.

Olivia S. Mitchell, *Introduction: New Models for Managing Longevity Risk.*
In: *New Models for Managing Longevity Risk.* Edited by Olivia S. Mitchell, Oxford University Press.
© Pension Research Council (2022). DOI: 10.1093/oso/9780192859808.003.0001

(2) Working longer can enhance retirement security, partly because it protects older employees against social isolation and the negative consequences of isolation, including mental health issues. It also reduces the drawdown of peoples' savings, and it usually boosts the value of public and private pensions drawn at the later claiming age.

(3) Many older people would prefer to age in place rather than entering long-term care facilities. This can be facilitated through PPPs providing coordinated care, community-based services, and adequate housing for the older population. Nevertheless, the supply of long-term care has proven to be inadequate in many countries.

(4) Technological innovation as well as public-private cooperation for insurance can help. Nevertheless, the rising rate of dementia among older persons requires much greater policy attention from both the private and public sectors.

(5) Innovative financial products such as pooled annuities and tontines can help defined contribution pensions provide assured lifetime income, thus protecting against longevity risk. Additionally, PPPs can help pension funds transfer longevity risk to the capital markets, thus enlarging the risk pools.

(6) Inasmuch as many older persons have net equity in their homes, PPPs can help the elderly find new ways to tap into this source of wealth. Reverse mortgages are one useful tool, and another is property tax deferral until such time as the homeowner sells the house. Both arrangements can be provided under the auspices of PPPs.

Next we offer a brief overview of the chapters to come, representing the perspectives of practitioners, academics, financial market specialists, medical experts, and gerontologists, among others, on how PPPs can help the world better manage longevity risk.

Part I. Understanding Longevity Risk

Here we define longevity risk as the chance that someone will outlive his or her retirement resources, potentially to fall into old-age poverty. One reason people may be vulnerable to such risk is that they might not understand the chances that they will live to older ages. In such an eventuality, workers might underestimate how much they need to save for retirement, and retirees could overestimate how much they can spend from their savings. In such circumstances, peoples' expectations about longevity as well as disability-free longevity could lead to suboptimal behavior.

Fortunately, many longitudinal data sets have elicited peoples' subjective survival expectations including the widely used Health and Retirement Study (HRS), a nationally representative panel of Americans over the age of

50 followed until their deaths. In Chapter 2, Kathleen McGarry (2022) uses the HRS survey waves from 1992 to 2016 to explore whether older people accurately perceive their survival chances, and whether these change over time in ways that are consistent with changes in their known risk factors. Her earlier work showed that men tended to overestimate their chances of survival to older ages, whereas women were more likely to underestimate them. This new research finds that the subjective expectations correlate closely with actual mortality experience, as well as known risk factors. Moreover, peoples' expectations are updated over time when health status changes. Accordingly, it appears that, on average, people are aware of their longevity risk when planning for retirement.

Despite this positive news, in Chapter 3, Douglas A. Wolf (2022) notes that retirees still face considerable uncertainty about how much of their remaining life years could be spent disabled. This is important since the disabled may require various forms of what is likely to be very costly long-term care. His chapter focuses on what demographers call peoples' 'active life expectancy' (ALE), during which no disability is present, versus the period after which people transition to being disabled. He points out that this transition usually signals a reduction in remaining total life years, and assets may need to be drawn down more rapidly. Wolf also uses the HRS to document that the prevalence of disability rises from about six percent at age 65, to nearly 20 percent at age 84. He also reports that a disability-free 65-year-old can expect to live nearly 15 more years, on average, while someone disabled at that age has a much lower expected remaining lifetime of just nine years. Nevertheless, being disabled often entails large out-of-pocket expenses (e.g. for nursing home care) and accelerates asset depletion. Indeed, many people spend down their assets after they enter a nursing home, after which the government Medicaid program supports subsequent nursing home costs. In this sense, the system functions as a sort of PPP, where after private assets are exhausted, public funds help support end-of-life care.

Another way in which people can make better provision against old-age insecurity is by working longer. This is because delayed retirement has the beneficial effects of boosting saving, reducing asset depletion, raising retirement benefits, and reducing social isolation which can cause depression and health problems. In Chapter 4, Maria D. Fitzpatrick (2022) shows that early retirement is bad for older Americans' health, particular for men: male mortality increases with early retirement and, in particular, for those claiming social security at age 62. She also reviews the literature from other countries as well, where the results are somewhat less conclusive.

In Chapter 5, Tim Driver and Amanda Henshon (2022) explore the links between working longer, social engagement, and longevity. The research suggests that older workers' employment quadruples their social interaction, thus protecting them against the isolation factor for poor physical and mental health. Moreover, the authors point out that older workers are less costly than generally perceived, since their wages are not higher than those of younger workers, and their health insurance premiums can be lower, particularly when they are Medicare-eligible. And last, they discuss the common misconception that hiring more older workers has a negative impact on younger workers. This 'lump of labor' fallacy has been widely disproved in the developed world. Accordingly, the authors call for PPPs to encourage continued employment of older individuals to the extent that members of this group are interested in working longer.

Part II. Public-Private Partnerships to Help Fill the Gaps

In Chapter 6, Nancy A. Hodgson (2022) notes that most older adults would prefer to remain in their homes as they age. A century ago, home care by family members was the norm for the very elderly, but few relatives can provide such care today. This is particularly a concern for the 'oldest old,' or persons age 85+, who have increasingly tended to live alone until a health or safety issue sends them to institutionalized care. Moreover, poor housing conditions and limited financial resources are barriers to aging in place for many older adults. To encourage aging in place, Hodgson argues that PPPs can help provide safer built environments, more accessible housing, and better-coordinated care and services. She also provides several real-world examples of models that encourage and support keeping older adults in their homes, both in the US and in Europe. Finally, she identifies several 'age-tech' innovations making it easier for medical professionals and family members to monitor older persons' safety, provide meals and transportation, and manage their medication.

In Chapter 7, Dozene Guishard and William J. Dionne (2022) also discuss PPPs that have helped extend older peoples' ability to remain in the community rather than enter care facilities. The Carter Burden Network is a nonprofit organization partly funded by the Department for the Aging in New York City, and its mission is to reduce food insecurity and malnutrition, lower hospitalization, and reduce social isolation in the target population. This work extends a long history of collaboration between government and social programs and services embedded in the 1965 Older American Act (OAA). The authors argue that without PPPs in the aging area, elders' longevity would fall and the risk of disrupting aging services delivered by the community-based nonprofit sector would rise.

By 2030, one in five US residents will be over the age of 65, according to Nora Super, Arielle Burstein, Jason Davis, and Caroline Servat (2022) in Chapter 8. Their chapter also notes that 70 percent of them will require long-term care at some point in their lifetimes. Nevertheless, few Americans have saved enough to pay for the staggering costs of long-term care, and past efforts to implement reform at the national level have failed. Moreover, the number of private insurers offering long-term care insurance (LTCI) has plummeted from over 100 in 2002, to about a dozen today. For this reason, the authors conducted interviews with over 50 experts to glean useful and practical ideas for incremental solutions to the long-term care crisis. Among the solutions generated was the creation of tax incentives to ensure that LTCI becomes an integral part of the retirement financial planning conversation. The authors also note that increases in health savings account contribution limits and tax-advantaged withdrawal limits would better accommodate LTCI premiums, as would a new savings vehicle specifically created to encourage LTCI contributions. Another path might be to enhance program experimentation at the state level, exploring back-end 'catastrophic' coverage options in addition to variations on the front-end approach. There is also room for technological solutions, which could take off with seed funding.

Chapter 9 by Adelina Comas-Herrera (2022) reviews an extensive body of work on policy responses to the growing costs of dementia. She notes that there are many different stakeholders in the dementia arena, in addition to the elderly; they include, among others, medical and nursing home establishments and their employees, the financial and insurance sectors, family members and caregivers, economists concerned with the cost of dementia, and those concerned with retirement insecurity. As a result, policymakers in most developed nations are beginning to develop models to estimate the fiscal cost of dementia in their aging economies. She concludes that dementia care costs will be high, yet she worries that policymakers have long favored 'hopeful' policies in relation to dementia, such as spending for Alzheimer's 'cures,' rather than tackling health and long-term care capacity shortfalls.

Part III. Implications for the Financial Sector and Policymakers

In Chapter 10, Richard K. Fullmer and Jonathan Barry Forman (2022) describe two new longevity assurance products and explain how these could be integrated into state-sponsored defined contribution pensions. Specifically, these would provide assured lifetime income to retirees, though benefit payments would not be insured or guaranteed. These products can pay retirees more than mutual funds since investors who survive each year receive not only investment returns but also survival credits. The authors describe both pooled annuities and tontines, both of which they argue can help participants in state-sponsored defined contribution pensions who want lifetime income. Moreover, these vehicles could also be used in emerging economies which lack a robust life insurance sector.

Delving deeper into the markets for longevity risk, in Chapter 11, John Kiff (2022) notes that these are often driven by defined benefit (DB) pension plans seeking to purchase reinsurance, and in turn, the reinsurers seeking to transfer annuity-related risks to other reinsurers. One explanation for the growth in such markets is that strict new pension rules have mandated disclosure and additional protections. Cumulative pension risk transfer is only about $550 billion in the three countries with the largest DB pension sectors, versus about $16 trillion of DB-related obligations. The reinsurer capacity for longevity risk transfer could be enlarged if the longevity risk they assume could be distributed to capital markets. One step in that direction would be to develop an agreement between market participants about which mortality models they can use to create and price longevity-linked deals. Additionally, governments could provide the much-needed granular longevity and demographic data required to estimate the models.

A different sort of PPP is envisioned in Chapter 12 by Alicia H. Munnell, Wenliang Hou, and Abigail N. Walters (2022), who evaluate ways to help older households more readily tap into their home equity. Specifically, they propose that homeowners age 65+ be permitted to defer paying their state property taxes until they sell their homes, at which time the state would recoup both the principal and interest on the loan. Although property tax deferral programs would be self-financing in the long term, the authors point out that the program would require start-up money from governments and/or the private sector at the outset, since the loans are not repaid until the homeowner passes away.

An alternative way to tap one's home equity is to take out a reverse mortgage, explain Christopher Mayer and Stephanie Moulton (2022) in Chapter 13. After examining the size and growth of equity release programs in the UK and North America, the authors offer several explanations for why few Americans tend to borrow on their homes using these instruments (far higher percentages of the elderly use reverse mortgages in the UK and Canada). They conclude that institutional barriers in the US have discouraged brand name companies from entering the market, thus limiting the distribution of reverse mortgages here. According to the authors, additional PPPs could help dismantle some of these barriers.

Conclusions

Despite the global tragedy of illness and death wreaked by the COVID-19 virus, the world must still prepare for the long-term extension of the human lifespan. The average baby born today has a one in three chance of living to age 100, so we must prepare for 100-year—or longer—lives. Yet it appears that we cannot finance such long lifespans simply from either the public purse or the private purse. Rather, the two sources of financing need to be combined. It is therefore imperative for plan sponsors, insurers, financial analysts, and policymakers to plan ahead and design new PPPs to manage longevity risk in our aging economy.

This volume shows that peoples' expectations about their chances of survival generally agree with data on the factors predictive of longer life-times, yet people also confront much uncertainty about how likely they are to become disabled in old age. One way to enhance retirement security is to work longer. Another way is to help the elderly age in place, facilitated by PPPs providing coordinated care, community-based services, and adequate housing. Technological innovation will also be useful, as are pooled annuities and tontines protecting against longevity risk. Additionally, PPPs can help pension funds transfer longevity risk to the capital markets, thus enlarging risk pools, while reverse mortgages can assist older homeowners tap their home equity. Nevertheless, the rising rate of dementia at older ages is sure to require much greater policy attention and efforts expended by both the private and public sectors.

Note

1. For a range of international examples, see World Bank Group (2016).

References

Comas-Herrera, A. (2022). 'Building on Hope or Tackling Fear? Policy Responses to the Growing Costs of Alzheimer's Disease and Other Dementias.' In O.S. Mitchell, ed., *New Models for Managing Longevity Risk: Public/Private Partnerships.* Oxford, UK: Oxford University Press, pp. 150–167.

Driver, T. and A. Henshon (2022). 'Working Longer Solves (Almost) Everything: The Correlation Between Employment, Social Engagement, and Longevity.' In O.S. Mitchell, ed., *New Models for Managing Longevity Risk: Public/Private Partnerships.* Oxford, UK: Oxford University Press, pp. 70–88.

Fitzpatrick, M. (2022). 'Does Working Longer Enhance Old Age?' In O.S. Mitchell, ed., *New Models for Managing Longevity Risk: Public/Private Partnerships.* Oxford, UK: Oxford University Press, pp. 57–69.

Fullmer, R.K. and J.B. Forman (2022). 'State-sponsored Pensions for Private Sector Workers: The Case for Pooled Annuities and Tontines.' In O.S. Mitchell, ed., *New Models for Managing Longevity Risk: Public/Private Partnerships.* Oxford, UK: Oxford University Press, pp. 171–206.

Guishard, D. and W.J. Dionne (2022). 'Public/Private Partnerships Extend Community-based Organization's Longevity.' In O.S. Mitchell, ed., *New Models for Managing Longevity Risk: Public/Private Partnerships.* Oxford, UK: Oxford University Press, pp. 105–21.

Hodgson, N. (2022). 'Aging-in-Place: The Role of Public/Private Partnerships.' In O.S. Mitchell, ed., *New Models for Managing Longevity Risk: Public/Private Partnerships.* Oxford, UK: Oxford University Press, pp. 91–104.

Kiff, J. (2022). 'New Financial Instruments for Managing Longevity Risk.' In O.S. Mitchell, ed., *New Models for Managing Longevity Risk: Public/Private Partnerships.* Oxford, UK: Oxford University Press, pp. 207–30.

Mayer, C. and S. Moulton (2022). 'The Market for Reverse Mortgages Among Older Americans.' In O.S. Mitchell, ed., *New Models for Managing Longevity Risk: Public/Private Partnerships.* Oxford, UK: Oxford University Press, pp. 258–300.

McGarry, K. (2022). 'Perceptions of Mortality: Individual Assessments of Longevity Risk.' In O.S. Mitchell, ed., *New Models for Managing Longevity Risk: Public/Private Partnerships.* Oxford, UK: Oxford University Press, pp. 11–33.

Munnell, A.H., W. Hou, and A.N. Walters (2022). 'Property Tax Deferral: Can a Public/Private Partnership Help Provide Lifetime Income?' In O.S. Mitchell, ed., *New Models for Managing Longevity Risk: Public/Private Partnerships.* Oxford, UK: Oxford University Press, pp. 231–57.

Stepler, R. (2016). 'World's Centenarian Population Projected to Grow Eightfold by 2050,' FactTank.com. https://www.pewresearch.org/fact-tank/2016/04/21/worlds-centenarian-population-projected-to-grow-eightfold-by-2050/

Super, N., A. Burstein, J. Davis, and C. Servat (2022). 'Innovative Strategies to Finance and Deliver Long-term Care.' In O.S. Mitchell, ed., *New Models for Managing Longevity Risk: Public/Private Partnerships.* Oxford, UK: Oxford University Press, pp. 122–49.

Wolf, D.A. (2022). 'Disability-Free Life Trends at Older Ages: Implications for Longevity Risk Management.' In O.S. Mitchell, ed., *New Models for Managing Longevity Risk: Public/Private Partnerships.* Oxford, UK: Oxford University Press, pp. 34–56.

World Bank Group (2016). 'About Public-Private Partnerships,' Public-Private Partnership Legal Resource Center. https://ppp.worldbank.org/public-private-partnership/about-public-private-partnerships

Part I
Understanding Longevity Risk

Understanding Longevity Risk

Chapter 2

Perceptions of Mortality

Individual Assessment of Longevity Risk

Kathleen McGarry

A financially successful retirement depends, in large part, on how people manage their longevity risk. Individuals need to save during their working lives to cover expenses in retirement, and then spend down those savings over the remainder of their lives to finance their consumption. This is the behavior predicted by the standard life cycle model in economics. The longer an individual expects to live, the longer he or she must work and/or save to finance consumption in retirement. Underestimating one's longevity could lead one to consume assets 'too quickly,' exhausting resources while one is still very much alive. In contrast, overestimating life expectancy would lead to a loss of utility, as savings would, in some sense, be wasted by not being consumed.[1]

The appeal of financial instruments such as life insurance and annuities also depends on peoples' estimates of their longevity. For instance, annuities are more valuable to those with longer life expectancies, while those anticipating shorter lifespans would find life insurance more appealing, along with estate planning. Despite the centrality of individuals' expectations regarding life expectancy, we know little about how these expectations are formed initially or how they evolve as an individual ages. Though a relatively recent strand of the economics literature has begun to explore subjective probabilities, much of the focus to date has been on the statistical properties of these distributions, and there is a great deal more to learn.

This chapter examines the evolution and validity of subjective survival probabilities, specifically the probability that an individual anticipates living to a target age. I examine the correlates of these reported probabilities when initially measured, how they change over time, and in particular, how they change with major life course events like the onset of a medical condition or the death of a close relative. Finally, I explore briefly their validity with respect to actual survival to that age.

Kathleen McGarry, *Perceptions of Mortality*. In: *New Models for Managing Longevity Risk*.
Edited by Olivia S. Mitchell, Oxford University Press.
© Pension Research Council (2022). DOI: 10.1093/oso/9780192859808.003.0002

As was true in past work, we confirm that subjective expectations of survival vary with known risk factors such as smoking status, sex, and health. I also find strong evidence that measures of individual expectations contain important information—information that goes beyond that gleaned from life tables, and thus has the potential to help researchers better understand individual financial decisions. Furthermore, individuals appear to incorporate new information regarding their health status as it becomes available; the diagnosis of a medical condition significantly affects one's projection of survival probabilities.

This chapter is organized as follows. First, I discuss the recent literature most relevant to this study, particularly drawing on research that uses the survey data and subjective probability question employed here. Next, I discuss the data in more detail, followed by a focus on the subjective probability measures themselves, particularly their validity and evolution over time. A final section concludes and provides some discussion of how these expectations might be informative with regard to financial outcomes.

Prior Research

Subjective probabilities figure prominently in economic models of behavior, and much research examining the validity and usefulness of subjective probabilities has focused on survival probabilities.[2] These studies have shown that subjective survival probabilities are, on average, close to actual survival probabilities, though there is substantial variation among groups. For example, men seem to overestimate their survival probabilities on average, while women underestimate them (Hurd and McGarry 1995, 2002). Similarly, subjective survival probabilities vary with known risk factors such as smoking status and schooling level, and they are also predictive of actual outcomes. For instance, Bassett and Lumsdaine (2001) examined subjective probability reports for a number of outcomes and concluded that these subjective measures varied with observable characteristics in expected ways (e.g. married women reported lower probabilities of working at later ages than did single women). The survival probabilities examined here and elsewhere have been used to study decision-making in several contexts including social security claiming, saving behavior, and retirement (Hurd et al. 2004; Bloom et al. 2006).

Despite these successes, there are reasons to question how useful such probabilities are in economic models. One of the most notable issues is the propensity of individuals to provide 'focal responses,' particularly probabilities of zero, one, or 0.50, since the actual probabilities for the chance of surviving to a given age cannot truly take a value of zero or 100 percent. Therefore, such reports can be problematic when included in economic models. For instance, a reported value of 50 percent could be the individual's true belief, or instead it could be a value close to 50 percent but rounded to a focal number. Alternatively, 50 percent could indicate a substantial amount of uncertainty, or even an unwillingness to think about the issue. Bruine de Bruin et al. (2000) examined what they termed the '50 blip' in probability questions, noting that individuals use wording such as a 50–50 chance, or 50 percent probability, to indicate that they were uncertain about the outcome, rather than intending to imply a specific probability. Additionally, that paper suggested that people might respond with '50 percent' to avoid thinking about 'negative and uncontrollable events' (p.127). Clearly, asking respondents about their chances of survival prompts them to consider their own mortality risk, for many a negative (and unpleasant) thought. Nevertheless, by contrast, Bissonnette et al. (2017: e294) concluded that there was 'little support for the idea that 50 percent-point answers are used to avoid answering questions.'

Despite the obvious statistical issues regarding such misreporting, most evidence indicates that these self-assessment survival reports contain some useful information that cannot be obtained elsewhere, and that they ought not to be completely dismissed. An individual reporting a 100 percent chance of surviving to age 75 likely intends to convey that he or she feels healthy and very much expects to live to that age and beyond. While analysts would be more comfortable were he or she to report a probability of, say, 90 percent, the person's report is nonetheless likely to be useful in understanding retirement and savings decisions. Furthermore, as van Santen et al. (2012) noted, excluding respondents who give focal responses not only leads to a smaller sample but also one that is likely to be biased. In particular, a researcher who excludes focal responses is likely to omit proportionately less-educated individuals.

For the analyst who needs to incorporate probabilities with focal responses into models, Kleinjans and van Soest (2014) have proposed a method of adjusting these responses. Their method, and similar techniques, have been successfully employed elsewhere, particularly with respect to survival probabilities (Hurd et al. 2004; Bloom et al. 2006; Bissonnette et al. 2017.

Another issue in the realm of reporting error relates to the magnitudes of the probability of related events. When comparing probabilities of two (or more) scenarios, such as the probabilities of working to ages 62 and 65, or the probabilities of living to ages 75 and 85, a small fraction of respondents in the HRS report a larger probability for the *latter* scenarios, for example a greater probability of living to age 85 than to age 75. This behavior clearly indicates a misunderstanding of probabilities, and such results are typically impossible to employ in economic models of behavior or, in the case of survival probabilities, used in deriving survival curves.

The usefulness of the information contained in an individual's subjective expectation report will also depend on how well self-reports compare with known population averages or actuarial predictions. In the case of survival probabilities, this standard of comparison would be with survival probabilities obtained from life tables. It may be that the individual's own report is more informative or contains information supplemental to life tables. For instance, Elder (2013) found that life table probabilities had far greater explanatory power in models of survival than did subjective expectations, in a subsample of respondents for whom mortality status was known. Nevertheless, his results also showed that the subjective expectations were positively and significantly linked to surviving to the target age, even when controlling for the life table probability. This result strongly suggests that there is important information contained in subjective survival measures. Moreover, when analyzing behavior, what an individual believes with regard to various measures is crucial, regardless of actuarial probabilities.

Data

The data set used in this analysis comes from the Health and Retirement Study (HRS), a panel survey of the US population age 51 or older.[3] These surveys collect extremely detailed information on respondents' health, financial resources, family, and personal characteristics; and they also ask respondents about the likelihood of various events, including the probability of surviving to a particular age, working to a given age, entering a nursing home, and leaving an inheritance. The database has also been linked with administrative records, most notably the National Death Index, Social Security Administration data, and Medicare records, providing researchers with the opportunity to merge data not typically associated with nationally representative surveys. The initial cohort of sample members was first interviewed in 1992 and consisted of those born between 1931 and 1941 and their spouses or partners. Additional cohorts of both older and younger individuals were added in 1998 to create a sample that, when appropriately weighted, is approximately nationally representative of the population over the age of 50. New cohorts have since been added every six years to fill in the lower end of the relevant age distribution. HRS respondents are interviewed biennially until their deaths (or until they attrite from the survey for other reasons),[4] with the most recent available data collected in 2016.[5]

The exceptionally long panel available for the original cohort, stretching from 1992 to 2016, means that respondents in the original HRS cohort who have not died or attrited from the survey have been interviewed 13 times over 24 years. It is thus possible to observe these individuals throughout much of their remaining lives, providing a near-complete picture of the various shocks people have faced as they have aged. Of particular note is that, by 2016, the youngest members of this cohort had (or could have) attained age 75. This is important because the primary subjective survival probability question, delineated below, asks respondents to report their chances of living to age 75. I can thus assess the predictive power of individual reports of survival probabilities for nearly the entire sample. To my knowledge, this is the first research study to do just that.

The question of interest (and its preface) in the initial HRS survey wave is:

> Next I would like to ask you about the chances that various events will happen in the future. Using any number from zero to 10, where zero equals absolutely no chance and 10 equals absolutely certain . . . What do you think are the chances that you will live to be 75 or more?

Later waves broadened the scale to range from zero to 100. For consistency, the responses in this first wave are multiplied by 10 in this analysis.[6]

There are similar questions about living to age 85 (in waves 1–4) and about the probability of living approximately 10 more years. Here I limit my analysis to the age 75 question, because it is the only one that is consistent across waves and that also allows me to observe the true outcome for the original respondents.

The analysis focuses on individuals in the initial HRS cohort; I exclude persons born after 1941 and who were thus too young to provide measures of mortality up to age 75. I also exclude proxy respondents because they were not asked the subjective probability questions. This leaves me with an analysis sample of 8,529 individuals.[7] Note that, over time, as individuals died or were lost to follow-up, the number of respondent interviews in each wave declines. In addition, because the primary variable in the analysis, the subjective probability of surviving to age 75, was not asked of respondents over the age of 65 for most of the survey (in all waves other than the first), the number of responses regarding survival probabilities declines as respondents 'aged out' of the question. Importantly, however, those individuals continue to contribute information regarding their longevity throughout the 13 waves of data, regardless of age, and thus they provide the important information regarding the accuracy of subjective expectations.

Descriptive statistics for a number of economic and demographic characteristics in the HRS analysis sample are reported in Table 2.1. Here I show the means and standard errors for the entire sample in the first two columns, and then I repeat these statistics separately for those respondents who survived to age 75 and those who did not. The values for the variables listed on the left hand side of the table are measured as of the first observation.

TABLE 2.1 Summary statistics (weighted)

	ALL (n = 8,529*)		Decedent (n = 2,210)		Survivor (n = 5,070)	
	Mean	SE	Mean	SE	Mean	SE
Demographic characteristics:						
Prob live to age 75	64.42***	0.318	56.45	0.691	67.29	0.389
Prob live to age 85	42.52***	0.347	44.88	0.440	35.97	0.701
Age	56.26***	0.031	56.15	0.062	56.47	0.040
Male	0.47***	0.005	0.57	0.100	0.43	0.007
Married 0/1	0.77***	0.004	0.70	0.009	0.79	0.005
Years of schooling	12.35***	0.031	11.73	0.064	12.59	0.039
Number of children	3.22	0.021	3.30	0.045	3.26	0.027
Nonwhite/Non-Hispanic 0/1	0.13***	0.003	0.17	0.008	0.12	0.004
Hispanic 0/1	0.06	0.002	0.06	0.005	0.06	0.003
Health status/ conditions						
Excellent health	0.24***	0.004	0.12	0.007	0.27	0.006
Very good	0.30***	0.005	0.21	0.008	0.33	0.006
Good	0.27**	0.005	0.29	0.009	0.26	0.006
Fair	0.13***	0.003	0.21	0.008	0.10	0.004
Poor	0.07***	0.003	0.16	0.007	0.04	0.003
Underweight	0.01***	0.001	0.02	0.003	0.01	0.001
Obese	0.23***	0.004	0.27	0.009	0.22	0.005
Ever smoked	0.38***	0.005	0.79	0.008	0.59	0.006
Current smoke	0.26***	0.005	0.44	0.010	0.21	0.005
Active 3+ times/week	0.21***	0.004	0.18	0.008	0.22	0.006
Family:						
Mother alive	0.41***	0.005	0.37	0.010	0.42	0.007
Father alive	0.16**	0.004	0.13	0.007	0.16	0.005
Number of siblings	2.85**	0.025	2.73	0.050	2.88	0.032
Household financial characteristics:						
Working	0.68***	0.005	0.58	0.010	0.71	0.006
Household income	85,161***	972	66,682	1,630	91,000	1,282
Household total wealth	257,146***	5,647	153,032	7,285	292,143	7,720

Note: Values are measured at the first interview. Dollar values are in 2018 dollars. Stars indicate if the difference between the survivors and decedents is significant at the ***1 or **5 percent levels. The two rightmost columns do not sum to the total, because a third category, those who attrit from the survey prior to age 75 and for whom the mortality outcome is unknown, are excluded from the breakdown by outcome.
Source: Author's calculations from the Health and Retirement Study.

The average age of respondents was 56, slightly fewer than half of these respondents were male, and over three-quarters were married at baseline. Respondents' health was good at the outset: using the self-assessed health measure, where respondents could report being in excellent, very good, good, fair, or poor health, only seven percent said they were in poor health. Sadly, rates of obesity and smoking were high: 23 percent reported values for their height and weight such that the respondent was classified as obese,[8] and 26 percent smoked (in 1992). Only 21 percent reported engaging in vigorous activity three or more times a week. Given the typical age difference between husbands and wives, and the shorter life expectancy for men, the probability that the respondent had a living mother was 41 percent compared to just 16 percent for a father.

Unsurprisingly, there are large differences in the means of these variables between those who survived to age 75 and those who did not, all significantly different from zero except for the number of children and the probability of being of Hispanic ethnicity (both of which are similar across groups).[9] Perhaps most interesting for the present study are the large differences across the two groups in subjective survival probabilities. The average reported probability of surviving to age 75 for those who did not survive is 56 percent, while the average for those who did survive was 67 percent. Similarly large differences are found for the probability of living to ages 85–45 versus 36 percent. The well-known differences in life expectancy by sex are apparent, with 57 percent of decedents being male compared to just 43 percent of survivors.

With respect to other measures, survivors were advantaged in every way. They had more schooling, were less likely to be nonwhite, and reported being in better health. Only four percent of survivors reported being in poor health, compared to 16 percent of decedents. Thus subjective health, like subjective survival probabilities, appears consistent, at least on average, with actual outcomes. Survivors were approximately half as likely to be smokers, less likely to be obese, and more likely to engage in vigorous activity than decedents. They also had a higher income and greater wealth.

In what follows, I examine how the subjective assessments by individuals of their likelihood of surviving to age 75 relate to actual mortality, to known risk factors for mortality, and how these expectations were updated over time with the arrival of new information.

Survival Probabilities
Cross-sectional properties

Table 2.2 provides statistics regarding the issue of focal responses, namely responses of zero, 50, or 100 percent. I report the distribution of focal responses in both the first wave and for all of the survey waves stacked

TABLE 2.2 Probability of focal response

	Percent of sample		
Type of response	All	Decedents	Survivors
First wave (n = 8,202)			
Non-focal response	50.5	47.5	50.8
Subjective probability = 0	6.5	12.0	4.8
Subjective probability = 50	21.7	22.4	22.7
Subjective probability = 100	21.3	18.1	21.8
Total	*100*	*100*	*100*
All waves (n = 35,463)			
Non-focal response	49.1	44.3	51.0
Subjective probability = 0	5.24	11.2	3.6
Subjective probability = 50	25.17	27.0	24.3
Subjective probability = 100	20.38	17.5	21.2
Total	*100*	*100*	*100*

Source: Author's calculations from the Health and Retirement Study.

together. The latter makes full use of the available data, but by construction those who live longer contribute more observations than shorter lived respondents. This can lead to potentially biased assessments of the properties of subjective probabilities if the two groups have different likelihoods of reporting focal values in general, or of probabilities of zero, 50, or 100 percent in particular. Here and in Table 2.3, I therefore present statistics for both the single wave and for the aggregate sample.

As others have reported, Table 2.2 shows a substantial heaping of respondents at 50 percent and 100 percent (just over 20% of the sample reported each of these values), but there is a much lower mass at zero percent. Clearly, from a probability standpoint, values of zero and 100 are inappropriate: a person saying zero or 100 percent where not trained in statistics could indicate that he or she felt certain of the outcome, whether low or high, and simply rounded to a convenient number. While some analysts have called into question the value of reported probabilities of 50 percent, as noted earlier, excluding those giving focal responses likely leads to biased results. Unsurprisingly, the bias is greater for less educated individuals who were less clear about probabilities, where the tendency to report zero, 50, or 100 percent was greatest.

There are also differences between decedents and survivors in the prevalence of focal responses, as one would expect, with more reported values of zero and fewer reports of 100 percent among those who did die before age 75, but with a similar percentage reporting a probability of 50 percent. Interestingly, nearly 20 percent of those who died before age 75 reported a 100 percent chance of surviving to that age.

The second panel illustrates similar patterns for the stacked sample including observations in all waves. This combined sample is weighted

TABLE 2.3 Regression of survival probability on individual characteristics

Variable	Coefficient	(Standard error)
Personal Characteristics:		
Male	−3.30***	(0.50)
Age	0.44***	(0.06)
Schooling	0.50***	(0.13)
Nonwhite	5.30***	(0.71)
Hispanic	−3.57**	(1.04)
Married	0.95	(2.05)
Health:		
Excellent	11.59***	(0.03)
Very good	5.42***	(0.53)
Good (omitted)	–	–
Fair	−8.66***	(0.76)
Poor	−20.56***	(1.20)
Existing Medical Condition:		
High blood pressure	−1.07**	(0.48)
Stroke	−1.33	(1.22)
Diabetes	−1.60**	(0.78)
Cancer	−2.90***	(0.84)
Lung problems	−3.92***	(1.05)
Heart problems	−4.09***	(0.72)
Arthritis	−0.24	(0.45)
Behaviors:		
Physically active	0.83***	(0.18)
Smokes now	−4.07***	(0.62)
Smoked ever	1.05**	(0.52)
Family:		
Mom alive	9.53	(5.54)
Mom's age	0.02	(0.07)
Mom's age at death	0.11***	(0.02)
Dad alive	8.80	(8.26)
Dad's age	0.02	(0.09)
Dad's age at death	0.11***	(0.02)
Mean of dependent variable	65.12	
Number of observations	31,711	
Number of respondents	7,834	

Note: Stars indicate if the coefficient estimates are significantly different from zero at the ***1 or **5 percent levels.
Source: Author's calculations from the Health and Retirement Study.

toward those who were the longest lived, and thus likely younger at the outset. Interestingly, the patterns are similar to those identified before, though differences between survivors and decedents are slightly more pronounced. Approximately one-half of the observations were non-focal responses; there

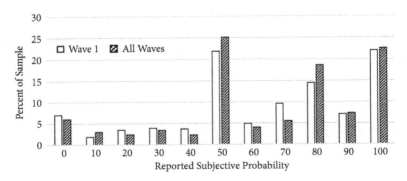

Figure 2.1 Distribution of HRS survival probabilities: wave 1 and all waves
Source: Author's calculations from the Health and Retirement Study.

were a large number of observations at probabilities of 50 percent and 100 percent, and fewer at zero.

Figure 2.1 shows the entire distribution of reports as a percentage of the sample for each of the 11 possible probabilities.[10] The lighter bars are for the first wave and the darker bars for the stacked waves (which again, skew right). The spikes in the percentage reporting 50 and 100 percent are clearly visible. Nonetheless, one can also see the distribution of non-focal responses which span the full probability range. Of note, the average life table probability for this sample was 69.3, so the distribution and the means in Table 2.1 compare well with this value. Additional differences are explored in more detail below.

Regression estimates

While Table 2.1 illustrated the strong correlation between numerous individual characteristics and actual survival, many of these factors are also correlated with subjective survival probabilities, suggesting that the individuals may be consciously or unconsciously incorporating known risk factors into the assessments of their own survival probabilities. Table 2.3 explores some of these correlations in a multivariate regression of the subjective survival probability on characteristics such as sex, health, smoking status, etc., all of which are likely to factor into actual survival probabilities and thus into respondents' assessment of their survival probabilities. Here I stack all observations for an individual and correct the standard errors for these multiple measures.[11] Because these estimates are similar to those reported elsewhere (Hurd and McGarry 1995), I discuss them only briefly and use a parsimonious specification to convey the main points although here we have more observations.

Consistent with known differences in life expectancies, men report a significantly lower survival probability, 3.3 percentage points lower, than do women. (The average difference in life table values is approximately twice that.) Probabilities rise with age, as they should given the shorter time until age 75 for older respondents, and they rise as well with schooling. All else constant, nonwhite respondents forecast a substantially greater chance of survival, and Hispanic respondents, less.[12]

A key factor in assessing one's probability of surviving is one's health status. The HRS offers several ways to measure health: a first is self-reported health, on a scale of one through five, ranging from excellent to poor. It also asked people to assess their current medical conditions, taking the form:

> Has a doctor ever told you that you had a heart attack, coronary heart disease, angina, congestive heart failure, or other heart problems?

A similar question was asked about high blood pressure, stroke, diabetes, cancer, lung problems, and arthritis. Finally, I include measures of peoples' health behaviors: physical activity, smoking status (current and former), and measures of obesity or being underweight.

Unsurprisingly, these health measures are strong predictors of individuals' survival probabilities. For the general measure of overall health, differences in outcomes between the various states of health are large. Moving from excellent to poor health results in a predicted decline of 32 percentage points in the probability of survival or approximately 50 percent.

Each of the medical conditions captured by the HRS has a negative effect on expectations, and all but stroke and arthritis have effects that are significantly different from zero, typically at the one percent level. Behaviors such as being physically active and smoking have the expected effects, and they are similarly highly significantly different from zero. There is a large negative relationship between smoking currently and subjective survival probabilities, with smokers reporting a lower probability by approximately four percentage points or six percent. This result holds, despite prior work finding that smokers underestimate their risk, indicating that the true difference could be even greater (Khwaja et al. 2007; Bissonnette et al. 2017).

Finally, in examining the relationship between survival probabilities and the mortality experience of family members, there is a positive and significant relationship between the age at death of a parent and the respondent's own expectations.

Comparison of subjective expectations

As noted above, the time span of the data allows me to follow the original HRS respondents (approximately age 51–61 in 1992) for 24 years, until the

TABLE 2.4 Survival probabilities

	All	Women	Men
Wave 1			
Actual survival probability	70.9	76.2	64.7
Subjective survival probability	64.1	65.8	62.0
Life table value	69.4	75.8	61.9
Ratio subjective/life table	0.93	0.87	1.00
Number	7000	3820	3180

Note: Sample is limited to those who report a value for the subjective survival probability and for whom actual survivor status is known.
Source: Author's calculations from the Health and Retirement Study.

youngest reached age 75. With these data, I can compare the subjective survival probabilities reported at younger ages with actual outcomes. Similarly, I can compare the predictive power of subjective assessments with objective assessments from life tables which depend here only on age and sex.

The first column of Table 2.4 shows that life table estimates are a more accurate assessment, on average of survival than subjective reports, with a mean self-reported probability of surviving to age 75 of 69.4, compared to the actual survival probability of 70.9. The average of the subjective reports was just 64.1, indicating that, on average, respondents underestimated their survival probabilities. This underestimate could be a potential liability with respect to adequate savings for retirement and financial well-being later in life. Much of the difference between the subjective assessments and actual outcomes or life table values stems from the substantial underreporting by women, a result that is consistent with the poor financial outcomes for women at older ages relative to men. (In 2018, 11.1% of women age 65+ were poor, compared to 8.1% of men in the same age range; US Bureau of the Census 2020).[13]

Figure 2.2 further examines the validity of these reported survival probabilities. Here I assign respondents to a subjective probability bin based on their first reported probability of living to age 75, and then I calculate the actual survival probability to age 75 for individuals in that bin. There is a positive, nearly monotonic, relationship between reported survival probabilities and actual survival. The non-monotonicity at the endpoints, zero and 100, points to measurement error for these responses. Those reporting zero have a very low subjective probability, similar to those reporting 10 percent, suggesting that these respondents may have simply been 'rounding down' to zero. At the other end of the distribution, those reporting living to

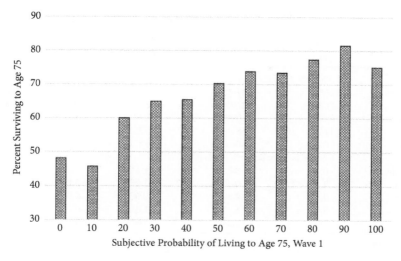

Figure 2.2 Percentage surviving to age 75 by subjective probability, HRS
Source: Author's calculations using the Health and Retirement Study.

age 75 with certainty, did have a high survival probability but less than that for those reporting a 90 or even an 80 percent chance, again suggesting strong rounding.

In other words, while I conclude that the subjective survival measures are not perfect, they do seem to correlate well with actual mortality experience and with known correlates of mortality risk.

Updating of survival probabilities

Of particular interest is how people update or change their expectations over time in response to new information.[14] Table 2.5 illustrates the change in subjective survival probabilities associated with a change in self-reported health status. It extends Hurd and McGarry (2002) with many more waves of data than the two waves used in that study. Relying on the additional years of information available here, I follow respondents to older ages and thus observe more transitions into fair or poor health status than in earlier work. It is in these worsening health categories that one might expect survival probabilities to be most impacted, as opposed to movements from excellent to very good health that would be expected earlier in the life course.

The rows of Table 2.5 correspond to the five health status categories in a given wave (wave T)—excellent, very good, good, fair, or poor—and the columns denote health status in the subsequent wave (T+1). The top panel of the table illustrates the number of individuals in each cell, corresponding

TABLE 2.5 Changes in subjective health and survival

Wave T	Wave T+1				
	Excellent	Very good	Good	Fair	Poor
	Numbers Transitioning				
Excellent	2654	1169	346	66	19
Very good	1623	4402	1815	260	37
Good	541	2099	3933	1048	137
Fair	114	381	1234	1907	544
Poor	26	66	213	5391	897
	Change in Survival Probabilities				
Excellent	−0.36	−3.01	1.11	−14.43	−3.77
Very good	0.99	−0.43	−1.22	−5.27	−3.34
Good	0.50	2.22	−0.53	−2.56	−6.33
Fair	6.99	6.97	1.61	−0.03	−4.95
Poor	17.58	11.34	15.41	5.50	−0.56

Source: Author's calculations from the Health and Retirement Study.

to the reporting of a particular transition between two health states. The bottom panel shows the average change in the reported values for the subjective probability of surviving to age 75 between the two waves. For instance, 66 respondents reported excellent health in one wave and fair health in the next. Among this group, the average decline in the probability of surviving to age 75 was 14.43 percentage points (or 22% based on the sample-wide average of 65).

As is apparent, respondents revised down their subjective survival probabilities as their perception of their health status declined. There is only one cell in the table which did not exhibit this pattern—the transition from excellent to good health—and the change in average survival probabilities for those in that cell was relatively small—just a 1.11 percentage point increase in survival probability. Interestingly, all diagonal values of the table (i.e. the changes in subjective probabilities for those who report being in the same broad health category in each of the two waves) were negative. For example, for the 3,933 respondents who reported being in good health in both waves, the average change in subjective probability of survival was −0.53. This pattern indicates a slight decline in expected survival with age, despite no change in their subjective health reports in terms of the five-point excellent to poor scale. This result suggests that the 100-point scale used in the probability question offers a more finely defined gradient for measuring health than general measures of overall health.

A more formal measure of health related to questions about the onset of medical conditions diagnosed by a doctor. To the extent that the onset of various medical conditions such as a heart attack or cancer was unexpected, their onset would likely be associated with a reduction in the subjective survival probability. These questions regarding new medical conditions parallel those asked initially:

> Since WAVE X MONTH/YEAR, has your doctor told you that you had a heart attack, coronary heart disease, angina, congestive heart failure, or other heart problems?

Again, the questions covered high blood pressure, stroke, diabetes, cancer, lung problems, and arthritis, in addition to the heart problems in the question above.

This measure is imperfect, in that while a heart attack or stroke is unlikely to be missed, the incidence of high blood pressure will depend on whether an individual had seen a doctor. In employing the onset of disease as a measure of the change in health, we could also miss a more gradual degradation of health not attributable to one of these factors. With these caveats in mind, Table 2.6 examines the change in probabilities for those reporting the onset of a new medical condition. I divide the sample into those who had an onset of the particular condition ('Developed condition') and those who did not ('No condition'), and I note the average subjective probabilities both 'Before' and 'After' for each group, as well as the change between the two waves.

Perhaps unsurprisingly, the largest changes in the subjective survival probabilities were among those who had a diagnosis of cancer, followed by that of a stroke, then of heart disease, and finally of lung problems. Conditions such as high blood pressure, diabetes, and arthritis had only small effects on expected survival chances. This result is consistent with the medical literature, and it suggests that people do update their probabilities with the arrival of new information. Furthermore, these changes across time for those determined to have a health condition were larger than changes for those not so diagnosed, for all but high blood pressure and arthritis. Nearly all of the differences are significant at a one percent level.

Some of the changes associated with a given condition could be seen as relatively small relative to the expected increase in mortality risk, note that the 'Before' expectations ought to include all information known to the respondent at the time of the survey. Someone with a higher risk of heart attack, perhaps based on family history, smoking status, or obesity, might have already incorporated much of this risk into his or her expectation. In such a case, the onset/event itself would be unlikely to convey entirely new information. Given our data, we cannot assess how much new information the event conveys.

In addition to medical and health information, new information about a respondent's own mortality risk could arise from the death of a close family member. This could include data about a genetic risk via the death of a

TABLE 2.6 Onset of medical conditions and family mortality

| | Subjective survival probabilities | | | | | |
| | Developed condition | | | No condition | | |
Event	Before	After	Change	Before	After	Change
Health conditions:						
High blood pressure	65.41	64.14	−1.27	65.68	65.73	0.05
Stroke	54.80	50.88	−3.93	65.76	65.78	0.03**
Diabetes	60.47	59.78	−0.70	65.77	65.78	0.02***
Cancer	63.89	56.47	−7.43	65.72	65.84	0.12***
Lung problems	56.15	53.00	−3.14	65.78	65.81	0.04**
Heart problems	61.30	57.97	−3.33	65.77	65.86	0.08***
Arthritis	65.41	64.53	−0.88	65.78	65.73	−0.17
Any condition	63.14	61.10	−2.04	66.14	66.53	0.39***
Deaths in the family						
Parent died	68.35	68.81	0.46	65.43	65.39	−0.04
Mother died	68.05	68.49	0.44	65.49	65.47	−0.01
Father died	69.43	69.64	0.21	65.60	65.58	−0.02
Sibling died	63.66	64.95	1.28	65.94	65.87	−0.07
Spouse died	61.61	62.53	0.91	65.73	65.73	−0.01
Parent-in-law died	66.85	66.37	−0.48	65.59	6.60	0.01
Mother-in-law died	66.28	66.71	0.43	65.60	65.57	−0.04
Father-in-law died	67.50	65.42	−2.08	65.63	65.42	0.03
Sibling-in-law died	64.49	63.86	−0.63	65.87	65.90	0.02

Note: Stars indicate if the changes in the subjective survival probabilities for those who experience the onset of a condition and those who do not are significantly different at the ***1 percent or **5 percent levels.
Source: Author's calculations from the Health and Retirement Study.

blood relative, or simply about mortality risk in general, say from the death of a spouse or in-law. The lower portion of Table 2.6 assesses the potential impact of the death of different relatives on reported survival probabilities. Despite the intuition, there is little evidence that respondents update their expectations in light of the death of a parent, sibling, spouse, or in-law. In results not reported here in detail, these conclusions remain unchanged if I allow for separate effects for men and women—testing to see if perhaps the death of a same-sex parent resonates more than the death of an opposite-sex parent. The lack of a response could stem from the age of the respondents. Because they were already in their 50s at the study's baseline, their parents were likely already rather old; the mean age for mothers in the sample at the initial interview was 80, and for fathers, 82. New information stemming from a parent (or parent-in-law) death at these later ages might not provide much information about the respondent's own probability of surviving to age 75. Thus, while the age at which a parent died was a significant predictor of the survival probability as show in Table 2.3, the actual death of a parent at these ages did not significantly alter the assessment.

TABLE 2.7 Regression of change in subjective probability

Variable	Coeff	(std err)
Health:		
Much better	2.07**	(0.87)
Somewhat better	1.49**	(0.65)
Same (omitted)	–	–
Somewhat worse	−1.98***	(0.50)
Much worse	−8.78***	(1.25)
Onset of condition:		
High blood pressure	−0.66	(0.96)
Stroke	−3.01	(2.46)
Diabetes	0.66	(1.41)
Cancer	−5.01***	(1.48)
Lung problems	−1.53	(1.96)
Heart problems	−2.18	(1.27)
Arthritis	−1.08	(0.87)
Family:		
Mom died btw waves	0.57	(0.78)
Mom's age at death	0.005	(0.003)
Dad died btw waves	0.82	(1.03)
Dad's age at death	−0.006	(0.005)
Mean of dependent var	−0.056	
Number of observations	24,294	
Number of respondents	7,341	

Note: Stars indicate if the coefficient estimates are significantly different from zero at the *** 1 or **5 percent levels.
Source: Author's calculations from the Health and Retirement Study.

Finally, in Table 2.7, I examine the relationship between changes in self-reported health, changes in medical conditions, changes in the status of close relatives, and changes in survival probabilities in a single regression to assess their relative importance in a more formal manner. The measure of the change in self-assessed health used here is drawn directly from a question asking respondents to report how their health changed from the previous wave, rather than by comparing two independent reports of current health across waves. Specifically, the question reads:

> Compared with your health (2 years ago / [in the prior wave]), would you say that your health is much better now, somewhat better now, about the same, somewhat worse, or much worse than it was then?

A total of 10.5 percent of respondents reported that their health was much better or somewhat better, two-thirds said their health was about the same, and 23 percent reported somewhat or much worse health.

As seen in Table 2.5, changes in self-assessed health are strongly correlated with changes in survival probabilities. The coefficients for all four categories are significantly different from zero and relatively large. Someone who reported his or her health as 'much better' than in the prior wave had an expected increase in his or her probability of surviving of 2.07 percentage points. With a mean change between waves of close to zero, this is a large amount. The largest change in the table was for those whose health became 'much worse.'

For the onset of conditions, the relationships are all negative with the exception of the diagnosis of diabetes, although few coefficients are significantly different from zero. The strongest effect is for the diagnosis of cancer, which results in a decline of five percentage points. The coefficient for heart problems is also significantly different from zero and larger in magnitude than all but the 'much worse' health change. The advent of a stroke has a large effect in terms of magnitude but was not significantly different from zero because of the large standard error.

Once again, we confirm that the death of family members has no statistically significant effect on respondents' subjective survival probabilities.

The validity of survival probabilities

Tables 2.6 and 2.7 provide clear evidence that individuals adjust their expectations with the arrival of new information (recognizing that what is 'new' information to the researcher may not be entirely new to the respondent). Next, I ask whether and to what extent these updates in survival probabilities improve the predictive validity of the subjective expectations questions. In so doing, I compare subjective probabilities with life table values and then with eventual survivorship status at age 75. To see more clearly how the subjective probabilities evolve over time, I limit my sample to those who survived and remained in the survey through at least wave six, and I then examine the trends in reported probabilities across those six waves.

Table 2.8 shows the average of the self-reported survival probability in each survey wave (SSP), the average life table values (LT), and the average of the ratio of the two probabilities (Ratio). The first triplet of columns (All) pertains to the full sample. The next two sets of columns pertain to survivors and decedents, respectively. There are several patterns contained in these data that are worth noting. First, the subjective survival probabilities are relatively constant across years. For the full sample, the average in the first wave was 68, while in the sixth wave (equivalent to 10 years of time), the average was 67.5—a minor change. Values for intervening years are similar. Second, the life table probabilities show a monotonic increase as probability theory implies. The conditional probability of surviving to age 75, having survived an additional year, is greater than the original probability. With these two trends, the ratio of the subjective to life table probability values steadily declines.

TABLE 2.8 Ratio of subjective survival probability to life table value

	All (n = 1825)			Survivors (n = 1468)			Decedents (n = 357)		
	SSP	LT	Ratio	SSP	LT	Ratio	SSP	LT	Ratio
Wave 1	68.0	68.4	1.0	70.0	68.8	1.02	59.8	66.9	0.90
Wave 2	66.4	69.4	0.96	68.3	69.7	0.99	58.4	67.9	0.86
Wave 3	67.9	70.9	0.96	70.1	71.2	0.99	58.9	69.5	0.85
Wave 4	67.2	72.7	0.93	69.6	73.1	0.96	57.6	71.4	0.81
Wave 5	68.0	74.8	0.91	70.5	75.1	0.94	57.7	73.6	0.79
Wave 6	67.5	77.6	0.87	70.3	77.9	0.91	56.3	76.5	0.74

Note: Sample is those individuals for whom survivorship status at age 75 is known and who were interviewed through at least wave 6 with reported values for the probability of living to age 75 at each interview. The sample is thus balanced. SSP is the subjective survival probability, LT is the life table probability, and Ratio is the ratio of SSP to LT.
Source: Author's calculations from the Health and Retirement Study.

When comparing the figures across the survivors and decedents, we see that the subjective probabilities for survivors are uniformly higher than those for decedents. In fact, these differences are surprisingly large, given that the decedents in this sample, by construction, must survive for at least six waves or 10 years beyond the first report. They are thus the longest lived/healthiest of the decedents, with ages in wave 6 ranging from approximately ages 61–71. The differences in life table reports are far smaller than those for self-reports, because they rely solely on age and sex, factors that do not differ sizably for the two groups. There is no measure of underlying health or other individual-specific measures used in constructing the life table values. For both survivors and decedents, the life table values rise monotonically, and thus the ratios for self-reported to life table probabilities decline. For survivors, these ratios remain close to one, indicating relatively accurate reporting in terms of actuarial values, although one might expect a value greater than one because these individuals do survive. In contrast, self-reports for decedents are (accurately) well below the actuarial predictions. This result for decedents indicates that individual reports contain additional information missed in population averages: they predict a lower survival probability, on average, than actuarial tables, and they are correct in the sense that, *ex-post*, they did not survive.

To compare more directly both the subjective reports and the life table values with observed outcomes, Table 2.9 presents the correlations between each of these probabilities and actual survival to age 75. Again, the comparisons are carried out by wave. The correlations for both sets of probabilities are all positive and significantly different from zero, but they are substantially higher for the subjective probabilities than for the life table values. In Table 2.6 we saw that the self-reported probabilities for women were closer to life table values than those for men, and thus in this table, the correlations between subjective probabilities for men and actual survival are

TABLE 2.9 Correlation between subjective and life table probabilities and outcomes

	All		Women		Men	
Wave	Subjective	Life table	Subjective	Life table	Subjective	Life table
Wave 1	0.145	0.106	0.105	0.091	0.167	0.117
Wave 2	0.147	0.108	0.108	0.085	0.176	0.127
Wave 3	0.161	0.110	0.143	0.082	0.171	0.115
Wave 4	0.174	0.114	0.173	0.094	0.165	0.117
Wave 5	0.193	0.121	0.164	0.099	0.220	0.131
Wave 6	0.207	0.124	0.189	0.085	0.220	0.127

Source: Author's calculations from the Health and Retirement Study.

also greater than those for women. Also, note that as the respondent ages and gets closer to the target age of 75, there is less uncertainty regarding survival and the correlations increase.

Discussion and Conclusion

The advent of 'big data' has proved to be a boon to researchers in a variety of fields. Yet as important as these data are to scientific research, survey information is still needed to address many of the most important questions. The data discussed and analyzed in this chapter, namely information on subjective probabilities, provide a prime example of the value of collecting information directly from individuals. In many ways, the HRS has managed to take the best from both worlds, with links to administrative data sets such as Medicare and Social Security Administrative data. The HRS allows researchers to access enormous amounts of high quality information on respondent behavior. In addition, however, the survey data collected from individual interviews allow for insight into the motivation behind observed behavior.

Here my focus has been on a relatively different and important type of question, namely older peoples' subjective probability of living to age 75. Despite evidence of measurement error, the subjective probabilities do reveal information beyond that gleaned from life tables, notwithstanding the prevalence of rounding to focal responses. Furthermore, as new information arises, particularly that related to the respondent's health, the respondent updates those probabilities and these updates too contain useful information beyond the life tables. As work continues in this area, we can anticipate refinements in questioning and in statistical methods that will allow researchers to make the most of these data and to improve the accuracy of our economic models.

Notes

1. Some life cycle models allow for a bequest motive in which individuals receive utility from leaving bequests to their heirs (cf. Dynan et al. 2002).
2. Other studies have analyzed expectations regarding stock market returns (Dominitz and Manski 2011b; Lumsdaine and Potter van Loom 2017), returns to schooling (Dominitz and Manski 1996), and income (Dominitz and Manski 2011a).
3. Specifically, I use data from the RAND version of the HRS.
4. Although the original samples are drawn from the non-institutionalized population, respondents are followed into nursing homes. Individuals who are unable to answer the survey questions are interviewed via a proxy. Additionally, non-respondents are retained in the survey and attempts are made to recontact them in subsequent waves. Attrition from the survey has been exceptionally low; see HRS (2017) for detailed information on response rates.
5. Data for the 2018 interview were not available at the time of this writing.
6. Perozek (2008) noted that the change in scale did not seem to affect the likelihood of 'rounded' responses, and there is little evidence to suggest that this change would alter the conclusions of her study or other similar efforts.
7. Because I use population weights in the analysis, also excluded from the sample are those with zero weight.
8. This level likely contains substantial bias such that the body mass index (BMI) is underreported (e.g. Keith et al. 2011).
9. The number of observations for the full sample is larger than the sum of survivors and decedents, because the mortality status for some who left the survey is unknown.
10. Recall that respondents were asked to report a value between zero and 10 inclusive. These reports were scaled to represent probabilities of zero to 100.
11. Despite having multiple observations per respondent, I do not estimate this regression as a fixed effects model because variables of primary interest such as schooling, race, and sex do not vary over time in the data and are thus not identified. Other variables such as smoking status also show little variation. The estimated effects for health-related variables are substantially unchanged in a fixed effects framework, and I explore the effect of changes in these variables below.
12. Hispanics can be of any race.
13. Perozek (2008) estimated survival probabilities using subjective reports from the HRS. She similarly found survival probabilities based on reports from women were lower than those from the life tables used by social security. In contrast the subjective survival probabilities for men were higher than life table values. Interestingly, the Social Security Administration later raised their estimate of male life expectancy and lowered the estimate female life expectancy. Her results thus suggest that the subjective responses in the HRS are valuable, and reflect more than a simple reading of actuarial values.
14. Bissonnette et al. (2017) found in panel data that respondents seemed update their assessment of near-term mortality risk as they aged.

References

Bassett, W. and R. Lumsdaine (2001). 'Probability Limits: Are Subjective Assessments Adequately Accurate?' *Journal of Human Resources*, 36(2): 327–363.

Bissonnette, L., M. Hurd, P-C. Michaud (2017). 'Individual Survival Curves Comparing Subjective and Observed Mortality Risks,' *Health Economics*, 26: e285–e303.

Bloom, D., D. Canning, M. Moore, and Y. Song (2006). 'The Effect of Subjective Survival Probabilities on Retirement and Wealth in the United States,' Program on the Global Demography of Aging, Working Paper Series, No. 17, November.

Bruine de Bruin, W., B. Fischhoff, S. Millstein, and B. L. Halpern-Felsher (2000). 'Verbal and Numerical Expressions of Probability: "It's a Fifty-Fifty Chance,"' *Organizational Behavior and Human Decision Processes*, 81(1): 115–131.

Dominitz, J. and C. Manski (1996). 'Eliciting Student Expectations of the Returns to Schooling,' *Journal of Human Resources*, 31: 1–16.

Dominitz, J. and C. Manski (2011a). 'Using Expectations Data to Study Subjective Income Expectations,' *Journal of the American Statistical Association*, 92: 855–867.

Dominitz, J. and C. Manski (2011b). 'Measuring and Interpreting Expectations of Equity Returns,' *Journal of Applied Economics*, 26: 352–370.

Dynan, K. E., J. Skinner, and S. P. Zeldes (2002). 'The Importance of Bequests and Life-cycle Saving in Capital Accumulation: A New Answer,' *American Economic Review*, 92(2): 274–278.

Elder, T. (2013). 'The Predictive Validity of Subjective Mortality Expectations: Evidence from the Health and Retirement Study,' *Demography*, 50: 569–589.

Health and Retirement Study (2017). 'Sample Sizes and Response Rates,' https://hrs.isr.umich.edu/sites/default/files/biblio/ResponseRates_2017.pdf

Hurd, M. D. and K. McGarry (1995). 'Evaluation of the Subjective Probabilities of Survival in the Health and Retirement Study,' *Journal of Human Resources*, 30: S268–S292.

Hurd, M. D. and K. McGarry (2002). 'The Predictive Validity of Subjective Probabilities of Survival,' *The Economic Journal*, 112(482): 966–985.

Hurd M. D., J. Smith, and J. Zissimopoulos (2004). 'The Effect of Subjective Survival on Retirement and Social Security Claiming,' *Journal of Applied Econometrics*, 19: 761–775.

Keith, S. W., K. R. Fotaine, N. M. Pajewski, T. Mehta, and D. B. Allison (2011). 'Use of Self-reported Height and Weight Biases the Body Mass Index-mortality Association,' *International Journal of Obesity*, 35(3): 401–408.

Khwaja, A., F. Sloan, and S. Chung (2007). 'The Relationship between Individual Expectations and Behaviors: Mortality Expectations and Smoking Decisions,' *Journal of Risk and Uncertainty*, 35: 179–201.

Kleinjans, K. J. and A. van Soest (2014). 'Nonresponse and Focal Point Answers to Subjective Probability Questions,' *Journal of Applied Econometrics*, 29(4): 567–585.

Lumsdaine, R. and R. J. D. Potter Van Loon (2017). 'Do Survey Probabilities Match Financial Market Beliefs?' *Journal of Behavioral Finance*, 19(2): 209–220.

Perozek, Ma (2008). 'Using Subjective Expectations to Forecast Longevity: Do Survey Respondents Know Something We Don't Know?' *Demography*, 45(1): 95–113.

US Bureau of the Census (2020). *Historical Poverty Tables: People and Families—1959–2018.* https://www.census.gov/data/tables/time-series/demo/income-poverty/historical-poverty-people.html

Van Santen, P., R. Alessie, and A. Kalwij (2012). 'Probabilistic Survey Questions and Incorrect Answers: Retirement Income Replacement Rates,' *Journal of Economic Behavior and Organization*, 82: 267–280.

Chapter 3

Disability-free Life Trends at Older Ages

Implications for Longevity Risk Management

Douglas A. Wolf

Longevity risk is typically defined as the problem of people living longer than expected. From an aggregate perspective, for example the one adopted by a pension fund manager, increasing life expectancy—that is, an increase in the *average* age at death of a covered population—implies that financial reserves may be inadequate to meet payment obligations. From an individual perspective, the problem is one of 'outliving one's assets,' but that problem can arise from having too few assets as well as from living longer than anticipated. The aggregate form of longevity risk is sometimes characterized as one associated with the *uncertainty* attached to future lifetimes, rather than simply the *length* of future lifetimes (e.g. Brouhns et al. 2002; de Waegenaere et al. 2010). The present chapter is concerned primarily with the length, rather than the variability, of remaining lifetimes.

At its core, longevity risk involves two dimensions: the level of assets, from which an income stream is to be generated, and the length of remaining life, which defines the period of time for which the income stream is needed. This chapter explores the possible role for a third dimension of the problem of longevity risk, namely the role of *active* (or 'disability-free') *life*—an individual-level phenomenon—and *active life expectancy* (ALE), which is an aggregate or cohort-level phenomenon. An individual's 'active' status can change during her or his lifetime, and it can improve as well as worsen (Wolf et al. 2007). Thus, during a person's remaining lifetime, the total period of time spent disabled (or, in the complementary *active* state) can be viewed as a random variable whose values range from zero to the entirety of remaining life.

ALE is defined as the average of the individual-level random variable 'cumulative time spent without disability' (or 'total active life'), and it can refer to either an actual population (i.e. a cohort) or an artificial population (e.g. in period terms). Nevertheless, there appear to be no available data that record the entirety (and few that record even a portion) of the process

Douglas A. Wolf, *Disability-free Life Trends at Older Ages.*
In: *New Models for Managing Longevity Risk.* Edited by Olivia S. Mitchell, Oxford University Press.
© Pension Research Council (2022). DOI: 10.1093/oso/9780192859808.003.0003

through which time spent with (or without) a disability steadily accumulates during individuals' lives. The most common form of individual-level longitudinal data on disabled or disability-free status presents a series of biannual (or in some cases annual) snapshots of individuals' statuses. An exception is the National Health and Aging Trends Study (NHATS), which includes *monthly* measures of respondents' receipt of help from others with personal-care tasks (such as eating, bathing, and dressing) and mobility-related tasks (such as getting into or out of bed) (Freedman et al. 2015). But to date, at most eight years of these monthly indicators can be produced using available NHATS public-use data, limiting its usefulness in characterizing the full picture of active status from age 65 to death. Instead, a large and vigorous literature has developed to produce estimates of ALE despite an absence of individual-level data on the length of active life, the phenomenon for which ALE is the supposed average (Imai and Soneji 2007; Laditka and Laditka 2009).

In what follows, we first review trends in life expectancy and ALE—aggregate-level phenomena, in both cases—and consider the implications of ALE for longevity risk. The section concludes that ALE trends add little or nothing to the understanding of aggregate longevity risk. The second section of the chapter turns to the individual perspective on longevity risk, considering the implications of active life—or alternatively, life spent with a disability—for longevity risk. Within the constraints imposed by data limitations noted above, we conclude that there are very striking implications of disability status for longevity risk, although given the complexity of the situation revealed by the data, clear-cut behavioral rules based on these findings are not evident. In a brief final section, we discuss interactions between public and private responses to disability late in life.

Trends in Life Expectancy and Active Life Expectancy

It is a well-known fact that period life expectancy has been increasing from year to year—with a handful of exceptions—for many decades. Although the available evidence is more limited, it suggests that ALE has been increasing in recent years as well.

While there are large differences in life expectancy by sex, race, and other background characteristics, for simplicity's sake I will limit attention mainly to both sexes/all races data. Moreover, given the focus of this chapter on longevity risk in retirement, I will limit attention to life expectancy at age 65. Figure 3.1 plots life expectancy as computed by the National Center for Health Statistics for the period 1950 to 2018 (Figure 3.1 also shows estimates of ALE from several sources, as described below). Despite the

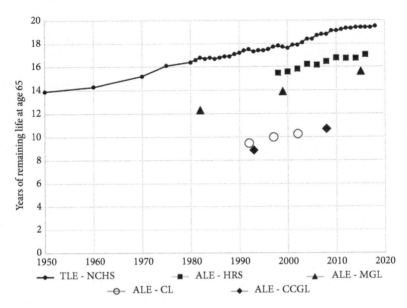

Figure 3.1 Trends in total and active lifetime at age 65

Sources: National Center for Health Statistics (2018) (NCHS); HRS (2019), author's calculations; Manton et al. (2006) (MGL); Cai and Lubitz (2007) (CL); Chernew et al. (2016) (CCGL).

existence of several brief periods of decline, the predominant pattern for life expectancy is clearly one of improvement during this period. A recent analysis of death rates—the inputs into computation of life expectancy—for roughly the same period (1969–2013) found statistically significant 'break points' in the trend line for overall mortality in 1978, 2002, and 2010 (Ma et al. 2015). The downward trend in overall mortality continued, but its slope changed somewhat, at each such breakpoint. An analogous pattern can be seen in the pattern for life expectancy at age 65 in Figure 3.1.

The more-or-less regular trend of increasing period life expectancy over a nearly 70-year period would seem to suggest that pension fund managers could develop forecasting tools that anticipate and therefore eliminate the problem of longevity risk. Moreover, the slowdown—and apparent cessation, since 2014—of the trend toward growing life expectancy at age 65 might, in turn, imply that the problem of longevity risk could diminish on its own.

Turning from life expectancy, defined by the unambiguous and irreversible transition from living to dead, to ALE, defined by a partitioning of remaining life years into those spent with or without disability, introduces several complexities into the analysis. Formally, ALE is the area under a survival curve that is multiplied by the proportion 'active' at each age (Imai and Soneji 2007). In practice, calculating period ALE using the most widely used technique, the so-called 'Sullivan' method, is simple: the calculations entail multiplying elements of the person-years-lived column of a life table by the corresponding elements of an array of age-specific disability (or non-disability) prevalence rates. The great majority of applications of this approach use a binary distinction between 'disabled' and 'disability-free' (or 'healthy' versus 'unhealthy,' or 'active' versus 'inactive,' or any number of other health- or functioning-related categories).

A large literature devoted to ALE has developed since the early contributions of Sullivan (1971) and Katz et al. (1983), and this literature supplies many and varied estimates for ALE. One reason for the proliferation of ALE estimates is the variety of measures of 'active' status that have been used—the distinction between 'disabled' and 'disability-free' is not nearly as straightforward, in concept or measure, as is the distinction between 'alive' and 'dead.' For this chapter, I have produced a series of period ALE estimates for 1998, 2000 ..., 2016 using disability measures from the US Health and Retirement Study (HRS) in combination with life tables published by the National Center for Health Statistics. The HRS is an ongoing large-scale population-based panel survey that began in 1992, employing biennial surveys thereafter. While the initial sample was limited to the non-institutionalized population age 51–61, various additions to the sample since then permit me to compute ALE estimates for 65-year-olds beginning in 1998 (Health and Retirement Study 2019). The disability measures used here are binary indicators of whether the sample person receives help from another person with any of six Activities of Daily Living (ADLs), namely eating, dressing, toileting, bathing, getting in or out of bed, and walking. Getting help from another person for a basic personal-care task such as these corresponds to a conceptualization of 'disability as dependency'; it is useful in a discussion of longevity risk because help from others entails the use of concrete resources—time or money—and therefore has implications for financial well-being. The ADL indicators used here are taken from a public-use file produced by the RAND Corporation (Bugliari et al. 2019a). The ALE calculations use the abridged life table setup found in Jagger et al. (2014), which implements the Sullivan method for calculating period ALE.

Age-specific disability prevalence rates based on the HRS variables are plotted in Figure 3.2. There are no apparent trends over this 18-year period among the two youngest age groups (65–74 and 80–84), ages at which disability prevalence rates are quite low. Among the older age groups (85–94 and 95+) the trends are not uniform throughout the period, but they are clearly predominantly downward, ending (in 2016) well below their initial values (in 1998).

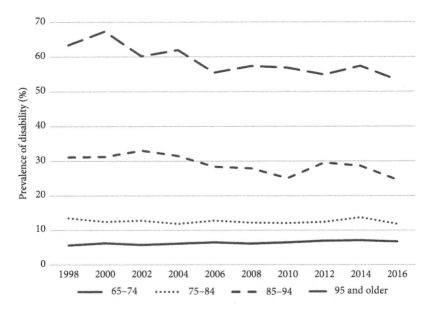

Figure 3.2 Trends in disability prevalence by age group, 1998–2016
Source: Author's calculations based on the Health and Retirement Study (2019).

The 1998–2016 HRS-based calculations of ALE are plotted, along with analogous points taken from three previous publications, in Figure 3.1. All the ALE estimates shown in Figure 3.1 pertain, like the total life-expectancy figures, to the total population; in addition, most also use the Sullivan method. Differences in levels across sources derive principally from the different criteria used to distinguish the 'disabled' from the 'disability-free' portion of the population. Crimmins et al. (2016), for example, define the 'active' population as those free of any limitation of activities, which is the broadest definition used among the sources shown here; this definition, in turn, produces the lowest estimates of ALE. My 'disability as dependency' definition is, in contrast, the most restrictive, and in turn produces the highest estimates of ALE. The other data points plotted in Figure 3.1 use disability criteria that fall between these two extremes. Cai and Lubitz (2007) use the criterion having *difficulty* performing either ADL or Instrumental ADL (e.g. shopping, meal preparation) tasks to define having a disability. Manton et al. (2006) use measures based on the National Long Term Care Survey data, which count as disabled those getting help from other people, along with those using special equipment, to perform daily tasks, and also include those with unmet needs for help dealing with health-related difficulties performing daily tasks.

Figure 3.1 reveals a strikingly consistent pattern of improvement in ALE at age 65 over time. While the levels of ALE differ by the criteria used to measure disability, changes over time in ALE based on each of these measures are close to parallel. Demographers and gerontologists are also interested in the 'compression of morbidity,' a phenomenon associated with the *percentage* of remaining lifetime lived in a disabled state (Cai and Lubitz 2007). With respect to morbidity compression, however, the estimates shown in Figure 3.1 are unclear: when converted to percentages of total life expectancy (not shown), none of the four ALE series plotted in Figure 3.1 shows a clear trend.

Implications for longevity risk

ALE appears to be closely tied to longevity: Figure 3.1 shows that trends in ALE tend to parallel the trend in life expectancy. But whatever the trends in ALE—examined in isolation or relative to total life expectancy—these trends most likely have little or no relevance for aggregate longevity risk. The payout obligations of a pension fund are usually unchanged by the disability status of its beneficiaries. Researchers have pointed out that common factors contribute to improvements in both total life expectancy and ALE (Chernew et al. 2016; Stallard 2016), suggesting that once such factors are incorporated into a mortality forecast, the level or trend in ALE should not add anything to the determination of longevity risk. In other words, whereas ALE is surely associated with the quality of life of pensioners, it seems to have no bearing on the longevity risk faced by pension fund managers.

Active Life and Individual Longevity Risk

In what follows, we discuss individual-level longevity risk from the vantage point of a 65-year-old person, that is, someone close to the typical US age of retirement. At that point, an individual has a given level of assets but faces an uncertain remaining lifetime. If the longevity risk issue is expressed narrowly as the risk of outliving one's assets, then the decision problem facing this individual can be factored into two parts: first, one must—at least implicitly—form an expectation regarding the number of life years that remain; and second, conditional on the first, one must decide either to annuitize assets or to draw them down, presumably following a careful and well-informed plan. The 'annuitize' option, in turn, can be further subdivided into one of buying a fixed-term (usually 10- or 15-year) income stream or buying a lifelong income stream.[1]

With a fixed-term annuity, considerable longevity risk is likely to remain; in contrast, a whole-life annuity eliminates longevity risk but does so at the cost of providing a notably smaller income stream during one's remaining lifetime. Introducing 'active lifetime' as a third factor adds yet another domain of uncertainty into the analysis. A fourth dimension of economic well-being during retirement is, of course, the size of one's social security benefit (for the over 95% of the 65+ population that do, or ultimately will, receive a benefit; Whitman et al. 2011). Although the social security system is subject to political forces and is therefore not immune to adjustment, it is nominally an asset that cannot be outlived; we largely ignore social security in what follows.

We address the dimensions of longevity, wealth, and disability using data from the 1998–2016 HRS, discussed earlier. To the 'disability' indicator already described, we add a measure of the net value of nonhousing wealth, also available in a public-use data file produced by the RAND Corporation (Bugliari et al. 2019b). We also adopt a cohort perspective, focusing on individuals age 65 (or 66) during any of the 1998–2016 interviews, and who were followed thereafter until lost to death or attrition from the sample by the last observation in 2016.[2] This limits the analysis, inasmuch as the maximum age to which surviving members of these biannual cohorts can be followed is 84.

Nevertheless, the most limiting feature of the data used here is the use of biennial indicators of current disability status (i.e. getting help from another person with one or more ADL tasks) as a proxy for continuous but possibly interrupted episodes of disability. At most, we can observe up to 10 biennia—baseline plus follow-up—within the continuously observed cohort subsample, and thereby obtain a partial measure of cumulative (in)active life over the follow-up period. Whether this measure understates or overstates the underlying, but unobserved, continuous active-years measure cannot be determined. If two consecutive HRS interviews are coded 'disabled,' the sample individual cannot be assumed to have been continuously disabled for two years (Wolf and Gill 2008). Similarly, if both of two successive interviews reveal someone to be disability-free at the time of the interview, we cannot assume that the person remained disability-free throughout the interval between interviews.

Moreover, by initiating the observation at age 65, we understate the lifetime experience of disability by an unknown amount: someone coded as disabled at age 65 has been in that state for an unknown period of time, and someone coded as disability-free at age 65 may have had a period with disability that ended at an earlier age. Finally, episodes of disability are right censored by death, given that death and accumulating life years with disability are semi-competing risks: an episode of having a disability can be censored by the event of death, but the reverse is not true (Varadhan et al. 2014). Subject to these data limitations, I report on three relevant random variables: survivorship from age 65, the level of assets held at age 65, and the period of life spent disabled, or free of disability, from age 65 onward. We first consider the marginal distribution of each variable in isolation, and then we consider some relevant associations among them.

Remaining lifetime at age 65

Period-based data on years of remaining life are readily available from conventional life tables. Based on the US period life table for 2007, the midpoint of the years spanned by the HRS sample, life expectancy at age 65 was 18.6 years (Arias 2011). Thus, average remaining lifetime for 65-year-olds slightly exceeded the 18-year follow-up period allowed in the HRS sample used here. Consequently, there is a great deal of censoring of age at death in the cohort sample. Moreover, as is well known, there is a great deal of variability in remaining lifetime (Edwards 2011). For example, the standard deviation of remaining lifetime at age 65, again based on the 2007 period life table for the full US population, was 8.8 years.

The substantial variability in the length of remaining lifetime underscores the challenges people face in deciding how to manage whatever assets they have at the time of retirement. Even if people could do a good job of forecasting the mean of their years-of-remaining-life distribution, there would remain a sizeable probability that they would underestimate the chances of living substantially longer than expected. More problematic, however, is the possibility of bias in people's forecasts of anticipated remaining lifetime. Perozek's (2008) analysis of HRS respondents' answers to survey questions regarding their beliefs about the chances that they will live to age 75, and to age 85, imply survival probabilities that are reasonably accurate for men, but understated for women. Such biases might, in turn, imply that women would tend to draw down their retirement-age assets too quickly. Similar findings appear in McGarry (2022) (Chapter 2, this volume), who additionally demonstrates that HRS respondents tend to adjust downwards their subjective survival probabilities in response to the experience of a serious health shock such as a stroke, the occurrence of heart problems, or receiving a cancer diagnosis.

Assets at age 65

There is a great deal of inequality in wealth holdings in the population generally, and this inequality persists into retirement years (Poterba et al. 2018; Eggelston and Munk 2019). Table 3.1 presents several indicators of the distribution of nonhousing wealth at age 65 in the HRS sample. These indicators are based on a pooled sample of people age 65 or 66 in 1998, 2000. . ., 2016, with wealth values expressed in 2019 dollars. The 2008–2009 years of the global financial crisis are included in this pooled sample, which undoubtedly distorts the wealth picture to some degree. Also, household

TABLE 3.1 Net nonhousing wealth for 65-year-old HRS respondents, 1998–2016

	All		With positive wealth	
Mean	$104,156		$144,489	
Median	$6,950		$25,200	
20th percentile	$0		$2,880	
40th percentile	$1,972		$13,755	
60th percentile	$17,850		$44,640	
80th percentile	$90,200		$146,300	
Given annual rate of return of	2%		4%	6%
percentage with wealth sufficient to buy an annuity providing . . .				
. . . mean annual income . . .				
. . . for 10 years	5.1%		5.6%	6.2%
. . . for 15 years	3.2%		3.8%	4.4%
. . . for life	2.1%		2.7%	3.3%
. . . mean annual income less social security . . .				
. . . for 10 years	11.3%		12.4%	13.3%
. . . for 15 years	8.1%		9.2%	10.4%
. . . for life	5.6%		7.2%	9.6%

Notes:
[a]Annuity pricing data provided by Benny Goodman of TIAA. These calculations are all based on annuity pricing data from pre-Covid-19 crisis times; the public health and financial situations of early 2020 have led to big changes in the demand for, the supply of, and the pricing of retirement annuities.
Source: Author's calculations based on data from Health and Retirement Study (2019).

wealth has been divided by two for married individuals; this may understate people's claims on wealth in the case of an emergency, but it may be reasonably close to what would be available for annuitization.

Confirming results in other studies, Table 3.1 shows that, on average, financial assets at the threshold of retirement are quite low and the distribution of those assets is extremely skewed. Nearly 28 percent of 65-year-olds have negative or zero net assets, and among all 65-year-olds, the average holdings are only $104,156. The median, however, is much lower, $6,950 (the maximum wealth in this sample, not shown in Table 3.1, is over $20 million).

The income streams potentially generated by these wealth holdings would be modest for a great majority of the population. To illustrate this point, Table 3.1 shows the percentage of the age 65 population with wealth sufficient to purchase an annuity that would generate an annual income equal to the population average for this age group, or—more realistically— an average income beyond what is provided by social security on average. For example, Census Bureau data tell us that the average annual income in 2018 of people age 65–74 was $46,325 (US Census Bureau 2019). The average monthly social security benefit among all retired workers age 65–69 in

December 2017 was $1,926 (Social Security Administration 2019), imply-ing an annual benefit of $23,106. Using prototypical annuity pricing, for $100,000 one could purchase a 10-year annuity that, in 2019, generates $917.81 per month, assuming a 2 percent rate of return on the assets used to buy the annuity. Based on these figures, one would have needed $420,601 to buy an annuity sufficient to produce annual income equal to the average annual total income received by individuals in 2018. More real-istically, a smaller amount—$193,790—would buy a 10-year annuity that generates income equal to the *difference* between average total income and average social security income, i.e. to 'top off' one's social security bene-fit. Yet, according to Table 3.1, only 11.3 percent of the age 65 population has enough financial wealth to buy even the smaller annuity. For those with substantial housing wealth and both the ability and willingness to 'downsize,' housing assets could be sold, adding to their annuity purchas-ing power, but doing so would entail incurring transaction and moving costs. To ensure that one will not outlive one's assets, a whole-life annuity is required, but as Table 3.1 makes clear, only a very small percentage of elders have sufficient assets to achieve an average retirement income using this strategy.

With respect to longevity risk, the main message from Table 3.1—which examines only the asset component of the issue—is that regardless of how long people expect they will live, the great majority of 65-year-olds have either already outlived their assets or they will soon do so. Moreover, any assets they do own will, at best, provide only a modest increment to their social security income. However, the importance of social security to retirees is well documented. For example, one recent study found that roughly half of the aged population lives in households that receive at least 50 percent of their total income from social security, while about one-quarter of the aged live in households that receive at least 90 percent of their family income from social security (Dushi et al. 2017). The data presented in Table 3.1 underscore the fact that the great majority of the population is ill-equipped to achieve a retirement income that is much larger than their social security benefit.

Years of active life

As explained earlier, empirical measurement of years of active life at the individual level is difficult using available survey data. Continuous measures of cumulative time spent disabled do not exist, and the limited time periods covered by most panel surveys place restrictions on the part of the life cycle that can be observed. Using the HRS measures and cohort sample previ-ously described, we can examine the age profile of current and cumulative (since 65) *biennial* indicators of disability. In order to accurately portray the distribution of years of active life beginning at age 65, it would be necessary to model it as a random variable subject to censoring by death; moreover, it would be desirable to build into that model the likely correlation between the two outcomes. That exercise, however, is beyond the scope of this chapter. Instead, I present simple descriptive information on the age profile of disability status among survivors at each age within the age 65 cohort subsample taken from the HRS.

Figure 3.3 shows three age profiles. For each, the data points plotted represent the average in each biennial survey (1998, 2000..., 2016) of age at each biennial measurement and (a) the prevalence—that is, the current value—of the disability indicator; (b) the cumulative incidence, during the follow-up period, of the disability indicator; and (c) the total number of biennia for which an individual is coded as 'disabled,' during the follow-up period. These profiles are, of necessity, limited to survivors at each follow-up interview and limited to those for whom complete measurements (from the interview in which they were age 65 or 66) to the present are available. The most that someone can be tracked using this cohort design is 10 waves. Therefore, while the origin of each line includes people age 65 or 66 in all 10 interviews, the second data point is limited to those age 65 or 66 in 1998–2014 and still alive two years later; the tenth and final data point on each line is limited to those age 65 or 66 in 1998 and still alive to respond to the 2016 interview.

Figure 3.3 plots current and cumulative disability patterns from age 65 to roughly the mean age at death—about 84—of survivors, and thus misses the ages where the risk of becoming or remaining disabled are highest (cf. Figure 3.2). The current-prevalence figures rise from about six percent at age 65 to nearly 20 percent at age 84; the cumulative-incidence curve (representing those 'ever disabled' starting with age 65) is only modestly higher, consistent with some degree of recovery among those previously disabled. The average number of biennia with disability curve is well above the other two, but even it suggests only modest 'lifetime' (since age 65) experience with disability among survivors to age 84. Not shown in this figure is the fact that among survivors to the 10th biennial interview, nearly 77 percent have *never* been coded 'disabled.' Thus, the available (and admittedly limited) information presented here suggests that whatever the implications of active life years are for longevity risk, those implications are manifested for only a minority of the population.

The preceding paragraphs have considered each of three dimensions of the longevity risk issue—years of total life, level of assets, and years of active life—in isolation. However, it is likely that these dimensions are associated, so we now turn to a consideration of selected pairwise associations of these dimensions. The analyses undertaken here are intended to be exploratory, not comprehensive.

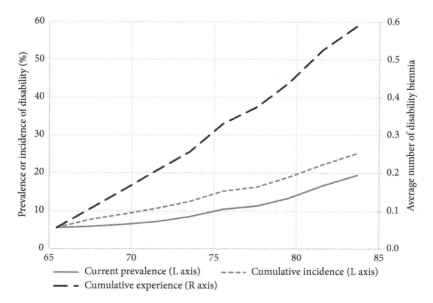

Figure 3.3 Presence of disability by age, HRS respondents, 1998–2016

Note: 'Current prevalence' is the percentage of respondents reporting a disability at the time of interview; 'Cumulative incidence' is the percentage of respondents that have reported a disability at the time of interview or at an earlier interview; 'Cumulative experience' is the average number of interviews, beginning at age 65, at which disability has been reported.
Source: Author's calculations based on data from the Health and Retirement Study (2019).

Wealth predicts longevity

Income has been shown to be strongly associated with longevity (Chetty et al. 2016), and it is to be expected that wealth will have a similar association. To assess the role of wealth at age 65 as a predictor of remaining life years, we estimated a censored regression (i.e. Tobit) model using a pooled sample of individuals observed to be 65 or 66 in 1998. . . 2016 (n = 11,478). As explained before, these individuals are followed for up to nine subsequent biennial interviews, at which time their remaining lifetime is right censored. Others—albeit only a small minority, about 21 percent—are observed to die during the follow-up period. The dependent variable in this regression is the log of survival time. Wealth at age 65 is represented as a categorical variable, with categories corresponding to the quintiles of wealth given that it is positive (those with negative or zero net wealth represented the reference group). The results of this simple bivariate regression are illustrated in Table 3.2. As shown in the table, zero-wealth age 65 individuals are expected to live only 11 more years, while those in each successive quintile of positive net wealth have longer average lifetimes, up to a maximum of 15.5 years for those in the top wealth quintile. Other than for

TABLE 3.2 Remaining lifetime at age 65, by wealth at age 65

	Zero wealth	Quintile of positive wealth:				
		First	Second	Third	Fourth	Fifth
Average remaining lifetime (years)	11.0	11.6	13.5	14.2	15.1	15.5

Source: Author's calculations based on data from the Health and Retirement Study (2019).

the difference between zero-wealth and first-quintile individuals, all the other longevity differences shown in the table correspond to statistically significant regression coefficients (with $p < 0.0001$).

Wealth is associated with reduced chances of becoming disabled

Just as wealth is positively associated with longevity, it is expected to be associated with a longer life free of disability. To test this hypothesis, we created a pooled sample of person-biennia observations for the HRS cohort sample. Each of the 11,478 baseline individuals used in the preceding analysis are now represented in the analysis sample for as many biennia that they remain alive; the pooled sample thus contains 51,993 observations. The analysis consists of a random-effects logit model of disability prevalence (i.e. 'having a disability' = 1) at each biennial interview, controlling for age, wealth quintile, and the lagged value of 'cumulative number of biennia with disability.' The latter variable is included because when it is equal to zero, the person has not yet experienced any disability, and thus the dependent variable represents the initial onset of disability.

The results of this disability-onset model show the dramatic consequences of wealth as a protective factor against becoming disabled. Figure 3.4 plots the key features of the results: for the ages shown (65–80), the probability of disability onset rises rapidly among those with zero wealth, and much more slowly for those in even the lowest quintile of positive wealth (for the sake of simplicity we show only the first, third, and fifth positive-wealth quintiles). The age profile of disability onset is particularly low for those at the upper end of the wealth distribution: someone previously disability-free at age 80, but with zero wealth at age 65, has a probability of disability onset that is more than 15 times larger (with probability equal to 0.156) than an otherwise comparable person who at age 65 was in the top positive-wealth quintile (with probability of only 0.01).

Disability onset predicts reduced longevity

Finally, we consider the consequences of experiencing disability for one's anticipated remaining lifetime. For this we use the same pooled person-biennium sample just described, but now adopt a random-effects

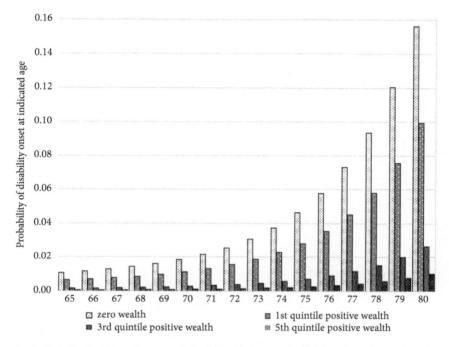

Figure 3.4 Probability of onset of disability by age and wealth at age 65

Note: Heights of bars in this histogram represent the probabilities of first reporting having a disability at each indicated age, for those with zero wealth at age 65 and those in the first, third, and fifth quintiles of positive wealth at age 65.

Source: Author's calculations based on data from the Health and Retirement Study (2019).

Tobit model for remaining years of life at each interview. The controls for disability experience include indicators of one, two, and three or more cumulative biennia with disability; the reference group consists of those with no experience of disability to date. For the reference group, shown in the uppermost line in Figure 3.5, average remaining lifetime is about 15 years at age 65, dropping steadily at later ages (as it must). The most dramatic differences shown in Figure 3.5 are between the disability-free population and those who have, to date, experienced just one biennium of disability (whether current or lagged). For example, a disability-free 65-year-old can expect to live nearly 15 more years, on average; however, someone disabled at that age has a much lower expected remaining lifetime of just nine years. The greater the cumulative experience of disability, the greater the reduction in remaining lifetime, although each additional increment to the number of biennia with disability produces a smaller reduction in remaining lifetime than the one before. Finally, the differences in residual life expectancy between disability classes narrow with age.[3]

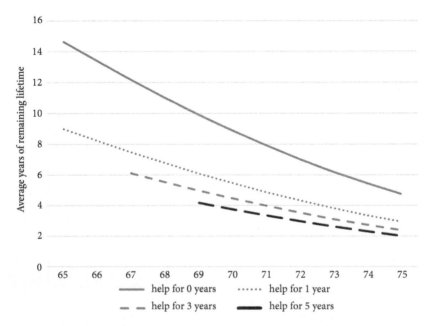

Figure 3.5 Average number of years of remaining lifetime, by current age and duration of current episode of disability

Source: Author's calculations based on data from the Health and Retirement Study (2019).

Longevity Risk, Late-Life Disability, and Public-Private Collaboration

Public-private partnerships, a blanket term that encompasses a broad array of institutional and contractual forms involving a diverse set of public and private actors, have become a major presence in recent decades. It is generally agreed that the sharing of risks across the public and private sectors is a central consideration in these partnerships (Hodge and Greve 2007). With respect to individual-level longevity risk, construed here as outliving one's financial assets, a spectrum of risk sharing arrangements can be observed. A prospective retiree entitled to social security benefits but without any additional private savings or other financial assets faces no longevity risk—presuming the continued operation of the social security program throughout her or his lifetime—thanks to the fact that this risk has been fully transferred to the public sector. Social security is, in effect, the 'public option' for sharing the risk of lack of retirement income. At the other extreme, someone with a pool of financial assets and an intention to self-manage those assets, i.e. to draw them down in keeping with some sort of financial plan, may indeed outlive their private assets, and end up dependent on social security. Private pension plans, and the regulatory apparatus governing them, represent intermediate points along this spectrum of longevity risk.

Introducing active life—or, its complement, late-life disability—into the longevity risk picture adds some interesting features. As shown above, the onset of disability may signal a shorter-than-expected remaining lifetime, which might indicate that assets could be drawn down more rapidly without raising one's longevity risk. On the other hand, the onset of disability signals what might prove eventually to be a need for high-cost long-term care services, which would in turn force the issue of drawing down one's assets more quickly than planned and raise one's longevity risk.

For the disabled older population—defined here as those getting help with everyday tasks—the primary source of help is unpaid family members, or 'informal caregivers.' Johnson and Wiener (2006) using data from 2002 indicate that among those getting help, about 61 percent were community-dwelling individuals getting unpaid help only, while nearly 26 percent were either nursing home residents or community-dwelling individuals receiving paid help only; the remaining 13 percent were community dwellers receiving help from both paid and unpaid sources.

The help provided to disabled elders by family members—mainly by their adult children—might otherwise generate large out-of-pocket costs; family caregiving, in other words, may help avoid longevity risk. It also may delay or completely avert high-cost institutional care (Van Houtven and Norton 2004; Charles and Sevak 2005). By doing so, family caregiving might have as one of its consequences the preservation of bequeathable assets; it might, in other words, have *positive* implications for intergenerational patterns of longevity risk. Yet family caregiving is widely understood to impose substantial costs on the individuals that provide it, and on the families of which they are a part. For example, according to a 2014 survey about 60 percent of informal caregivers are, or at one time while providing care were, employed (NAC/AARP 2015). Alternatively—changing denominators—about 18 percent of the employed population are simultaneously engaged in care provision (Wolf 2019). Employed caregivers report a broad range of care-related costs, among which are missing work, taking unpaid leave (and consequently lowering income), changing to a lower paid or part-time job, or quitting work entirely (Witters 2011; NAC/AARP 2015). Thus, there are good reasons to imagine that family caregiving has *negative* implications for intergenerational patterns of longevity risk.

For those disabled elders whose care is provided in the community by paid caregivers, or in nursing homes (and, therefore, necessarily by paid caregivers), the majority of care costs are borne by Medicaid (Reaves and Musumeci 2015). Paid care services are strongly connected to longevity risk, in view of the fact that eligibility for Medicaid depends in part on passing a stringent asset test. Moreover, there is a great deal of state-to-state variation in the stringency of the asset test: in 2018, for example, the level of allowable assets ranged from a low of $1,500 (in New Hampshire), to a high of $7,560 (in California and South Carolina) (Musumeci and Chidambaram 2019).[4] Thus, in order to be Medicaid eligible, someone must have either arrived at old age without assets or have 'spent down' their assets—quite likely on paid care services—to the low level needed to achieve eligibility. Moving into a nursing home as a self-pay patient is one way of accomplishing spend-down. One analysis of survey data linked to administrative data showed that, among community residents not initially enrolled in Medicaid, fewer than three percent were observed to enroll in Medicaid during a four-year follow-up period if they never moved into a nursing home; meanwhile, 22 percent (20 percent, 19 percent, 17 percent) did transition onto Medicaid by the end of the follow-up period if they had moved into a nursing home within one year (or 2, 3, or 4 years, respectively) after baseline (Spillman and Waidmann 2014). The high cost of nursing homes, in other words, provides the means by which many people deplete their financial assets.

Together, these facts support a somewhat oversimplified characterization of one form of public-private 'partnership' that has arisen to cope with the intersection of longevity risk with active life, as follows: the **private** component of risk sharing consists of family caregivers providing needed care services, protecting insofar as possible their parents' assets (and, indirectly, their own inheritances), while saving the public the expense of paying for 'formal' care services. Under this approach, the costs that do arise are borne narrowly by individuals and their families and may even have intergenerational repercussions. The **public** part of this partnership consists of the provision of expensive care services, in the community or in a nursing home, to a population of disabled elders that have been impoverished by the process of establishing Medicaid eligibility. Those in the latter group have necessarily outlived whatever assets they once had. Costs are borne broadly by society through the taxpayer-funded Medicaid program. This is, at best, a rather haphazard 'partnership' (hence the quotation marks around that word), is one that is not the result of a deliberate design, and is moreover one with substantial between- (and probably within-) state variability.

There is limited space in the aforementioned partnership for private institutions other than families, for example, private long-term care insurance. Indeed, 30 years ago Pauly (1990) showed how nonpurchase of private insurance was a rational response to (among other things) the availability of family members as potential providers of care. Rates of private coverage of this risk continue to be quite low (Brown et al. 2012). Nevertheless, we will mention two policy domains that have the potential to alter the terms of this public-private partnership.

Consumer-directed care

Consumer-directed care refers to an increased role of consumers in managing their own health and health care services. Consumer direction is believed to improve the quality while lowering the costs of health care (Buntin et al. 2006). In the area of long-term care, the principal manifestation of this policy idea has been the Cash and Counseling program, which has been implemented on a limited basis in 15 states (De Milto 2015). In this program, Medicaid beneficiaries eligible for long-term care services receive a cash budget with which to purchase services, and the cash can be used to pay family members to provide at-home care. Because this program operates as a component of Medicaid, the asset-depletion feature of Medicaid is in force here, as well. Yet, by allowing payments to family members, Cash and Counseling could offer a means of reducing some of the costs that would otherwise be borne by family caregivers.

Paid leave

Paid family caregiving leave provisions may allow some people to receive 'paid care' from an employed family member while not requiring that the benefit—the payment for care services—be conditioned on the depletion of the care recipient's assets—i.e. on Medicaid eligibility. While this type of benefit is both capped and limited in duration, it (like Cash and Counseling benefits) has at least some potential to offset what would otherwise be a cost borne by family caregivers; consequently paid caregiving leave has the potential to change the nature of the public-private partnership that has arisen with respect to elder care.

As of 2019, eight states plus the District of Columbia had passed laws mandating the provision of some form of paid family leave by nearly all private employers (National Partnership for Women and Families 2019). Because some of these states have relatively large populations, in 2018 nearly 21 percent of total US employment was in the four states that by then had implemented a paid family leave law; over 28 percent of total US employment (in 2018) was in states that by 2023 will have implemented their paid family leave program.[5] In all cases, these laws require that paid leave be extended to those providing care to parents as well as to the parents of newborn children, the more typical target of such policies.

The first Federal requirement for paid care-related leave emerged with the Families First Coronavirus Response Act (FFCRA) and in the Coronavirus Aid, Relief, and Economic Security (CARES) Act, both of which were passed in March 2020. Both bills were enacted in response to the major and rapidly evolving public health and economic crises associated with the COVID-19 pandemic of 2020. Prior to 2020, Federal policy governing family caregiving leave for private-sector workers was limited to the Family and Medical Leave Act of 1993, which mandated the provision of unpaid leave while exempting those working for small firms and those who fail to meet length-of-service requirements (Klerman et al. 2014). While the FFCRA and CARES Act represent a major shift in Federal leave policy, neither is likely—nor are they intended—to alter the extent or costs of family-provided care to disabled elders: benefits in the new programs are closely tied to quarantining associated with COVID-19 exposure, or to the needs of children unable to attend school. Moreover, the programs were temporary, expiring on December 31, 2020. These initiatives may, however, prove to be the first step toward a more permanent and widespread Federal paid-leave mandate.

Conclusion

Longevity risk can be analyzed as either an aggregate or an individual-level issue. From the aggregate perspective—for example, that adopted by a pension fund manager—an imbalance between the average lifetimes of those in a covered population and the adequacy of fund reserves appears to be little altered by consideration of ALE for that population. Individual-level longevity risk—the prospects for outliving one's financial assets—is, as well, of little relevance to the substantial proportion of the population that reaches retirement age with zero or only modest asset levels. For those people, the problem is one of living on one's social security benefit rather than worrying about annuitizing or drawing down one's savings. Nevertheless, there are important associations among the three dimensions of remaining lifetime, one's level of financial assets, and the experience of disability. The onset of disability in late life provides a signal about the length of one's active life (the individual-level variable of which ALE is a population average); this signal, in turn, indicates that remaining lifetime will be shorter than expected, or that care costs will be greater than expected, or both.

Care needs for most people are addressed through the provision of unpaid care services provided by family members, and this type of care may preserve one's assets as well as protect one's children's inheritance, albeit at what might be a substantial cost to the care providers. In the absence of informal care from family members, or the presence of care needs too severe to be met by family members, one's care needs may end up being publicly financed through Medicaid, but this outcome will generally be accompanied by the exhaustion of one's assets—a full-scale realization, in other words, of longevity risk.

Acknowledgements

Julia Carboni and Benny Goodman made helpful contributions to this chapter.

Notes

1. The annuities market offers a number of additional features and variations on these basic plans, which for the sake of simplicity I ignore.
2. The two-year sample inclusion is a consequence of the biennial interviewing design used by the HRS. Thus, respondents age 65 or 66 in 1998 are 67 or 68 in 2000, 69 or 70 in 2002, and so on. The same approach is applied to those age 65 or 66 in 2000, 2002, or later, but with correspondingly shorter follow-up periods.
3. The results plotted in Figure 3.5 are admittedly, but to an unknown extent, an artifact of the functional form and model specification adopted for this purely descriptive analysis. I have not, for example, explored interactions between age and cumulative experience of disability, both of which are time-varying covariates.
4. Arizona was the only state not to impose an asset test on seniors and people with disabilities in 2018.
5. Author's calculations using the annual Local Area Unemployment Statistics data from US Bureau of Labor Statistics (2020).

References

Arias, E. (2011). *United States Life Tables, 2007.* National Vital Statistics Reports 59(9). Hyattsville, MD: National Center for Health Statistics.

Brouhns, N., M. Denuit, and J. K. Vermunt (2002). 'Measuring the Longevity Risk in Mortality Projections,' *Bulletin of the Swiss Association of Actuaries*, 2: 105–130.

Brown, J. R., G. S. Goda, and K. McGarry (2012). 'Long-term Care Insurance Demand Limited by Beliefs About Needs, Concerns About Insurers, and Care Available from Family,' *Health Affairs*, 31: 1294–1301.

Bugliari, D., N. Campbell, C. Chan, O. Hayden, et al. (2019a). *RAND HRS Longitudinal File 2016 (V1) Documentation.* http://hrsonline.isr.umich.edu/data/index.html

Bugliari, D., N. Campbell, C. Chan, O. Hayden, et al. (2019b). *RAND HRS Detailed Imputations File 2016 (V1) Documentation.* http://hrsonline.isr.umich.edu/data/index.html

Buntin, M. B., C. Damberg, A. Haviland, et al. (2006). 'Consumer-directed Health Care: Early Evidence about Effects on Cost and Quality,' *Health Affairs*, w516 (web exclusive). https://www.healthaffairs.org/doi/full/10.1377/hlthaff.25.w516

Cai, L. and J. Lubitz (2007). 'Was There Compression of Disability for Older Americans from 1992 To 2003?' *Demography*, 44: 479–495.

US Census Bureau (2019). 'Table P-10. Age–People (Both Sexes Combined–All Races) by Median and Mean Income: 1974 to 2018,' *Historical Income Tables: People.*

Washington, DC: US Department of Commerce. https://www.census.gov/data/tables/time-series/demo/income-poverty/historical-income-people.html

Charles, K. and P. Sevak (2005). 'Can Family Caregiving Substitute for Nursing Home Care?' *Journal of Health Economics*, 24: 1174–1190.

Chernew, M., D. M. Cutler, K. Ghosh, and M. B. Landrum (2016). 'Understanding the Improvement in Disability Free Life Expectancy in The US Elderly Population,' NBER Working Paper No. 22306. Cambridge, MA: National Bureau of Economic Research.

Chetty, R., M. Stepner, S. Abraham, et al. (2016). 'The Association between Income and Life Expectancy in The United States, 2001–2014,' *Journal of the American Medical Association*, 315: 1750–1766.

Crimmins, E. M., Y. Zhang, and Y. Saito (2016). 'Trends Over 4 Decades in Disability-Free Life Expectancy in the United States,' *American Journal of Public Health*, 106: 1287–1293.

De Milto, L. (2015). *Program Results Report—Cash & Counseling*. Robert Wood Johnson Foundation (updated version of February 28, 2015).

De Waegenaere, A., B. Melenberg, and R. Stevens (2010). 'Longevity Risk,' *De Economist*, 158: 151–192.

Dushi, I., H. Iams, and B. Trenkamp (2017). 'The Importance of Social Security Benefits to the Income of the Aged Population,' *Social Security Bulletin*, 77: 1–12.

Edwards, R. (2011). 'The Cost of Uncertain Life Span,' NBER Working Paper No. 14093. Cambridge, MA: National Bureau of Economic Research.

Eggelston, J. and R. Munk (2019). 'Net Worth of Households: 2016,' Current Population Reports, P70BR-166 (October).

Freedman, V. A., D. A. Wolf, and V. Mor (2015). 'Mobility and Self-Care Accommodation Duration Measures in the National Health and Aging Trends Study,' NHATS Technical Paper #12. Baltimore: Johns Hopkins University School of Public Health. www.NHATS.org

Health and Retirement Study (2019). *The Health and Retirement Study*. Institute for Social Research: University of Michigan. https://hrs.isr.umich.edu/about

Hodge, G. A. and C. Greve (2007). 'Public-Private Partnerships: An International Performance Review,' *Public Administration Review*, 67: 545–558.

Imai, K. and S. Soneji (2007). 'On the Estimation of Disability-Free Life Expectancy: Sullivan's Method and Its Extension,' *Journal of the American Statistical Association*, 102: 1199–1211.

Jagger, C., H. Van Oyen, and J.-M. Robine (2014). *Health Expectancy Calculation by the Sullivan Method: A Practical Guide* (4th edn). https://reves.site.ined.fr/en/resources/computation_online/sullivan/

Johnson, R. W. and J. M. Wiener (2006). 'A Profile of Frail Older Americans and Their Caregivers,' Occasional Paper Number 8. Washington, DC: The Urban Institute.

Katz, S., L. G. Branch, M. H. Branson, et al. (1983). 'Active Life Expectancy,' *New England Journal of Medicine*, 309: 1218–1224.

Klerman, J. A., K. Kaley, and A. Pozniak (2014). *Family and Medical Leave in 2012: Technical Report*. Cambridge, MA: Abt Associates Inc. https://www.dol.gov/agencies/oasp/evaluation/fmla/fmla2012

Laditka, S. B. and J. N. Laditka (2009). 'Active Life Expectancy: A Central Measure of Population Health,' in P. Uhlenberg, ed., *International Handbook of Population Aging*. New York: Springer, pp. 543–565.

Ma, J., E. M. Ward, R. L. Siegel, and A. Jemal (2015). 'Temporal Trends in Mortality in the United States, 1969–2013,' *Journal of the American Medical Association*, 314: 1731–1739.

Manton, K. G., X. Gu, and V. L. Lamb (2006). 'Long-Term Trends in Life Expectancy and Active Life Expectancy in the United States,' *Population and Development Review*, 32: 81–105.

McGarry, K. (2022). 'Perceptions of Mortality: Individual Assessments of Longevity Risk.' In O.S. Mitchell, ed., *New Models for Managing Longevity Risk: Public/Private Partnerships*. Oxford, UK: Oxford University Press, pp. 11–33.

Musumeci, M. B., and P. Chidambaram (2019). *Medicaid Financial Eligibility for Seniors and People with Disabilities: Findings from a 50-State Survey*. Kaiser Family Foundation Issue Brief. https://www.kff.org/medicaid/issue-brief/medicaid-financial-eligibility-for-seniors-and-people-with-disabilities-findings-from-a-50-state-survey/

NAC/AARP (National Alliance for Caregiving and AARP Public Policy Institute) (2015). *Caregiving in the US*. https://www.aarp.org/ppi/info-2015/caregiving-in-the-united-states-2015.html

National Center for Health Statistics (2018). *Health, United States, 2017: With Special Feature on Mortality*. Hyattsville, MD: National Center for Health Statistics.

National Partnership for Women & Families (2019). *State Paid Family and Medical Leave Insurance Laws*. https://www.nationalpartnership.org (August).

Pauly, M. V. (1990). 'The Rational Nonpurchase of Long-Term-Care Insurance,' *Journal of Political Economy*, 98: 153–168.

Perozek, M. (2008). 'Using Subjective Expectations to Forecast Longevity: Do Survey Respondents Know Something We Don't Know?' *Demography*, 45: 95–113.

Poterba, J., S. Venti, and D. A. Wise (2018). 'Longitudinal Determinants of End-Of-Life Wealth Inequality,' *Journal of Public Economics*, 162: 78–88.

Reaves, E. L. and M. B. Musumeci (2015). *Medicaid and Long-Term Services and Supports: A Primer*. Kaiser Commission on Medicaid and the Uninsured publication #8617-02. http://files.kff.org

Social Security Administration (2019). *Annual Statistical Supplement to the Social Security Bulletin, 2018*. Washington, DC: SSA Publication No. 13–11700. https://www.ssa.gov/policy/docs/statcomps/supplement/2018/supplement18.pdf

Spillman, B. and T. Waidmann (2014). *Rates and Timing of Medicaid Enrollment among Older Americans*. Report to the Office of Disability, Aging and Long-term Care Policy of the US Department of Health and Human Services. Washington, DC: The Urban Institute.

Stallard, E. (2016). 'Compression of Morbidity and Mortality: New Perspectives,' *North American Actuarial Journal*, 20: 341–354.

Sullivan, D.F. (1971). 'A Single Index of Mortality and Morbidity,' *HSMHA Health Reports*, 86: 347–354.

US Bureau of Labor Statistics (2020). *Local Area Unemployment Statistics*. Washington, DC: United States Department of Labor. https://www.bls.gov/lau/data.htm

Van Houtven, C. and E. Norton (2004). 'Informal Care and Health Care Use of Older Adults,' *Journal of Health Economics*, 23: 1159–1180.

Varadhan, R., Q-L. Xue, and K. Bandeen-Roche (2014). 'Semicompeting Risks in Aging Research: Methods, Issues and Needs,' *Lifetime Data Analysis*, 20: 538–562.

Whitman, K., G. L. Reznik, and D. Shoffner (2011). 'Who Never Receives Social Security Benefits?' *Social Security Bulletin*, 71(2): 17–24. https://papers.ssrn.com/sol3/papers.cfm?abstract_id=1831635

Witters, D. (2011). 'Caregiving Costs US Economy $25.2 Billion in Lost Productivity.' The Gallup Poll. https://news.gallup.com/poll/148670/caregiving-costs-economy-billion-lost-productivity.aspx

Wolf, D. A. (2019). 'Effects of Paid Caregiving Leave on Government Costs.' Presented at the AEI-Brookings Conference on Paid Caregiving Leave, Washington DC, November 18.

Wolf, D. A. and T. M. Gill (2008). 'Fitting Event-History Models to Uneventful Data,' Working Paper 65. Syracuse, NY: Syracuse University Center for Policy Research. https://surface.syr.edu/cpr/65/

Wolf, D. A., C. F. Mendes De Leon, and T. A. Glass (2007). 'Trends in Rates of Onset of and Recovery from Disability at Older Ages: 1982–1994,' *Journal of Gerontology: Social Sciences*, 62B: S3–S10.

Chapter 4

Does Working Longer Enhance Old Age?

Maria D. Fitzpatrick

Managing longevity risk is an important component driving the financial and labor market decisions of older Americans. Historically, most research on the relationship between health and retirement focused on the effects of poor health or negative health shocks on the labor market and financial decision-making of older workers. More recently, research has expanded to focus on how labor market decisions about when to retire affect health outcomes. This chapter summarizes the research of the effects of retirement on health and longevity. I distill the growing set of studies into a set of themes, and focus on those most relevant for those interested in managing longevity risk for Americans.

How Might Retirement Affect Health?

Understanding the relationship between retirement and health is difficult because retirement typically involves multiple related changes to people's lives. Most prominent is the change to people's activity, particularly physical and social. The term retirement is often used to refer to someone moving from full employment to no employment, but it has many different meanings to different people and transitions are not as clearly defined as one might think (Chan and Stevens 2008). Here, I will use the term in the way that most people do: a transition from working at some person-specific historic level to working less than that, with the possibility of an associated start of collecting retirement benefits.

There are multiple ways in which the activity changes with retirement might be beneficial for people's health, well-being, and longevity. For example, from the perspective of someone employed in a physically demanding job, retirement may prove beneficial to health as it allows the person to limit or refrain from the strenuous activity. Retirement may allow people to invest more time in self-care and healthy behavior, including eating more healthily and exercising. If so, there are likely to be positive effects with these types of health investments. Also, in many cases, retirement is associated with a switch from a stressful and taxing work environment to a more relaxed

Maria D. Fitzpatrick, *Does Working Longer Enhance Old Age?*.
In: *New Models for Managing Longevity Risk*. Edited by Olivia S. Mitchell, Oxford University Press.
© Pension Research Council (2022). DOI: 10.1093/oso/9780192859808.003.0004

and carefree schedule and experience. This may have beneficial effects on peoples' physical, mental, and emotional health, possibly also resulting in increased longevity.

Changes in activity with retirement may also have detrimental effects on people's health, well-being, and longevity. If employment and work give people's lives meaning and/or involve positive social interactions, then retirement may lead people's health to deteriorate. Additionally, there is a medical literature showing that physical inactivity can lead to increases in negative health shocks like infection. Therefore, if retirement means going from an active working life to a sedentary home life, people's health may deteriorate. Also, if people replace their work time with negative healthy behaviors (e.g. more drinking or smoking), this can erode health and longevity.

The transition to retirement can bring on changes to income and other financial resources. Upon retirement, people typically shift from having an earned income from their employer to (i) collecting pension benefits from their employer and/or withdrawal of funds from retirement savings accounts, (ii) collecting public pension benefits, or (iii) some combination of the two. They may also begin drawing down other types of assets. Depending on the size of earnings compared to the generosity of employer-provided and public pension benefits, as well as a person's own retirement savings, income could increase, decrease, or stay the same. Most often, it decreases or stays the same. For example, the replacement rate in the US social security system in 2005 was 64 percent of final earnings for the median quintile of earners ages 64 and 65 (Biggs and Springstead 2008). Relatedly, Chetty et al. (2016) found that longevity increases through the income distribution, which may, but does not necessarily, mean that changes to income will lead to changes in longevity. More relevant to this discussion, Snyder and Evans (2006) showed that changes to retirement wealth driven by a change in social security benefit rules led to higher mortality.

Another shift occurring in retirement that may have effects on health is access to health insurance. In 2018, 61 percent of adults ages 19 to 64 were covered by employer-provided health insurance (Kauffman Family Foundation 2018). That proportion would be even higher if the sample were limited to those employed nearing retirement. As people transition out of employment and into retirement, many will lose their employer-provided health insurance. If they are age 65 plus, they will have access to and will likely utilize Medicare, so the effects on their health will depend on the coverage of their employer-provided insurance relative to Medicare. If they are not yet age 65, some (mostly those employed in the public sector) may have access to retiree health insurance through their former employers. Others must decide whether to forgo health insurance or to purchase it in the private market. Forgoing health insurance may prove detrimental to health and longevity, particularly for older people who forgo or postpone preventative or diagnostic measures when they lack health insurance coverage.[1]

The combined effect of the above may differ across individuals and will therefore vary across populations, a point we will return to as we summarize the literature below. Similarly, the effects of retirement on health and longevity may be different, even of opposite sign, depending on the measures used. For example, it is possible that retirement might lead people to be happier and less stressed, while also involving negative physical shocks that might lead them to die earlier.

Finally, changes to activity and health shocks may have immediate effects and may also serve to influence health and longevity in the long term. This is highlighted in canonical health economics models (e.g. Grossman 1972), which show that health is a stock measure resulting from both current and past inputs. For any given individual, the move to retirement may have positive or negative effects on health, depending on the horizon of interest.

Relationships between Retirement and Health

To determine the relationship between retirement and health, one might be tempted to compare the health and longevity of retired Americans to those not retired. This comparison is flawed for a few reasons. First, older Americans are more likely to be retired and to have poorer health and higher mortality rates than those even just a bit younger. Figure 4.1 presents information on the retirement rates and death rates of Americans by age for ages 50 to 80.[2] From this figure, one can see that retirement and mortality increase with age. For example, the proportion of men in retirement goes from eight percent at age 50 to 45 percent at age 60, and 96 percent by age 70. At the same time, male mortality is low (just 0.5% probability) at age 50, then doubles by age 60, doubles again by age 70, and again by age 80. By age 80, 57 males out of every 1,000 have died. Other health measures decline with age in similar ways to the mortality increase. Therefore, comparison of health outcomes for those retired versus those not retired would lead us to overestimate the relationship between retirement and health, because it would be attributing some of the effects of aging to the decision to retire.

One might think the solution to this is to compare the health of people of the same age who are retired with those still working. But, health and retirement decisions are intertwined in ways that make it difficult to identify the causal effects of retirement on health in this way. Most importantly, poor health is a common factor driving people to stop working and enter retirement. Therefore, on average, even among people of the same age, retirees may be in poorer health than those who have not yet retired.

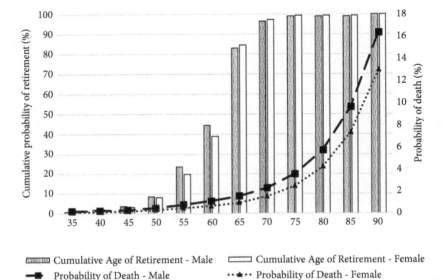

Figure 4.1 Probability of being retired (left axis) and mortality (right axis), by age
Sources: Federal Reserve Board (2016) and Social Security Administration (2019).

This is evident when we examine the health of retirees versus non-retirees. Insler (2014) used the HRS to show the health levels and changes in health by age separately for groups of retired people and those who are not retired. He found that average reported health was higher at every age for those not yet retired. Also, people who are retired had more negative changes in their health than those who had not yet retired. This is illustrative of the fact that unhealthier people retire earlier and healthier people work longer.

Because the relationship between retirement and health is multidirectional, studies have used a variety of techniques to identify the effects of retirement on people's health and well-being. Many of these involve making use of pension plan rules that create different incentives to retire for people who are otherwise quite similar. Using these rules in this way helps overcome the problem that differences in the types of people who are retired may drive differences in health outcomes rather than retirement itself.

The First Generation of US Studies: The Health and Retirement Study

One of the first studies to examine how health changed during retirement was Charles (2004). In order to study this question, the author used the rich information included in the Health and Retirement Study (HRS), an ongoing nationally representative panel survey of Americans above age 50. Charles focused on men in their 60s and 70s. He also used the Survey of Asset and Health Dynamics among the Oldest Head and the National Longitudinal Survey of Mature Men. To explore relationship between retirement and health, Charles used the fact that retirement patterns of the cohorts of men in his study were influenced by social security rules—and changes to those rules over time—and by the elimination of mandatory retirement in the US. Social security eligibility changes quite a bit as people age, as do take-up rates for social security benefits and their labor supply. At age 62, most Americans are first eligible for Social Security's Retirement and Survivors Insurance, and many claim at this age. For cohorts born before 1937, relevant to Charles's analysis, the full retirement age under the social security rules was set at 65.

Between ages 62 and 70 (or 72 for some cohorts in the analysis), there were changes to the incentives to either retire or continue working driven by the social security benefit formula and the social security earnings test. The social security benefit formula encourages continued work after early eligibility by increasing the size of the benefit if one delays claiming. The earnings test taxes away social security benefits based on one's earned income, making it less attractive to continue working while collecting benefits or, conversely, to claim benefits while still working. In the 1980s, the earnings test rules were changed to make continued work and postponing benefit collection even more attractive. In addition, some of the cohorts covered in the Charles study were making decisions about retirement before mandatory retirement policies were prohibited in the US.

Using a statistical method called instrumental variables estimation, Charles used these differences in eligibility and incentives to essentially compare the subjective well-being of men who retired at younger versus older ages because of these rules. Doing so allowed him to argue that the comparison returned an estimate of the effect of retirement itself on subjective well-being, at least for those whose retirement behavior was influenced by these rules. He found that retirement had the effect of increasing men's reported well-being.[3] An open question, however, is whether this was a change in the true underlying health of these men, or a change in their own perception of their health. Surely, improvements in subjective well-being are valuable and important, but they may not translate into changes in physical health.

In a similar setup, Neuman (2008) used the HRS and information about public and private sector pensions to estimate the effect of retirement on a wider set of health outcomes than those in Charles (2004). In addition to the social security benefit rule changes, Neuman used eligibility rules in survey respondents' employer-provided pensions. He also used the tendency for spouses to retire at the same time, even if they were different ages; this means that one spouse's decision to retire may be affected by the other spouse's age and eligibility for social security. Neuman found that retirement has a positive effect on subjective measures of health, but more objective measures of physical health, like mobility, were either not affected at all or were negatively affected. As in Charles (2004), it may be the case that these changes in subjective health in the HRS reflect changes in respondents' perceptions of their health rather than their underlying health conditions. Also using the HRS, Coe and Lindeboom (2008) and Coe et al. (2012) studied the effects of retirement on health and cognitive functioning, using the offer of early retirement windows by employers to their employees.

Since employers cannot offer these opportunities to employees of varying health status, these windows should drive retirement but be unrelated to people's health. Also, these windows are typically offered for short periods of time and are unanticipated by the workers, potentially making it harder for people to adjust their retirement decisions in ways related to their health than changes to social security eligibility rules. The authors showed small positive effects, if any, of retirement on subjective health outcomes measured in the first year or two after retirement, and no effects on objective health outcomes. Relatedly, there were small increases in cognitive functioning for blue-collar workers, but, they faded out over time. The authors concluded there was little relationship between increases in the length of working life and in longevity in the US.

Dave et al. (2008) take a different empirical approach using the HRS. To control for the tendency of less healthy people to retire earlier, the authors used a statistical technique called individual fixed effects, implying that the estimates of the relationship between retirement and health result from comparing individuals' health after they retired to their health before they retired. Results showed deterioration across a range of health measures. For example, mental health measures declined by six to nine percent, mobility measures decreased by five to 16 percent, and rates of illness increased by five to nine percent. Nevertheless, if negative shocks to people's health (like an injury or a diagnosis) lead to retirement, these estimates are too negative because they attribute some of the pre-retirement shock to the retirement itself. This is partly why these estimates differ from those previously mentioned.

Insler (2014) took a slightly different tack. Instead of using the rules of pension plans to help make appropriate comparisons of individuals, he makes use of people's expectations of their retirement date in an instrumental variables strategy. The intuition is that he is removing the effect of unanticipated health shocks (the type that might be problematic in the Dave et al. (2008) study) by using people's predictions of when they will retire. To further remove differences in anticipated health, Insler (2014) controls for a rich set of covariates. He finds that retirement leads to improvements in a general measure of health that he had constructed. These improvements seem to be related to decreases in smoking and increases in exercise. If the set of controls included does not adequately adjust for underlying health differences in people who expect to retire at different ages, it may be the case that these estimates are biased.

Gorry et al. (2018) follow Charles (2004) to use age-based variation in eligibility for social security retirement benefits, applicability of the social security earnings test, and eligibility for retirement benefits in an employer-sponsored pension, to create arguably causal estimates of the effects of retirement on physical and mental health, life satisfaction, and health care utilization. The idea is that these age-based retirement eligibility measures should not be directly correlated with health, except through their effects on retirement behavior, as they do not prompt discrete jumps in health status at these ages beyond what is controlled for with age trends. The authors reported that retirement improved measures of physical and mental health (significant after more than four years of retirement), and life satisfaction (significant in the first four years of retirement). They found no evidence that improvements were driven by increases in health care utilization.

The Next Generation of US Studies: Administrative Data

With a wealth of information on respondents, the HRS is a remarkable resource for research on older Americans, yet it provides a relatively small sample. As a result, researchers have relatively low statistical power to identify effects of retirement on health, particularly if these are small. Without large samples, it can be difficult to use certain statistical techniques aimed at identifying causal effects and others aimed at identifying effects across different subgroups of the population, because such techniques are 'data-hungry,' requiring larger amounts of data than do traditional techniques.

Another concern about the HRS, which is true of all survey data, is that it provides mainly self-reported information about health status and health conditions. A shift in retirement status may lead people to feel differently about their health or interpret their health conditions differently. For example, retiring from a physically strenuous job may make people with physical limitations feel less restricted by those limitations. Alternatively, becoming less active and more socially isolated may make people feel as though a health condition has worsened. Therefore, survey responses on the effects of retirement on health capture some combination of the effects on underlying health and changes in the individual's interpretation of his or her health status.

More recent work in the US, and, as I detail below, in Europe, has succeeded in bringing administrative data to bear on the question of how retirement affects health. Administrative data often contains all the individuals in some population (e.g. a country), so it usually has more observations, and potentially more statistical power, than a survey like the HRS. Also, measures of health in administrative data often derive from health records, like death or hospital records. Analyzing the effect of retirement on health using these objective health measures is more likely to capture changes in underlying conditions or health care utilization, compared to survey respondents' perceptions. Yet, these benefits come at a cost, since most administrative data, particularly in the US, lack rich information about household composition, savings, and other factors relevant for understanding retirement and health.

An example of research utilizing administrative data in the US is Fitzpatrick and Moore (2018). There, we make use of the early retirement age for social security eligibility at age 62. Around 30 percent of Americans claim social security from the very month they turn age 62. Using the census of all death records in the US from the Center for Disease Control's Multiple Cause of Death Records, we document that there is a two percent increase in male mortality precisely at age 62. This increase in mortality is larger for single men, as well as for men with low levels of educational attainment. This increase in male mortality is the increase in male mortality in the entire population, not necessarily just among those who retire. Although about 10 percent of men retire at this age, the death records data do not have information on employment and retirement, so we cannot directly identify a link between the two. Nevertheless, there are no other discontinuous changes to people's lives that occur exactly at age 62 that could possibly be driving the increase in male mortality. We also show that there are no similar increases in mortality at any other age, including other birthday-related ages, between ages 55 and 75, which suggests that this is not just a 'birthday effect.' And we show that this increase in mortality at age 62 is only present for cohorts eligible for social security at age 62, not for those whose eligibility starts at other ages.

To discover whether the increase in male mortality at age 62 is due to a shift in activity, a change in income levels, or a change in health insurance status, we couple our analysis of the administrative death records with a set of analyses from the HRS. We look for correlations between the size of the mortality increases at age 62 among various subgroups with the size of their changes in other measures at age 62. There is little to no correlation between the size of the mortality changes and either income or health insurance coverage. Yet, there is a clear positive correlation between increases in mortality and drops in male labor market participation.

What Can We Learn from Studies in Other Countries?

Sometimes studies from other countries can be useful for showing what might occur in a particular context. There have been many studies conducted in other countries, particularly in European settings, that have investigated the effect of retirement on health. The European studies can be separated into two groups, as with the US research. The first round of these studies used HRS-like data and variation in retirement eligibility rules in pension systems, or sometimes across different pension systems in different countries, to identify the effects of retirement on health (Bound and Waidmann 2007; Coe and Zamarro 2011; Behncke 2012; Lucifora and Vigani 2018; Bertoni et al. 2018; Delugas and Balia 2019). The second round used variation in pension eligibility rules, sometimes long-standing eligibility rules and other times unanticipated early retirement windows, coupled with administrative data on health outcomes, health expenditures, and health care usage (Bloemen et al. 2017; Hallberg et al. 2015; Hagen 2018; Shai 2018; Zhang et al. 2018; Frimmel and Pruckner 2018; Rogne and Syse 2018; Zulkarnain and Rutledge 2018; Nielsen 2019; Grøtting 2019; Giesecke, 2019; Kuhn et al. 2019).

In both sets of studies using European data, the results are generally inconclusive. Some of this undoubtedly results from the fact that the studies use different outcome measures, ranging from subjective measures to mental health, to expenditures on health, to mortality. Some of the heterogeneity also stems from different methods used. In addition, they use different populations, aged from their 50s to their 70s, army employees to entire populations, and men or women. Yet, ultimately, some of the heterogeneity may result from the fact that there are many pathways through which retirement affects health, producing different estimates of the net effect.

Conclusions

The past 15 years have seen an explosion in economics research aimed at understanding the effects of retirement on health and longevity. Seeing how health factors enter the retirement decision is important for interpreting the resulting effect that retirement has on health. Many studies in the US and Europe have used a variety of data sources and methodologies to investigate this question, but the results are largely inconclusive. The pattern of evidence from studies of retirement in the US suggests there may be benefits to retirement relating to mental health and subjective well-being, but there may also be costs in terms of decreased physical health and increased mortality. In sum, the clearest conclusion from this review of the literature is that much more research is necessary. Large data sets with rich information on health inputs and outcomes, linked to administrative records, will likely be necessary to help us more fully understand the full nature of how health affects retirement, both on average and for specific population subgroups.

Importantly, the latest research showing that retirement has negative effects on health and increases mortality indicates that the relationship between retirement and longevity is more complicated than one might have thought. It has long been known that people take their expectations of longevity into account when making decisions about retirement. Now, we know that people's decisions about retirement may also affect their health and longevity in crucial ways. This makes planning for retirement by individuals more complicated than if the relationship were unidirectional.

The research also has implications for companies with older employees and for governments working to design optimal retirement and pension policy. For example, it may be the case that taking up bridge jobs or part-time work would help individuals to avoid the negative health consequences of retirement. Employers may find it easier to retain older workers by offering them these kinds of flexible work arrangements, which could in turn benefit worker health and longevity. Another incentive to delay retirement might come from government policies aimed at delaying enrollment for social security payments that may have the benefit of improving the health of older Americans as well as making them more financially secure during retirement. Future research should be aimed at understanding more about how well the tools of business and government could help reduce the negative health consequences of retirement.

Notes

1. It is worth noting that some of the options and decision-making around health insurance coverage for workers who retire before age 65 is likely to have changed with the Affordable Care Act (ACA). By providing the opportunity to purchase health insurance coverage through the exchanges, the ACA gives more options to people retiring before Medicare eligibility.
2. Information on cumulative probability of retirement comes from the 2016 Survey of Household Economics and Decisionmaking. Information on mortality rates is for 2016 and comes from the 2019 Social Security Administration Office of the Chief Actuary Report.

3. This was in contrast to a negative relationship when he does not use these techniques to control for the fact that men in poor physical and emotional health are likely to retire earlier.

References

Behncke, S. (2012). 'Does Retirement Trigger Ill Health?' *Health Economics*, 21(3): 282–300. https://doi.org/10.1002/hec.1712

Bertoni, M., S. Maggi, and G. Weber (2018). 'Work, Retirement, and Muscle Strength Loss in Old Age,' *Health Economics*, 27(1): 115–128. https://doi.org/10.1002/hec.3517

Biggs, A. G., and G. R. Springstead (2008). 'Alternate Measures of Replacement Rates for Social Security Benefits and Retirement Income,' *Social Security Bulletin*, 68(2). https://www.ssa.gov/policy/docs/ssb/v68n2/v68n2p1.html

Bloemen, H., S. Hochguertel, and J. Zweerink. (2017). 'The Causal Effect of Retirement on Mortality: Evidence from Targeted Incentives to Retire Early,' *Health Economics*, 26(12): e204–e218. https://doi.org/10.1002/hec.3493

Bound, J., and T. Waidmann. (2007). 'Estimating the Health Effects of Retirement,' *SSRN Electronic Journal*. https://doi.org/10.2139/ssrn.1082047

Chan, S., and A. H. Stevens, (2008). 'What You Don't Know Can't Help You: Pension Knowledge and Retirement Decision-Making,' *The Review of Economics and Statistics*, 90(2): 14.

Charles, K. K. (2004). 'Is Retirement Depressing? Labor Force Inactivity and Psychological Well Being in Later Life,' *Research in Labor Economics*, 23: 269–299.

Chetty, R., M. Stepner, S. Abraham, S. Lin, B. Scuderi, N. Turner, A. Bergeron, and D. Cutler. (2016). 'The Association between Income and Life Expectancy in the United States, 2001–2014,' *JAMA*, 315(16): 1750–1766. https://doi.org/10.1001/jama.2016.4226

Coe, N. B. and M. Lindeboom (2008). 'Does Retirement Kill You? The Evidence from Early Retirement Windows,' CentER Discussion Paper Series No. 2008–93. Tilburg, ND: Tilburg University. https://papers.ssrn.com/sol3/papers.cfm?abstract_id=1295315

Coe, N. B. and Z. Con Gaudecker (2011). 'Retirement Effects on Health in Europe,' *Journal of Health Economics*, 30(1): 77–86. https://doi.org/10.1016/j.jhealeco.2010.11.002

Coe, N. B., H. M. Von Gaudecker, M. Lindeboom, and J. Maurer (2012). 'The Effect of Retirement on Cognitive Functioning,' *Health Economics*, 21(8): 913–927.

Dave, D, I. Rashad, and J. Spasojevic (2008). 'The Effects of Retirement on Physical and Mental Health Outcomes,' *Southern Economic Journal*, 75(2): 497–523.

Delugas, E. and S. Balia (2019). 'A Life Change for the Better? The Health Consequence of Retirement.' Working paper presented at 60th Annual Conference (RSA) of the Italian Economic Association, Oct. 2019. https://siecon3607788.c.cdn77.org/sites/siecon.org/files/media_wysiwyg/227-delugas-balia.pdf

Federal Reserve Board (2016). *Survey of Household Economics and Decisionmaking*. https://www.federalreserve.gov/consumerscommunities/shed_data.htm

Fitzpatrick, M. D., and T.J. Moore (2018). 'The Mortality Effects of Retirement: Evidence from Social Security Eligibility at Age 62. ' *Journal of Public Economics*, 157: 121–137. https://doi.org/10.1016/j.jpubeco.2017.12.001

Frimmel, W. and G. J. Pruckner (2018). '2018 Retirement and Healthcare Utilization.' Working Paper, No. 1802. Johannes Kepler University of Linz, Department of Economics, Linz. http://hdl.handle.net/10419/183261

Giesecke, M. (2019). 'The Retirement Mortality Puzzle: Evidence from a Regression Discontinuity Design.' Rurr Economic Papers #800. RWI—Leibniz-Institut für Wirtschaftsforschung Hohenzollernstr. Essen, Germany. https://doi.org/10.4419/86788928

Gorry, A., D. Gorry, and S.N. Slavov (2018). 'Does Retirement Improve Health and Life Satisfaction?' *Health Economics*, 27(12): 2067–2086. https://doi.org/10.1002/hec.3821

Grossman, M. (1972). 'On the Concept of Health Capital and the Demand for Health,' *Journal of Political Economy*, 80(2): 223–255.

Grøtting, M. W. (2019). *Empirical Essays on Health and Aging*. Doctoral Thesis, University of Bergin. 190. http://bora.uib.no/bitstream/handle/1956/20407/Dr.thesis_2019_Maja%20W%20Grøtting.pdf?sequence=1&isAllowed=y

Hagen, J. (2018). 'The Effects of Increasing the Normal Retirement Age on Health Care Utilization and Mortality,' *Journal of Population Economics*, 31(1): 193–234. https://doi.org/10.1007/s00148-017-0664-x

Hallberg, D., P. Johansson, and M. Josephson (2015). 'Is an Early Retirement Offer Good for your Health? Quasi-experimental Evidence from the Army.' *Journal of Health Economics*, 44: 274–285. https://doi.org/10.1016/j.jhealeco.2015.09.006

Insler, M. (2014). 'The Health Consequences of Retirement,' *Journal of Human Resources*, 49(1): 195–233.

Kauffman Family Foundation (2018). 'Employer Sponsored Coverage Rates for the Nonelderly by Age.' https://www.kff.org/other/state-indicator/rate-by-age-2/?currentTimeframe=0&selectedDistributions=adults-19-64&sortModel=%7B%22colId%22:%22Location%22,%22sort%22:%22asc%22%7D (accessed July 11, 2020).

Kuhn, A., S. Staubli, J. Wuellrich, and J. Zweimüller (2019). 'Fatal Attraction? Extended Unemployment Benefits, Labor Force Exits, and Mortality,' *Journal of Public Economics*, 104087. https://doi.org/10.1016/j.jpubeco.2019.104087

Lucifora, C. and D. Vigani. (2018). 'Health Care Utilization at Retirement: The Role of the Opportunity Cost of Time,' *Health Economics*, 27(12): 2030–2050. https://doi.org/10.1002/hec.3819

Neuman, K. (2008). 'Quit Your Job and Get Healthier? The Effect of Retirement on Health,' *Journal of Labor Research*, 29(2): 177–201.

Nielsen, N. F. (2019). 'Sick of Retirement?' *Journal of Health Economics*, 65: 133–152. https://doi.org/10.1016/j.jhealeco.2019.03.008

Rogne, A. F. and A. Syse (2018). 'The Effect of Retirement on Male Mortality: Quasi-experimental Evidence from Norway,' *European Sociological Review*, 34(5): 501–517. https://doi.org/10.1093/esr/jcy023

Shai, O. (2018). 'Is Retirement Good for Men's Health? Evidence Using a Change in the Retirement Age in Israel,' *Journal of Health Economics*, 57: 15–30. https://doi.org/10.1016/j.jhealeco.2017.10.008

Snyder, S.E. and W.N. Evans (2006). 'The Effect of Income on Mortality: Evidence from the Social Security Notch,' *Review of Economics and Statistics*, 88(3): 482–495.

Social Security Administration (2019). *Historical Probabilities of Death*. https://www.ssa.gov/oact/HistEst/Death/2019/DeathProbabilities2019.html

Zhang, Y., M. Salm, and A. Van Soest (2018). 'The Effect of Retirement on Health-care Utilization: Evidence from China,' *Journal of Health Economics*, 62: 165–177. https://doi.org/10.1016/j.jhealeco.2018.09.009

Zulkarnain, A., and M.S. Rutledge (2018). 'How Does Delayed Retirement Affect Mortality and Health?' *SSRN Electronic Journal*. https://doi.org/10.2139/ssrn.3261325

Chapter 5

Working Longer Solves (*Almost*) Everything

The Correlation between Employment, Social Engagement, and Longevity

Tim Driver and Amanda Henshon

For more than a century, the overall population of the United States and the world has been aging steadily,[1] and though the increase in the proportion of older adults differs throughout the world, between 2015 and 2050, the number of adults over 65 will nearly double as a percentage of population overall (Figure 5.1).[2] Data from the United States Census Bureau indicate that more than 10,000 people in the US will turn 65 each day for the next 20 years (US Census Bureau 2017).

According to the latest Bureau of Labor Statistics data, based on 2016 figures, 'older households'—defined as those headed by someone age 65 and older—spend an average of $45,756 per year, or roughly $3,800 a month. That is about $1,000 less than the monthly average spent by all US households combined (US Bureau of Labor Statistics 2017b). Assuming retirement at 65, an average person would have to earn nearly 1.5 times his or her yearly expenditures over the course of a 40-year career in order to save enough to support a 25-year retirement.[3]

Additionally, early retirement and early initiation of social security benefits results in a failure to maximize those benefits. It has been estimated that 90 percent of Americans begin collecting social security retirement benefits at or before their full retirement age, with the most popular age being 62, the earliest eligible age, and the average age to begin receiving benefits being 64 (Munnell and Chen 2015). This choice of drawing earlier benefits has a lasting impact, reducing the monthly benefits received by as much as 25 percent when compared to waiting until age 66 and an additional 32 percent for those who wait until age 70 (Social Security Administration 2020).

The very concept of retirement is no more than a social construct with an arbitrarily selected age. Age 70 was designated as the appropriate age for mandatory retirement in the first state-sponsored age-based social insurance

Tim Driver and Amanda Henshon, *Working Longer Solves (Almost) Everything*.
In: *New Models for Managing Longevity Risk*. Edited by Olivia S. Mitchell, Oxford University Press.
© Pension Research Council (2022). DOI: 10.1093/oso/9780192859808.003.0005

(a)

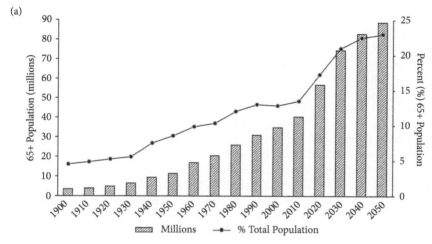

(b)

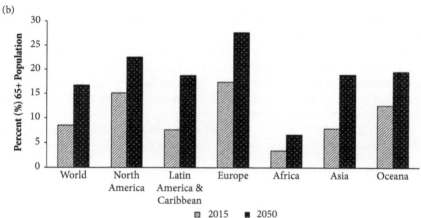

Figure 5.1 For more than a century, the United States and the world have been aging steadily

Note: Though the world population is aging, the pace of that aging is not the same around the world. Regions vary in the size and projected growth of their populations age 65 and over. Many of the oldest countries are in Europe, a trend that will continue through 2050. The older population in Asia and Latin America will more than double between 2015 and 2050.
Source: Federal Interagency Forum on Aging Related Statistics (2019).

program adopted by Otto von Bismarck in late 19th-century Germany as a means of staving off calls for radical socialist responses to political unrest caused, in part, by high youth unemployment rates. The age of 70 had nothing to do with ability or anything else relevant to competence, and its selection was likely more to do with the fact that most workers did not live to this advanced age. Germany later lowered the retirement age to 65 in 1916, an age still well beyond the life expectancy of most workers. Likewise, social security eligibility age calculations in the United States were determined more by life expectancy in the early 20th century and the need to open up jobs for younger workers, as the US was struggling to emerge from the Great Depression, than on any carefully constructed policy determination about when employees should no longer work (Laskow 2014).

Working longer provides additional lifetime earnings and the opportunity for incremental saving, and it also augments the size of eventual pension and social security benefits (especially if receipt of social security benefits, which rise by about 8% per year of delay, is postponed while one continues to work). Longer worklives also reduce the number of years of retirement during which these augmented assets will be consumed. Even without considering any health benefit, deferred retirement results in greater resources amassed to support fewer years of retirement.

The Business Case for Older Workers

Retaining older adults in the workforce benefits employers. Employers are always in need of experienced, well-trained, and productive workers. As the overall population ages, the perception of what constitutes the 'working age' is evolving to include older adults in their late 60s and beyond. Moreover, that population is growing as a proportion of the total population faster than any other age group (Figure 5.2).

In early 2020, prior to the COVID-19 pandemic, we saw historically low unemployment rates, with many jobs unfilled due to labor shortages. This

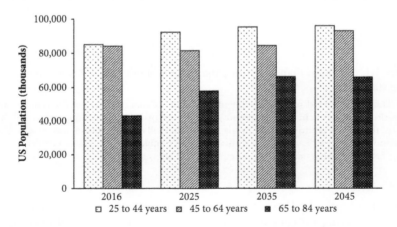

Figure 5.2 US working-age population is getting older, population projections, 2016–2045

Source: US Census Bureau (2017).

labor scarcity was heightened by restrictions on immigration. The only increasing pool of workers from which employers could fill their needs was those age 55 and over. Yet with the recession brought on by the pandemic, early indicators suggest that older workers will struggle to find work. During the Great Recession, it took unemployed older workers twice as long to find work as their younger counterparts (Johnson 2012). And like in 2009, there is now a surge in consumers seeking jobs on sites like RetirementJobs.com. But COVID-19 complicates the situation, not only in the lack of predictability of any economic recovery, but also in the categorization of older employees as 'at risk.' More than ever, older workers are seeking jobs they can perform from home, which may further limit employment options. Yet no matter the economic situation, overcoming misconceptions about older workers is crucial to expanding their access to employment.

More experienced

Employers benefit from both the work experience and life experience that older workers provide. Job-specific abilities may require years to acquire and develop. This is true not only of the skills required by specialists like architects, musicians, and craftspeople, but also of skills obtained through accumulated knowledge by salespeople, drivers, factory workers, and others. Experiential familiarity allows salespeople to communicate vast arrays of information to customers, and manufacturing workers to anticipate and avoid mistakes. Institutional knowledge accumulated by older employees as well as time-earned interpersonal skills can add value to mentoring relationships and assist in training younger workers. Additionally, older workers have established professional networks that expedite access to partners, funders, and others who can facilitate job execution.[4]

The assumption that performance declines with age as employees burn out or slow down is not supported by data. In fact, long-recognized meta-studies of employee productivity by age using objective measures of production output show a small, but statistically significant, positive correlation between age and performance (Waldman and Avolio 1986). A study of a Mercedes Benz assembly facility suggests that older workers made fewer severe errors on the assembly line. Though that study was conducted at a single German plant, the authors believe the results are generalizable to other similar large-scale manufacturing facilities worldwide (Borsch-Supan and Weiss 2016).

Lower turnover rate and increased workforce flexibility

Lower turnover among employees benefits employers in several distinct ways. First, unanticipated turnover forces an employer to absorb the unforeseen costs of recruiting and training replacement workers. Studies have shown typical turnover cost to equal approximately 20 percent of a worker's annual salary (Boushey and Glynn 2012).[5] Unanticipated departures also may result in unfinished tasks, increased workloads, and overtime costs. Lowering turnover of staff also has been shown to improve customer satisfaction and increase profitability (John Larson and Company, 2018).

Lowering staff turnover equates to longer tenured employees. It is well known that older workers, on average, have a longer tenure than their younger counterparts. Figure 5.3 shows that the average 30–35-year-old remains at a job for 4.4 years, while a comparable 55–60-year-old remains at a job for 12.7 years.

Older workers also are a valued resource when employers need a more flexible workforce or in situations when people are needed for short-term assignments. For example, following a natural disaster, an insurance company might have an urgent need for on-call, trained, insurance adjusters who can relocate with little notice for a short-term assignment (Johnson 2017).

Improved customer satisfaction

Longer tenure produces not only a significant economic benefit to employers in terms of the cost savings related to acquiring and training replacement workers, but also through increased customer satisfaction. Workers improve in performance over time as they gain knowledge and comfort, and develop personal relationships. A longer tenured staff often works better as a team, develops a better understanding of customers, and is more cognizant of the

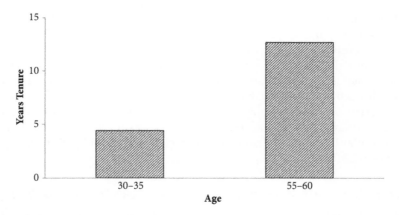

Figure 5.3 Older workers have much longer average tenure than younger workers
Source: Panel Study on Income Dynamics (2015).

resources available to serve customers' needs. Additionally, customers are more willing to seek assistance from employees with whom they are familiar. Recent proprietary data from a large office supply retailer confirm the value of employee tenure. Stores with more long-tenured employees have more satisfied customers, and stores with more satisfied customers have higher rates of profit growth. This makes sense, as a longer tenured employee is better able, for example, to show a customer where an item is located because he or she has more store experience. A more satisfied customer is more likely to make a return visit and may even develop a rapport with store staff. Even slight increases in customer satisfaction dramatically impact store profitability (Figure 5.4).

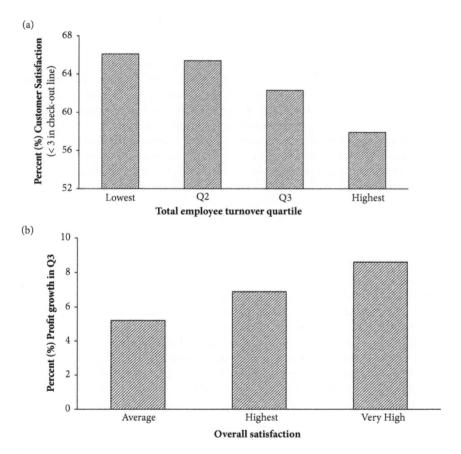

Figure 5.4 Stores with low turnover do better

Source: John Larson and Company (2018).

Augment diversity programs

The analyses that drove diversity initiatives around race and ethnicity also apply to age. Studies have identified a statistically significant correlation between the diversity (including age) of management teams, and overall innovation (Bersin and Chamorro-Premuzic 2019). Those companies that reported above-average diversity in their management teams also reported 19 percent higher innovation revenue, versus companies with below-average leadership diversity. More diverse companies also reported better overall financial performance (Rocío et al. 2017). *Wall Street Journal* researchers ranked companies based on diversity (including age) and determined that the 20 most diverse companies not only had better operating results on average than the least diverse firms, but also that their stocks generally outperformed those of the less diverse companies (Holger 2019). Companies that establish and maintain more diverse workplaces—by gender, nationality, race, and age—perform better.

Additionally, employers benefit from having a workforce that mirrors the customer base. Not only will diverse employees promote innovations that serve diverse populations, but they will also mirror increasingly diverse clientele. Building diversity into a team so that it reflects the customer base supports a deeper understanding of customer needs and increases opportunities to form personal connections with them. Promoting personal connections with older consumers is especially significant, as their purchasing power far outweighs their numbers. In 2017, the total economic activity of Americans over age 50 totaled $7.6 trillion. While these older consumers represented approximately 35 percent of the 2017 population, they controlled more than half of the investable assets in the US. If this were a separate economy, it would have ranked third in the world, behind only the United States and China (Oxford Economics 2016).

Finally, considerable evidence suggests that firm productivity is enhanced by using mixed-age teams. Analysis of German data found that intergenerational collaboration blended the distinct talents of older and younger workers (Zwick and Gobel 2013). The *Wall Street Journal* has highlighted how teaming older workers with younger workers helps drive innovation by pairing experience with new ideas to bring an idea to fruition. An example can be seen in the software industry, which though long known for glorifying the young genius inventor, relies on more experienced employees to nurture an innovation into a viable and profitable product (Wadhwa 2013).

Do older workers' strengths offset possible increased costs?

Despite the benefits of employing older adults, some of which are discussed above, there are perceived costs, as well. The size of these costs, however, may not be as large as generally thought. The theory that older workers remaining in the workforce longer reduces job opportunities for younger workers has been used to provide economic justification for early and mandatory retirement. But research at the Boston College Center for Retirement Research based on data from the Current Population Survey, which includes detailed questions about labor force participation, wages, and income from various sources, suggests that 'greater employment of older persons leads to better outcomes for the young—reduced unemployment, increased employment, and a higher wage' (Munnell and Wu 2012). Not only did this analysis disprove the notion that higher employment rates for older workers adversely impacted employment and wage rates for their younger counterparts, it in fact suggested that the opposite is true. Whether the economy is strong or in recession, increased employment of older workers does not negatively impact younger workers.

Older workers also are perceived to be significantly more costly in terms of wages when compared to younger workers. But as more employers shift to performance-based rather than tenure-based compensation, this cost differential has narrowed. In 1992, 61 percent of large employers offered performance-based pay, increasing to 80 percent in 2002. The trend continued over the next decade, with 90 percent of large employers reporting compensation structures based on performance by 2012. Additionally, Mercer pay research based on more than a million observations revealed that, across all job levels, pay increased during the earlier years, plateaued mid-career, then decreased as employees aged. This data showed that for less skilled and administrative jobs, 25-year-olds and 55-year-olds earned comparable amounts, as did 35-year-old and 60-year-old professionals and middle managers (Mercer 2019). Given that cash compensation comprises 74 percent of total employee cost, it is no longer true that older workers are significantly more costly based on their wages (Aon Hewitt 2015).

The link between age and retirement costs also has diminished as employers have shifted away from defined benefit (DB) pensions toward defined contribution (DC) plans. This shift has been dramatic: large employers offering DB plans decreased from 68 percent in 2004 to 22 percent in 2015 (Aon Hewitt 2015). Conversely, the availability of DC plans has increased from 32 percent to 78 percent over the same period (Aon Hewitt 2015). This trend toward DC plans with no age-related employer contributions further neutralizes the cost differential to employers of older versus younger workers.

Nevertheless, health care continues to be more costly for older workers versus younger workers (Burtless 2017). On the other hand, increases in life expectancy have been accompanied by gains in overall health: not only are people living longer, they also are staying healthy longer. In fact, older workers report good health in comparable numbers to their younger counterparts (Irving et al. 2018). As a result, the health insurance cost age differential is shrinking. Health care costs for both employers and employees have increased steadily across all age groups over the past decade. Figure 5.5 indicates that, despite the continued increase, the rate of increase is slower for workers over age 50 than for younger workers (Tejada et al. 2017).[6] The overall increase in health care costs result in employer-provided health insurance becoming a larger component of total employee compensation, but the narrowing gap between the costs of health care for older and younger workers makes the relative cost of employing older workers closer to that for younger employees.

There is an important exception to this rule: the cost to small employers for providing health care to older workers can actually be less than the cost for health care for younger employees. Employers with more than 20 employees are prohibited from creating more than one employee health care plan, even if one is a Medicare supplement plan. Nevertheless, federal law permits smaller employers to establish a separate Medicare supplement plan for employees age 65+. Thus, while younger workers will continue to be covered by the employer's basic health care plan, older workers may choose to file for Medicare parts A and B, and the employer is permitted to provide a supplemental plan (Cooney 2020).

Older workers may choose to switch to Medicare for lower deductibles, copayments, and premiums. Employers may provide their employees with

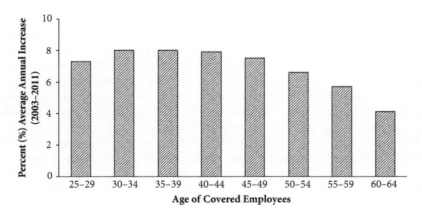

Figure 5.5 Average annual health care claims cost increase for large employers by age of employee

Note: Truven claims data covering over 14.6 million medical plan participants (employees and dependents); costs shown include total company-paid medical claim costs per employee for the employee plus all covered dependents.

Source: Aon Hewitt (2015).

information about Medicare and other health care options, but they may not *entice* an employee to switch to Medicare with a bonus or other incentive. Yet the provision of a Medicare supplement plan by a small employer likely would reduce the necessary employee contribution to below that required under the employer's basic health care plan. The financial benefit to the employee may incentivize employees age 65+ to switch to Medicare. Of course, the savings to the employee are mirrored by savings to the employer. Medicare supplement plans, even those with low deductibles and copayments, can be purchased less expensively than all-inclusive health insurance.

This exception is noteworthy as about 20 million people in the US (18% of all US employees) work for businesses with fewer than 20 employees (US Bureau of Labor Statistics 2017a). The Affordable Care Act requires only businesses with 50 or more employees to provide health care benefits to employees, yet more than 60%of businesses with 20 or fewer employees provide such a benefit (National Small Business Association 2015). Less expensive health care benefits for older workers therefore nullifies an important objection to employing older workers; in fact, it may even incentivize small businesses to seek out older workers.

The business case for employing older workers is strong. Their experience, length of employment, and diversity of opinion benefit employers, perhaps even increasing business revenue. And the presumed cost to employers of hiring or retaining such workers is either declining or non-existent.

The Societal Health Case for People Working Longer

Working longer is also beneficial to the economy as a whole, increasing gross domestic product (GDP), providing skilled and less skilled labor, reducing the cost and burden of caring for older adults, and helping to shore up the federal social security system as workers continue to make contributions through payroll taxes.

Social security could use this help. By 2033, 77 million Americans will be eligible for retirement benefits, a substantial increase from 47 million in 2015 (US Census Bureau 2017). Some experts project the Social Security Trust Fund will be depleted by 2034, after which the program can pay out only 75 percent of benefits (Goss 2010). Americans have favored the federal safety net since its creation in 1935. Surveys have consistently shown the popularity of social security and the desire for the government to increase benefits (Williams 2015). However, there has also been widespread doubt and uncertainty about its future solvency. Gallup polling historically has found that Americans 'would rather raise social security taxes than reduce benefits' (Newport 2019). Since its creation, Americans have strongly believed in the preservation of social security for future generations, even if they have to pay more for this. For many, preventing cuts to social security benefits is not just a desire, they believe it is a necessity. According to an April 2019 Gallup survey, 57 percent of retirees indicate social security is a 'major source of income in their retirement' (Newport 2019).

Making it easier for people to work longer has been a topic attracting attention from employers, nonprofit advocates, and policymakers at the federal, state, and local level. In the US Senate, bills such as the Older Worker Opportunity Act have been introduced. The bill's sponsor, former US Senator Herb Kohl, then-chair of the Senate Special Committee on Aging, specifically highlighted the importance of programs recognizing employers who welcome older workers, such as the Certified Age Friendly Employer program, an initiative started in 2005 by the Age Friendly Foundation. Nonprofit organizations such as Changing the Narrative and the Frameworks Institute have partnered with the Age Friendly Foundation in promoting certification of Age Friendly Employers, and they also work to change the way we think and talk about agism, to promote more productive policies and practices that leverage the strengths and talents of older people.

In Massachusetts, Governor Charlie Baker established a Council to Address Aging with bipartisan support. A top recommendation of the council was the broadening of an age friendly employer designation to propel employers toward being more willing to recruit and retain older employees.

Policymakers, nonprofit organizations, and employers themselves will need to build on these efforts to accelerate the participation rate of older adults in the labor force and volunteer ranks. They can accomplish this through more prominent awareness initiatives and convenings of senior leaders who can then educate each other about the business and health case for employing older adults. The benefits of working longer far outweigh the costs, and public policy is likely to evolve to facilitate working longer (Rappaport and Driver 2018).

Benefits to Older Workers

Older workers benefit from continued participation in the workforce: work provides a means for older adults to remain engaged in their communities. In addition to reaping economic benefits from employment, they will be healthier for it, less isolated, and happier. Objective social isolation has repeatedly been found to be a risk factor for poor mental and physical health, including higher prevalence of disease and increased risk of mortality (Streeter et al. 2020).

Work provides opportunities for learning, reasoning, and social engagement, all of which help stave off the adverse effects aging can have on the brain.[7] After retirement, there is often a decline in older adults' cognitive abilities (Xue et al. 2018). A long-term study in England assessed memory in more than 3,000 civil servants over a 30-year period covering the final part of their careers and the early years of their retirement. Results showed that verbal memory, which declines naturally with age, deteriorated 38 percent faster after retirement (Xue et al. 2018). Other analyses have suggested that cognitive declines nearly double post-retirement (Sap and Denier 2017). Underscoring the impact extended work has on longevity, mortality rates decreased among those who worked past age 65 (Wu et al. 2016). These post-retirement deteriorations stemmed not from the absence of work, but from smaller social networks and increased isolation. Study participants who continued to work into their older years had a 25 percent increase in the size of their social networks, while people who retired saw their social networks shrink. Given that social isolation has been identified as a health determinant equal to smoking 15 cigarettes per day (Holt-Lunstad et al. 2010), the reduced social networks resulting from retirement are cause for significant concern.

Employment for older workers may lead to as much as four times as much social interaction compared to those who had retired. A survey conducted by RetirementJobs.com and the Age Friendly Foundation in January 2020 compared the difference in interpersonal interactions among working older adults versus those who were unemployed (RetirementJobs.com and the Age Friendly Foundation 2020). The survey, which was sent to more than 300,000 older adults (age 55 and over), asked respondents how many different people they spoke to *in person* during an average day.[8] Overall, more than one-third of the 1,438 respondents reported speaking to 10 or more different people each day. Those respondents who identified themselves as unemployed reported significantly fewer social interactions than those who self-identified as employed. While only approximately 15 percent of the unemployed respondents spoke to at least 10 different people each day, more than 60 percent of employed respondents reported that they interacted with at least 10 people each day. Even those who worked remotely reported significantly higher in-person interactions, with more than 40 percent speaking to at least 10 people each day (Figure 5.6). These data lend further weight to the theory that continued employment helps stave off social isolation and its resulting ill health effects among older adults.

Older adults who have a 'retirement job' also often volunteer. It is quite possible then that social interaction can be maintained if older adults choose to volunteer rather than work. Research on the benefits of volunteering by older adults is more extensive and has been going on for

(a)

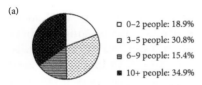

☐ 0–2 people: 18.9%

☐ 3–5 people: 30.8%

⊟ 6–9 people: 15.4%

■ 10+ people: 34.9%

Panel A: All respondents: How many different people do you speak to in-person on an average weekday?

Note: Out of 1,438 total respondents, 272 respondents spoke to two or fewer people, 443 respondents spoke to between three and five people, 221 respondents spoke to between six and nine people, and 502 respondents spoke to 10 or more people.

(b)

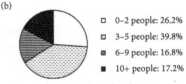

☐ 0–2 people: 26.2%

☐ 3–5 people: 39.8%

■ 6–9 people: 16.8%

■ 10+ people: 17.2%

Panel B: Not currently employed: How many different people do you speak to in-person on an average weekday?

Note: Out of 1,438 total respondents, 587 were employed and 851 were not. Of the 851 unemployed respondents, 223 spoke to two or fewer people each day, 339 spoke to between three and five people each day, 143 spoke to between six and nine people each day, and 146 spoke to 10 or more people each day.

(c)

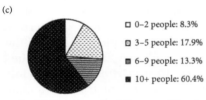

☐ 0–2 people: 8.3%

☐ 3–5 people: 17.9%

⊟ 6–9 people: 13.3%

■ 10+ people: 60.4%

Panel C: Currently employed: How many different people do you speak to in-person on an average weekday?

Note: Out of the 587 respondents who were employed, 49 spoke to two or fewer people each day, 105 spoke to between three and five people each day, 78 spoke to between six and nine people each day, and 355 spoke to 10 or more people each day.

(d)

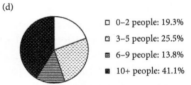

☐ 0–2 people: 19.3%

☐ 3–5 people: 25.5%

⊟ 6–9 people: 13.8%

■ 10+ people: 41.1%

Panel D: Work remotely: How many different people do you speak to in-person on an average weekday?

Note: Of the 587 respondents who were employed, 148 worked remotely. Among that group, 29 spoke to two or fewer people each day, 38 spoke to between three and five people each day, 20 spoke to between six and nine people each day, and 61 spoke to 10 or more people each day.

Figure 5.6 Interpersonal interactions among working versus non-working older adults

Source: RetirementJobs.com and the Age Friendly Foundation (2020).

longer than research on older paid employees. Although not conclusive, there is a correlation between volunteering and improved health outcomes, including larger social networks (Chambré 1987).

In addition to the benefits derived from increased social interaction, for many people, life derives some meaning, purpose, affiliation, and structure from the fact that they are working. Maintaining a satisfying career can help older people sustain their sense of worth and contribute to their happiness (Koenig 2018). David Weir's research with the University of Michigan Health and Retirement Study supports this, also suggesting that people who retire early report lower rates of satisfaction in retirement than those who wait (Koenig 2018).

It is noteworthy that nearly half of older adults seeking work after an initial retirement prefer a job that is new to them. The RetirementJobs.com and the Age Friendly Foundation survey asked respondents who had previously considered themselves retired whether they were pursuing an opportunity in a new field or were employed doing something similar to what they had done in the past (Figure 5.7). While 55.9 percent continued to perform a job similar to what they had done in the past, interestingly, 44.1 percent of respondents had found something in a new field (RetirementJobs.com and the Age Friendly Foundation 2020).

This switch to a new type of work can be attributed to a variety of factors. Some people chose work that could be performed part-time; others sought less intensive work conditions; and some simply wanted to try something new. In fact, it is not uncommon for older workers to express a willingness to trade a pay cut for a more desirable job. At the age 50+ life stage, people tend to value their time somewhat differently, which can lead them down a different path (Table 5.1). Post-COVID-19, jobs that allow an employee to work from home are likely to become more desirable. Financial considerations also play an important role. As the retirement job often is a buttress to standard forms of retirement income such as the 401k, pension, and social security, the amount that a job pays may be important, but it may not need to be as high as earlier in their working life. Work also can be seen primarily as a source of reliable health insurance, rather than primarily as a source of income. Additionally, there are age-dependent implications with respect to how much one can earn without impacting social security payout, thus making a *lower* income preferable in some situations.

There is a trend underway toward working longer, suggesting people are willing and feeling the need to convert their sustained health into more years of work. Realizing this change, however, does not necessarily come

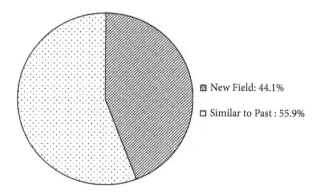

Figure 5.7 Survey: Are you pursuing an opportunity in a new field or are you employed doing something similar to what you have done in the past?

Source: RetirementJobs.com and the Age Friendly Foundation (2020).

TABLE 5.1 Job characteristics valued by employees age 50+

Positive job characteristics for older workers	Negative job characteristics for older workers
• Flexibility: Partial day, week or year • Staying closer to home/Telecommuting • Being an *individual contributor* where you complete shorter, assigned tasks whose outcome you mostly control • Being managed by someone younger • Finding a fun, challenging, secure, and stable job and staying in it for a long time • A readiness to trade income for work/life balance (job pay is a supplement to investment and social security income) • Competing for business results in the marketplace • Providing advice to people who value your work and life experience • Mentoring younger workers • Developing relationships with customers who value your reliable and service-oriented style, trust you because they're older too, and may know you from previous personal or business dealings in the community • Giving back to society • Working for 'meaning' • A readiness to be trained and learn new skills, such as specific computer programs	• 60-hour workweeks • Long commutes • Frequent work travel • Managing large teams • Taking on big organizational mandates with significant risk and stress. • Job hopping to improve pay or title • Needing big raises every year to meet rising living and/or child-rearing costs • Competing with peers for promotions within the company and face-time with the boss • Being mentored by a mature, experienced worker • Developing relationships through heavy time investments (e.g. industry conferences) • What's in it for me? • Not having time to focus on learning new things

Note: Compiled from results of 12 years of survey data collected by RetirementJobs.com.
Source: RetirementJobs.com (2017).

easily for all older adults. Today, nearly one in three people age 65–69 and one in five age 70–74 are working (Mislinski 2020). These labor force participation rates are up about 50 percent in the last 20 years.

Working longer addresses economic pressure on older adults and adds health benefits. Yet it remains a substantial challenge for these older adults to find jobs in later years. Historically, older workers have remained unemployed longer than younger workers—about 37 weeks for people age 55+ compared with 25 weeks for workers age 35 to 44 (US Bureau of Labor Statistics 2017a). Many employers still need to be convinced of the value of employing older workers.

Conclusion

There is a strong positive correlation between employment, social engagement, and longevity. Facilitating continued or new employment of older workers not only adds more years to those individuals' lives, but also adds more 'life' to their later years. When looking at increases in longevity, we need to characterize these additional years as added to the *middle* of one's life rather than the *end*. Moreover, though age discrimination in the workplace remains widespread, it is declining: a 2009 survey by RetirementJobs.com found that virtually all (96%) older job seekers believed age bias was a 'fact of life in the workplace.' Ten years later, in 2019, four of five (83%) said this was the case, a decline of 13 percentage points (RetirementJobs.com 2019). This represents the beginning of a shift in cultural acceptance. In tight job markets, employers have little choice but to tap this 'alternative' candidate pool, but even in times of recession, employment opportunities for older workers benefit all.

Notes

1. By 2035, more people in the United States will be over age 65 than under 17. According to data from the United Nations, one in six people in the world will be over age 65 (16%), up from one in 11 in 2019 (9%). By 2050, one in four persons living in Europe and North America could be age 65+. In 2018, for the first time in history, persons age 65+ outnumbered children under five years of age globally. The number of persons age 80+ is projected to triple, from 143 million in 2019 to 426 million in 2050. (United Nations Department of Economic and Social Affairs 2019).
2. In this model, work includes both full- and part-time work, either ongoing or periodic. Additionally, volunteering can be understood as a form of working. For those who do not require the economic assistance of working longer, volunteering not only benefits communities, but it can also provide the volunteer with the same physical, social, and emotional benefits as paid employment (Chambré 1987).
3. This is a rough estimate based on figures from the 2016 US Bureau of Labor Statistics Consumer Expenditure Surveys. It is not adjusted for inflation, investment income, possible social security income, or other benefits.
4. One very simplistic example might be that of an experienced salesperson in a large box store who will not only be familiar with the location of products within the store, but also will have acquired knowledge about the products themselves, as well as the necessary frequency of restocking or returns.
5. For the 90 percent of US workers who earn $75,000 or less, typical turnover costs amount to one-fifth of the worker's annual salary (Boushey and Glynn 2012).
6. This decrease in the health care costs for older adults when compared to their younger counterparts is due to reduced incidence of certain high-cost diseases

such as heart disease among adults ages 50–65. Better diagnostic care and drug solutions, and improved overall health also contribute to the cost reduction (Tejada et al. 2017).
7. People not only need and want to work longer, increasingly they can. Unlike a century ago, when 80 percent of jobs were physically demanding manufacturing jobs unsuited to older workers, 80 percent of today's economy is service-based. Technology, most notably artificial intelligence and self-driving cars, loom as unpredictable variables in the future equation of work for older adults. Yet these could well be offset by other major shifts in the mass market landscape. For example, the cashier positions today may rapidly turn into the caregiver positions of the future.
8. The survey was distributed between more than 300,000 older adults from among RetirementJobs.com members.

References

Aon Hewitt (2015). 'A Business Case for Older Workers Age 50+: A Look at the Value of Experience,' *AARP*, March. https://doi.org/10.26419/res.00100.001

Bersin, J. and T. Chamorro-Premuzic (2019). 'The Case for Hiring Older Workers,' *Harvard Business Review*. September 26: http://www. https://hbr.org/2019/09/the-case-for-hiring-older-workers

Börsch-Supan, A. and M. Weiss (2016). 'Productivity and Age: Evidence from Work Teams at the Assembly Line,' *Journal of the Economics of Ageing*, 7(C): 30–42.

Boushey, H. and S. J. Glynn. (2012). 'There Are Significant Business Costs to Replacing Employees,' *Issue Brief*. Washington, DC: Center for American Progress.

Burtless, G. (2017). 'Age Related Health Costs and Job Prospects of Older Workers.' SIEPR Working Paper: 2017 Working Longer and Retirement Conference. Stanford, CA: Stanford Institute for Economic Policy Research. https://siepr.stanford.edu/system/files/BURTLESS_Age-Related-Health-Costs_1st-Draft_Oct-2017.pdf

Chambré, S. M. (1987). *Good Deeds in Old Age: Volunteering by the New Leisure Class.* Lexington, MA: Lexington Books.

Cooney, M. (2020). Personal communication from Matthew J. Cooney, CEBS, President of Cooney Health, Framingham, MA. On file with the authors.

Federal Interagency Forum on Aging Related Statistics (2019). *Population Aging in the United States: A Global Perspective.* Washington, DC: GPO. https://agingstats.gov/infographics.html

Goss, S. (2010). 'The Future Financial Status of the Social Security Program,' *Social Security Bulletin*, 70(3). https://www.ssa.gov/policy/docs/ssb/v70n3/v70n3p111.html

Holger, D. (2019). 'The Business Case for More Diversity,' *Wall Street Journal*, Oct. 26: https://www.wsj.com/articles/the-business-case-for-more-diversity–11572091200

Holt-Lunstad, J., T. B. Smith, and J. B. Layton, (2010) 'Social Relationships and Mortality Risk: A Meta-Analytic Review,' *PLoS Medicine*, 7(7). http://dx.doi.org/10.1371/journal.pmed.1000316

Irving, P., R. Beamish, and A. Burstein (2018). *Silver to Gold: The Business of Aging.* Santa Monica, CA: Milken Institute Center for the Future of Aging. https://milkeninstitute.org/sites/default/files/reports-pdf/FINAL-Silver-to-Gold-0226.pdf

John Larson and Company and RetirementJobs.com (2018). *Proprietary Analysis of Survey Data from a Large Office Supply Retailer.* On file with the authors.

Johnson, D. (2017). 'Hurricanes Reveal Need for More Catastrophe Adjusters,' *Claims Journal,* October 2: https://www.claimsjournal.com/news/national/2017/10/02/280852.htm

Johnson, R. W. (2012). 'Older Workers, Retirement and the Great Recession,' *Stanford Center on Poverty and Inequality.* https://inequality.stanford.edu/sites/default/files/Retirement_fact_sheet.pdf

Koenig, R. (2018). '4 Reasons to Work Longer,' *US News & World Report.* June 1: https://money.usnews.com/careers/salaries-and-benefits/slideshows/4-reasons-to-work-longer

Laskow, S. (2014). 'How Retirement Was Invented,' *The Atlantic,* October 24. https://www.theatlantic.com/business/archive/2014/10/how-retirement-was-invented/381802/

Lorenzo, R., N. Voigt, K. Schetelig, A. Zawadzki, I. Welpe, and P. Brosi (2017). 'The Mix That Matters: Innovation through Diversity,' *BCG,* April 21. https://www.bcg.com/publications/2017/people-organization-leadership-talent-innovation-through-diversity-mix-that-matters.aspx

Mercer (2019). 'Next Stage: Are You Age Ready?' https://www.mercer.com/content/ dam/mercer/attachments/private/gl-2019-6009756-mn-experienced-worker-POV-mercer.pdf

Mislinski, J. (2020). 'Demographic Trends for the 50-and-Older Workforce,' *Advisor Perspectives,* June 10. https://www.advisorperspectives.com/dshort/updates/2020/02/11/demographic-trends-for-the-50-and-older-work-force

Munnell, A. H. and A. Chen (2015). 'Trends in Social Security Claiming,' *Center for Retirement Research at Boston College,* May 15–8.

Munnell, A. H. and A.Y. Wu, (2012) 'Are Aging Baby Boomers Squeezing Young Workers out of Jobs?' *Center for Retirement Research at Boston College,* October 12–18.

National Small Business Association (2015). *Small Business Healthcare Survey.* Washington, DC: NSBA. https://www.nsba.biz/wp-content/uploads/2015/11/Health-Care-Survey-2015.pdf

Newport, F. (2019). 'Social Security and American Public Opinion,' *Gallup.* https://news.gallup.com/opinion/polling-matters/258335/social-security-american-public-opinion.aspx

Oxford Economics (2016). *The Longevity Economy: How People Over 50 Are Driving Economic and Social Value in the US.* September: https://www.oxfordeconomics.com/recent-releases/the-longevity-economy

Rappaport, A. and T. Driver (2018). 'Working Longer to Improve Retirement Security: Improving Public Policy,' *Society of Actuaries.* https://www.soa.org/resources/essays-monographs/2018-securing-future-retirements/

RetirementJobs.com (2017). *12-year Survey of What Older Workers Want in a 'Retirement Job*. On file with the authors.

RetirementJobs.com (2019). *Analysis of Survey Data on Perception of Age Bias in the Workplace*. On file with the authors.

RetirementJobs.com and the Age Friendly Foundation (2020). *Analysis of Survey Data*. On file with the authors.

Rocío, L., Voigt, N., Schetelig, K., Zawadzki, A., Welpe, I. M., and P. Brosi (2017). 'The Mix That Matters - Innovation Through Diversity.' The Boston Consulting Group, Inc.

Sap, C. and N. Denier (2017). 'Mental Retirement and Health Selection: Analyses from the US Health and Retirement Study,' *Social Science & Medicine*, 178: 78–86.

Social Security Administration (2020). *Benefits Planner: Retirement*. Washington, DC: Social Security Administration.

Streeter, J. L., S. Raposo, and H-W. Liao (2020). 'Sightlines Project Special Report: Social Engagement,' *Stanford Center on Longevity*. http://longevity.stanford.edu/sightlines-project-social-engagement-special-report/#top

Tejada, V. B., B. Bastian, E. Arias, A. Lipphardt, J. M. Keralis, L. Lu, and Y. Chong (2017). *Mortality Trends in the United States, 1980–2015*. Atlanta, GA: CDC, National Center for Health Statistics.

United Nations Department of Economic and Social Affairs (2019). *2019 Revision of World Population Dynamics*. New York, NY: United Nations Department of Economic and Social Affairs.

US Bureau of Labor Statistics (2017a). *Unemployed Persons by Duration of Unemployment*. Washington, DC: United States Bureau of Labor Statistics.

US Bureau of Labor Statistics (2017b). *Consumer Expenditure Surveys*. Washington, DC: United States Bureau of Labor Statistics.

US Census Bureau, Population Division (2017). *Main Projections Series for the United States*. Washington, DC: United States Census Bureau, Population Division.

Wadhwa, V. (2013). 'There's No Age Requirement for Innovation,' *The Wall Street Journal*, October 28: https://blogs.wsj.com/accelerators/2013/10/28/vivek-wadhwa-theres-no-age-requirement-for-innovation/

Waldman, D. A. and B. J. Avolio (1986). 'A Meta-analysis of Age Differences in Job Performance,' *Journal of Applied Psychology*, 71(1): 33–38.

Williams, A. (2015). 'Social Security 80th Anniversary Survey Report,' *AARP*, August: https://www.aarp.org/research/topics/economics/info-2015/social-security-80th-anniversary-report.html

Wu, C., M. C. Odden, G. G. Fisher, and R. S. Stawski (2016). 'The Association of Retirement Age with Mortality: A Population-based Longitudinal Study among Older Adults in the United States,' *Journal of Epidemiology and Community Health*, 70: 917–923.

Xue, B., D. Cadar, M. Fleischmann, S. Stansfeld, E. Carr, M. Kivimaki, A. McMunn, and J. Head (2018). 'Effect of Retirement on Cognitive Function: The Whitehall II Cohort Study,' *European Journal of Epidemiology*, 33: 989–1001.

Zwick, T. and C. Göbel (2013). 'Are Personnel Measures Effective in Increasing Productivity of Old Workers?' *Labour Economics*, 22(C): 80–93.

Part II

Public-Private Partnerships to Help Fill the Gaps

Chapter 6

Aging in Place

The Role of Public-Private Partnerships

Nancy A. Hodgson

The US population of adults age 65+ grew over 15 percent in the last decade, yet the largest growth occurred in individuals age 85+ (Johnson and Parnell 2017). It is estimated that, by 2050, those age 85+ will constitute one-fifth of the older US adult population (Ortman et al. 2014). This demographic shift prompts numerous social and economic concerns. One important question is where older adults, particularly the oldest old, will reside, given that most older adults value their ability to maintain independence and prefer to remain in their home and community.

There is a pressing need for home care and other community-based services to enable older adults to live safely and comfortably in their home and community (Farber et al. 2011). At the same time, the number of family members available to care for elders at home has declined, and the number of professional and paraprofessional workers trained to care for elders at home has fallen. Although most (84%) of older adults depend on family members for care (Herbert and Molinsky 2019), the projected decline in family caregiver support, referred to as the family-care gap, raises additional questions about who will care for the growing number of older adults hoping to age in their homes (Gaugler 2020). Changes in family composition and geographic dispersion have resulted in many older adults living alone as they age, hoping to remain in their homes as long as possible (Mather et al. 2015). Often geographically separated due to educational and job opportunities, working children struggle to provide care for their aging parents from a distance. Concerns about the well-being of an aging family member eventually trigger worried relatives to move an older adult into an institutional care setting. As a result, many older adults seek unsatisfactory and costly institutional care, rather than the home- and community-based care that they would prefer.

This chapter explores the concept of aging in place and summarizes opportunities for public-private partnerships (PPPs) in this arena. We first

Nancy A. Hodgson, *Aging in Place*. In: *New Models for Managing Longevity Risk*.
Edited by Olivia S. Mitchell, Oxford University Press.
© Pension Research Council (2022). DOI: 10.1093/oso/9780192859808.003.0006

provide a description of 'aging in place,' and then we review several challenges to supporting older adults in their home and community. This is followed by a review of successful PPP models of aging in place, comparing the features of each. We conclude with an assessment of prospects for the future.

Aging-in-Place

Close to 90 percent of older adults in the US express the goal of aging in place, and an estimated 80 percent of persons age 65+ live independently in their own homes (Farber et al. 2011). 'Aging in place' is a term that has emerged in the last decade to describe people's desire to stay in their home as they age. It is defined as the ability to live in one's home and community safely, independently, and comfortably, regardless of age, income, or ability level (CDC 2017). Aging in place has two aspects, physical and social, and is more than staying in one's home. A goal of aging-in-place services is to improve and sustain the interactions between older adults and the larger community environments. Efforts to promote aging in place 'enhance well-being and quality of life for older people at home and as integral members of the community' (Thomas and Blanchard 2009: 12).

The three core elements in models of aging in place include attention to individual preferences, to the built environment, and to the availability of community-based services supporting health and well-being (Bigonnesse and Chaudhury 2019). Aging-in-place models allow older adults to age in the least restrictive environment of their choice, and these have demonstrable economic and financial benefits. Therefore, aging in place is considered the preferred residential alternative to the current fragmented models of long-term care (Marek et al. 2012; Popejoy et al. 2015). Rather than requiring older adults to move from one setting to another as their care needs change, aging-in-place models provide the necessary services that older adults may eventually require in the home so there is no need to move to a different place.

Challenges to Aging in Place

Despite elders' preferences for aging at home and in their own community, three factors make this challenging: (1) illness and disability rates among older adults; (2) poor housing conditions; and (3) limited financial resources. As a result, the choice to age in place becomes dependent on older adults' resources and the range of programs, services, and settings available to them.

The acute or gradual accumulation of illness and disability is the first leading challenge to aging in place, regardless of sex/gender or race/ethnicity. Over 95 percent of adults age 85+ have at least one chronic condition (Centers for Medicare and Medicaid Services 2013); 73 percent have at least one disability (He and Larsen 2014); and 43 percent of people age 80+ report having mobility limitations (Herbert and Molinsky 2019). Approximately 70 percent of those age 65+ will require extensive health care services during their lifetime (Genworth Financial, Inc. 2015; Osterman 2017). Approximately 40 percent of older adults have some type of age-related difficulty that constrains their ability to fully engage in activities of daily living (ADL) or instrumental activities of daily living (IADL). Fifteen percent of adults age 85+ report difficulty with cleaning, preparing meals, grocery shopping, or transportation, and another 60 percent struggle with at least one activity of daily living such as bathing, toileting, dressing, or feeding themselves (Centers for Medicare and Medicaid Services 2013). Between 10 and 15 percent report difficulties with hearing or vision, and one-quarter of older adults report difficulties going in or out of their homes.

The built environment and housing conditions in many communities serve as the second challenge to aging in place (Lehning 2012). One reason is that most communities were designed for a mobile and non-disabled population. The need for residential and commercial spaces within walking distance is rarely considered in most urban planning or new building construction efforts. Instead, most communities are organized to accommodate active, non-disabled adults without attention to the supportive social and physical environment needed by older adults. (Herbert and Molinsky 2019). Over 40 percent of the housing units occupied by older adults were built in 1969 or earlier, and often the supportive qualities of these homes receive little attention. Only 3.5 percent of homes in the US offer single-floor living, a no-step entry, and extra wide halls and doorways that can accommodate a wheelchair and other mobility devices (Herbert and Molinsky 2019).

As a result of these challenges, effective strategies are needed to foster and facilitate age-friendly renovations across the diverse range of the aging housing stock (Cohen and Passel 2016). These include systematic home assessments, increased public awareness about the role of the environment, and the creation of programs providing affordable home modification and repair services. In many cases, major renovations are required, but with the average costs of renovations estimated at $50,000, these modifications can be cost-prohibitive particularly for minority populations (Johnson and Appold 2017). Home retrofitting offers one solution to accommodate older adults continuing to live at home as they age, but only a fraction of home renovators are 'aging-in-place' certified (a certification to indicate that they have received special training to provide remodeling of housing for older adults).

Low financial resources are a major drawback to meeting the social and physical needs of an aging society, and are the third leading challenge to aging in place. Over half of the US population is at risk of not having enough money to maintain its standard of living in retirement, and 52 percent of households age 55+ are estimated to have no retirement savings (US Government Accountability Office 2015). Over 20 percent of married social security recipients and 43 percent of single recipients depend on social security for 90 percent or more of their income (Dushi et al. 2017). Over 30 percent of older adults report having no money at the end of each month or report debt after meeting essential expenses. As a result, many older adults who wish to age in place may lack the monetary resources to pay for in-home care and must rely on the support of family.

The Role of Public-Private Partnerships

New funding models are needed to provide financially viable aging-in-place models (see Munnell et al. 2022; Chapter 12, this volume). PPPs can help by allowing private sector companies to collaborate with the public sector. Given the demand for aging-in-place models, PPPs in which the private aging and housing sectors assist the public health and social service sector to address aging-in-place challenges have received significant attention, as this collaboration allows for increased investment of time, money, and focus (White House Conference on Aging 2015). In the next section of this chapter, we review existing examples of PPP aging-in-place models. The core features of the models are compared in Table 6.1.

Tiger Place Institute

Tiger Place Institute was developed at the University of Missouri in 2004 to create a cost-effective alternative to nursing home care. It is an aging-in-place model offering integrated care coordination and health care services to older adults living in specially designed apartments or in their own homes. (Rantz 2008). Core features include:

- A built environment with attention to improving health outcomes, mobility and independence, and involvement in life and community activities;
- Integrated care coordination and on-site health care services;
- Health-monitoring technology for early detection and treatment; and
- Environmentally embedded sensor technology to identify falls and fall risk, and to prolong independence.

TABLE 6.1 Examples of public-private partnership models facilitating aging in place

	Built Environment		Community-based Services					
	Health care	Housing	Transportation	Social services & supports	Activities of daily living	Socialization	Food	Technology
TigerPlace Institute	x	x	x	x	x	x	x	x
PACE	x	x	x	x	x	x	x	
Village to Village		x	x	x	x	x	x	x
Westchester County	x	x	x	x	x		x	x
Interim Healthcare, Inc.	x	x	x	x	x	x	x	
NORCs	x	x	x	x		x		

Sources: Greenfield, et al. (2012); Centers for Medicare and Medicaid Services (2013); Westchester County PPP (2018).

Tiger Place Institute's public and private stakeholders include the University of Missouri, AmeriCare, and the Cerner Corporation (a NASDAQ-traded health care and information technology firm).

Program of All-Inclusive Care for the Elderly

Program of All-Inclusive Care for the Elderly (PACE) is a patient-centered, integrated care and social support model. PACE operates as both an insurer and provider that assumes full risk for medical care and long-term services for adults age 55+ who are sufficiently frail to be categorized as 'nursing home eligible' by their state's Medicaid program. Program benefits include the following Medicaid- and Medicare-covered services:

* Built environment with on-site dentistry, primary care and medical specialty services, physical and occupational therapy.
* Community-based services including meals and nutrition counseling, home modifications, home care, transportation, recreational therapy, and social work counseling.

The PACE model is evolving, and becoming more flexible in its design. Historically, PACE programs were operated by nonprofit organizations, but they are now open to private investment. Approximately 10 percent of the over 135 PACE's programs in the United States are currently operated by for-profit companies (Clark 2016; Gleckman 2019).

Westchester County Public-Private Partnership for Aging Services

Westchester County Public-Private Partnership for Aging Services (WPPP) was launched in 1991 as a partnership of government, business, and voluntary service agencies, with a mission to improve the quality of life for a diverse, aging population through creative programing. This umbrella organization asks corporations to contribute funds, sponsor specific programs, and donate in-kind support for local community initiatives.

New York State's Westchester County residents age 85+ are the county's fastest growing sector, and over 90 percent of Westchester County's older residents report the desire to age in place. At the same time, over one-quarter of the older residents are women who live alone, and about 9,000 seniors in this area live below the poverty level, with over 37,000 senior households having less than the income needed to afford rent. Examples of programs developed by the WPPP to address these needs include:

* Health for Life, six-week peer-learning programs;
* Age-Friendly Networking Conference;

- Livable Communities Villages (304 villages);
- Livable Communities Collaborative (18 groups);
- Annual Senior Hall of Fame Awards gala;
- Annual Salute to Seniors Business Expo;
- CarePrep caregiver training and education; and
- Telehealth Intervention Programs for Seniors (TIPS) that delivers remote patient monitoring with help from college students trained in a 'high tech meets high touch' approach for intergenerational care.

WPPP's innovative programming has been adapted by other communities around the country. It is one of the founding members of the WHO Global Network of Age-friendly Communities in the US. Participating organizations and companies include local government agencies; businesses such as hotels, insurance, legal, and financial firms; and nonprofit organizations such as the Jewish Federation (Westchester County PPP Annual Report 2018).

Village to Village

The Village to Village (VtV) model was initially developed by Beacon Hill Village (BHV), a grassroots organization located in Boston. BHV offers fee-paying members preferred access to social and cultural activities, health and fitness programs, household and home maintenance services, and medical care, by negotiating with and partnering regional service providers. The goal of the VtV is to offer members all the benefits found in an independent or assisted living facility, without requiring them to move from their homes. Core features of VtV include:

- A comprehensive, coordinated approach to home-based and community services on a one-stop-shopping basis;
- Use of a consumer-driven organization model that requires membership fees, though some villages have attempted to provide scholarships or reduced rates to increase low and moderate income elders' access;
- Provision of information about resources and providers, and assistance with transportation and grocery shopping, covered by membership fees;
- Home care services, home repair and maintenance services, and other services, paid for privately on a fee-for-service basis, usually at a slightly (around 20%) discounted rate negotiated by the village on behalf of members;
- A wide variety of community-building activities, including interest groups, exercise classes, cultural and educational field trips; and
- Organized volunteering, with members helping each other or organizations in their community. Some villages use a 'time banking' model to structure their volunteer time.

Since its foundation, BHV has collaborated with NCB Capital Impact, with funding from the MetLife Foundation and other sources, to develop a VtV Network that offers web-based assistance for communities seeking to establish their own villages. Philanthropic organizations, such as the SCAN Foundation and the Archstone Foundation, have also invested in developing and evaluating 'villages' in other areas of the US (Clark, 2016).

Naturally Occurring Retirement Communities

Similar to the BHV model, Naturally Occurring Retirement Communities (NORCs) are community-level initiatives that bring together older adults and diverse stakeholders within a residential area (e.g. an apartment building, neighborhood, town) with a large number of older adults, to facilitate and coordinate a range of activities, relationships, and services to promote aging in place (Greenfield et al. 2012). NORCs refer to locations that were not planned as senior housing, yet, over time, have developed a sizable proportion of older residents due to long-time residents remaining in their homes into later life as well as in-migration of older adults.

The first NORC with 'supportive service programs'—known as a NORC-SSP—was the Penn South Houses Program in New York City. Started by the United Hospital Fund in 1985–1986 with funding from the UJA (United Jewish Appeal) Federation, the Penn South program became a model for others to follow and customize to their own communities. Today, there are NORC-SSP programs in 25 American states that are part of the National NORCs Aging In Place Initiative organized by the United Jewish Communities. In New York State alone, there are now 41 sites that have adopted this model and secured state and municipal funding to build the scope of services offered. NORC programs aim to create partnerships among diverse stakeholders—including residents, local government, housing managers and owners, and local service providers—to coordinate services and programs for residents within communities designated as NORCs (Vladeck 2004). The key components of the NORC model include:

- A geographical location where many elders live close to each other but have little previous social connection to one another before the NORC. NORCs are most commonly found in urban areas but may also be located in a rural area;
- A multigenerational, age-integrated building or neighborhood, where younger residents can interact with elders and in some cases provide assistance, while elders share their skills and experiences with the youth;

• Empowering elders through active involvement and planning of services and governance; and

• Partnerships with one or more local service providers—social services, health care services, educational and recreational opportunities, volunteer opportunities, and services such as transportation and home repairs.

NORC programs have secured both private philanthropic and local government funds to support the expansion of the model to other areas throughout the US.

Interim Healthcare Aging-in-Place Program

The Interim Healthcare Aging-in-Place Program is a private-equity-based venture in partnership with Medicare that is comprised of a franchise network of home care, senior care, home health, and hospice and health care staffing services. Interim Healthcare's Aging-in-Place Program provides reimbursement to Medicare-certified facilities where older residents are 'homebound' by Medicare's definition. The program focuses on companionship, preparing meals, running errands, helping with ADL and transportation needs. Facilities are provided with nurses, home aides, therapists, and companions. Medical services are offered, such as wound dressing, physical therapy, health care education, and medication reminders.

Public-Private Partnerships in Other Countries

In addition to these US-based examples, other countries have also leveraged PPPs to advance models of aging in place adapted to the specific needs of their societies. In some countries, such as Japan and the Netherlands, PPPs are the norm, and the boundaries between public and private enterprise are blurred. Many of these experiments in social innovation are promoted as part of the World Health Organization's Global Network for Age-friendly Cities and Communities (World Health Organization 2018). Examples from Japan and France are provided below.

Japan

Japan has adapted the Western-style convenience store to provide a range of services beyond those offered in the US. Since they are now in every town throughout the country, they serve as community hubs that reach deep into isolated rural areas. 7-Eleven, for example, provides healthy, cooked meals with free delivery, utility-bill payment, and package pickup services. Another government initiative is subsidizing a pilot program of mobile convenience stores to reach even the most remote mountain villages.

Akita-city, in the mountainous northeastern region in Japan, created the Age-Friendly Partner Program to serve as a model throughout Japan. In their public-private model, the municipal government acts as an umbrella organization providing support for 88 local, privately owned firms, delivering a variety of services to the aging population. For example, Minamiyama Daily Service Company trains community health workers to make weekly milk deliveries while also checking on the condition of each person. The workers offer nutritional advice, ask about elders' needs, and help prevent social isolation (World Health Organization 2018).

Dijon, France

Aging in place not only means staying in one's home, but also having access to the local community. Dijon's age-friendly initiatives are city-wide services and activities that allow their elders to continue to contribute to the city's civic and social life. Dijon is a medium-sized city in the Franche-Comté region of France. About 22 percent of the population is age 60+ and those age 85+ has doubled over the past 20 years. Dijon's age-friendly initiatives assume an intergenerational approach with a variety of stakeholders including private firms, public agencies, academic institutions, and individual citizens. The partnership has invested heavily in transportation and mobility infrastructure for seniors. The city has also pedestrianized certain areas and enhanced the accessibility of its tram platforms, improving access to the city center. Benches and chairs have been added and pavement curbs lowered, to increase walkability; and public toilets have been provided. A new opportunity for social interaction has been created through a seniors' restaurant initiative. Participants are transported by professionals and volunteers from their houses to a neighborhood restaurant for sociable group meals. In addition, a 'mobility day of activities' encourages Dijon residents to remain mobile as they age through the use of mobility aids adapted to needs and capacities. Dijon's residents have the opportunity to try different modes of transport, such as bicycles, tricycles, electric bicycles, and motorized scooters, and to learn more about the different mobility aids that are available as they age (World Health Organization 2018).

Technology Opportunities for Public-Private Partnerships in Aging in Place

Meeting the aging-in-place needs of millions of aging individuals with different incomes, health conditions, and living situations is complex, with no one-size-fits-all solution. While there is no 'typical' older adult, there are traits, preferences, and physical realities that are common for older adults. Surveys of older adults suggest that opportunities for physical activity, safety, and socialization are important priorities for individuals seeking to age in place (Nielsen 2014). Nevertheless there are gaps between the services available and those that older consumers actually need and want.

To address this market demand, the coming years are likely to witness a huge increase in the types of technological advances for Baby Boomers determined to age in place. Beyond the aging-in-place models presented in this chapter, additional innovation opportunities for shared public-private investments to keep older adults in their homes longer offer huge potential social and financial benefits to individuals and society. Examples of age-tech innovations that support aging in place range from technologies that promote health awareness via wearable health trackers or sensing technologies, to help from the 'gig' economy where collaborative consumption business models provide meal or medication delivery, as well as transportation services. These new technologies, developed by private start-ups in partnership with government and/or academic institutes, offer potential approaches to meeting the care needs of older adults who wish to age in place (Ward and Coughlin 2016; Kim et al. 2017).

Conclusion

Innovative financial models are needed to support new models of aging in place (see Munnell et al. 2022; Chapter 12, this volume). Most older adults today prefer to age in place, and this is unlikely to change in the future. The examples of PPPs in this chapter summarize current practices and trends, yet there is much more that can be done to leverage financial investments to meet the health and housing needs of the aging population and honor their preference for aging in place. Future efforts to strengthen the cooperation between public and private partners in aging in place will require an understanding of the needs of older adults in terms of the built environment and the need for coordinated, affordable care to make it possible for older adults to remain in their homes, with access to personal and health care services, and to facilitate meaningful social connections.

Private industry may be well positioned to innovate on existing models if they better understand the changing market dynamics and preferences of the aging demographic. The opportunities to age in place in the future will be impacted by the increasing diversity of health, housing, and social needs of older adults. While the current older adult population in the US is predominantly white, it will become far more heterogeneous in the next 20 years and will require diverse models of aging in place to meet a range of housing, health, and social needs (Johnson and Parnell 2017). Collective impact will only be achieved through the commitment of key stakeholders from different public and private sectors (e.g. health care, housing, technology) coming together to promote aging in place that is inclusive of all older adults.

Acknowledgements

The author thanks Steven Dennis, Sonia Talwar, Emily Summerhayes, and Laurel Caffeé for their research assistance. Opinions and conclusions expressed herein are solely those of the author.

References

Bigonnesse, C. and H. Chaudhury (2019). 'The Landscape of Aging in Place in Gerontology Literature: Emergence, Theoretical Perspectives, and Influencing Factors,' *Journal of Aging and Environment*, DOI: 10.1080/0276389.

Centers for Disease Control (2017). 'Healthy Aging: Promoting Well-being in Older Adults.' https://www.cdc.gov/grand-rounds/pp/2017/20170919-senior-aging.html (updated October 2018).

Centers for Medicare and Medicaid Services (2013). 'Characteristics and Perceptions of the Medicare Population.' https://www.cms.gov/research-statistics-data-and-systems/research/mcbs/data-tables.htm

Clark, M. et al. (2016). 'Innovative Public-Private Partnerships to Enhance Aging in Place in the United States,' *Huamin Research Center Research Report #26.* New Brunswick, NJ: Rutgers School of Social Work. https://socialwork.rutgers.edu/sites/default/files/report_26_revised.pdf

Cohen, D. and J. Passel (2016). 'A Record 60.6 Million Americans Live in Multi-generational Households,' Fact Tank, Pew Research Center. http://www.pewresearch.org/fact-tank/2016/08/11/arecord-60-6-million-americans-live-in-multigenerational-households

Dushi, I., H. M. Iams, and B. Trenkamp (2017). 'The Importance of Social Security Benefits to the Income of the Aged Population,' *Social Security Bulletin*, 77(2). Washington, DC: SSA. https://www.ssa.gov/policy/docs/ssb/v77n2/v77n2p1.html

Farber, N. et al. (2011). 'Aging in Place: A State Survey of Livability Policies and Practices,' A Research Report by the Conference of State Legislatures and the AARP Public Policy Institute. AARP; NCSL. http://assets.aarp.org/rgcenter/ppi/livcom/aging-in-place-2011-full.pdf

Gaugler, J. (2020). *Bridging the Family Care Gap*. Philadelphia, PA: Elsevier Press.

Genworth Financial, Inc. (2015). 'Genworth 2015 Cost of Care Survey: Home Care Providers, Adult Day Health Care Facilities, Assisted Living Facilities and Nursing Homes.' https://www.genworth.com/dam/Americas/US/PDFs/Consumer/corporate/130568_040115_gnw.pdf

Gleckman, H. (2019). 'Reimaging the Delivery of Care,' *Generations. Journal of the American Society on Aging*, 43(1): 78–84.

Greenfield, E. A., A. E. Scharlach, A. J. Lehning, and J. Davitt (2012). 'Fostering Communities to Support Aging in Place: NORC-SSPs and Villages as Promising Models,' *Journal of Aging Studies*, 26: 273–284.

He, W. and L. Larsen (2014). *Older Americans with a Disability: 2008–2012. American Community Survey Reports*. ACS-29. Washington, DC: GPO.

Herbert C. and J. H. Molinsky (2019). 'What Can Be Done to Better Support Older Adults Aging Successfully in their Homes and Communities?' *Health Affairs*, 38(5): 860–864.

Johnson Jr, J. H. and S. J. Appold (2017). *US Older Adults: Demographics, Living Arrangements and Barriers to Aging in Place*. Chapel Hill, NC: Kenan Institute.

Johnson Jr., J. H. and A. Parnell (2017). 'The Challenges and Opportunities of the American Demographic Shift,' *Journal of the American Society on Aging*, 40(4): 9–15.

Kim, K. I., S. S. Gollamudi, and S. Steinhubl (2017). 'Digital Technology to Enable Aging in Place,' *Experimental Gerontology*, 88: 25–31. doi:10.1016/j.exger.2016.11.013

Lehning, A. (2012). 'City Governments and Aging in Place: Community Design, Transportation and Housing Innovation Adoption,' *The Gerontologist*, 52(3): 345–356.

Marek, D. M., et al. (2012). 'Aging in Place versus Nursing Home Care,' *Research in Gerontological Nursing*, 5(2): 123–129.

Mather, M., L. A. Jacobsen, and K. M. Pollard (2015). 'Aging in the United States,' *Population Reference Bureau*, 70(2). http://www.prb.org/pdf16/aging-us-population-bulletin.pdf

Munnell, A.H., W. Hou, and A.N. Walters (2022). 'Property Tax Deferral: Can a Public/Private Partnership Help Provide Lifetime Income?' In O.S. Mitchell, ed., *New Models for Managing Longevity Risk: Public/Private Partnerships*. Oxford, UK: Oxford University Press, pp. 231–57.

Nielsen Report (2014). 'The Age Gap,' *Nielsen Report: Demographics* https://www.nielsen.com/us/en/insights/report/2014/the-age-gap/

Ortman, J. M., V. A. Velkoff, and H. Hogan (2014). 'An Aging Nation: The Older Population in the United States,' *Current Population Reports*. Washington, DC: United States Census Bureau P25–1140.

Osterman, P. (2017). *Who Will Care for Us? Long-Term Care and the Long-Term Workforce*. New York, NY: Russell Sage Foundation.

Popejoy, L. L., et al. (2015). 'Comparing Aging in Place to Home Health Care: Impact of Nurse Care Coordination on Utilization and Costs,' *Nursing Economics*, 33(6): 306–313.

Rantz, M. J., et al. (2008). 'TigerPlace: A State-Academic-Private Project to Revolutionize Traditional Long-Term Care,' *Journal of Housing for the Elderly*, 22(1–2): 66–85.

Thomas, W. H. and J. Blanchard (2009). 'Moving Beyond Place: Aging in Community,' *Generations. Journal of the American Society on Aging*, 33(2): 12–17.

United States Government Accountability Office (2015). *Most Households Approaching Retirement have Low Savings*. Washington, DC: GAO. https://www.gao.gov/assets/680/670153.pdf

Vladeck, F. (2004). *A Good Place to Grow Old: New York's Model for NORC Supportive Service Programs.* New York, NY: United Hospital Fund.

Ward, C. and J. Coughlin (2016). *Comparing Costs of Aging at Home with Sharing Economy Services vs. Residential Care.* MIT AgeLab Issue Brief. Cambridge, MA: Massachusetts Institute of Technology.

Westchester County Public-Private Partnership for Aging-in-Place (2018). *2018 Annual Report.* www.westchesterpartnership.org

White House Conference on Aging (2015). *White House Conference on Aging: Final Report.* US Department of Health & Human Services. http://www.whitehouseconferenceonaging.gov/2015-WHCOA-FinalReport.pdf

World Health Organization (2018). *The Global Network for Age-friendly Cities and Communities: Looking Back over the Last Decade, Looking Forward to the Next.* Geneva, SUI (No. WHO/FWC/ALC/18.4). https://www.who.int/ageing/publications/gnafcc-report-2018/en/

Chapter 7

Public-Private Partnerships Extend Community-based Organization's Longevity

Dozene Guishard and William J. Dionne

Public-private partnerships (PPPs) play a critical role in projects from public infrastructure development (e.g. roads, bridges, etc.) to community-based programs and services. PPPs are traditionally contractual agreements between government entities and the private sector, and they contribute to the longevity of projects through financial support, a mutually agreed upon scope of services and timelines. This chapter focuses on aging services nonprofit organizations and the influence of PPPs on the survival of aging-in-place community-based programs and service delivery through the lens of Carter Burden Network (CBN). CBN is an aging service nonprofit organization serving older adults in New York City (NYC).

Background

CBN's mission is to promote the well-being of seniors age 60+ through a continuum of services, advocacy, arts and culture, health and wellness, and volunteer programs, all oriented to individual, family, and community needs. CBN is dedicated to supporting the efforts of older people to live safely and with dignity. Established in 1971 by then NYC Council Member Carter Burden, the organization was created to assist the large number of older residents living in his district who were poor, in declining health, and isolated. Since CBN's humble beginnings with a single employee in the councilman's office, it has transformed into a network of 12 programs in seven locations, and in CY 2019 CBN served 5,623 clients.

In 2016, the organization underwent a rebranding process and changed its name from The Carter Burden Center for the Aging to the CBN, in order to reflect its growth in size and scope. It was no longer one center but a network of centers, programs, and services that work together with government, corporate, individual, and community partners to lead the way in aging services in NYC. CBN's history is a great illustration of the power of public-private collaboration to lead to organizational longevity. CBN also

Dozene Guishard and William J. Dionne, *Public-Private Partnerships Extend Community-based Organization's Longevity.* In: *New Models for Managing Longevity Risk.* Edited by Olivia S. Mitchell, Oxford University Press.
© Pension Research Council (2022). DOI: 10.1093/oso/9780192859808.003.0007

contributes to overall quality of life enhancements, which may influence its clients' longevity.

CBN's programs and services are built on a four pillar framework comprised of senior centers, social services, arts and culture, and health and wellness. Technology is a critical component of the overall framework. Each pillar contributes to the organization's capacity to enrich the lives of community-dwelling older adults age 60+. Below are illustrations of the four pillar framework and technology:

Senior center framework

The Senior Center Framework is achieved through CBN's extensive meal service programs operating through its senior centers. Senior centers are at the core of CBN's work. The organization operates four centers in Manhattan—two in East Harlem, including one in an NYC Housing Authority (NYCHA) complex; one on the Upper East Side; and one on Roosevelt Island. The suggested cost of a hot nutritious breakfast (in some instances a plated meal) is 25 cents and $1 for a hot nutritious lunch. One of the East Harlem centers is open seven days per week, and is designated as a one of the New York City Department for the Aging's (NYCDFTA) 18 Innovative Senior Centers.

CBN serves a culturally diverse population of nearly 3,800 senior center members annually, with approximately 400 members served daily. While the neighborhoods served by CBN are socioeconomically disparate, CBN serves low to moderate income and vulnerable seniors, who face financial challenges, diminishing health, and declining social networks. Food insecurity is a common problem. As such, CBN's centers provide 113,000 meals annually through congregate meals (i.e. meals provided at senior centers), thereby addressing nutritional and socialization needs. The centers are also a resource hub for social service, recreational, and health and wellness programs.

Social services framework

Equally critical are CBN's robust social services programs, assisting clients through its senior centers, offices, and home visits. Ongoing case management offers comprehensive services including benefits assistance, advocacy, counseling, money management, end-of-life planning, and monthly support/discussion groups. In providing these activities, 18,190 contacts were made with over 1,500 clients across the CBN's social services programs in the last fiscal year. Through its Community Elder Mistreatment and Abuse Prevention Program (CEMAPP), designed to combat elder abuse, over 3,900 hours of case assistance were provided to 200 clients throughout

Manhattan. This assistance included individual counseling, installation of security devices, legal advocacy, and safety planning.

Health and wellness framework

The health and wellness framework is a newer and actively expanding component of CBN's overall service delivery, comprised of programming and research. Health and wellness initiatives offer a full range of health workshops, lectures, physical fitness classes (e.g. Tai-Chi), evidence-based programsand health screenings, which all contribute to seniors' physical and psychological well-being. In an effort to inform health and wellness programming and services, CBN partners with academic institutions to conduct numerous research projects to better understand client needs, and to share best practices with the aging service provider network.

An illustration of CBN's research partnerships is its engagement with Rockefeller University Clinical and Translational Science Center, Rockefeller University Bio Nutrition Program, and the Clinical Directors Network (CDN) to conduct a study on healthy aging. Looking at physiologic data and psychosocial and nutritional information of clients in East Harlem, significant needs were identified: 83 percent of participants were overweight, 33 percent had a history of diabetes, and 84 percent had uncontrolled high blood pressure. These findings helped CBN create targeted, culturally appropriate workshops, and to secure its first US Administration on Community Living federal grant, funding an innovative nutritional intervention to reduce high blood pressure by introducing the DASH (Dietary Approaches to Stop Hypertension) Diet Intervention in congregate meals at two senior centers.

Additionally, research collaborations include a partnership with the research division of the Visiting Nurse Service of New York (VNSNY). Together, CBN and VNSNY deployed the AdvantAge survey in East Harlem and Roosevelt Island. The customized age-friendly survey helps determine how well communities and organizations are supporting older residents by analyzing quality of life characteristics, particularly health and wellness. Through the East Harlem study, CBN identified fall prevention as a key need and developed an evidence-based comprehensive model to decrease falls through environmental, medical, and preventive approaches. Following the recent conclusion of the survey on Roosevelt Island, CBN is convening with seniors and other Island stakeholders in town halls to develop long-term collaborative solutions to the key issues identified.

Arts and culture framework

The arts are central to CBN's programming. CBN's signature Making Art Work (MAW) creative arts education program offers classes in painting, ceramics, print-making, sewing, quilt-making, clothing construction, mixed media, dance, and choir. The program's tailored services nurture creative expression and promote psychological and physiological benefits associated with regular artistic practice and expression. In 2019, CBN offered over 2,100 art classes through its four centers, attended by 915 seniors. In 2009, CBN reinforced its commitment to the arts by opening the Carter Burden Gallery. The first of its kind in the nation, the gallery, located in the Chelsea arts district, exclusively exhibits significant and vibrant works of artists over 60, giving a voice to re-emerging older professional artists and combating agism in the art world. In 2019, the gallery mounted 35 exhibitions, featuring the work of 120 artists.

Technology

Technology education is also a key component of CBN's innovative programming. In 2019, CBN, in partnership with organizations such as Older Adults Technology Services (OATS) and Cornell Tech, provided over 1,200 technology classes and open computer lab sessions attended by nearly 400 seniors. From beginners to advanced, these classes helped seniors leverage technology to advance their education, enhance their connections, and manage their practical needs. Technology education is an effective strategy to help reduce social isolation, particularly for homebound older adults.

In 2019, CBN implemented a technology pilot titled Tech Pals designed to leverage the use of smart screen technology to enhance independence and connectedness for homebound seniors and individuals with disabilities who live on Roosevelt Island. Tech Pals pilot is housed in the NYCDFTA-supported CBN Roosevelt Island Senior Center, conducted in collaboration with the Roosevelt Island Disabled Association (RIDA). The Tech Pals pilot is funded with generous philanthropic support from New York Community Trust, a community foundation. The pilot provides participants with an Amazon Echo Show (smart screen device) and one-on-one technological support and education to enhance independence and connectedness. Through the Echo Show, participants engage with the NYCDFTA-supported case management team, receive access to a plethora of education sessions, engage in Roosevelt Island Senior Center activities, and engage in a Facebook group created for participants.

CBN's timeline (Table 7.1) reflects the start of the organization, as well as the infusion of government, corporate, and philanthropic support over its history from 1971 to 2019.

Historical Context of Aging Services

The previous discussion focused on CBN's history and development. Next we explore the historical context surrounding the funding, development,

TABLE 7.1 Carter Burden Network timeline

Milestones	1971–1989	1990–1999	2000–2005	2006–2012	2013–2016	2017–2019
	• Councilman Carter Burden establishes agency: 1971 • Walk-in unit: 1971 • Homebound unit: 1973 • Yorkville Luncheon Club launched in collaboration with Jan Hus Church of the Epiphany: 1975 • Graduate MSW Student Program: 1975 • Crime Victims Assistance Program: 1978 • Volunteer Services: 1979	• Volunteer Services for the Elderly of Yorkville (VSEY) merger: 1993 • Assumed sole sponsorship of the Yorkville Luncheon Club and renamed it the Carter Burden Luncheon Club: 1997 • C.V. Starr Adult Day Services: 1999 • Opened new Headquarters at 1484 1st Ave. in collaboration with the New York Presbyterian Wright Center: 1999 • VOLS Legal Clinic: 1999	• Graduate MSW Student Program now in-house: 2001 • Hunter Nursing Student Program: 2001 • Graduate Occupational Therapy Program: 2001 • Community Elder Mistreatment and Abuse Prevention Program (CEMAPP): 2003 • Begins catering home delivered meals with the Stanley M. Isaacs Neighborhood Center: 2004	• Cultural Connections: 2006 • Friendly visiting program expanded in collaboration with City Meals: 2006 • Mental Health Services hosted in collaboration with SPOP: 2006 • Social Service Unit (Homebound and Walk-in Units): 2008 • Expansion of Case Management Unit in collaboration with Lenox Hill Neighborhood House and Search Care: 2008 • Gallery 307: 2009 • Making Art Work: 2009 • Elder Craftsman merger: 2009	• Carter Burden/ Leonard Covello Senior Program: 2013 • Carter Burden Gallery: 2013 • Metro East 99th St. Adult Day Program: 2014 • Caregiver Resource Program: 2015 • Lehman Village Senior Center (Covello satellite): 2015 • Roosevelt Island Senior Center (Carter Burden Luncheon Club satellite): 2016 • Collaborations initiated with Cornell Tech and Rockefeller University: 2016	• The Carter Burden Center for the Aging launches its new brand identity and becomes the Carter Burden Network: 2017 • CBN Headquarters relocates to 415 E. 73rd St: 2017 • CBN receives its first federal grant from the Dept of Health and Human Services Administration for Community Living (ACL) to implement the DASH diet at two of its centers: 2018
Participants	75–400	500–25,00	2,500–3,000	3,500–4,000	4,000–5,000	ect. 5,000
Volunteers	15–20	25–1,500	1,200–2,000	2,000–2,700	3,000–3,500	ect. 3,500
Budget	1971: $45,000 1980: $279,717 1981: $353,272	1990: $756,000 1992: $910,725	2000: $2,200,000 2001: $2,650,000	2006: $3,165,000 2011: $3,532,800	2013: $3,942,800 2016: $7,742,264	2017: $8,205,196 2018: $8,003,000 2019: $8,672,324

Source: Carter Burden Network (2020).

growth, expansion, and stagnation of programs and services for older adults in the US. The context of aging services dates back to the mid-16th century, when the colonists of Plymouth authorized a governmental entity to offer support to the vulnerable residents of its time, which presumably included older adults (Achenbaum and Carr 2015). In the mid-16th–century, aging services were conceptualizedas care for the vulnerable, with an emphasis on the informal network of families, neighbors, and religious institutions that continues to be a critical source of care for today's older adults.

Formal aging services have increased markedly in the last century, as evidenced by the passage of the Social Security Act in 1935 as well as thethe Congressional appropriation in 1952, which provided the first federal funds to support social programs and services before the establishment of the Older American Act (OAA) legislation in 1965. Along with the enactment of Medicare and Medicaid legislation, OAA is the bedrock of the aging services network, and it created the Administration on Aging (AOA), an agency in the US Department of Health and Human Services. The aging services network is comprised of programs and services specifically designed to support older adults' capacity to remain in the community (VCU Libraries Social Welfare History Project 2020).

AOA is one of the nation's largest providers of home-and-community-based care for older persons and their caregivers. It seeks to provide a coordinated and cost-effective system of long-term care which helps seniors age in place. Elected officials initiated landmark legislative actions to address the humanitarian crisis of food insecurity, shelter, and housing (VCU Libraries Social Welfare History Project 2020), which are the basic human requirements identified in Maslow's (1943) Hierarchy of Need (Figure 7.1), to address the growing rate of poverty in older adults and children. CBN's programs and services align with fulfilling each of the five levels of need described in Figure 7.1.

The OAA disburses funding to the states' aging services units, which is then shared with Area Agencies on Aging. The latter offers direct services or contracts with local groups to deliver health services, meals and nutrition services, caregiver support, and senior employment, as well as adult day care and other services (National Association of Area Agencies on Aging 2017). In New York State, the Office on Aging receives the federal funds, which are passed through to the NYCDFTA. CBN contracts with NYCDFTA to provide the mandated programs and services under Title III such as congregate meals (breakfast and lunch at the senior centers), case management, social services, assisted transportation, and elder abuse protection. It has been estimated that by 2030, the population age 60+ in the state will exceed 25 percent of the population (New York State Office for the Aging 2019).

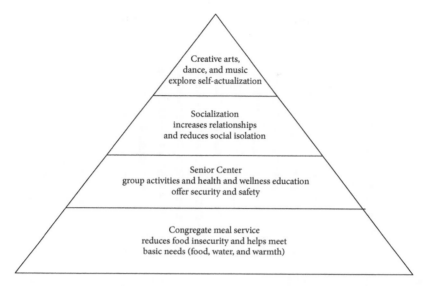

Figure 7.1 Carter Burden Network programs and services offered based on the tenets of Maslow's Hierarchy of Needs

Source: McLeod (2018).

Funding for Aging Services

Federal funding for aging services has not kept pace with the rapidly growing needs of the burgeoning 60+ population (O'Shaughnessy 2011). Figure 7.2 reports results of an 18-year retrospective examination of Annual Funding Appropriations for the OAA programs from 2001 to 2019 (Fox-Grage et al. 2019).

'Overall, annual OAA discretionary funding has declined over the 10-year period from FY2010 to FY2019 (not adjusted for inflation). Since FY2010, total OAA funding levels have remained below the FY2010 level when discretionary funding was at its highest amount of $2.328 billion' (Fox-Grage et al.2019). In 2011, the first of the Baby Boomers turned 65. Concomitantly, the US life expectancy increased from age 68.14 in 1950 to 78.93 in 2020, a 16 percent rise (Macrotrends 2020).

Carter Burden Network Public-Private Partnership Initiatives

CBN is keenly aware that the limited government funding has not kept pace with inflation. The growing needs of a burgeoning older adult population and the limited philanthropic support for aging services are now driving

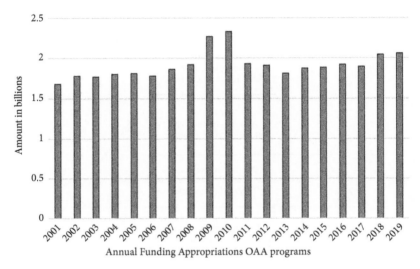

Figure 7.2 Annual Funding Appropriations for the Older Americans Act Programs, 2001–2019

Source: AARP Public Policy Institute (2019).

forces for development of innovative PPPs to address the needs of older adults. According to a report by the Silver Century Foundation,

> [e]very year, American grant makers donate tens of billions of dollars to nonprofits, to help make the world a better place. Yet only one percent of those dollars goes to aging-related projects, according to the Foundation Center, which analyzed grants of over $10,000 made in 2015 by 1000 of the largest US foundations. By contrast, 28 percent goes to projects for children and youth. (Hubbard 2018)

Giving USA, a nonprofit organization, reported in 2017 that nonprofit aging services organizations that provide community-based services and long-term care facilities represented about 6 percent of nonprofit organizations in the country that filed tax returns, while approximately 24.5 percent of American households are headed by someone age 65 or older (Giving USA 2017).

John Feather leads Grantmakers in Aging, the national society of grantmaking foundations and other organizations that work to improve the lives of older people. Dr Feather stated, 'As the number of older Americans is set to double to more than 20 percent of the population in the next twenty years, the percentage of charitable giving in aging has remained the same' (Feather 2015: 68).

CBN's three strategic PPP initiatives were driven by funding inequities in aging services and a desire to meet the demands of a growing older adult population where people are living longer with multiple chronic health conditions and inappropriate housing. These initiatives address the mind, body, and spirit of seniors at CBN through its senior centers' nutritional meal programs, creative arts, and health and wellness programming to promote positive health outcomes and contribute to older adults' overall well-being. While aging services funding remains stagnant overall, CBN was an early adopter of PPPs as a strategy to best serve the needs of the older adults. To illustrate, three of CBN's public-private initiatives—senior centers, creative arts collaborations, and health and wellness—are discussed below.

Senior centers

The creation of CBN was based on a public-private collaboration from its inception in 1971 when Council Member Carter Burden, an elected official, and his private family foundation, formed a partnership to address the needs of older vulnerable constituents that were food insecure and inappropriately housed (e.g. multiple floor walk-up apartments; insufficient income for food and medication). Recognizing food insecurity as a critical challenge of his district's older adult population, Councilman Burden partnered with Jan Hus Church and Church of the Epiphany in 1975 to develop the Carter Burden Luncheon Club. The opening of the Luncheon Club in 1975 occurred at a time in US history when Congress was passing legislation to address the needs of the vulnerable older adult population. For instance, the Nutrition Services Program was enacted between 1973 and 1975.

The Luncheon Club served a vital role in addressing food insecurity by offering hot lunches to the seniors on the Upper East Side. Shortly thereafter, CBN received funding from the NYCDFTA, one of 622 Area Agencies on Aging nationwide. Since then, CBN has opened three additional senior centers: Leonard Covello NYCDFTA-designated Innovative Senior Center (open seven days a week); Lehman Village Senior Center housed in a NYCHA building for low income residents; and Roosevelt Island Senior Center. CBN also operates four of NYCDFTA's 250 senior centers throughout NYC.

CBN also received support for the Luncheon Club through the federal Title III C Nutrition and Meals Services, and it continues to receive funding to support its three senior centers serving roughly 113,000 hot breakfast and lunch meals daily. For some seniors, the meals at the senior center may be the only meal of the day. In addition to nutritious meals, CBN also offers creative arts programming.

Creative arts collaboration

MAW and CBN's range of programming and services provide outlets for creative expression during difficult times and vital coping skills to respond to challenges. MAW is partially funded by NYCDFTA, and additional support for the Creative Art Center at the Leonard Covello Senior Center was donated by Macy's. Every year, the Covello Senior Center hosts its annual fashion show, with clothes made by the seniors in clothing construction classes. Macy's provides support for the fashion show through its employees, who volunteer their time for make-up and clothing adornment. In 2019, CBN offered 2,100 art classes through its four centers, attended by 900 seniors. A major recent endeavor of MAW was the Love Wall project, where participants created over 250 handmade ceramic tiles over a one-year period, reflecting the theme of love from each artist's unique perspective. The arts have the power to foster a connected, resilient, and welcoming community for all.

In 2009, CBN opened the Carter Burden Gallery. This group has not received any government support, but it has received private support from the Macquarie Group, an international financial firm, as well as the Thompson Family Foundation and Ford Foundation.

Health and wellness initiatives

CBN has developed a Health and Wellness Initiative Framework (H&WF) designed to address the increased longevity of older adults and the desire of more than 90 percent of older adults to remain in their own homes and communities. CBN is committed to providing health and wellness programs and services that promote positive health outcomes, contributing to older adults' capacity to live independently and with dignity in their communities. The framework is focused on interventions targeting social determinants of health including food insecurity, social isolation, health illiteracy, and income inequality.

Through specifically designed programs and services with community partners, the H&WF engages the older adult's mind, body, and spirit at senior centers and community settings throughout CBN's catchment areas. The framework consists of the following components: education, advocacy, research, community partnerships, technology, funding, and physical fitness.

CBN partners large health care systems serving its catchment area such as the NYC Health + Hospitals (NYC H+H), one of the country's largest public hospital systems; the Lenox Hill Hospital Northwell Health System; and New York Presbyterian Hospital. Northwell Health is New York's largest private employer and health care provider. The New York Presbyterian Hospital is a nonprofit academic medical center in NYC affiliated with two Ivy League medical schools: Columbia University Vagelos College of Physicians and Surgeons and Weill Cornell Medical College. Each of the health care providers offers critical health education on topics including diabetes and cancer, and conducts health screenings.

Metro East 99th Street Hybrid Adult Day Program (Day Program) and the DASH Diet Intervention are H&WF initiatives highlighted in this section to illustrate public-private collaborations. The two initiatives seek to help improve health outcomes and contribute to overall quality of life through education, screenings, services, and programming.

Metro East 99th Street Day Program In 2014, CBN received its first New York State Department of Health funding to support the Day Program Demonstration Project through the Balancing Incentive Program (BIP) under the New York State Medicaid Redesign Team (MRT) to reduce the state's Medicaid expenditures. This approach serves frail adults age 60+ with developmental, cognitive, or physical impairments, providing clients with socialization, supervision and monitoring, personal care, and nutrition in a protective setting.

The Day Program was developed to examine the effects of community-based programming on post-nursing-home transitions for a mixed-age, chronically ill tenant population into independent living. According to the Genworth 2014 Cost of Care Survey (Genworth Financial 2014), the median cost for nursing home stays in New York was $124,100 (semi-private room) and $130,670 (private room) annually. The median cost for adult health day care was $16,900 annually, and the social adult day care model was even less.

Metro East 99th Street Project was a newly constructed apartment building in 2014 that accepted tenants as former in-patients from the decommissioned Goldwater Skilled Nursing Facility and Hospital on Roosevelt Island. Eligible patients from Goldwater were given an opportunity to apply for an apartment at Metro East, which was an innovative collaboration between NYC H+H, Housing Preservation & Development (HPD), New York State Homes and Community Renewal (NYHCR), New York State Department of Health-Office of Health Insurance, New York State MRT, NYCHA, NYCDF-TA, and SKA Marin, a private developer and property manager of the Metro East 99th Street Project. It was a newly constructed 176-apartment unit of affordable housing for tenants transitioning out of long-nursing home stays after five to 22 years of placement.

The Day Program and services were critical to the tenants' successful transition into independent living and sustained housing. The Day Program model was an interdisciplinary approach that addressed the mind, body, and spirit of this vulnerable population, and it was designed to enhance the impact of community-based programs and service interventions in an effort to reduce health care costs, improve health outcomes, and enhance quality of life for previously institutionalized individuals (National Adult Day Services Association 2020).

Patients transitioning from long-term care facilities were the focus of the New York State Department of Health Nursing Home Transition and Diversion Medicaid Waiver Program's strategic plan. The goal was to reduce the state's Medicaid expenditures with appropriate housing that promoted independent living with dignity, and increased access to community-based services that helped individuals to live independently, which was a part of the community transition strategy. The strategy was predicated on the 1999 Olmstead Decision to increase access to community-based services and programs that support community living and eliminate segregation of person with disabilities (US Department of Justice, Civil Rights Division 2020).

In addition, the Day Program was designed to collaborate with managed long-term care plans to create a sustainable financial reimbursement structure commensurate with the delivery of programs and services. The Day Program assisted in the reintegration of extended nursing home stay residents into independent living as a part of the community-based continuum of long-term care services.

CBN also partnered with Vital Care, Inc., a telehealth company which assesses the effectiveness of the Day Program through an evidence-informed strategy, measuring the ongoing metrics against the baseline to determine outcomes. The approach uses a tablet device and a web-based program designed to educate, monitor, and measure biometrics (blood pressure, weight, and oxygen levels).

The Day Program demonstrated a 30 percent reduction in the rate of hospitalization for the 68 adult day members who participated in the remote community-enabled Telehealth Program. All attended the Day Program. The Telehealth Program had a 70 percent retention rate, which was the highest of all Day Program activities. The rate of hospital avoidance was self-reported. At each Telehealth engagement, questions were asked about doctor visits and hospitalizations. The Day Program provided a variety of services/activities.[1]

The Day Program was one of a set of cost-effective strategies to reduce Medicaid expenditures for high health care users living with multiple chronic health conditions by using cost-efficient community-based programs as opposed to expensive institutional care for individuals who are capable of living independently with appropriate housing. The Day Program was considered a best practice model in the transition of institutionalized individuals' reintegration into community living in an affordable housing development without a supportive housing designation. Although there were extensive PPPs, and extensive efforts by CBN to secure funding from the philanthropic sector, it was not able to extend the longevity of the demonstration Day Program. The affordable housing building 301 East 99th Street remains a thriving part of the East Harlem community.

DASH Diet Intervention CBN formed a partnership in 2015 with The Rockefeller University Center for Clinical Translational Science Center (CCTS) and CDN to conduct an academic community-based research study about seniors aging in place. The CCTS two-year funded Healthy Aging Study was conducted by the partnership from 2016 to 2018 to assess the health status and health priorities of seniors receiving CBN services at two of the East Harlem locations: one at a congregate meal site and the other a social model adult day program. The study revealed a prevalence of hypertension in 83 percent, with 23 to 46 percent meeting age-adjusted criteria for uncontrolled hypertension depending on the guidelines (Kost, Tobin, et al. forthcoming).

These study findings provided the impetus for further exploration of factors that contribute to overall health, such as food, physical fitness, and more. CBN provides congregate meal services by offering daily breakfast and lunch meals at senior centers, providing an opportunity to explore the impact of diet on health outcomes, and to learn about implementation challenges. Table 7.2 describes the project and reveals the percentage of those with blood pressure levels within the normal range and those determined to be uncontrolled. The study findings revealed that of 217 seniors in the study, 84 percent had high uncontrolled blood pressure (Kost, Tobin, et al. forthcoming). The results of the Healthy Aging Study prompted CBN and its partners to create a nutritional intervention to improve dietary habits for seniors and to address hypertension.

TABLE 7.2 Healthy Aging Study: Blood pressure in CBN pilot population

RU/CBN/CDN[a]: Carter Burden Healthy Aging Study Pilot 2016–2018	
Purpose: To collect information on the health of CBN seniors to assess the impact of services on health	Blood Pressure in CBN Pilot Population (n = 217)
Method: Pulse, blood pressure, walk/balance test, rsurveys on health, nutrition, and social factors, etc.	17% Normal blood pressure 16% Elevated blood pressure (SPB 120–129 mm Hg)
Highlights:	23% Hypertension stage 1 (SPB 130–139 mm Hg)
• Enthusiastic enrollment of 218 seniors • 99% completed the study • An important finding about blood pressure	42% Hypertension stage 2 (SPB >140 mm Hg) 2% Hypertension crisis (SPB >180 mm Hg)

Note: [a]Research for the Healthy Aging Study was conducted via partnership between Rockefeller University Clinical Translational Science Center, CBN, and Clinical Director Network.
Source: Kost, Tobin, et al. (forthcoming).

Nationally, cardiovascular disease (CVD) poses significant health risks for seniors, with two-thirds of those age 60 to 79, and approximately 85 percent of those age 80+ having one or more CVD risk factors. Blood pressure is one of the major modifiable risk factors for cardiovascular morbidity and mortality, with even moderate reductions playing a major role in preventing cardiovascular events. In 2018, CBN, in partnership with CCTS and CDN, was awarded a two-year US Department of Health and Human Services / Administration on Community Living Innovation in Nutrition grant to address seniors' cardiovascular risk through implementation of a dietary intervention at two of its senior centers—the Leonard Covello Senior Program in East Harlem and the Carter Burden Luncheon Club on the Upper East Side.

A community academic partnership was developed to implement nutritional and social behavioral interventions to reduce hypertension among seniors aging in place through DASH Diet Intervention (Kost, Coller, et al. forthcoming). The project implemented the National Heart, Lung and Blood Institute (NHLBI)'s DASH diet, through meals provided at senior centers; it also studied the impact of implementing this intervention in senior centers on blood pressure control. The DASH diet has been tested by two major studies backed by the National Institutes of Health (NIH), demonstrating ability to lower blood pressure in as little as 14 days (US Department of Health and Human Services 2006). The DASH diet is plant-focused, rich in fruits, vegetables, and nuts, with supplementary inclusion of non-fat and low-fat dairy products, whole grains, poultry, fish, lean meats, and heart healthy fats. The DASH diet had not been previously been tested in the setting of congregate meals among community living seniors. The project also offered educational workshops on blood pressure, nutrition, exercise, home blood pressure self-monitoring, and medication adherence, and their relations to cardiovascular health. Nutrition demonstrations with ingredients from the farmers' market and food pantry will show seniors how to maintain the DASH diet at home within their budget (Kost, Coller, et al. forthcoming). Results are anticipated soon.

Conclusion

PPPs can be critical for longevity of community-based organizations focused on aging services. CBN has worked with a network of public-private partners for the past 49 years, staying committed to its philosophy of collaboration and partnership as a driving force for sustainability of the organization, while contributing to the overall longevity of the older adults served. CBN's programs and services illustrate the value of partnerships as a conduit for sustainable programming, evident by its four senior centers that address the issues of food insecurity and social isolation, and its contribution to overall improved quality of life of its clients. One of CBN's clients who attended the Leonard Covello Senior Center recently said:

> When I first came to the Covello Senior Center, I wasn't active, didn't exercise, [and] was depressed and lonely. Covello has helped me to be more active, more outspoken, and more energetic through exercise programs, awareness, walking classes, and better eating habits. Now, I'm a totally new person—more healthy, more active, and more aware. (Covello Member and Active Zumba Participant)

In order for CBN and its colleagues in the aging service network to address the growing demands of the aging population, increased funding is required from government, corporations, and private philanthropy. Aging is everyone's business, so it will take a network of funders to help offer vulnerable older adults the safety nets necessary to remain independent in their homes and communities. The PPPs of CBN and other nonprofit aging service providers do offer a return on investment. For each of the nearly 6,000 seniors served and the 113,000 meals provided annually, CBN is contributing to a reduction in health care costs by improving health outcomes and reducing hospitalizations. Evidence of effectiveness was provided through the Metro East 99th Street Day Program, and additional data will be available following evaluation of the DASH Diet Intervention and its attempt to lower high blood pressure. The creative arts program also contributes to reduced social isolation, a social determinant of health. Through internal studies, the art programming has been shown to increase self-efficacy, reduce anxiety, and enhance social connectedness.

As discussed, funding for aging services has not kept pace with inflation or the increasing longevity of millions of older adults. Accordingly, PPPs extend the life of the aging service network and the longevity of nonprofit organizations like CBN that aim to improve the quality of life of older adults, especially significant today with the increasing life expectancy of older persons. Other nonprofit organizations similar to CBN, such as Westchester Public-Private Partnership Services for Aging Services (WPP) located in Mt Vernon, New York, recruit corporations to contribute unrestricted funds, underwrite specific programs, and donate in-kind services that expand needed services for the older adult population (Westchester Public-Private Partnership for Aging Services 2020). LiveOn NY (2015) is another nonprofit membership organization that uses direct assistance and innovative programs to help serve millions of older New Yorkers.

PPPs are equally important to other organizations, including Generations United a nonprofit organization which focuses on intergenerational collaboration and a multisectoral approach to support successful aging in place (Generations United 2020).

Without PPPs, CBN and similar community-based organizations around the country could not provide the safety net services needed to help the millions of older adults seeking to age in place. These include congregate meals offered at senior centers, assisted transportation, health and wellness education programs, physical fitness programs, case management and social services, in-home visits, and elder abuse protection services. Any reduction or indeed the elimination of PPPs could increase the risk of disrupting current and future aging services delivered by the community-based nonprofit sector.

Acknowledgements

We thank several reviewers of and contributors to the chapter including Velda Murad, Rina Desai, Clewert Sylvester, Janna Heyman, and Karen Dybing.

Note

1. Personalized plan of care, meal services, intergenerational technology training, cultural activities (on and off site), cooking and nutritional training sessions (e.g. grocery shopping, meal preparation), current issues discussion groups, book clubs, horticultural programs (e.g. in partnership with a local elementary school), media art classes, and Telehealth Program.

References

AARP (2019). *AARP Public Policy Institute*. Washington, DC: AARP. www.aarp.org/ppi

Achenbaum, W. A. and L.C. Carr (2015). 'A Brief History of Aging Services in the United States,' *American Society on Aging*. https://www.asaging.org/blog/brief-history-aging-services-united-states

Carter Burden Network (2020). 'History,' *Carter Burden Network*. http://www.carterburdennetwork.org/

Feather, J. (2015). 'Engaging Private Philanthropy in Aging: It's Time for a New Approach,' *Journal of the American Society on Aging*, 39(3): 68–71.

Fox-Grage, W., Houser, A., and K. Ujvari (2019). 'Spotlight: Older Americans Act.' *AARP Public Policy Institute Spotlight 34*. Washington, DC: February.

Generations United (2020). 'Who We Are,' *Generations United*. https://www.gu.org/who-we-are/

Genworth Financial (2014). *2014 Cost of Care Survey: Home Care Providers, Adult Day Health Care Facilities, Assisted Living Facilities and Nursing Homes*. Richmond, VA: NYSE: GNW. https://www.genworth.com/dam/Americas/US/PDFs/Consumer/corporate/130568_032514_CostofCare_FINAL_nonsecure.pdf

Giving USA (2017). 'A Giving USA Report Looks at the Importance of Philanthropy in the Aging Services Sector,' The Giving Institute. https://givingusa.org/philanthropy-may-be-imperative-for-the-future-of-aging-services-2/ (updated Feb. 17, 2017).

Hubbard, L. A. (2018). 'What's Missing in Philanthropy?' *Silver Century Foundation.* https://www.silvercentury.org/2018/10/whats-missing-in-philanthropy/ (updated October 8, 2018).

Kost, R., J. N. Tobin, K. Vasquez, W. J. Dionne, and D. Guishard (forthcoming). 'Healthy Aging Study,' Rockefeller University Clinical Translational Science Center, Clinical Director Network, and Carter Burden Network.

Kost, R., B. Coller, J. N. Tobin, K. Vasquez, A. Ronning, N. Moufdi, C. Coffran, D. Guishard, C. Sylvester, G. George-Alexander, D. Vasquez, T. Ezeonu, C. Khalida, W. Dionne, D. Diaz, C. Jiang, N. Singh, and V. Baez (forthcoming). 'Improving Cardiovascular Health through Implementation of a Dietary Approaches to Stop Hypertension (DASH)-Diet-based Multi-component Intervention with Senior Services Programs,' Rockefeller University Clinical Translational Science Center, Clinical Director Network, and Carter Burden Network.

LiveOn NY (2015). 'Our Work Improves the Life of 3 Million Older New Yorkers,' LiveOn NY. https://www.liveon-ny.org/ (updated 2020).

Macrotrends (2020). 'US Life Expectancy: 1950–2020,' Macrotrends LLC. https://www.macrotrends.net/countries/USA/united-states/life-expectancy

Maslow, A. H. (1943). 'A Theory of Human Motivation,' *Psychological Review,* 50(4), 370–396.

McLeod, S. (2018). 'Maslow's Hierarchy of Needs,' Simply Psychology. https://www.simplypsychology.org/maslow.html

National Adult Day Services Association (2020). 'About Adult Day Services.' https://www.nadsa.org/learn-more/about-adult-day-services/

National Association of Area Agencies on Aging (2017). 'Local Leaders in Aging and Community Living,' National Association of Area Agencies on Aging. https://www.n4a.org/Files/LocalLeadersAAA2017.pdf (updated March 2017).

New York State Office for the Aging (2019). 'Older Adults: An Economic Powerhouse,' New York State: The Official Website of New York State. https://aging.ny.gov/news/older-adults-economic-powerhouse (updated October 19, 2019).

O'Shaughnessy, C.V. (2011). 'The Aging Services Network: Serving a Vulnerable and Growing Elderly Population in Tough Economic Times,' Background Paper No. 83. Washington, DC: The George Washington University National Health Policy Forum. http://www.nhpf.org/library/background-papers/BP83_AgingServices_12-13-11.pdf

US Department of Health and Human Services (2006). 'Your Guide to Lowering Your Blood Pressure with DASH,' NIH Publication No. 06–4082. Washington, DC: National Institutes of Health; National Heart, Blood, and Lung Institute. https://www.nhlbi.nih.gov/files/docs/public/heart/new_dash.pdf

US Department of Justice, Civil Rights Division (2020). *Olmstead: Community Integration for Everyone.* Washington, DC: ADA. https://www.ada.gov/olmstead/olmstead_about.htm

VCU Libraries Social Welfare History Project (2020). 'US Administration on Aging.' https://socialwelfare.library.vcu.edu/federal/u-s-administration-on-aging/

Westchester Public/Private Partnership for Aging Services (2020). 'About Us.' http://westchesterpartnership.org/home/

Chapter 8

Innovative Strategies to Finance and Deliver Long-term Care

Nora Super, Arielle Burstein, Jason Davis, and Caroline Servat

Americans reaching age 65 today can expect to live, on average, until age 85—and about one-quarter of them will live past 90 (CDC 2019). While some will enjoy decades of active, purposeful living, over half will need a high degree of assistance with eating, bathing, and other activities of daily living (ADLs). The aging of the Baby Boomers will double the number of Americans needing long-term care (LTC) to 27 million by 2050; see Figure 8.1 (Favreault and Dey 2015). To identify new care delivery and funding models, we at the Milken Institute's Center for the Future of Aging and Innovative Finance have analyzed the most pressing barriers to effectively meeting the LTC needs of Americans. Based on this research, we have identified actionable suggestions on how to improve the financing and delivery of LTC in the United States.

The costs of formal LTC services are staggering. In 2019, the price of a nursing home stay averaged about $102,200 per year, or well-over two times an older (age 65+) middle-income family's income. The median rate for a private, one-bedroom unit in an assisted living facility was $49,000 per year, while the cost of adult day services averaged $19,500 annually (Genworth 2019). Today, defined benefit pension plans are not available to most Americans, and very few have saved sufficiently for retirement. A typical American age 65–74 has financial assets of just $95,000, and only $81,000 in home equity (Jacobson et al. 2017).

Long-term services and support (LTSS) refer to a wide range of services that help people live more independently by assisting with health care needs and ADLs. In the US, Medicaid pays for around 34 percent of LTSS costs, primarily for low-income people or those who have spent down their financial assets to qualify for coverage. Private LTC insurance (LTCI) pays for less than three percent (Favreault and Dey 2015). According to the United States Department of Health and Human Services (HHS), on average roughly 52 percent of LTSS costs are paid out of pocket for individuals age 65 through death; see Figure 8.2).

Nora Super et al., *Innovative Strategies to Finance and Deliver Long-term Care.*
In: *New Models for Managing Longevity Risk.* Edited by Olivia S. Mitchell, Oxford University Press.
© Pension Research Council (2022). DOI: 10.1093/oso/9780192859808.003.0008

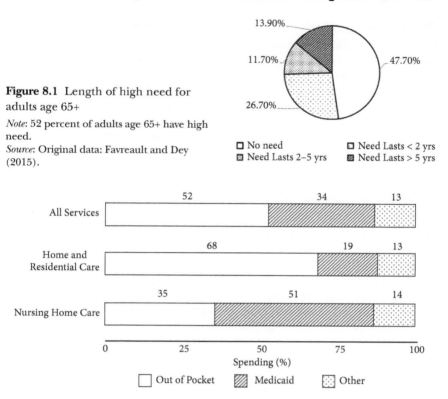

Figure 8.1 Length of high need for adults age 65+

Note: 52 percent of adults age 65+ have high need.
Source: Original data: Favreault and Dey (2015).

Figure 8.2 Average lifetime long-term care spending for adults age 65+ by source
Source: Favreault and Dey (2015).

By the year 2030, one in five US residents will be age 65+ (US Census Bureau 2018), and 70 percent of them will require LTSS at some point in their lives (BPC 2017). A decline in the number of family caregivers and limited financial resources will make adequate care harder to find for many Americans. In other words, as a nation, we are woefully underprepared for this impending crisis.

With the onset of the coronavirus (COVID-19) outbreak, the market failures and funding gaps in providing LTC stand out in stark relief. Public and private providers and payers face a uniquely daunting challenge in delivering LTC for those at high risk of severe illness and mortality. This new paradigm has impacted everything from the provision of care for socially isolated older adults, to the delivery of technology solutions as telehealth benefits expand in the wake of the crisis. In the long term, the associated economic downturn will further strain families' and individuals' ability to save for supportive housing and care.

Methodology

In 2019, the Milken Institute conducted market research related to LTC funding and delivery models including over 50 interviews with key stakeholders and subject-matter experts from a wide variety of fields including academia, financial services, government, insurance, health care, and technology. Despite initial claims that the system is fundamentally broken and needs to be entirely reworked, over 80 percent of interviewees offered concrete suggestions for incremental solutions to address the gaps in funding and delivery systems.

During this research, we developed several suggestions to improve the current state of LTC funding and delivery. In what follows, we focus on three of the most promising approaches:

(1) Facilitate private and public insurance product design with increased funding to allow for better testing of models that expand the market for insurers and decrease costs for consumers and government.
(2) Increase Medicare coverage of LTSS through the expansion of Medicare Advantage (MA) supplemental benefits, refinement and development of the Value-Based Insurance Design (VBID) model, and testing of new benefit offerings that will allow insurers to gather the data needed to measure health outcomes and related cost savings.
(3) Improve cost savings and efficiency through better integration of technology with care delivery, and by scaling successful funding models to allow for greater adoption.

Below we expand upon each in turn.

Public and Private Long-Term Care Insurance Solutions

Over the last two decades, the private LTCI market has changed considerably, contracting from over 100 insurers offering LTCI coverage in 2004 to roughly a dozen in 2018 (NAIC 2020).

Current state of the LTCI market

Market shrinkage has resulted from faulty actuarial assumptions made before the mid-2000s in pricing LTCI policies as well as a failure to accurately predict interest rates, mortality rates, lapse rates, and claims rates. In the early 2000s, stand-alone individual policy sales reached over 750,000 policies per year, but as of 2018, that number had dwindled to about 57,000 (Cohen 2019; see Figure 8.3). Those insurers who remained in the market

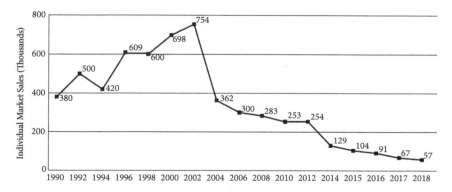

Figure 8.3 Annual sales of stand-alone individual policies have been declining for almost 20 years

Note: Authors' analysis based on AHIP, LIMRA and LifePlans sales surveys, 1990–2016. LIMRA data after 2016. Beginning in 2009, LTC Partners data for annuitants included in counts. *Source*: Cohen (2019).

needed to increase premiums significantly to stay financially solvent and generate financial return, causing trepidation among consumers.

Accordingly, the popularity of traditional stand-alone LTCI products has waned due to the high cost of policies, concern about premium increases, the misperception that Medicare or health insurance benefits include coverage for LTC, and a general lack of product understanding by the consumer (Ujvari 2018). Yet there is room for significant growth in the LTCI market, given that private insurance only covers less than three percent of overall LTSS expenditures (Favreault and Dey 2015).

More recently, the coronavirus outbreak has resulted in a number of shifts within the LTCI market. Some LTCI providers have made qualifying for coverage more difficult by limiting eligibility to those over a certain age, as well as requiring a waiting period for individuals who have tested positive for COVID-19. Additionally, the cost of LTCI may be affected by the pandemic's negative impact on the economy and the resulting low interest rates. Insurers contending with lower interest earnings may look to make up for those losses through higher pricing (Lankford 2020).

Promising new approaches

In response to a declining market for traditional LTCI products, insurers have been experimenting with hybrid policies that integrate existing benefits into life insurance (whole or universal) or annuity products, often through an LTC rider. This enhancement allows the policyholder to access a portion, or the entirety, of a death benefit to pay for qualified LTC expenses.

Hybrid policies may protect against sharp premium increases because many require an upfront lump premium payment or have structured yearly premiums over a defined time period. Also, underwriting that is less stringent than for traditional LTC products makes qualifying for these policies easier for individuals with pre-existing conditions. In 2018, 85 percent of LTC product sales were for hybrid LTC products, including products with a chronic illness rider (Society of Actuaries 2019). Hybrid policies do cost more than stand-alone LTCI, typically by three to 15 percent annually (ElderLawAnswers 2018).

Insurers have also experimented with variations on traditional stand-alone LTCI that borrow features from other segments of the industry. For example, in 2018 New York Life (2018) launched its My Care product. In its basic form, without riders or customizations, My Care offers four levels of benefits between the $50,000 Bronze level and the $250,000 Platinum level. Benefits are defined by specific dollar thresholds instead of by the benefit period of three to five years typical in other stand-alone LTCI policies. This product contains features similar to health insurance that keep down the cost of premiums, such as a one-time cash deductible payment and cost-sharing by the policyholder of 20 percent (coinsurance). Market testing these types of products offers insight into the right balance of benefits versus premiums to attract a larger group of enrollees.

Several of our interviewees recommended using health savings accounts (HSAs) as an option to pay for LTCI premiums. HSAs act as tax-advantaged investment vehicles, available to individuals and families enrolled in high-deductible health insurance plans increasingly provided by employers. HSAs are designed to help cover consumers' share of deductible and coinsurance payments; they can also be used to pay for direct LTC costs or premiums for qualified LTCI policies. The tax benefits associated with HSAs are substantial.

Unfortunately, the premium structure of some hybrid policies makes them inappropriate for qualified HSA distributions. Moreover, the potential for HSAs to become a significant future source of LTC funding is limited by current contribution limits. Today, most account holders think of their HSA balance as money to be spent on current expenses, partly because familiarity with 'use it or lose it' flexible spending arrangements (FSAs) means they do not realize that they are not required to spend down their HSA balances every year. Others lack access to longer term investment options within their HSA. The result is that, to date, only a tiny percentage of HSAs are currently invested in covering future health care and LTC needs. Increases in permitted HSA contributions would allow individuals to set aside more money earlier in their lives to help pay those costs in the future.

Losses experienced across the LTCI industry have also deterred potential market entrants. General Electric recognized a $9.5 billion pre-tax charge in 2018, stemming mostly from improperly priced LTCI policies sold in the 1980s and 1990s (Scism 2018). In addition to more accurate pricing for new products, insurers could potentially look to the catastrophe (CAT) bond market as a model for guarding against extreme losses. This insurance market developed CAT bonds to shift risk from insurance companies to investors, and to provide insurers with capital if and when a natural disaster occurs that meets clearly defined thresholds. Given the high costs of LTC and the inherent risk for insurers active in the LTCI market, creating a capital market product similar to CAT bonds could help provide capital should claims reach catastrophic levels. Providing additional forms of liquidity to insurance companies could, in turn, make the market more profitable and allow for increased flexibility in policy construction. More research is needed to model and understand general underwriting issues around triggers that are not incident-specific, such as a natural disaster, and based on a pool of policyholders (Milken Institute 2008).

LTCI state program experimentation

The Affordable Care Act (ACA) of 2010 established the federal Community Living Assistance Services and Supports (CLASS) plan, a voluntary, publicly administered federal LTCI program; this Act was subsequently repealed after it was determined to be financially nonviable. Since then, federal policymakers have not addressed LTCI comprehensively, though some states have begun to advance public programs.[1] When designing public LTCI programs, states have taken three distinct approaches: (1) a full coverage approach to provide benefits after a short waiting period, typically 90 days, with no lifetime claims limit; (2) a front-end approach that has a similarly short waiting period but a limited benefit timeframe (e.g. two years); and (3) catastrophic (back-end) coverage that has a longer waiting period (e.g. two years), with no lifetime claims limit (Gleckman 2019).

The full coverage plan provides coverage without any gaps, but it carries the highest cost. Favreault et al. (2015) estimated that a 1.35 percent payroll tax would be needed to fund a mandatory full coverage program. A front-end approach complements Medicare's post-acute care (PAC) coverage,[2] and the costs are more predictable, making it easier for government actuaries to model. Nevertheless, critics have warned that front-end coverage could discourage people from planning for their own needs, does not complement private LTCI, and fails to meaningfully help those with catastrophic needs. Also, this approach is not seen as progressive because wealthy individuals receive the same benefits as do low-income individuals (Gleckman 2019).

Over the years, some insurers and policymakers have emphasized the advantages of government-sponsored catastrophic LTC coverage, because it would significantly reduce the risk of covering the approximately 15 percent of older adults with lifetime costs over $250,000 (BPC 2017). In fact the Bipartisan Policy Center (BPC) concluded that government-sponsored catastrophic insurance would need to be mandatory 'to spread risk and remain financially feasible' (BPC 2017: 26). Such a backloaded social insurance approach (when combined with a safety net for those without adequate means) could provide a more easily explained and manageable front-end obligation, for which an individual's assets or the purchase of LTCI policies could help cover the gaps.

In 2019, Washington State Governor Jay Inslee signed into law the Long-term Care Trust Act, establishing the nation's first state-level LTCI program based on the front-end coverage model. This program provides a maximum lifetime benefit of $36,500 per person ($100 per day), indexed to inflation. Funding comes from mandatory payroll taxes paid by all Washington W-2 workers of 58 cents per every $100 of income. Eligibility is limited to Washington residents who have paid into the program for a specified period. To access benefits, an individual must need assistance with at least three ADLs. It has been estimated that Medicaid savings will be $34 million in the first year that benefits are distributed, growing to a total of roughly $4 billion by 2052 (Katz 2019; Washingtonians for a Responsible Future 2019). This state program is likely to generate much-needed data about how a front-end approach can help finance LTC. Critics have noted that the benefits of the program are too small to pay for the full costs of care, but they generally view it as a step in the right direction.

The Minnesota 'LifeStage Protection Product' proposal was put forward in December 2018 under the Minnesota Department of Human Services 'Own Your Future' initiative. It is a flexible insurance product that acts as term-life insurance during the policyholders' working years, and then it converts to LTCI at age 65 with coverage amounts and premiums remaining constant. The product, designed to be affordable, specifically targets adults between 35 and 55 years of age earning $50,000 to $125,000 per year (e.g. a 45-year-old male with a $100,000-policy would pay $63 per month; O'Leary Marketing Associates LLC 2018). Such a product could be attractive to parents who seek to safeguard their children through life insurance during the parents' working lives and to convert the policy to pay for LTC expenses after their children are grown.

Barriers to expansion

Another reason Americans have been slow to buy LTCI is that insurers have failed to demonstrate the value proposition to consumers. Several of our interviewees noted that the regulatory process for bringing new insurance products to the market can be quite lengthy. Insurers and actuaries also indicated that the review process for obtaining approval of rate increases is cumbersome. In response, the National Association of Insurance Commissioners (NAIC) asked its LTCI task force to draft a proposal outlining a streamlined and consistent LTCI rate review process. The new process would avoid duplication of work by state insurance departments and the insurers themselves, and also address 'cross-state rate subsidization' (Hilton 2020).

Path forward

Our research therefore identifies several strategies that show promise, including the following:

- Create better tax incentives that ensure LTCI (including all forms of hybrid policies) becomes an integral part of the retirement finance conversation, given that LTC costs are the most significant unmet retirement income security threat for most Americans.
- Increase HSA contribution limits and tax-advantaged withdrawal limits to better accommodate LTCI premiums, or create a new savings vehicle specifically for LTC modeled after HSAs.
- Enhance LTCI program experimentation at the state level, exploring back-end 'catastrophic' coverage options in addition to variations on the front-end approach.
- Explore similarities with the catastrophic risk insurance market and the CAT bond market to improve predictive modeling and provide a secondary market opportunity.

Medicare Expansion Solutions

While some experts look to new product design and state-based approaches to boost LTCI insurance, others point to the health insurance industry for lessons on how to manage the risk and cost of insurance.

Current state of Medicare market

Ample evidence suggests that social determinants of health, including access to housing, nutrition, and transportation, can positively impact health outcomes and reduce health care use and spending for vulnerable populations (Nichols and Taylor 2018). Social determinants, including health behaviors, social, and economic factors, account for 80 percent of health outcomes in a population, compared with 20 percent attributed to clinical care (Magnan 2017). To address this reality, the health care industry has been moving services out of clinical settings and into the communities where people live (Servat and Super 2019).

Historically, the US Medicare program has paid only for acute care services such as hospital stays, physician visits, and other services determined to be medically necessary by a physician. In particular, Medicare does not provide LTC coverage for nursing homes or personal care needs such as help with bathing or dressing (HHS 2017). Many Americans mistakenly believe that Medicare pays for these services and are surprised to find out it does not (Insured Retirement Institute 2019).

MA, originally named the Medicare+Choice program, was created under the 1997 Balanced Budget Act in response to growing support for private alternatives to traditional Medicare. Private health plans have been part of the Medicare program since its inception in 1965, first operating under risk-based contracts with health maintenance organizations (HMOs), which grew substantially from the 1980s onward. MA plans are required to submit estimates of the costs of providing traditional Medicare benefits and, if their payment rates exceed those costs, to provide additional benefits to their enrollees equal to the value of the surplus. MA plans traditionally include benefits such as prescription drug benefits, and vision and dental care as a means to attract more enrollees.

The 2004 Medicare Prescription Drug, Improvement, and Modernization of Act (MMA) further changed how private plans (now named MA) are paid under Medicare. Under the current bidding process, MA plans that bid below the county-level spending benchmarks are offered rebates in the amount of the value of the surplus, which then converts to additional benefits to the enrollee. MMA also paved the way for more private plan options within MA including regional preferred provider options (PPOs), Special Needs Plans (SNPs), and a coordinated care plan designed to deliver targeted care to address the needs of specific vulnerable populations. Today, 13 percent of MA enrollees are in SNPs, with 85 percent of those being dually eligible for Medicaid and Medicare (Jacobson et al. 2019). Enrollment in MA has nearly doubled over the past decade. In 2019, the majority of the 64 million people on Medicare were covered by traditional Medicare, but one-third (34%) were enrolled in MA plans (Jacobson et al. 2019). The Congressional Budget Office (CBO) projects that MA enrollment will continue to grow over the next decade, with plans enrolling about 47 percent of beneficiaries by 2029, compared with 34 percent in 2018 (Jacobson et al. 2019; see Figure 8.4).

Promising new approaches

With growing evidence confirming that provision of supportive services saves costs in the long run, Medicare has begun experimenting with

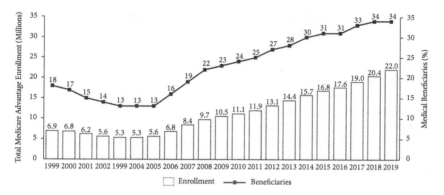

Figure 8.4 Enrollment in Medicare Advantage has nearly doubled, 2010–2019

Note: Includes cost plans as well as Medicare Advantage plans. About 64 million people were enrolled in Medicare in 2019.
Source: Kaiser Family Foundation (2019).

covering non-medical services, such as transportation and home-meal delivery. Accordingly, the line has blurred between supporting social determinants of health and providing LTSS.

Medicare Advantage special supplemental benefits Through the 2019 enactment of the Creating High-Quality Results and Outcomes Necessary to Improve Chronic (CHRONIC) Care Act, MA plans for the first time can pay for services that are not primarily health related. These 'special supplemental benefits' can be targeted to meet the needs of certain chronically ill enrollees. With Centers for Medicare & Medicaid Services (CMS) guidance, MA plans have been granted significant flexibility around who is eligible for these benefits and the services they receive (Anne Tumlinson Innovations & Long-Term Quality Alliance 2019). Analysis of publicly available data from CMS indicates that 512 plans (16% of all MA plans) will offer at least one of the new supplemental benefits (Long-Term Quality Alliance & ATI Advisory 2020).

Value-based insurance design In 2017, CMS began testing the MA VBID model, providing insurers with the ability to offer beneficiaries diagnosed with select chronic diseases various incentives (e.g. reduced cost-sharing and additional supplemental benefits) for utilization of services that providers considered to be of high clinical value. The model aims to 'reduce Medicare program expenditures, enhance the quality of care for Medicare beneficiaries, including dual-eligible beneficiaries, and improve the coordination and efficiency of health care service delivery' (CMS 2019). The model was initially made available to seven states covering seven chronic diseases; CMS then expanded it to all 50 states and territories (Murphy-Barron et al. 2019).

The scope of MA's VBID program has also expanded. Initially, the Center for Medicare and Medicaid Innovation (CMMI) allowed participating MA plans to target enrollees with any of only seven chronic conditions: diabetes, chronic obstructive pulmonary disease, congestive heart failure, past stroke, hypertension, coronary artery disease, and mood disorders. In 2018, rheumatoid arthritis and dementia were added to the list. Consequently, the uptake from insurers has been significant. The number of MA members enrolled in plans with value-based payment designs more than tripled from 2019 to 2020. CMS announced expansions to the VBID model, to include further customization of plans based on socioeconomic status, increasing access to telehealth services, and incentives for wellness program participation, including premium reduction and, eventually, a hospice benefit.

Overall, the VBID program offers MA plans a great deal of flexibility to offer person-centered care, which could make available some LTSS to Medicare beneficiaries. The potential benefits of the VBID model to MA plans are many and include (Murphy-Barron et al. 2019):

- Possible savings due to avoidance of costly medical care
- Improved health outcomes
- Future increases in enrollment due to enhanced benefits or reduced cost-sharing
- Broadened networks due to telehealth services
- Plan flexibility

Given this new regulatory flexibility, major payers have developed specific evaluation frameworks around non-medical benefits to enrollees. For example, Humana (2019) is targeting social determinants with its Bold Goal Initiative, focused on food insecurity, loneliness, and social isolation 'because of their direct impact on healthy days and clinical outcomes,' the company states. These initiatives include a predictive model allowing care managers and clinicians to identify patients at risk of loneliness and isolation. In December 2019, the company announced a new partnership with Philips, a leading technology company, to implement remote monitoring solutions as a fall prevention benefit for at-risk members.

Aetna is partnering with Meals on Wheels America to focus on technology-based care coordination to track the well-being of members in the home environment. Through this partnership, Meals on Wheels created a technology-based platform to allow Meals on Wheels volunteers to track noticeable health changes in free-meal recipients. The current project is operating in four markets, serving 50 clients per market (Bryant

2019). Meals on Wheels also has a larger scale project in three markets with Humana to address social determinants of health (e.g. food insecurity, loneliness, and medication management). Aetna's MA plan also includes a new fall prevention supplemental benefit for qualifying members in the form of an annual allowance on home safety features (Aetna 2019).

New benefits in traditional Medicare Medicare is receiving a great deal of political attention, yet most discussions on the Democratic side have focused on ways to expand coverage to all Americans, rather than on how to increase benefits to address the growing LTC crisis. Both Senators Bernie Sanders (I-VT) and Elizabeth Warren's (D-MA) proposals for 'Medicare for All' suggested expanding Medicare to cover LTSS. These proposals harken back to 2005 when some policymakers proposed the creation of Medicare Part E (or Extra) to help pay for prescription drugs and other out-of-pocket expenses (Cooper et al. 2005). Prescription drug coverage was added to Medicare as Part D under the MMA in 2016. To date, President Joe Biden has crafted a plan modeled after the 2019 Credit for Caring Act, which would allow some of America's 40 million family caregivers to receive a tax credit of up to $3,000 to help defray LTSS costs; Biden's proposal increases the tax credit to $5,000.

In 2018, Republican Frank Pallone (D-NJ), chairman of the House Energy and Commerce Committee, offered a draft Part E amendment, the Medicare Long-Term Care Services and Supports Act (House Energy and Commerce Committee, 2018). This proposal would establish a cash benefit within Medicare for beneficiaries to use toward all LTSS, including nursing facility care, adult daycare programs, home health aide services, personal care services, transportation, and assistance provided by a family caregiver. Draft legislation has not yet been introduced in the House since it was proposed two years ago.

New Medigap options Medicare Supplement Insurance or Medigap policies are private plans, available from insurance companies or through brokers, but not on the CMS website (Medicare.gov). Medigap plans are designed to fill the gaps in Medicare coverage for costs such as copayments, coinsurance, and deductibles. They differ from MA as the latter provides coverage for all health services. Medigap plans do cover some of the benefits that traditional, fee-for-service Medicare does not, and they are standardized and regulated at the state level. Labeled Plans A, B, C, D, F, G, K, L, M, and N.2 each have a different coverage set standardized by Medicare. Essential for those with pre-existing conditions, only four states (Connecticut, Massachusetts, Maine, New York) require either continuous or annual guaranteed issue protections for beneficiaries regardless of medical history (Boccuti et al. 2018).

While Medigap plans have not traditionally covered LTSS, states that are not subject to federal uniformity standards (i.e. Massachusetts, Minnesota, and Wisconsin) may have more flexibility to experiment with adding non-medical benefits to address the needs of those enrolled in traditional Medicare. States with larger shares of enrollees in Medigap plans tend to be located in the Midwest and Plains states where access to MA plans is lower. In 2018, the Minnesota Department of Human Services proposed to provide a home care benefit for Medigap and MA plans. Actuaries calculated that a one-year, $100-a-day home care benefit would add about $21 to a monthly Medigap premium (John Cutler Consulting 2018).

Barriers to expansion

Opportunities to expand MA supplemental benefits depend on the availability of rebate dollars which vary widely across geographic markets. Rebates, which average $107 per month in 2019 across the nation, can range from as little as $2 in North Dakota to $159 in Florida (Skopec et al. 2019).

CMS criteria for targeting supplemental non-medical benefits also present implementation challenges. According to the rules, non-medical benefits can be targeted based on *clinical criteria* rather than *social needs*, and coding can vary significantly across providers, making eligibility criteria challenging to navigate. Due to issues related to licensing and payment, MA plans are also concerned with how to provide these new benefits across multiple states (Long-term Quality Alliance 2018).

Actuaries have had difficulty modeling the real cost of providing discrete supplemental benefits, which has created an atmosphere of uncertainty and may partly account for the relatively slow and conservative rollout of such services. MA plans cautiously rolled out these new benefits in 2020, and experts anticipate that a broader distribution of benefits across markets in the future will enable more reliable economic analyses.

Critics of MA expansion efforts note that the model is not available everywhere in the US, and MA plans restrict access to doctors outside of their plans' network. Moreover, MA plans have not penetrated rural areas and are found mainly in more densely populated markets. Thus, in six states (Florida, Hawaii, Minnesota, Oregon, Pennsylvania, and Wisconsin) and Puerto Rico, over 40 percent of Medicare beneficiaries are enrolled in an MA plan. By contrast, in two more rural states (Alaska and Wyoming), fewer than 10 percent of all beneficiaries are enrolled in MA plans (Jacobson et al. 2019).

House Ways and Means Committee Chairman Richard Neal (D-MA) has also invited NAIC to explore the financial feasibility of adding LTC to Medigap policies. NAIC (2019) concluded that the addition of LTC benefits could make such coverage cost-prohibitive for most Medicare beneficiaries. The entity also noted other barriers to Medigap coverage of including LTC, such as anti-selection, plan uniformity across states versus optional riders, and potential market disruption.

While the majority of Medicare beneficiaries are enrolled in tradition-al (or fee-for-service) Medicare, almost all innovation in recent years has occurred in MA plans and other shared-risk programs. This may be because it is challenging to bundle packages of services under traditional Medicare due to its fee-for-service nature.

To summarize, several promising strategies to use Medicare as a vehicle to provide coverage for some LTSS are as follows:

- Continue to test the expansion of MA special supplemental benefits (e.g. home-meal delivery and transportation services) to measure the economic and health impacts;
- Test and expand the delivery of LTSS under VBID model; and
- Create new Medicare Part E in traditional Medicare to cover LTSS or new Medigap plans to cover LTC costs.

Technological Solutions

With a rapidly aging population and high costs for care, technology offers deep potential to fill a wide gap between the demand for and the availability of services.

Current state of technology

LTSS typically requires high touch interaction, but technology can help meet needs for those who cannot afford to pay for services or who live in remote areas where access is limited. Technology will not replace human interaction, yet it can bring supportive services into the home and com-munity. This was especially seen when care delivery was rapidly adapted to reduce transmission risk of COVID-19 across the globe in 2020, including for those providing or receiving in-person LTSS. Safety requirements, such as sharply restricting visitors to nursing homes and assisted living facilities, have increased the risk of social isolation and lack of access to routine med-ical care for millions of older adults. Technology can serve as a bridge when in-person care is not a viable option; however, COVID-19 has also exposed the limitations of a technology, especially for older adults who do not have access to broadband or personal computers.

During our interviews, numerous ideas for technology came up, rang-ing from remote monitoring to robots. Still, two main questions arose: who will pay for the integration of the technology, and how likely is it that it will be demonstrably cost-effective? New technology, from wearables and home surveillance to predictive analytics, promises to help lower costs and improve quality of care. Yet many programs are still in the pilot phase, requiring additional funding and coordination to achieve scale. To date, there is little evidence of incremental cost savings, and monitoring and evaluation costs add to the funding gap for start-ups and care providers.

Promising new approaches

Emerging technologies have significant potential to assist older adults as they age and to better coordinate LTSS. Health and LTCI companies, as well as CMS, will play essential roles in adoption rates because many of these tools can be given or shared at a discount to participants in order to encourage use, as a potentially more effective distribution channel than a purely direct-to-consumer model. We see four emerging technologies that could maximize the independence of aging Americans and reduce the economic and health impacts of cognitive and physical limitations: (1) predictive analytics; (2) telehealth; (3) remote monitoring; and (4) assisted mobility. Also, we've identified several models that could be enhanced to ensure funding is available to test and then scale up these emerging technologies.

Predictive analytics With the availability of big data, predictive analytics have become ubiquitous. This capability allows predicting the future using data from the past (Davenport 2014), a valuable tool for diagnosticians and providers looking to improve the quality of care and lower costs. According to Deloitte (2019), the main areas of potential benefit from predictive analytics are the improvement of business operations, personal medicine to improve diagnosis and treatment, and cohort treatment and epidemiology to assess potential risk factors for public health. The Society of Actuaries (2017) found that 93 percent of health organizations say predictive analytics is vital to the future of their business, and an impressive 89 percent of providers claimed that they are currently using predictive analytics or are planning to adopt the technology within the next five years.

Data generated by new technologies may also allow service providers and insurers to intervene earlier and with more specificity to lower costs and improve quality. Tech giant Google has already made strides using predictive analytics to improve diagnostics and has had several high-profile successes. Google-owned DeepMind developed an algorithm that identified acute kidney disease 48 hours before physicians did (Tomasev et al. 2019).

The LTCI industry traditionally has had to estimate how many people would file claims, set their premiums, and enroll participants, hoping projections were accurate; but the forecasts were often not accurate. Many experts we interviewed observed that the health insurance industry has become much more aggressive about intervening to reduce risk, based on data analytics. The LTCI industry could take advantage of these new techno-logical tools to better manage risk, from improved underwriting with data on cohort characteristics, to coordinated claim management with a better understanding of specific issues such as falls prevention.

In partnership with the John A. Hartford Foundation, CVS Minute Clinics have agreed to integrate 'Age-Friendly Health Systems' practices into 1,100 clinics across the US (CVS 2014). They identified the 4Ms as evidence-based practices that emphasize:

- What Matters: Care aligned with each older adult's health goals and care preferences.
- Medication: Use of age-friendly medications that do not interfere with goals and preferences, mobility, or mentation.
- Mentation: Prevention, treatment, and management of dementia, depression, and delirium.
- Mobility: Ensuring that older adults move safely every day to maintain function and do what matters.

By implementing these care principles delivered in convenient care settings with electronic data exchange capabilities, CVS seeks to provide more inte-grated care for treatment of chronic conditions associated with aging such as diabetes and hypertension (Dolansky and Pohnert 2019). The nurse prac-titioners who provide care to these older adults will be able to share data regarding the visits with participants' health plans and providers.

Telehealth Broader adoption and reimbursement for telehealth could rev-olutionize the speed of health and LTC delivery as it can facilitate commu-nication between providers and patients and expedite the delivery of care in emergencies. Telehealth is currently used mainly to manage certain chronic conditions such as diabetes and heart failure (CDC 2019a). The Centers for Disease Control and Prevention (CDC)'s National Diabetes Prevention Pro-gram has increased access and flexibility for the program by offering 200 of its curricula and handouts online (CDC 2019b).

Telehealth can also help reduce barriers to care for people who live far away from their providers, especially in rural communities, and for those who have transportation or mobility limitations. According to Eldercare Locator, a government-sponsored, national, toll-free hotline, the num-ber one reason older adults call the hotline is because of transportation problems (National Association of Area Agencies on Aging 2020). Trans-portation barriers are frequently mentioned by patients as a major reason for missing appointments, and missed medical appointments are associated with increased medical costs for the patient, delayed care and communication between providers and patients, and increased use of emergency departments. For instance, Sviokla et al. (2010) reported that missed appointments cost the US health care system $150 billion each year.

Despite its potential, telehealth use is not yet widespread, and has not been widely reimbursed for the patient or the provider. Due to COVID-19, however, we saw a rapid increase in telehealth by providers and patients.

In March 2020, CMS responded to the COVID-19 crisis and the need to provide necessary care to at-risk individuals by temporarily relaxing certain requirements for telehealth usage by Medicare providers. Prior to COVID, individuals had to live in rural areas, to be at an 'originating site' or designated medical facility to receive telehealth services. Under the new rules, telehealth has been expanded to cover almost all Medicare beneficiaries, including its use on smartphones, and the expansion of coverage to include non-COVID-related care (CMS 2020). In the past, getting patients to use telehealth was often a stumbling block for telehealth adoption. But in the wake of COVID-19, use of telehealth services expanded rapidly. From March to April 2020 alone, Medicare beneficiaries increased their use of telehealth by nearly 120-fold, from 11,000 to 1.3 million (Alliance for Connected Care 2020).

Remote monitoring Technology also permits providers to monitor their patients remotely and extend data gathering beyond the clinical setting (Center for Connected Health Policy 2019). Such remote monitoring can reduce hospital readmission rates, though more extensive studies are needed to compute return on investment for health outcomes (Center for Connected Health Policy 2018).

Of late, several high-profile technology firms have focused on remote monitoring. In 2019, Apple made a significant partnership with an MA plan to collect data from the Apple wrist watch, and additional Apple partnerships with Medicare private plans are likely (Peters 2019). Humana has also partnered with Philips to provide its high-risk MA members with Philips' Lifeline medical alert service, a remote monitoring device (Reuter 2019).

Health plans are increasingly supplying their members with tools including iPads that patients can take home for a limited period following a hospital stay. CareMore Health, an integrated delivery system owned by Anthem, also offers remote monitoring as part of its suite of services to help patients manage their chronic conditions. For example, patients in their heart failure program are given a wireless scale to use at home that provides data directly to their clinician. The clinician will see whether a patient has experienced rapid weight gain, an indication that medical attention is required (Hostetter et al. 2017). New partnerships with existing consumer channels also show significant potential to improve access to data. The new company model created by the merger of CVS Health and Aetna is poised to make such conveniences commonplace, using pharmacies as a significant delivery disruption. With stores located in virtually every US neighborhood, and the ability to integrate consumer and payer data, CVS predicts that the combined effort will improve the consumer health experience and build healthier communities (Servat and Super 2019).

One of the indirect impacts of the COVID-19 crisis on older adults, particularly in LTC facilities, is the enforcement of isolation to reduce risk of transmission. While the individuals in these care settings are the most at risk for adverse outcomes from the virus, the health risks from loneliness and social isolation can also significantly increase the likelihood of chronic illnesses and premature death. In response, the Advancing Connectivity during the Coronavirus to Ensure Support for Seniors (ACCESS) Act was introduced in April 2020 to expand access to technology for those in nursing homes and care facilities, and to allow residents to utilize telehealth services and virtual visits with loved ones while remaining socially distanced for their safety (US Senate, Office of Amy Klobuchar 2020). This legislation creates an environment that supports better connections for patient care and potentially improves health outcomes with both medical and non-medical intervention strategies without increasing patients' risk of COVID-19 transmission.

Health information technology can support advancements in care coordination and sharing of essential health information as individuals transition across care settings such as through long-term and post-acute care (LTPAC). Enhanced care coordination between acute care and LTPAC providers will enhance the quality of care provided in LTPAC facilities and reduce costs. Individuals receiving LTPAC services today frequently have chronic conditions and co-morbidities; transitions between care settings are common, creating the risk of complications, and often resulting in hospital readmission (Banger et al. 2020).

Assisted mobility As noted above, lack of access to transportation makes it difficult for some older adults to keep their health care appointments. Medicaid has long offered transportation as a covered benefit, but MA plans have only recently been offering this option. Some health plans have also begun offering vouchers for rideshare services such as Uber and Lyft. In 2016, CareMore Health recognized the cost savings potential of providing non-emergency medical transportation and carried out a pilot with rideshare service Lyft. It found that transportation costs decreased by 32 percent, among other positive outcomes, and so the firm expanded the service to 75,000 members nationally (Powers et al. 2016, 2018). Outside of medical appointments, transportation challenges limit older adults' independence and their ability to engage socially with their communities, a factor proven to be relevant to health outcomes. Recognizing the difficulty of getting around, the city of Monrovia in Southern California partnered with Lyft to offer subsidized rates with rides costing as little as 50 cents and up to $3.50 (Servat and Super 2019).

Another development is delivery via apps for everything from groceries to home projects. An MIT AgeLab study found that using App-directed services (e.g. for household errands, transportation, and home-meal delivery) for aging adults wishing to remain in their own homes cost less than the average monthly cost of assisted living, even with the need for services increasing with individuals' diminishing physical capability (Miller et al. 2018).

Funding vehicles We also identified several models that could be enhanced to ensure existing funding is more efficiently allocated, and to allow for new types of financing to bridge existing gaps across a continuum of capital from grants to investments. These include:

- **The State Grants for Assistive Technology**, which increase accessibility to assistive technology for individuals with disabilities of all ages (ACL 2019). This program provides one grant to each state and territory, based mainly on population. Approximately $28.1 million in grants was awarded in 2019, and many of those whom we interviewed agreed that there was insufficient funding for testing new technologies, and specifically for LTC applications. Government grants provide capital that is 'cost-free' in that the funding would not be repaid, which is critical for private companies that are reliant on generating revenue to pay investors. Given the success of the existing program, it could be expanded to the LTC market more broadly.
- **The Small Business Innovation Research (SBIR) and Small Business Technology Transfer (STTR) Programs** were created by the National Institute on Aging (NIA) to bring innovative technologies and treatments to market (NIA 2019). SBIR is designed to encourage American small businesses to engage in federal research and development with commercialization as the ultimate goal. The model achieved success, and in 2019 it provided an estimated $105 million to start-ups in this space (Hannon 2020). The SBIR program is unique in that it can drive new research and technology innovation, and it will also support small businesses to grow and scale up new products that show potential. Additional investments could be instrumental in bringing more technologies to scale (SBA Office of Investment & Innovation 2015).
- **Impact investment funds** and other forms of capital can provide funding opportunities beyond government grants for new technology adoption. Impact investors tend to be those seeking some financial return but who may need less than the market rate if the social return is quantifiable. For example, the Clean Energy Trust Impact Fund provides seed funding to 'cleantech' companies which require assistance to move a product from

pilot to commercialization. The fund is structured to catalyze additional investment by providing capital at one of the riskiest stages of development. Parallels can be drawn from untested cleantech companies and those in the LTC space, as both have high costs to move past the pilot stage to scale up their operations, and both need customers, individual and strategic, for product adoption. Many cleantech companies have to rely on uptake from agencies like utility firms, much like LTC tech products that may need to be integrated into government or nonprofit service providers. Navigating public-private partnerships and gaining low cost capital could be a useful way to bring to scale new technology for LTC.

Barriers to expansion

Adoption of technology in the LTC space has slowed in part because providers have not been eligible for the subsidies granted to hospitals and doctors under the 2019 Health Information Technology for Economic and Clinical Health (HITECH) Act. Even when adopted, many new technologies are still relatively unproven, and better data are required to show demonstrable improvements to care. Thus far, interventions from remote monitoring to predictive analytics have been structured as pilot programs while the results are gathered on efficacy and efficiency.

To improve and scale up the four promising practices listed above, the communication pathways and accuracy of the information moving between primary care doctors, specialists, hospital settings, and skilled nursing facilities must be reliable and easily shared. Interoperability (i.e. the capacity for different systems, devices, and applications to access, exchange, integrate, and cooperatively use data) remains a substantial challenge, especially for operations outside of hospital-based systems and physicians' offices. Poor communication can have serious medical consequences, while smooth transitions can improve care (JaWanna et al. 2018). The Office of the National Coordinator (ONC) for Health Information Technology showed that, as of 2017, seven of 10 hospitals studied still received summary care records via mail or fax (Johnson et al. 2018).

In March 2020, the ONC of Health Information Technology, in conjunction with CMS, released the 21st Century Cures Act Final Rule for expanding interoperability between patients, health care providers, and medical professionals. New requirements include the implementation of patient application program interface (API) services that facilitate access to information on health care costs and limited clinical information; patient clinical data exchange systems that create cumulative medical history records and ease patient transfer between payers; and the requirement of hospitals to notify a patient's other care providers of a change in patient status (e.g. admission, transfer, or discharge) (HHS 2020). The government can continue to improve interoperability by creating additional standards for implementation and software; increasing transparency regarding data and privacy; and incentivizing the appropriate use of electronic health information to improve health and well-being (DeSalvo 2015).

In summary, important hurdles remain for funding research and design efforts for new technology and scale successful programs. To advance technology solutions improving LTC financing and delivery, several public-private strategies are available and worth exploring further:

- Pilot test technology that has worked in the health care sector (e.g. predictive analytics, telehealth, remote monitoring, and assisted mobility in multiple locations across different settings of care).
- Improve interoperability by creating additional standards for implementation and software; increasing transparency regarding data and privacy; and incentivizing the appropriate use of electronic health information to improve health and well-being.
- Close the funding gap for technology to support LTC by establishing a federal-level small business seed fund targeting aging-related technology companies, modeled after the State Grant for Assistive Technology program; creating an impact investment fund to support the development of emerging technologies; and scaling up public-private subsidy programs for insurers and care providers to offer technology at low or no cost to users.

Conclusion

Though new models to provide LTC are a pressing concern, Medicare today only covers minimal aspects of LTSS, and Medicaid eligibility is limited to individuals who meet strict income and asset requirements. However, most Americans are underprepared to self-fund the high cost of care and the private LTCI market has suffered severe restrictions in recent years. This study has identified a menu of potential solutions to help address the related LTC funding gaps, market failures, and care delivery needs.

Because of the urgency created by this impending crisis, it is crucial for all stakeholders to ask how each participate in this exploratory phase. Many new models for funding and service delivery warrant more testing and design. Our organization, the Milken Institute, seeks to continue this work through our Financial Innovations Lab series.[3]

Acknowledgements

The authors thank Transamerica Institute for its generous support of this research, and Randy Hardock, Gretchen Alkema, Caitlin MacLean, Paul Irving, and Lauren Dunning for helpful comments. They especially appreciate Cara Levy for her excellent research assistance.

Notes

1. In addition to Washington State, several other states are also working on LTC access and affordability, including Arizona, California, Hawaii, Illinois, and Michigan. Lawmakers in California, Illinois, and Michigan have approved studies that will explore residents' needs and a variety of potential LTC solutions. Arizona has embarked on a two-year pilot program in 2020 that supports caregivers by providing grants to reimburse for caregiving expenses, up to $1,000 (Wiltz 2019). Hawaii has implemented the Kūpuna Caregivers Program, which supports unpaid family caregivers who also work outside the home for at least 30 hours per week. Program participants are eligible for up to $70 per day in benefits, which can be applied toward a variety of services. The program aims to ease the financial burden of caregiving and help the family caregiver maintain his or her employment outside of the home (Paying for Senior Care 2015).

2. PAC includes rehabilitation or palliative services that people receive after, or in some cases instead of, a stay in an acute care hospital. Depending on the intensity of care the patient requires, treatment may include a stay in a facility, ongoing outpatient therapy, or care provided at home (Medicare Payment Advisory Commission 2020).

3. The Milken Institute Financial Innovations Labs are miniature think tanks designed to devise new business models, policy recommendations, capital structures, and financial technologies that can achieve concrete goals. By bringing together a diverse group of stakeholders, Financial Innovation Labs encourage collaboration between players who may not normally interact.

References

ACL (Administration for Community Living) (2019). *ACL State Grants for Assistive Technology Awards (ATSG) for the States/Territories FY 2019 Final Allocation*. ACL. Washington, DC: ACL.

Aetna (2019). 'Aetna's 2020 Medicare Plans Connect Members with More Personalized Care and Benefits in their Homes and Communities,' Press Release, Hartford, CT, October 24.

Alliance for Connected Care (2020). 'Medicare Members Using Telehealth Grew 120 Times in Early Weeks of COVID-19 as Regulations Eased,' Alliance for Connected Care Blog, May 28. http://connectwithcare.org/medicare-members-using-telehealth-grew-120-times-in-early-weeks-of-covid-19-as-regulations-eased/

Anne Tumlinson Innovations & Long-Term Quality Alliance (2019). *A Turning Point in Medicare Policy: Guiding Principles for New Flexibility under Special Supplemental Benefits for the Chronically Ill*. Washington, DC: Long-Term Quality Alliance.

Banger A., S. Rizk, J. Bagwell, and A. Ortiz (2020). *National Health IT Priorities for Research*. Washington, DC: The Office of the National Coordinator for Health Information Technology. https://www.healthit.gov/sites/default/files/page/2020-01/PolicyandDevelopmentAgenda.pdf

Boccuti, C., G. Jacobsen, K. Orgera, and T. Neuman (2018). *Medigap Enrollment and Consumer Protections Vary Across States*. San Francisco: Kaiser Family Foundation. https://www.kff.org/medicare/issue-brief/medigap-enrollment-and-consumer-protections-vary-across-states/

BPC (Bipartisan Policy Center) (2017). *Financing Long-Term Services and Supports: Seeking Bipartisan Solutions in Politically Challenging Times.* Washington, DC: Bipartisan Policy Center.

Bryant, B. (2019). 'Meals on Wheels Turns to Home Care to Help Win Medicare Advantage Partners,' *Home Health Care News,* August 8. https://home healthcarenews.com/2019/08/meals-on-wheels-turns-to-home-care-to-help-win -medicare-advantage-partners/

CDC (Centers for Disease Control and Prevention) (2019). *United States Life Tables, 2017.* CDC NVSS-68-7. Washington DC: Centers for Disease Control and Prevention Division of Vital Statistics.

CDC (Centers for Disease Control and Prevention) (2019a). *Telehealth in Rural Communities: How the CDC Develops Programs That Deliver Care in New ways.* Atlanta, GA: Centers for Disease Control and Prevention https://www.cdc.gov/ chronicdisease/resources/publications/factsheets/telehealth-in-rural-communities.htm

CDC (Centers for Disease Control and Prevention) (2019b). 'National Diabetes Prevention Program: About the National DPP.' https://www.cdc.gov/ diabetes/prevention/about.htm

Center for Connected Health Policy (2018). 'Remote Patient Monitoring Research Catalogue.' https://www.cchpca.org/sites/default/files/2018-09/Remote%20 Patient%20Monitoring%20Research%20Catalogue%20%28Aug%202018%29. pdf

Center for Connected Health Policy (2019). 'About Telehealth: Remote Patient Monitoring (RPM).' https://www.cchpca.org/about/about-telehealth/remote-patient-monitoring-rpm

CMS (Centers for Medicare & Medicaid Services) (2019). 'Medicare Advantage Value-Based Insurance Design Model.' https://innovation.cms.gov/ initiatives/vbid/ (updated March 3, 2020).

CMS (Centers for Medicare & Medicaid Services) (2020). 'Medicare Telemedicine Health Care Provider Fact Sheet.' https://www.cms.gov/newsroom/fact-sheets/ medicare-telemedicine-health-care-provider-fact-sheet (updated March 17, 2020).

Cohen, M. A. (2019). 'Financing Long-Term Care: Challenges, Opportunities and Financing Alternatives,' Presentation to New York State Long Term Care Planning Project. Boston, MA: LeadingAge LTSS Center.

Cooper, B., M. Moon, C. Schoen, and K. Davis (2005). *Medicare Extra: A Comprehensive Benefit Option for Medicare Beneficiaries.* New York City, NY: The Commonwealth Fund. https://www.commonwealthfund.org/publications/ journal-article/2005/oct/medicare-extra-comprehensive-benefit-option-medicare?redirect_source=/publications/in-the-literature/2005/oct/medicare-extra—a-comprehensive-benefit-option-for-medicare-beneficiaries

CVS (2014) 'Age Friendly Slide Presentation.' Shared on January 14, 2020.

Davenport (2014). 'A Predictive Analytics Primer,' *Harvard Business Review,* Sept 2. https://hbr.org/2014/09/a-predictive-analytics-primer

Deloitte (2019). *Predictive Analytics in Health Care: Emerging Value and Risks.* https://www2.deloitte.com/us/en/insights/topics/analytics/predictive-analytics-health-care-value-risks.html

Department of Health and Human Services (2020). 'HHS Finalizes Historic Rules to Provide Patients More Control of Their Health Data,' Press Release, Washington, DC: March 9. https://www.hhs.gov/about/news/2020/03/09/hhs-finalizes-historic-rules-to-provide-patients-more-control-of-their-health-data.html#:~:text=The%20ONC%20Final%20Rule%20identifies,certified%20health%20IT%2C%20health%20information

DeSalvo (2015). 'Health Information Technology: Where We Stand and Where We Need To Go.' Health Affairs Blog. https://www.healthaffairs.org/do/10.1377/hblog20150424.047271/full/

Dolansky, M. and A. Pohnert (2019). 'Implementing the Age-Friendly Health System into CVS Minute Clinics,' *Innovation in Aging*, 3(1): 149–150. https://academic.oup.com/innovateage/article/3/Supplement_1/S149/5617219

ElderLawAnswers (2018). 'Hybrid Policies Allow You to Have Your Long-Term Care Insurance Cake and Eat It, Too,' *ElderLawAnswers*. https://www.elderlawanswers.com/hybrid-policies-allow-you-to-have-your-long-term-care-insurance-cake-and-eat-it-too–15541 (updated June 14, 2018).

Favreault, M. and J. Dey (2015). *Long-Term Services and Supports for Older Americans: Risks and Financing*. Washington, DC: HHS Office of the Assistant Secretary for Planning and Evaluation, Office of Disability, Aging and Long-Term Care Policy. https://aspe.hhs.gov/basic-report/long-term-services-and-supports-older-americans-risks-and-financing-research-brief (updated February 2016).

Favreault, M. M., H. Gleckman, and R. W. Johnson (2015). 'Financing Long-Term Services And Supports: Options Reflect TradeOffs For Older Americans And Federal Spending,' *Health Affairs*, 34(12): 2181-91.

Genworth (2019). *Genworth Cost of Care Survey 2019 Summary and Methodology*. Richmond, VA: Genworth. https://pro.genworth.com/riiproweb/productinfo/pdf/131168.pdf

Gleckman, H. (2019). 'Interest Grows In Social Insurance For Long-Term Care. What Should It Look Like?' *Forbes*, September 4. https://www.forbes.com/sites/howardgleckman/2019/09/04/interest-grows-in-social-insurance-for-long-term-care-what-should-it-look-like/#63c234715803

Hannon (2020). 'The Government Program Funding Startups for Older Adults,' *Forbes, Next Avenue*. https://www.forbes.com/sites/nextavenue/2020/02/07/the-government-program-funding-startups-for-older-adults/#17fa987128da

HHS (United States Department of Health and Human Services) (2017). 'What is Medicare and What Does It Cover?' LongTermCare.gov. https://longtermcare.acl.gov/medicare-medicaid-more/medicare.html (updated November 14, 2017).

Hilton, J. (2020). 'NAIC To Collect LTC Data In Bid To Create Uniform Price Hike Review,' *InsuranceNewsNet*. https://insurancenewsnet.com/innarticle/naic-collects-ltc-data-in-bid-to-create-uniform-price-hike-review#.XjyZ72hKiUl (updated January14).

Hostetter, M., S. Klein, and D. McCarthy (2017). *CareMore: Improving Outcomes and Controlling Health Care Spending for High-Needs Patients*. New York, NY. The Commonwealth Fund. https://www.commonwealthfund.org/publications/case-study/2017/mar/caremore-improving-outcomes-and-controlling-health-care-spending

Humana (2019). 'Social Determinants of Health.' https://populationhealth.
humana.com/social-determinants-of-health/

Insured Retirement Institute (2019). *Boomer Expectations for Retirement 2019: Ninth Annual Update on the Retirement Preparedness of the Boomer Generation.* Washington, DC: Insured Retirement Institute. https://www.myirionline.org/docs/default-source/default-document-library/iri_babyboomers_whitepaper_2019_final.pdf?sfvrsn=0

Jacobson, G., S. Griffin, T. Neuman, and K. Smith (2017). *Income and Assets of Medicare Beneficiaries, 2016–2035.* San Francisco, CA: Kaiser Family Foundation. https://www.kff.org/medicare/issue-brief/income-and-assets-of-medicare-beneficiaries-2016-2035/

Jacobson, G., M. Freed, A. Damico, and T. Neuman (2019). *A Dozen Facts about Medicare Advantage in 2019.* San Francisco, CA: Kaiser Family Foundation. https://www.kff.org/medicare/issue-brief/a-dozen-facts-about-medicare-advantage-in-2019/

JaWanna, H., Y. Pylypchuk, and V. Patel (2018) *Electronic Health Record Adoption and Interoperability among US Skilled Nursing Facilities and Home Health Agencies in 2017.* ONC Data Brief 41. Washington, DC: The Office of the National Coordinator for Health Information Technology. https://www.healthit.gov/sites/default/files/page/2018-11/Electronic-Health-Record-Adoption-and-Interoperability-among-U.S.-Skilled-Nursing-Facilities-and-Home-Health-Agencies-in-2017.pdf

John Cutler Consulting (2018). *Enhanced Home Care Benefit in Medicare Supplemental Plans.* St. Paul, MN: Minnesota Department of Human Services Own Your Future Initiative. https://mn.gov/dhs/assets/John-Cutler-final-report_tcm1053-373468.pdf

Johnson, C., Y. Pylypchuk, and V. Patel (2018). *Methods Used to Enable Interoperability among US Non-Federal Acute Care Hospitals in 2017.* ONC Data Brief 43. Washington, DC: The Office of the National Coordinator for Health Information Technology. https://www.healthit.gov/sites/default/files/page/2018-12/Methods-Used-to-Enable-Interoperability-among-U.S.-NonFederal-Acute-Care-Hospitals-in-2017_0.pdf

Kaiser Family Foundation (2019). *Medicare Advantage.* San Francisco, CA: Kaiser Family Foundation. https://www.kff.org/medicare/fact-sheet/medicare-advantage

Katz, R. (2019). 'Washington State: First Out of the Gate on LTC Financing,' *Leading Age.* https://www.leadingage.org/legislation/washington-state-first-out-gate-ltc-financing (updated May 1).

Lankford, Kimberly (2020). 'FAQs about Coronavirus and Long-Term Care Insurance,' *US News & World Report,* May 22.

Long-Term Quality Alliance. (2018). *Medicare Advantage's New Supplemental Benefit for 2019: Plan Views and Responses.* Washington, DC: Long-term Quality Alliance. http://www.ltqa.org/wp-content/themes/ltqaMain/custom/images/LTQA-Report-on-MA-Flexible-Supplemental-Benefits-FINAL-11-9-18.pdf

Long-term Quality Alliance and ATI Advisory (2020). *Medicare Advantage and Supplemental Benefits: New Data and Principles for Implementation.* Washington, DC. http://www.ltqa.org/medicare-advantage-and-supplemental-benefits-new-data-and-principles-for-implementation/

Magnan, S. (2017). *Social Determinants of Health 101 for Health Care: Five Plus Five* Washington, DC: National Academy of Medicine. https://nam.edu/social-determinants-of-health-101-for-health-care-five-plus-five

Medicare Payment Advisory Commission (2020). 'Post-Acute Care,' *Medpac.* http://www.medpac.gov/-research-areas-/post-acute-care

Milken Institute (2008). *Financial Innovations for Catastrophic Risk: Cat Bonds and Beyond Financial Innovations Lab Report.* Santa Monica, CA: Milken Institute.

Miller J., C. Ward, C. Lee, L. D'Ambrosio, and J. Coughlin (2018). 'Sharing is Caring: The Potential of the Sharing Economy to Support Aging in Place.' *Gerontology and Geriatrics Education, 10.1080.* https://www.tandfonline.com/doi/abs/10.1080/02701960.2018.1428575

Murphy-Barron, C. M., P. M. Pelizarri, and B. Regan (2019). *The Medicare Advantage Value Based Insurance Design Model: Overview and Considerations.* Seattle, WA: Milliman. https://www.milliman.com/insight/The-Medicare-Advantage-Value-Based-Insurance-Design-Model-Overview-and-considerations

NAIC (National Association of Insurance Commissioners) (2019). *Letter to Chairman of the House Ways and Means Committee, Richard E. Neal.* Kansas City, MO: NAIC. https://cdn2.hubspot.net/hubfs/2635471/NAIC%20Response%20to%20W&M%20LTSS%20Letter%20FINAL.pdf

NAIC (National Association of Insurance Commissioners) (2020). 'Long-Term Care Insurance,' National Association of Insurance Commissioners. https://content.naic.org/cipr_topics/topic_long_term_care_insurance.htm (updated February 4, 2020).

National Association of Area Agencies on Aging (2020). 'Eldercare Location,' *n4a.* https://www.n4a.org/eldercarelocator

NIA (National Institute on Aging) (2019). 'NIA Small Business Programs (SBIR & STTR).' https://www.nia.nih.gov/research/osbr

New York Life (2018). 'New York Life Reimagines Long-term Care Insurance with the Launch of NYL My Care,' Press Release, New York, NY, September 5.

Nichols, L. and L. Taylor (2018). 'Social Determinants as Public Goods: A New Approach to Financing Key Investments In Healthy Communities,' Health Affairs, 37(8). https://www.healthaffairs.org/doi/full/10.1377/hlthaff.2018.0039

O'Leary Marketing Associates LLC (2018). *LifeStage Protection Product Final Report Prepared for Minnesota Department of Human Services Own Your Future Initiative.* Schaumburg, IL: SOA. https://mn.gov/dhs/assets/LifeStage-protection-product%E2%80%93final-report_tcm1053-373463.pdf

Paying for Senior Care (2015). *Hawaii's Kupuna Caregivers Program: Helping Working Families to Care for their Loved Ones.* Charlotte, NC. https://www.paying-forseniorcare.com/hawaii/kupuna-caregivers

Peters, J. (2019). 'Medicare Insurers Are Starting to Offer Big Apple Watch Discounts,' *The Verge*, October 8. https://www.theverge.com/2019/10/8/20904804/apple-watch-medicare-insurance-discounts-devoted-health

Powers, B. W., S. Rinefort, and S. Jain (2016). 'Nonemergency Medical Transportation Delivering Care in the Era of Lyft and Uber,' *JAMA*, 316(9): 921–922.

Powers, B. W., S. Rinefot, and S. Jain (2018). 'Shifting Non-Emergency Medical Transportation to Lyft Improves Patient Experience and Lowers Costs,' Health Affairs Blog, September 13: https://www.healthaffairs.org/do/10.1377/hblog20180907.685440/full/

Reuter, E. (2019). 'Philips, Humana to Offer Remote Monitoring for at-Risk Seniors,' *MedCity News*, December 10. https://medcitynews.com/2019/12/philips-humana-to-offer-remote-monitoring-for-high-risk-seniors/

SBA (Small Business Administration) Office of Investment & Innovation (2015). 'SBIR-STTR Presentation.' SBA-HQ, Washington, DC. https://www.sbir.gov/sites/default/files/SBA_OII_SBIR_STTR_Presentation_for_General_Public_3-20-15.pdf

Scism, L. (2018). 'Millions Bought Insurance to Cover Retirement Health Costs: Now They Face an Awful Choice,' *The Wall Street Journal*. https://www.wsj.com/articles/millions-bought-insurance-to-cover-retirement-health-costs-now-they-face-an-awful-choice-1516206708?mod=article_inline (updated January 17, 2018).

Servat, C. and N. Super (2019). *Age-Forward Cities for 2030*. Santa Monica, CA: The Milken Institute Center for the Future of Aging. https://milkeninstitute.org/reports/age-forward-cities–2030

Skopec, L., C. Ramos, and J. Aarons (2019). *Are Medicare Advantage Plans Using New Supplemental Benefit Flexibility to Address Enrollees' Health-Related Social Needs?* Washington, DC: The Urban Institute.

Society of Actuaries (2017). '2017 Predictive Analytics in Healthcare Trend Forecast,' *SOA Health Trends Forecast 2017*. Schamburg, IL: Society of Actuaries.

Society of Actuaries (2019). *A Primer on the Hybrid LTC Market*. Schaumburg, IL: Society of Actuaries.

Sviokla, J., B. Schroeder, and T. Weakland (2010). 'How Behavioral Economics Can Help Cure the Health Care Crisis,' *Harvard Business Review*. https://hbr.org/2010/03/how-behavioral-economics-can-h

Tomasev N., X. Glorot, and J. W. Rae (2019). 'A Clinically Applicable Approach to Continuous Prediction of Future Acute Kidney Injury,' *Nature*, 572(7767): 116–119.

Ujvari, K. (2018). 'Disrupting the Marketplace: The State of Private Long -Term Care Insurance, 2018 Update.' *AARP Public Policy Institute Insight on the Issues*. Washington, DC: AARP Public Policy Institute, 138.

United States Census Bureau (2018). 'Older People Projected to Outnumber Children for First Time in US History,' Press Release, Washington, DC, March 13

United States House Committee on Energy and Commerce (2018). 'Medicare Long-term Care Services and Supports Act,' Discussion Draft, Washington, DC. https://energycommerce.house.gov/sites/democrats.energycommerce.house.gov/files/documents/LTSS%20Act%20May%202018.pdf

United States Senate, Office of Amy Klobuchar (2020). 'Klobuchar, Casey Introduce Legislation to Increase Seniors' Virtual Connection to Health Care and Community Amidst Coronavirus Outbreak,' Press Release, Washington, DC, March 19. https://www.klobuchar.senate.gov/public/index.cfm/2020/3/klobuchar-casey-introduce-legislation-to-increase-seniors-virtual-connection-to-health-care-and-community-amidst-coronavirus-outbreak

Washingtonians for a Responsible Future (2019). 'LONG-TERM CARE TRUST ACT: Our Long-Term Care System Makes Families Poor and Threatens to Bankrupt Our State's Budget,' Washingtonians for a Responsible Future, Washington, DC.

Wiltz, T. (2019). 'Getting Older, Going Broke: Who's Going to Pay for Long-term Care?' The Pew Charitable Trusts: July 25. https://www.pewtrusts.org/en/research-and-analysis/blogs/stateline/2019/07/25/getting-older-going-broke-whos-going-to-pay-for-long-term-care

Chapter 9

Building on Hope or Tackling Fear?

Policy Responses to the Growing Costs of Alzheimer's Disease and Other Dementias

Adelina Comas-Herrera

Dementia is a syndrome caused by a collection of progressive illnesses associated with an ongoing decline of brain function. The most common forms of dementia are Alzheimer's disease and vascular dementia. Symptoms vary somewhat by disease, but generally they involve changes in cognition, personality, and behavior, and people at the more severe stages require high levels of care and support, resulting in large costs.

A huge increase in the numbers of people living longer is a great achievement for humanity, but it has also brought with it important challenges. One of these is that the numbers of people living with dementia are growing at a rapid speed and scale. It has been estimated that the number of people living with dementia worldwide will grow from 46 million in 2015 to 131.5 million by 2050 (Prince et al. 2015), and that the societal costs of dementia will have reached $1 trillion globally by 2019 (Wimo et al. 2017).

Dementia Policy Choices

There are many reasons why policymakers are paying increasing attention to dementia. It is a condition with multiple and interdependent impacts: it can affect people's ability to live independently, perform self-care tasks, keep themselves safe, participate in society, continue in the labor market,[1] control their own finances; and it also affects others, usually family members, who often provide care and support for very long hours and may give up or reduce their paid employment in order to provide this care, and whose own health may be compromised. This multiplicity of impacts also means that dementia policy spans multiple government departments, and there is a wide range of stakeholders that can potentially have an interest in, and be part of, decision-making processes.

Adelina Comas-Herrera, *Building on Hope or Tackling Fear?*. In: *New Models for Managing Longevity Risk.*
Edited by Olivia S. Mitchell, Oxford University Press.
© Pension Research Council (2022). DOI: 10.1093/oso/9780192859808.003.0009

These multiple impacts also mean that there are many policy choices that can be made to address dementia, including: encouragement (financial, regulatory, and/or through research infrastructure) in the search for disease-modifying treatments for the causes of dementia; public health approaches toward risk reduction; legislation to protect the rights of people living with dementia; reforms to reduce the financial risk associated with needing (and providing) long-term care for extended periods; policies to improve health and long-term care system responses; policies to encourage the development of technological solutions; policies to reduce stigma and promote the social inclusion of people with dementia; and legal instruments to address the implications of loss of capacity (Binstock et al. 1992; OECD 2015; WHO 2017; Blank 2019).

An added complexity for policymaking in dementia is that policy decisions must be made in the face of great uncertainty and a relatively weak evidence base. There is uncertainty, for example, about the nature of the underlying diseases,[2] making it almost impossible to estimate the probability that investments in finding disease-modifying treatments will be successful. There is also uncertainty about the future costs of care, which means that traditional insurance mechanisms may not be suitable if insurers cannot estimate risks accurately (Barr 2010).

Additionally, the evidence base available to policymakers on dementia is limited. The health and care programs in most countries lack information systems to identify people with dementia and to allow monitoring of their situation and outcomes of their care (OECD 2018). In many countries, governments also lack population surveys providing basic data on, for example, how many people have dementia and how they are being cared for, as highlighted in the country summaries of the World Alzheimer Report 2016 (Prince et al. 2016). The research evidence base on non-pharmacological aspects of care treatment and support is weak, particularly for low- and middle-income countries, although it is improving (Prince et al. 2016; Livingston et al. 2017; WHO 2017; Alzheimer's Disease International 2018; Pickett et al. 2018; Salcher-Konrad et al. 2019). Pickett and Brayne (2019) analyzed dementia research investment between 2011 and 2016 in Canada, France, Germany, Italy, the United Kingdom (UK), and the United States (US). They found that, in that period, dementia research spending grew by nearly 140 percent, reaching 1,374 million euros in 2016, which represented 0.34 percent of the societal costs of dementia in those countries. They also found that most of this research funding was focused on biomedical research, with only 4.9 percent of the spending focused on health and social care research (Pickett and Brayne 2019).

While dementia advocacy groups focus on getting governments to commit to dementia-specific policies, addressing some of the major impacts of dementia requires policies that are broader in scope. For example, reducing the risk of dementia at the population level may require addressing broader economic inequalities. Ensuring better health care for people with dementia may require wider reforms of health care systems to improve the resources available for the management of non-communicable diseases and chronic conditions. Addressing workforce shortages in dementia is a key issue for the health and care sectors, and for the economy as a whole. Addressing the risk that the costs of dementia may be catastrophic requires addressing the financing of the long-term care system.

Dementia as an Economic Concern

The high costs of dementia are often cited as a motivation for policy action and used by advocates to draw attention to the condition. For example, the World Health Assembly's global action plan on dementia mentions the financial costs of dementia in its second paragraph (World Health Organization 2017). Advocacy groups have frequently commissioned research to estimate the costs of dementia: for example, see the Alzheimer's Society for the UK (Prince et al. 2014), Dementia Australia (Brown et al. 2017), and Alzheimer's Disease International (Prince et al. 2015). An emphasis on high costs (sometimes referred to as 'economic catastrophism') has been particularly strong in the context of making the case for investment in biomedical research to find a disease-modifying treatment. For example, at an international Dementia Forum event, the US Alzheimer Association CEO, Harry Johns (2019), was quoted on Twitter as saying, 'We have increased funding in dementia research by convincing Congress that the cost of dementia is not sustainable.'

Economic concerns surrounding dementia have been identified as including the impact on national economies (in terms of impact on government spending and on economic growth), the impact on individual finances, and the costs and benefits of different types of care (Keen 1993).

Of course, the economic impact of dementia depends on wider economic trends. Changes in economic growth may affect the amount of public spending on health and care services, for example following the Great Recession, and despite growing demand for services, the UK's public expenditure on adult social care fell in real terms from £22 billion in 2010–2011 to £20.23 billion in 2014–2015 (Bottery et al. 2019). Changes in labor markets will also shape the capacity to respond to dementia: in many countries, there are already major difficulties in the recruitment of health and social care workforce, and these difficulties are expected to become much larger in the near future (OECD 2016).

Dementia Costs and Sustainability

It is common to see academic articles and advocacy arguing that, because the costs of dementia are high and expected to grow substantially, they are unsustainable. Yet equating high (and growing) costs with being unsustainable is incorrect, as sustainability does not depend on the size of costs alone.

Thomson et al. (2009), when discussing the sustainability of health financing, argue that spending on care would be *economically sustainable* up to the point at which the societal costs of care exceed the value produced by that expenditure. So, if spending on dementia care sufficiently threatened other valued areas of economic activity, then dementia care would be considered to be economically unsustainable. They also discuss fiscal and political sustainability. *Fiscal sustainability* relates specifically to public expenditure and how that compares to public revenue. Thomson et al. further explain that fiscal sustainability can typically be addressed in three ways: (1) increasing public revenue to meet the desired level of public spending on care; (2) reducing public spending to the level that can be met by public revenue; and (3) improving the capacity of the care systems to convert resources into value. From a political perspective, sustainability requires that the way in which the government allocates public resources is in line with voters' expectations. From this *political sustainability* perspective, it could even be argued that current public spending on care for people with dementia is too low in many countries, particularly for social care in the UK, where there appears to be a consensus on the need for long-term care financing reform to increase the role of public funding, even if political consensus remains elusive as to the shape of this reform.

It is also interesting to observe that many who seek to emphasize the scale of the costs of dementia present estimates of the societal costs of dementia (which include the opportunity costs of unpaid care) as a percentage of gross domestic product (GDP), when GDP only includes formal (paid) economic activity. The correct comparison, between the percentage of GDP and the formal costs of care, would be less dramatic.[3]

In practice, economists have often drawn attention to the fact that formal costs of health and social care in relation to dementia are only a relatively small part of GDP. For example, a US report from 1991 entitled 'Alzheimers: Could It Bankrupt the Health-Care System?' included an interview with Joshua Wiener, who had carried out estimates of future long-term care expenditure:

> Joshua Wiener, a long-term care specialist with the Urban Institute's Health Policy Center in Washington, is sceptical of claims that more Alzheimer's cases will cripple the health-care system. He estimates inflation-adjusted spending on long-term care will roughly double from 1993 and 2018, from $75.5 billion to $168.2 billion, adjusted for inflation. But, assuming modest economic growth, that will only account for about 2.2 percent of the gross domestic product. 'It's a sizable increase, but I don't know if it's the end of civilization as we know it,' Wiener says.

> (Bettelheim 1991)

Dementia Workforce and Sustainability

Concerns about sustainability of dementia care are also expressed in relation to the future availability of formal health and social care workers and unpaid carers (OECD 2015). In most middle- and high-income countries, the population who would traditionally be of working age is rapidly decreasing in size compared to those needing care due to dementia or other age-related conditions. While in other sectors it is expected that automation will help reduce demand for labor, it is unlikely that this will happen to a significant extent in the care of people with dementia (Knapp et al. 2015; Pissarides 2018; Goodhart and Pradhan 2020).

As Goodhart and Pradhan (2020) explain, there is also a risk that large increases in the population that require care will require the redirection of an already shrinking labor force toward providing care. As the care sector is considered to have little potential for productivity growth, a shift of labor toward this sector would be expected to result lower productivity growth (Ngai and Pissarides 2007; Pissarides 2018). Nevertheless, automation means that there are many jobs in other sectors that will cease to exist. Pissarides (2018: 4) argues that the pay and social respect of jobs in the care and services sectors will need to change so that they become 'good jobs' if society is to win the 'war against the robots.'

Other Potential Economic Impacts of Dementia

There are other effects of dementia on the economy that can, at least in part, be attributed to the ways in which care systems are financed and organized. The first is that the absence of well-functioning collective mechanisms to pool the risk of incurring high costs of care as a result of dementia or other conditions may generate distortions in financial planning. Individuals may oversave, in an attempt to make sure that they have enough savings to cope with the highest possible costs of dementia, and reduce their consumption (Barr 2010), or people may put themselves at financial risk by spending down their savings and assets in order to qualify for public care where these are means-tested.

Another outcome that can result from the insufficient availability of good quality, affordable formal care and strong social norms, is the pressure on women to reduce or give up their employment when a relative requires care. As the educational attainment and labor force participation of women increases, the opportunity costs of women giving up paid work in order to provide care grow. This means that lack of opportunities to stay in the labor market by not being able to obtain replacement care (see Brimblecombe et al. 2018) may increasingly result in an inefficient use of human capital. As Korfhage (2019) shows in his analysis of the impact on lifetime earnings and social insurance entitlements of carers who have left employment in Germany, the opportunity costs are much higher at younger ages and at the higher end of the income distribution.

How Much Does Dementia Cost, and How Much Will It Cost in the Future?

There is no standardized methodology on how to estimate the present and future costs of dementia, and studies that produce these estimates do not always seek to answer the same research and policy questions. In practice, because demographic change is driving projected costs, most projection studies find that the costs of dementia will double or treble over the next 20 or 30 years. For example, in England, the costs of dementia have been projected to rise from £23 billion in 2015 to £80.1 billion by 2040, an increase of nearly 250 percent (Wittenberg et al. 2020). Globally, the costs of dementia were estimated to grow from $818 billion in 2015, to $1 trillion by 2018 and $2 trillion in 2030 (Wimo et al. 2017).

These projection models usually use as a baseline a cost of dementia study which, typically, seeks to include all the costs of dementia to society, the direct costs of medical and long-term care services, and at least some indirect costs (usually estimates of the costs of unpaid care) (Wimo et al. 2017; El-Hayek et al. 2019; Wittenberg et al. 2019). A recent review by El-Hayek et al. (2019) set out to consider all the potential costs of dementia and the methodological difficulties in properly measuring them. This work suggested that, in practice, most studies leave out significant costs, such as, for example, the costs of care for the period before dementia is diagnosable.

While differences in the methodologies used in projections of dementia costs studies are often due to data limitations, an important source of differences is also the fact that each poses different research and policy questions. This section considers five policy questions that may be answered using models of future costs of dementia and gives some examples of studies that have sought to address them:

What resources are needed to ensure that the availability of care matches expected changes in demand, and what resources are needed to deliver improved care, treatment, and support?

Most cost of dementia studies fall into this group. They usually measure the impact of demographic change, and sometimes also of expected epidemiological changes, on the future demand for care, treatment, and support for people who have dementia. They usually implicitly assume that the unit costs of care will rise in line with wages, and that this will guarantee that the supply of services will increase to meet demand (Wittenberg et al. 1998). The studies may also investigate the impact of other expected changes, for example, in the expected supply of unpaid care, improvements in access to care, and, in some cases, the impact of different ways of financing care. These studies increasingly attempt to take a societal approach by including the costs of unpaid care. Many of these studies highlight the increase in resources needed by reporting the costs of formal medical and long-term care as a percentage of GDP. In England, for example, it was estimated that the health and social care costs for people with dementia would rise from 0.8 percent of GDP in 2015 to 1.9 percent in 2040 (Wittenberg et al. 2019).

It has been estimated that, globally, 40 percent of the costs of dementia are due to unpaid care, 40 percent to formal long-term care services, and 20 percent to medical care (Wimo et al. 2018). Yet, it is difficult to compare the fractions across studies, due to differences in methods and data used (particularly to estimate the costs of unpaid care), and also due to different definition of boundaries between types of expenditure (particularly between medical/health care and long-term/social care). Relatively few studies report on the balance between publicly and privately financed care.

What would be the impact of new dementia treatments and prevention strategies?

Simulation models can be used to estimate the costs impact of a modifying treatment for Alzheimer's disease and other forms of dementia, or of successful risk reduction strategies. This has led to an increase in models based on studies that aim to separate the costs of care, treatment, and support attributable to dementia from costs that are due to other conditions, usually by comparing the service use of people with dementia to those of the same age and gender who do not have the disease (Hurd et al. 2013; White et al. 2019). One difficulty with these models is that usually they implicitly assume that the risk of developing dementia is independent from the risk of having other health conditions, an assumption that is not well-supported by epidemiological evidence (Bunn et al. 2014).

As the effects (and costs) of possible new drug treatments are not yet known, the models that simulate their impact are hypothetical, but they can be used, for example, to estimate the maximum price at which, given certain assumed effects, the new drugs would be cost-effective (Anderson et al. 2018).

When estimating the impact of changes in the course of the diseases, it is possible that new treatments and prevention strategies for Alzheimer's disease may result in increased longevity and could eventually lead to higher overall health and care costs, particularly if they slow progression. For example, a simulation model in the US showed that reducing the incidence of some of the risks that have been identified as being associated with dementia, such as diabetes and hypertension, could eventually lead to higher numbers of people living with dementia as a result of increased longevity (Zissimopoulos et al. 2018).

What will be the fiscal implications of dementia?

There are relatively few studies that specifically analyze the fiscal implications of dementia. The ones that do typically estimate the projected costs of the benefits paid out by the social insurance system as a result of dementia under current entitlement rules, and then they compare these to the projected growth in insurance contributions. As a result of these analyses, recommendations can be made to address the sustainability of the social insurance system which may result in increases in the social insurance contributions or the proportion of the costs of care met by taxes. Examples are analyses that were carried out to assess the implications of a major reform of the German long-term care insurance system in 2017, which extended the coverage to include dementia as a result of consensus that existing eligibility criteria left out people with dementia and also that the levels of benefits were too low. The reform increased access to benefits for people with dementia and the size of the benefits available to them, but it also increased the contribution rates to 2.55 percent of gross income (Häcker et al. 2009; Doetter and Rothgang 2017; Mosca et al. 2017; Nadash et al. 2018).

Analyses of fiscal sustainability will not usually focus on dementia specifically, but its costs will be included in, for example, long-term forecasts of public spending, as in the UK's Office for Budget Responsibility (2018) report. The European Commission regularly produces a report on aging which analyzes the fiscal impact of public spending on aging-related programs (European Commission Economic Policy Committee 2018). The European Commission's analyses show that, while demography is an important driver of future costs of care, the generosity of the public system is an even more important determinant of future costs.

While most of the debate on sustainability focuses on the costs of publicly funded services, there is increasing awareness of the fiscal impact of the provision of unpaid care (particularly where carers withdraw or reduce their involvement in the labor market). Pickard et al. (2018) estimated that the public expenditure costs of carers leaving employment in England in 2015/2016 amounted to £2.9 billion a year (£1.2 in forgone taxes and £1.7 in benefits claimed). This did not include the longer term impact of workers' difficulties returning to employment when the care episode ended. The cost of publicly funded formal long-term care in England in the same year was estimated to be £15.3 billion (Wittenberg and Hu 2015). In Germany, Korfhage (2019) has analyzed the fiscal implications of reduced tax and social insurance contributions as a result of unpaid carers withdrawing from the labor market: he showed that they then faced labor market frictions when they attempt to rejoin the labor market when the care episode ended.

What will be the impact of dementia on the economy?

A recent study for different regions in Japan suggests that the impact of labor market reductions as a result of dementia and stroke (due to people of working age developing these conditions and to unpaid carers withdrawing from the labor market) amounted to one percent of GDP. The impact was slightly mitigated in regions with higher investment in research and development (R&D) and higher private capital stock (Taghizadeh-Hesary et al. 2020).

What is the financial impact of dementia at individual or family level?

The lifetime costs of dementia, from diagnosis to the end of life, have been estimated to amount to $321,780 in 2015 US dollars. Of these, 70 percent were costs incurred by families, 14 percent by Medicaid, and 16 percent by Medicare (Jutkowitz et al. 2017). In the absence of strong mechanisms to share the risk of high costs of dementia among the population, these costs can have a very significant effect on a family's wealth and amplify economic inequalities. For example, Kaufman et al. (2018) estimated that, in the US, dementia was associated with a loss of 97 percent of wealth among black Americans compared with a 42 percent loss among non-black Americans. Their study did not find substantial differences in loss of wealth between families unaffected by dementia.

Unpaid carers who have left employment also face significant lifetime costs, in the US, Skira (2015) estimated that, for women in the mid-50s who exited work to provide care for a parent for two years, the median forgone income was $51,780.

Responding to Dementia as an Economic Concern

Policy responses to concerns about the growing economic costs of dementia can be broadly classified into two categories: policies to try to reduce or contain the costs of care (which could be considered hopeful policies), and policies to ensure that health, long-term care, and social protection systems can deliver levels of care and protection from risk that are in line with social expectations (policies to reduce fears).

Policies to attempt to reduce or contain the costs of care

These policies seek to reduce the size of the challenge posed by dementia, through a hopeful vision of future success in biomedical research, healthy aging, technological innovation, and the adoption of cost-saving interventions.

Such policies may be particularly appealing to policymakers because research into new treatments and risk reduction policies hold the promise of a future free of one of the most feared health conditions (Bond et al. 2005; Kessler et al. 2012; Peel 2014; Burke 2017; Evans 2018; Alzheimer's Disease International 2019). Also, the hope that investment in R&D will have positive outcomes contributing to economic growth can play a role in such policies finding favor with policymakers. Particularly in times of austerity, policymakers may also see these policies as a way to avoid having to make more difficult policy decisions such as, for example, addressing the financing of chronic health care and long-term care.

The evidence base for cost-effective (and even some cost-saving) care, treatment, and support interventions is growing (Knapp et al. 2013; NICE 2018; Nickel et al. 2018). The evidence so far suggests that, for persons living with dementia, treatment with the existing anti-dementia drugs (Donepezil and Memantine) (NICE 2018), physical exercise, occupational therapy, and cognitive stimulation therapy (Knapp et al. 2013; Nickel et al. 2018), some types of dementia care management (Michalowsky et al. 2019; Vroomen et al. 2016), and a person-centered care and psychological intervention for people in nursing homes called WHELD (Ballard et al. 2018) can be cost-effective. For dyads of persons with dementia and their care partners, self-management group rehabilitation, and cognitive behavioral therapy are also cost-effective (Nickel et al. 2018). For carers, a manual-based individual coping program (START) and an education and support intervention also seem cost-effective (Nickel et al. 2018).

This evidence base suggests that policymakers can potentially make more efficient resource allocations by making sure that these cost-effective interventions are made more widely available and, where possible, replace other interventions and approaches unsupported by evidence.

Policies to increase the capacity for health, long-term care, and social protection systems to respond to dementia

Fears around dementia are also linked to the perceived lack of good quality services to deliver care, treatment, and support; to concerns about being a burden to one's family; and to the fear of losing all savings and assets (Evans-Lacko et al. 2019). An assessment by the Organisation for Economic Co-operation and Development (OECD; OECD 2018) concluded that most OECD countries are poorly equipped to identify dementia, and uncovered evidence of poor quality of care in most countries, particularly for people with advanced dementia.

Policies needed to address this issue are wider than dementia, encompassing the medical, long-term care, and social protection sectors. Strong political champions tend to be required, to build consensus across different political groups and stakeholders, a process which in many countries can take considerable time. In Germany, the establishment of a mandatory long-term care insurance system took two decades of political debate before consensus was eventually reached across all the major political parties, the unions, employers, and sickness funds as well as private insurers (Götze and Rothgang 2014). In the UK, potential reforms of the public long-term care financing system have been under discussion since at least the 1990s.

Tackling the structure of health and care systems

The models for dementia health care predominant in high-income countries and in some low- and middle-income countries, are reliant on the role of specialist care, but in most countries there are already shortages of dementia specialists, particularly neurologists, old-age psychiatrists, and geriatricians (Hlávka et al. 2018). To respond to increasing numbers of people living with dementia, alternative models of dementia health care based on primary care and specially trained health workers could potentially be expanded to deliver a consistent quality of care to larger numbers of people, at a lower cost per person (see Prince et al. 2016).

It is also likely that the models of long-term care delivery that have developed in most high-income countries during the 20th century will need to change. The sharp divisions between 'health' and 'social' aspects of care is becoming increasingly obsolete, particularly as the proportion of older people with functional dependency but no other chronic conditions is likely to decline while the numbers rise of care users with dementia and three or more chronic conditions (Kingston et al. 2018). Long-term care systems will increasingly need to ensure that family and other unpaid carers do not need to give up their jobs in order to provide care, perhaps through a renewed focus on models of replacement care and care leave policies (Brimblecombe et al. 2018). This would mirror policy developments seen in relation to childcare in many countries. There is also growing interest in innovative care models, including new approaches to more attractive daycare and housing with care models, and better integrated services in the wider communities.

Addressing the workforce challenge

The care sector has the opportunity to attract workers that, due to technological change, are no longer able to work in their previous jobs. Yet this transition will need to be carefully managed, not least because most of those workers would have experienced higher levels of pay and better working conditions than those currently working in the care sector.

More innovative approaches to group care may have the potential to offer more attractive environments both for staff and care users, with the potential to use at least some economies of scale to deliver care that is more oriented to rehabilitation and social participation, and better rooted in the local community.

Tackling the financing of care Without collective risk pooling mechanisms to cover the whole population for the risk of catastrophic costs of long-term care as a result of conditions such as dementia, universal health coverage cannot be achieved. While some countries have been able to offer this (e.g. the Scandinavian countries), many others have either added long-term care to existing social health insurance schemes or developed separately financed long-term care social insurance systems. There are also still a few high-income countries where there has not been sufficient political and social support for universal coverage of long-term care needs. Both the UK and the US have public systems that only cover those lacking the means to pay for their own care. In the case of the US, those without pre-existing conditions who have high incomes may be able to buy private long-term care insurance. In the UK, the market for private long-term care insurance is virtually non-existent (Comas-Herrera et al. 2012). At least in the UK, there is growing recognition that public expectations and public policies on care are at odds. After many decades of debate on how long-term care funding should be reformed, there is at least a consensus that reform does need to happen, even if consensus about the type of reform has not yet been achieved.

Conclusion

'Hopeful policies' that support research on understanding the nature of the conditions that result in dementia, promote dementia risk reduction, and encourage technological care innovations have their place. Yet, they do not remove the need to address the more difficult policy decisions on how to ensure health, care, and social protection systems can deliver care, treatment, support, and financial protection for people living with dementia that is in line with public expectations and preferences.

Many barriers that policymakers encounter when seeking to address the capacity of care and social protection systems appear to be linked to concerns about the size of public spending and its potential impact on economic sustainability. As this review highlights, the economic impact of dementia needs to be considered in a wider economic and political context. At a time of increased automation in many other sectors, the care sector could benefit from policies that facilitate transitions of workers from other sectors, as well as improving current models of care and adopting cost-effective interventions.

As the number of people living with dementia grows, so does the number of people with personal experience of the implications of this condition to both the individuals themselves and their families. Thus, there is likely to be increased awareness of the limitations of current health, care, and protection systems. Unless these systems can be made to reflect societal norms and expectations, they too will become politically unsustainable.

Notes

1. Not all people who develop dementia are over retirement age.
2. Only recently a new form of dementia, LATE, has been identified. This form appears to mimic Alzheimer's type dementia and it is suggested that this may explain why some recent trials for treatments of Alzheimer's disease have not been successful (Nelson et al. 2019).
3. For example, Alzheimer's Disease International's (2015) infographic that represents the findings of their *World Alzheimer's Report 2015* aims to illustrate the scale of the societal costs of dementia by stating that 'If global dementia care were a country, it would be the 18th largest economy in the world exceeding the market values of companies such as Apple and Google' (Alzheimer's Disease International 2015).

References

Alzheimer's Disease International (2015). 'The Global Impact of Dementia.' https://www.alz.co.uk/sites/default/files/pdfs/global-impact-dementia-infographic.pdf

Alzheimer's Disease International (2018). *World Alzheimer Report 2018. The State of the Art of Dementia Research: New Frontiers.* London: Alzheimer's Disease International, London. https://www.alz.co.uk/research/WorldAlzheimerReport2018.pdf

Alzheimer's Disease International (2019). *World Alzheimer Report 2019: Attitudes to Dementia.* London: Alzheimer's Disease International, London. https://www.alz.co.uk/research/WorldAlzheimerReport2019.pdf

Anderson, R., M. Knapp, R. Wittenberg, R. Handels, and J. M. Schott (2018). *Economic Modelling of Disease-Modifying Therapies in Alzheimer's Disease.* https://www.lse.ac.uk/cpec/assets/documents/EconomicmodellingAD.pdf

Ballard, C., A. Corbett, M. Orrell, G. Williams, E. Moniz-Cook, R. Romeo, . . . and J. Fossey (2018). 'Impact of Person-centred Care Training and Person-centred Activities on Quality of Life, Agitation, and Antipsychotic Use in People with

Dementia Living in Nursing Homes: A Cluster-randomised Controlled Trial,' *PLoS Medicine*, 15(2): e1002500.   https://doi.org/10.1371/journal.pmed. 1002500

Barr, N. (2010). 'Long-term Care: A Suitable Case for Social Insurance,' *Social Policy & Administration*, 44(4), 359–374. https://doi.org/10.1111/j.1467-9515.2010. 00718.x

Bettelheim, A. (1991). 'Alzheimer's Disease: Could It Bankrupt the Health-Care System?' Congressional Quarterly, Inc. in conjunction with EBSCO Pub. https://library.cqpress.com/cqresearcher/document.php?id=cqresrre19980 51500

Binstock, R. H., S. G. Post, and P. J. Whitehouse (1992). *Dementia and Aging: Ethics, Values, and Policy Choices.* Baltimore, MA: Johns Hopkins University Press.

Blank, R. H. (2019). *Social & Public Policy of Alzheimer's Disease in the United States.* Singapore: Springer Singapore. https://doi.org/10.1007/978-981-13-0656-3

Bond, J., C. Stave, A. Sganga, B. O'Connell, and R. L. Stanley (2005). 'Inequalities in Dementia Care Across Europe: Key Findings of the Facing Dementia Survey,' *International Journal of Clinical Practice, Supplement*, 59(146): 8–14. https://doi. org/10.1111/j.1368-504x.2005.00480.x

Bottery, S., D. Ward, and D. Fenney. (2019). 'Social Care 360,' The King's Fund. https://www.kingsfund.org.uk/publications/social-care–360

Brimblecombe, N., J.-L. Fernandez, M. Knapp, A. Rehill, and R. Wittenberg (2018). 'Review of the International Evidence on Support for Unpaid Carers,' *Journal of Long-Term Care*, 25–40. https://doi.org/10.21953/lse.ffq4txr2nftf

Brown, L., E. Hansnata, and H. A. La (2017). *Economic Cost of Dementia in Australia 2016–2056.* Canberra. http://www.natsem.canberra.edu.au/

Bunn, F., A. M. Burn, C. Goodman, G. Rait, S. Norton, L. Robinson, and C. Brayne (2014). 'Comorbidity and Dementia: A Scoping Review of the Literature,' *BMC Medicine*, 12(1). https://doi.org/10.1186/s12916-014-0192-4

Burke, L. (2017). 'Imagining a Future without Dementia: Fictions of Regeneration and the Crises of Work and Sustainability,' *Palgrave Communications*, 3(52): 1–9. https://doi.org/10.1057/s41599-017-0051-y

Comas-Herrera, A., R. Butterfield, J.-L. Fernández, R. Wittenberg, and J. M. Wiener (2012). 'Barriers to and Opportunities for Private Long-term Care Insurance in England: What Can We Learn from Other Countries?' *The LSE Companion to Health Policy.* https://doi.org/10.4337/9781781004241.00026

Doetter, L. F. and H. Rothgang (2017). 'Quality and Cost-effectiveness in Long-term Care and Dependency Prevention: The German Policy Landscape.' https://docs.wixstatic.com/ugd/442c21_299a62535bac40179f7fe3500dcf71bd. pdf

El-Hayek, Y. H., R. E. Wiley, C. P. Khoury, R. P. Daya, C. Ballard, A. R. Evans, and A. Atri (2019). 'Tip of the Iceberg: Assessing the Global Socioeconomic Costs of Alzheimer's Disease and Related Dementias and Strategic Implications for Stakeholders,' *Journal of Alzheimer's Disease*, 70: 323–341. https://doi.org/10.3233/JAD-190426

European Commission Economic Policy Committee (2018). *The 2018 Ageing Report: Economic and Budgetary Projections for the EU Member States (2016–2070).* Brussels, Bel. https://doi.org/10.2765/615631

Evans, S. C. (2018). 'Ageism and Dementia,' in L. Ayolon and C. Tesch-Römer, eds., *Contemporary Perspectives on Ageism*. Cham: Springer, Cham, pp. 263–275. https://doi.org/10.1007/978-3-319-73820-8_16

Evans-Lacko, S., J. Bhatt, A. Comas-Herrera, F. D'Amico, N. Farina, S. Gaber, ... and E. Wilson (2019). 'Attitudes to Dementia Survey,' in Alzheimer's Disease International, ed., *World Alzheimer Report 2019, Attitudes to Dementia*. London: Alzheimer's Disease International, pp. 21–87. https://www.alz.co.uk/research/WorldAlzheimerReport2019.pdf

Goodhart, C. and M. Pradhan (2020). 'Dependency, Dementia and the Coming Crisis of Caring,' *The Great Demographic Reversal*. London: Palgrave Macmillan. https://doi.org/10.1007/978-3-030-42657-6_4

Götze, R. and H. Rothgang (2014). 'Fiscal and Social Policy: Financing Long-Term Care in Germany,' in K.-P. Companje, ed., *Financing High Medical Risk*. Amsterdam: AUP, pp. 63–100. Amsterdam: AUP. https://doi.org/10.2139/ssrn.2191995

Häcker, J., T. Hackmann, and S. Moog. (2009). 'Demenzkranke und Pflegebedürftige in der Sozialen Pflegeversicherung. Ein intertemporaler Kostenvergleich,' *Schmollers Jahrbuch*, 129(3): 445–471. https://doi.org/10.3790/schm.129.3.445

Hlávka, J. P., S. Mattke, and J. L. Liu (2018). *Assessing the Preparedness of the Health Care System Infrastructure in Six European Countries for an Alzheimer's Treatment*. https://www.rand.org/content/dam/rand/pubs/research_reports/RR2500/RR2503/RAND_RR2503.pdf

Hurd, M.D., Martorell, P., Delavande, A., Mullen, K. J., and Langa, K. M. (2013). 'Monetary Costs of Dementia in the United States,' *New England Journal of Medicine*, 368(14): 1326–1334. https://doi.org/10.1056/NEJMsa1204629

Johns, H. (2019). '@DementiaForumX,' DementiaForumX, May 15. https://twitter.com/DementiaForumX/status/1128583306369470464

Jutkowitz, E., R. L. Kane, J. E. Gaugler, R. F. MacLehose, B. Dowd, and K. M. Kuntz (2017). 'Societal and Family Lifetime Cost of Dementia: Implications for Policy,' *Journal of the American Geriatrics Society*, 65(10): 2169–2175. https://doi.org/10.1111/jgs.15043

Kaufman, J. E., W. T. Gallo, and M. C. Fahs (2018). 'The Contribution of Dementia to the Disparity in Family Wealth between Black and Non-black Americans,' *Cambridge University Press*, 40(2): 306–327. https://doi.org/10.1017/S0144686X18000934

Keen, J. (1993). 'Dementia: Questions of Cost and Value,' *International Journal of Geriatric Psychiatry*, 8(5): 369–378. https://doi.org/10.1002/gps.930080502

Kessler, E.-M., C. E. Bowen, M. Baer, L. Froelich, and H.-W. Wahl (2012). 'Dementia Worry: A Psychological Examination of an Unexplored Phenomenon,' *European Journal of Ageing*, 9(4): 275–284. https://doi.org/10.1007/s10433-012-0242-8

Kingston, A., A. Comas-Herrera, and C. Jagger (2018). 'Forecasting the Care Needs of the Older Population in England over the Next 20 Years: Estimates from the Population Ageing and Care Simulation (PACSim) Modelling Study,' *The Lancet Public Health*, 3(9). https://doi.org/10.1016/S2468-2667(18)30118-X

Knapp, M., J. Barlow, A. Comas-Herrera, J. Damant, P. Freddolino, K. Hamblin, and J. Woolham (2015). 'The Case for Investment in Technology to Manage the Global Costs of Dementia,' *PIRU Publication 2016–18*, November. http://eprints.lse.ac.uk/66482/1/__lse.ac.uk_storage_LIBRARY_Secondary_ libfile_shared_repository_Content_LSEE_The%20case%20for%20investment %20in%20technology.pdf

Knapp, M., V. Iemmi, and R. Romeo (2013). 'Dementia Care Costs and Outcomes: A Systematic Review,' *International Journal of Geriatric Psychiatry*, 28(6): 551–561. https://doi.org/10.1002/gps.3864

Korfhage, T. (2019). 'Long-run Consequences of Informal Elderly Care and Implications of Public Long-term Care Insurance,' *Ruhr Economic Papers No. 813.* https://ideas.repec.org/p/zbw/rwirep/813.html.

Livingston, G., A. Sommerlad, V. Orgeta, S. G. Costafreda, J. Huntley, D. Ames... and N. Mukadam (2017). 'Dementia Prevention, Intervention, and Care,' *The Lancet*, 360(10113). https://doi.org/10.1016/S0140-6736(17)31363-6

Michalowsky, B., F. Xie, T. Eichler, J. Hertel, A. Kaczynski, I. Kilimann, and W. Hoffmann (2019). 'Cost-effectiveness of a Collaborative Dementia Care Management—Results of a Cluster-randomized Controlled Trial,' *Alzheimer's and Dementia*, 15(10): 1296–1308. https://doi.org/10.1016/j.jalz.2019.05.008

Mosca, I., P. J. Van Der Wees, E. S. Mot, J. J. G. Wammes, and P. P. T. Jeurissen (2017). 'Sustainability of Long-term Care: Puzzling Tasks Ahead for Policy-Makers Key Messages,' *Kerman University of Medical Sciences*, 6(4): 195–205. https://doi.org/ 10.15171/ijhpm.2016.109

Nadash, P., P. Doty, and M. Von Schwanenflügel (2018). 'The German Long-Term Care Insurance Program: Evolution and Recent Developments,' *The Gerontologist*, 58(3): 588–597. https://doi.org/10.1093/geront/gnx018

Nelson, P. T., D. W. Dickson, J. Q. Trojanowski, C. R. Jack, P. A. Boyle, K. Arfanakis... and J. A. Schneider (2019). 'Limbic-predominant Age-related TDP-43 Encephalopathy (LATE): Consensus Working Group Report,' *Brain*, 142(6): 1503–1527. https://doi.org/10.1093/brain/awz099

Ngai, L. R. and Pissarides, C. A. (2007). 'Structural Change in a Multisector Model of Growth,' *American Economic Review*, 97(1): 429–443. https://doi.org/10.1257/aer.97.1.429

NICE (2018). *Dementia: Assessment, Management and Support for People Living with Dementia and their Carers: Guidance and Guidelines.* NICE: National institute for Health and Care Excellence. https://www.nice.org.uk/guidance/ng97

Nickel, F., J. Barth, and P. L. Kolominsky-Rabas (2018). 'Health Economic Evaluations of Non-Pharmacological Interventions for Persons with dDementia and their Informal Caregivers: A Systematic Review,' *BMC Geriatrics*, 18(1): 69. https:// doi.org/10.1186/s12877-018-0751-1

OECD (Organisation for Economic Co-operation and Development) (2015). *Addressing Dementia: The OECD Response.* https://doi.org/10.1787/ 9789264231726-en

OECD (Organisation for Economic Co-operation and Development) (2016). *Health Workforce Policies in OECD Countries: Right Jobs, Right Skills, Right Places.* OECD

Health Policy Studies, March, pp. 1–8. http://www.oecd.org/health/health-systems/health-workforce-policies-in-oecd-countries-9789264239517-en.htm

OECD (Organisation for Economic Co-operation and Development) (2018). *Care Needed: Improving the Lives of People with Dementia*. O.H.P. Studies. Paris: OECD. https://doi.org/10.1787/9789264085107-en

Office for Budget Responsibility (2018). *Fiscal Sustainability Report*. London: Her Majesty's Stationery Office. www.gov.uk/government/publications

Peel, E. (2014). '"The Living Death of Alzheimer's" Versus "Take a Walk to Keep Dementia at Bay": Representations of Dementia in Print Media and Carer Discourse,' *Sociology of Health & Illness*, 36(6): 885–901. https://doi.org/10.1111/1467-9566.12122

Pickard, L., D. King, N. Brimblecombe, and M. Knapp (2018). 'Public Expenditure Costs of Carers Leaving Employment in England, 2015/2016,' *Health & Social Care in the Community*, 26(1): e132–e142. https://doi.org/10.1111/hsc.12486

Pickett, J., C. Bird, C. Ballard, S. Banerjee, C. Brayne, K. Cowan . . . and C. Walton (2018). 'A Roadmap to Advance Dementia Research in Prevention, Diagnosis, Intervention, and Care by 2025,' *International Journal of Geriatric Psychiatry*, 33(7). https://doi.org/10.1002/gps.4868

Pickett, J. and C. Brayne (2019). 'The Scale and Profile of Global Dementia Research Funding,' *The Lancet*, 394(10212): 1888–1889. https://doi.org/10.1016/S0140-6736(19)32599-1

Pissarides, C. (2018). 'Labor Market Challenges in Europe: New Technology, Automation and Allocative Efficiency,' Eurogroup informal meeting, Vienna, September 7. https://www.consilium.europa.eu/media/36358/eurogroup-7-sep-18-pissarides-final-notes.pdf

Prince, M., A. Comas-Herrera, M. Knapp, M. Guerchet, and M. Karagiannidou (2016). *World Alzheimer Report 2016: Improving Healthcare for People Living with Dementia. Coverage, Quality and Costs Now and in the Future*. London: Alzheimer's Disease International. https://www.alz.co.uk/research/world-report-2016

Prince, M., M. Knapp, M. Guerchet, P. McCrone, M. Prina, A. Comas-Herrera. . . and D. Salimkumar (2014). *Dementia UK: Update* (Second). London: Alzheimer's Society. https://www.alzheimers.org.uk/sites/default/files/migrate/downloads/dementia_uk_update.pdf

Prince, M., A. Wimo, M. Guerchet, G.-C. Ali, Y.-T. Wu, M. Prina . . . and Z. Xia (2015). *World Alzheimer Report 2015. The Global Impact of Dementia: An Analysis of Prevalence, Incidence, Cost and Trends*. London: Alzheimer's Disease International. www.alz.co.uk/worldreport2015corrections

Salcher-Konrad, M., H. Naci, D. Mcdaid, S. Alladi, D. Oliveira, A. Fry . . . and A. Comas-Herrera (2019). 'Effectiveness of Interventions for Dementia in Low- and Middle-income Countries: Protocol for a Systematic Review, Pairwise and Network Meta-analysis,' *BMJ Open*, 9(6). https://bmjopen.bmj.com/content/9/6/e027851

Skira, M. M. (2015). 'Dynamic Wage and Employment Effects of Elder Parent Care,' *International Economic Review*, 56(1): 63–93. https://doi.org/10.1111/iere.12095

Taghizadeh-Hesary, F., N. Yoshino, A. Mortha, F. Roshanmehr, J. Fiallos, E. Tajra . . . and B. Kateb (2020). 'Economic Burden of Neurological Disorders in an Aging Society: The Example of Japan. A Panel Data Analysis,'

January 6. (Reprinted in *The Lancet Neurology*.) https://papers.ssrn.com/sol3/papers.cfm?abstract_id=3514749

Thomson, S., T. Foubister, and E. Mossialos (2009). *Financing Health Care in the European Union: Challenges and Policy Responses.* Observatory Studies Series No. 17. Copenhagen, DK. http://www.euro.who.int/__data/assets/pdf_file/0009/98307/E92469.pdf

Vroomen, J. M. N., J. E. Bosmans, I. Eekhout, K. J. Joling, L. D. Van Mierlo, F. J. M. Meiland . . . and S. E. De Rooij (2016). 'The Cost-effectiveness of Two Forms of Case Management Compared to a Control Group for Persons with Dementia and their Informal Caregivers from a Societal Perspective,' *PLoS ONE*, 11(9). https://doi.org/10.1371/journal.pone.0160908

White, L., P. Fishman, A. Basu, P. K. Crane, E. B. Larson, and N. B. Coe (2019). 'Medicare Expenditures Attributable to Dementia,' *Health Services Research*, 54(4): 773–781. https://doi.org/10.1111/1475-6773.13134

WHO (2017). 'Global Action Plan on the Public Health Response to Dementia 2017–2025,' *World Health Organization*, 52. https://doi.org/Licence: CC BY-NC-SA 3.0 IGO

Wimo, A., S. Gauthier, and M. Prince (2018). *Global Estimates of Informal Care.* London: Alzheimer's Disease International. https://www.alz.co.uk/adi/pdf/global-estimates-of-informal-care.pdf

Wimo, A., M. Guerchet, G.-C. Ali, Y.-T. Wu, A. M. Prina, B. Winblad . . . and M. Prince (2017). 'The Worldwide Costs of Dementia 2015 and Comparisons with 2010,' *Alzheimer's & Dementia: The Journal of the Alzheimer's Association*, 13(1): 1–7. https://pubmed.ncbi.nlm.nih.gov/27583652/

Wittenberg, R. and B. Hu (2015). 'Projections of Demand for and Costs of Social Care for Older People and Younger Adults in England,' PSSRU Discussion Paper No. 2990. www.pssru.ac.uk/pdf/DP2900.pdf

Wittenberg, R., B. Hu, C. Jagger, A. Kingston, M. Knapp, A. Comas-Herrera, D. King, A. Rehill . . . and S. Banerjee (2020). 'Projections of Care for Older People with Dementia in England: 2015 to 2040,' *Age and Ageing*, 49: 264–269. https://doi.org/10.1093/ageing/afz154

Wittenberg, R., M. Knapp, B. Hu, A. Comas-Herrera, D. King, A. Rehill . . . and A. Kingston (2019). 'The Costs of Dementia in England,' *International Journal of Geriatric Psychiatry*, gps.5113. https://doi.org/10.1002/gps.5113

Wittenberg, R., L. Pickard, A. Comas-Herrera, B. Davies, and R. Darton (1998). *Demand for Long-term Care: Projections of Long-term Care Finance for Elderly People.* London: PSSRU, University of Kent. https://kar.kent.ac.uk/id/eprint/27422

World Health Organization (2017). *Global Action Plan on the Public Health Response to Dementia 2017–2025.* Geneva: World Health Organization. https://www.who.int/mental_health/neurology/dementia/action_plan_2017_2025/en/

Zissimopoulos, J. M., B. C. Tysinger, P. A. StClair, E. M. Crimmins, and J. Zissimopoulos (2018). 'The Impact of Changes in Population Health and Mortality on Future Prevalence of Alzheimer's Disease and Other Dementias in the United States,' *Journals of Gerontology: Social Sciences*, 73(1): S38–S47. https://doi.org/10.1093/geronb/gbx147

Part III

Implications for the Financial Sector and Policymakers

Chapter 10

State-sponsored Pensions for Private-Sector Workers

The Case for Pooled Annuities and Tontines

Richard K. Fullmer and Jonathan Barry Forman

This chapter explains how state governments could create new low-cost lifetime assurance funds to help provide retirement income security for millions of private-sector workers who currently lack pension coverage and how these governments could do so with minimal risk. An assurance fund operates like a mutual fund held within a defined contribution (DC) plan, but with the added features of mortality pooling and fully funded lifetime payouts. As we envision them, assurance funds would be offered as annuity-like investment options on the new investment platforms being created by states like Oregon, California, and Maryland that offer their citizens the opportunity to participate in state-sponsored retirement savings plans (see, e.g., Pension Rights Center 2020; AARP Public Policy Institute 2020). Adding an assurance fund could effectively turn these retirement savings plans into lifetime pensions. Participants in these state-sponsored pensions could allocate their contributions between regular mutual funds and these new assurance funds, and, in partnership with various private-sector investment and record-keeping companies, the state-sponsored pension would manage and invest those designated contributions and make the appropriate payouts to retirees and their beneficiaries.

To ensure their sustainability, assurance funds would operate as either tontines or pooled annuities—sometimes referred to as participating annuities.[1] The term 'assurance' is used to differentiate these products from 'insurance' products, in that while they do pool longevity risk, they are not based in any way on the principle of indemnity or a contract of risk transfer. Like commercial annuities, assurance funds would provide lifetime income, but unlike commercial annuities, assurance funds would not guarantee a precise level of that income. Instead, assurance funds would adhere to a strict budget constraint that requires them to remain fully funded at all

Richard K. Fullmer and Jonathan Barry Forman, *State-sponsored Pensions for Private-Sector Workers*. In: *New Models for Managing Longevity Risk*. Edited by Olivia S. Mitchell, Oxford University Press.
© Pension Research Council (2022). DOI: 10.1093/oso/9780192859808.003.0010

times.[2] As a result, assurance fund payouts would vary as necessary to ensure their sustainability.

Not only would assurance funds be sustainable, they would also be efficient.[3] In particular, assurance-fund payouts would be significantly higher than payouts from traditional mutual funds. This follows naturally from the fact that assurance funds rely on the survivor principle—that the share of each participant, at death, is enjoyed by the surviving participants, resulting in higher payouts to survivors for as long as they live. Additionally, assurance funds should enjoy higher average payout rates than comparable commercial annuities, because assurance funds would have no need for reserves and would do away with the expense of compensating insurance companies for taking on any risk.

In a world with substantial levels of undersaving, economic efficiency is vital. Moreover, underfunding is a slippery slope, because once a hole develops, there is always a chance that it could grow deeper; and deeper holes are increasingly difficult to escape from. Truly sustainable solutions must always remain fully funded, because to tolerate underfunding is to invite sustainability risk. Assurance-fund income would not be fixed, and it would not be guaranteed. Rather, it would be variable and nonguaranteed. But it would always be *fully funded* and, therefore, *fully sustainable* . . . forever.

The useful properties of assurance funds extend beyond state-sponsored pensions in the United States. Indeed, the assurance-fund model could extend to other countries and to private-sector retirement plans, as well. For example, a country like Chile, which has a well-established annuity market, could include assurance funds in its universal DC pension system to provide its citizens a flexible alternative to the current choices of traditional programmed withdrawals or traditional annuities (OECD 2019a). A country like Colombia, which lacks a deep annuity market due to policies that discourage private insurers from participating, might introduce assurance funds as a relatively fast, low-cost alternative to developing an annuity market (OECD 2015).

Lifetime Assurance Funds

A lifetime assurance fund is essentially a DC pension plan designed to pay out what it can—no more and no less—in an objective manner that is fully disclosed to all participants. Economically, an assurance fund always abides by a strict budget constraint, in that the expected present value of the payouts must always equal the present value of the fund's assets. An assurance fund can do this because it relies on the principle of mortality risk pooling, and, assuming that the pool of investors is large enough, the assurance fund is able to discount future payouts by the probability that the pool's members will be alive to receive those payouts. The budget constraint effectively means that assurance funds are always grounded in economic reality, which we believe makes them an attractive option for states and retirees alike.

Through an assurance-fund pool, members diversify and share longevity risk among themselves. The investment balance of each investor is accounted for individually and reflects actual market values.[4] Participants in a retirement plan that offers assurance funds may make their own investment decisions within the set of assurance funds provided by the plan administrator, and their accounts are credited with their investment returns as usual. That is, a given retirement plan might offer a few different assurance funds in the same way that it offers a few different traditional mutual funds. In fact, these same mutual funds could serve as the underlying investments used by the assurance funds. For example, if a plan offered five different mutual funds as investment choices, it could elect to offer the same five investment choices as assurance funds.[5]

Contributions to these assurance funds would be irrevocable in order to enforce the condition that the risk-sharing arrangement is for life. In return, investors would receive mortality credits for as long as they lived: living investors would divide the assets from the accounts of the investors that die. These mortality credits would be in addition to the investment returns on the underlying investment assets. As we envision them, the payouts from assurance funds would vary over time to ensure that the actuarial expected value of each investor's future lifetime payouts always matches the current value of her account balance. In short, the payouts from assurance funds will vary according to investment performance and mortality experience, because those are the two factors that affect the investor's balance.

Assurance funds compared to traditional mutual funds. Assurance-fund payouts would be higher than the amounts that could be safely withdrawn from traditional mutual funds. The reason is that assurance funds offer not only investment returns, but also mortality credits. The return advantage to long-lived survivors would be especially significant because, as we will show, mortality credits would increase significantly with age.

Investments in assurance funds would differ in a major way from investments in mutual funds in that an investor in an assurance fund would *never* be allowed to withdraw her contributions (or investment earnings or mortality credits). The situation is identical to a commercial life annuity: once the premium is paid, there is no refund. Instead, a participant in an assurance fund would only receive payouts according to the lifetime-payout method that she elected. For example, a typical participant in an assurance fund could elect to receive relatively level monthly payments starting at her planned retirement age—say, age 65 (if she is alive then)—until her death. Alternatively, she could elect to have escalating payouts (say, to offset inflation) that would start lower (at age 65) but would end up much higher, the longer she survives. Either way, the payouts to survivors from an assurance fund would be significantly higher than the payouts from a regular investment due to the mortality credits.

Assurance funds compared to traditional life annuities

Assurance-fund payouts should also be higher than the payouts from a commercial life annuity. Assurance-fund payouts would follow directly from: (1) the investment returns on the underlying investment portfolio; (2) the mortality experience of the assurance-fund pool; and (3) the payout method that a member elects, which could be designed to be level or escalating. Because the assurance-fund sponsor would make no guarantees, it would only charge a trivial fee to administer the program; and no money would ever need to be set aside for insurance company reserves or risk-taking. All in all, assurance-fund payouts would mimic the high payouts that would come from being able to buy an actuarially fair variable income annuity (VIA), which by some estimates could be 10 or 15 percent higher than what a typical commercial life annuity would pay.[6]

Tontines and Pooled Annuities

As mentioned, assurance funds would be structured as either tontines or pooled annuities. This section explains how simple tontines work and then goes on to show how an assurance fund could be engineered as a tontine or pooled annuity.

A simple tontine

In the simplest type of tontine, a set of investors contributes equally to buy a portfolio of investments to be awarded entirely to the last surviving investor (Cooper 1972: 1–2). Alternatively, the balances of those who die can be divided up and redistributed to the surviving investors more frequently. The latter type of tontine can be used to develop new financial products that would provide reliable, pension-like income for retirees, like tontine annuities, tontine pensions, and individual tontine accounts (see, e.g., Goldsticker 2007; Sabin 2010; Newfield 2014; Milevsky and Salisbury 2015; Forman and Sabin 2015; Forman and Sabin 2016; Fullmer 2019; Fullmer and Sabin 2019a).

At the outset, imagine that 1,000 65-year-old retirees each contributed $1,000 to an investment fund that purchased a $1,000,000 treasury bond paying four percent interest coupons. The bond would generate $40,000 in interest per year, which would be split equally among the surviving investors of the tontine. A custodian would hold the bond, and because the custodian would take no risk and require no capital, the custodian would charge a trivial fee. If all the investors lived through the first year, each would receive a $40 dividend from the fund ($40 = $40,000/1,000). If only 800 original investors were alive a decade after the tontine started (when the survivors are age 75), then each would receive a $50 dividend ($50 = $40,000/800). If only 100 were alive two decades after that (when the survivors are age 95), then each would receive a $400 dividend ($400 = $40,000/100). Later, when only 40 remain, each would receive a $1,000 dividend ($1,000 = $40,000/40). If the terms of the tontine called for liquidation at that point, then each of the 40 survivors would also receive a liquidating distribution of $25,000 ($25,000 = $1,000,000/40).

More advanced tontines

Most retirees would likely prefer reasonably level benefits throughout their retirement years, rather than benefits that increased sharply at the very end of their lives. Fortunately, it is possible to design tontines with payouts that are expected to remain level, on average, throughout retirement or, alternatively, with payouts that increase gradually throughout retirement, say, to offset inflation (see, e.g., Forman and Sabin 2015; Milevsky and Salisbury 2015).

Tontines would be of little practical interest if the way that they redistributed forfeited balances was not fair to all investors. A growing set of 'fair tontine design' articles have examined the ways and conditions in which tontines can indeed offer fair, equitable bets to all investors (e.g. Sabin 2010; Donnelly et al. 2014; Forman and Sabin 2015; Milevsky and Salisbury 2016). Indeed, tontines can be designed to offer fair bets for all investors even if they are of different ages and genders, invest different amounts at different times, use different investment portfolios, and elect to receive different types of payouts. Furthermore, and crucially, fair tontines can be open-ended and perpetual. The key is to redistribute forfeited balances to the survivors in a very precise manner that reflects each survivor's individual account balance and probability of death. For example, Forman and Sabin (2015) showed how a tontine fund can fairly accommodate investors of different ages and account balances by deriving so-called 'fair-transfer-plan weights.' Tontine schemes can also be designed to permit investors to individualize their underlying investments and payout choices (Forman and Sabin 2015; Fullmer and Sabin 2019a).

Pooled annuities

The term 'pooled annuities' generally refers to insurance company annuities offered without any insurance company guarantees (Piggott et al. 2005; Donnelly 2015).[7] Instead, the annuitants bear all of the risks. For example, if the annuitant population lives longer than projected, everyone's payouts would go down. Like fair tontines, pooled annuities can be carefully designed to provide fair bets to all annuitants.

Pension Sustainability Challenges

The quest for retirement security faces significant challenges in virtually every country across the globe. These challenges involve both the saving/accumulation and the dissaving/decumulation phases of the retirement life cycle.

Demographics and economics

One challenge involves aging demographics in the form of increasing life expectancy and a lower ratio of workers to retirees. At the same time, low and even negative interest rates have dramatically increased the cost of financing retirement. Further, the uncertainty associated with longevity risk—both idiosyncratic (the diversifiable portion) and systematic (the non-diversifiable portion)—adds to the challenge by making the cost more uncertain. Simply put, retirement is expensive, and the act of promising *specific/exact* retirement benefits is both risky and expensive.

For this reason, it is not surprising that, despite the advantage of mortality risk pooling, economies of scale, and professional management, many defined benefit (DB) pension plans have disappeared, while many of those that remain are significantly underfunded (Forman 2020). Indeed, private-sector DB plans in the United States were underfunded by $401.3 billion at the end of the first quarter of 2020, at which time the plans were 89 percent funded, while state and local US government pension plans were underfunded by $4.9 trillion and were just 45 percent funded (Board of Governors of the Federal Reserve System 2020). Other analysts using different data sources offer different estimates of public plan funding status, but they generally agree that such plans are significantly underfunded in the aggregate (see, e.g., Aubry et al. 2018).

The shift from defined benefit to defined contribution plans

DB pension promises create liabilities that must be hedged or otherwise reserved against. The cost of this liability management ultimately reduces the amount that could otherwise be paid out to pensioners. One response to these costs and risks has been to shift the burden of retirement funding from institutions to individuals—largely by replacing DB plans with DC plans (see, e.g., Zelinsky 2004; Mackenzie 2010; Staff of the Joint Committee on Taxation 2016).

This shift toward DC plans, of course, presents other challenges. One significant issue is that DC plans in the United States and many other countries operate primarily as tax-advantaged savings vehicles rather than lifetime income vehicles (Staff of the Joint Committee on Taxation 2019). Also, unlike DB plans, DC plans usually make distributions as lump sum or periodic distributions rather than as lifetime pensions. Unfortunately, most individuals lack the financial literacy, acumen, and skills to effectively manage the drawdown of retirement savings over their highly uncertain lifespans (Lusardi and Mitchell 2014).

While it is true that individuals may elect to convert a portion of their savings into lifetime income by purchasing commercial life annuities, this is only true for those who live in countries in which life annuities are available in good supply. Yet even in countries with well-developed annuity markets, a demand problem often still exists, in that people rarely choose to buy annuities voluntarily (American Academy of Actuaries 2015). This is true even though annuitization would appear to be in the best economic interest of most people. Economists refer to this as the 'annuity puzzle' (Benartzi et al. 2011). Accordingly, many retirees within a DC system forgo any form of longevity protection and instead take their chances that they will not outlive their assets.

Inadequate access is another problem. Large segments of the population—for example, those that work in the informal economy or otherwise for small employers that do not provide retirement plan benefits—lack access to convenient ways to save efficiently and adequately. For example, as of March of 2019, just 71 percent of US private-sector workers had access to employer-sponsored pension plans, and only 56 percent of US private-sector workers participated (US Department of Labor, Bureau of Labor Statistics 2019). The probability of pension coverage is greater for older workers, for white workers, for highly educated workers, for full-time workers, for higher income workers, and for workers at larger firms (Copeland 2014). Participation in individual retirement accounts (IRAs) is even lower than participation in pensions; for example, while 36 percent of US households had an IRA in mid-2019, only around 12 percent of households made contributions to their IRAs in 2018 (Holden and Schrass 2019).

The Role for State-sponsored Defined Contribution Pensions

Ultimately, the risk of failure for retirees in the DC system may fall on society (and largely, on governments). It is in everyone's interest, therefore, to ensure that the retirement system functions efficiently. To that end we note that commercial life annuities have some of the same problems mentioned above regarding DB pensions, namely, guaranteeing a specific amount of income creates liabilities for the guarantor that must be hedged and reserved. Those guarantees can be achieved only at a cost, and that cost reduces the benefits that can be paid out to annuitants.

Assurance funds represent a low-cost alternative that can benefit states by providing them with an economically efficient way to provide retiring workers with universal access to pension-like lifetime income. Moreover, states would benefit in that assurance funds would be sustainable in perpetuity because they would never risk underfunding. Of course, a prerequisite is to ensure that workers have access to a retirement savings system in the first place, and states are increasingly taking a role in providing that access.

Expanding coverage with universal pensions

To expand pension coverage, many countries have established universal pensions—or at least universal retirement savings programs. Those that mandate participation enjoy high participation rates, while those that are voluntary naturally have lower participation rates (OECD 2019b).

The United States has a voluntary pension system that is not universal (Forman and Mackenzie 2013). Although the US federal government has not adopted a universal pension system, several state governments have begun to create their own universal systems for workers not covered by employer-sponsored pensions (Gale and John 2018; Pension Rights Center 2020; AARP Public Policy Institute 2020). A general theme is to encourage individuals to save in IRAs through automatic payroll deductions unless workers opt out. Moreover, workers who opt out may automatically be re-enrolled each year, again with the opportunity to opt out (i.e. automatic re-enrollment). The automatic escalation of their annual contribution rate is also a possibility. Such automatic enrollment features will almost certainly lead to high participation rates and to higher levels of retirement savings (OECD 2012). Contributions are often invested in a sensible default investment option such as a target-date fund, unless a worker elects otherwise (IRC § 404(c); US Department of Labor, Employee Benefits Security Administration 2013).[8]

The Oregon retirement savings plan for private-sector workers

While several states are in the process of setting up state-sponsored retirement savings plans for private-sector workers (Pension Rights Center 2020; AARP Public Policy Institute 2020), the state of Oregon is the furthest along (VanDerhei 2019). As of December of 2019, at least 54,000 Oregonians at some 3,637 businesses were enrolled (Stites 2019).

Oregon started its OregonSaves program in 2017 to provide a means of retirement saving for private-sector employees who were not eligible for an employer-sponsored plan (OregonSaves 2020). The program requires that Oregon employers without employer-sponsored plans automatically enroll their employees into payroll-deduction Roth IRAs managed by Oregon-Saves. The default contribution rate is five percent, although employees can opt out. Moreover, employee contributions are automatically increased by one percent each year until they reach 10 percent, unless the employee opts out.

OregonSaves uses a private-sector program administrator for record-keeping and other functions. Investor accounts are held as Roth IRAs, so contributions made in 2020 were limited to $6,000 (or $7,000 for individuals over the age of 50). Contributions to these Roth IRAs are not deductible, but investment earnings are tax-exempt and withdrawals are tax-free. The first $1,000 of a worker's contributions are invested in a money-market or capital-preservation fund (OregonSaves 2020). Further contributions are automatically invested in a target-date fund. OregonSaves also offers a growth fund alternative. OregonSaves charges an annual asset-based fee of around one percent to pay for the administration of the program and the operating expenses charged by the underlying investment funds. This fee is quite high although perhaps not surprisingly so given that the program is so new and has not yet achieved significant economies of scale. Presumably, the fee level will drop significantly as the program continues to grow.

From universal savings accounts to universal pensions

While expanded access to retirement savings plans is certainly helpful, these state-sponsored plans often lack a mechanism to turn retirement savings into lifetime retirement income. Thus, they act more like universal savings accounts than universal pensions. While individuals might use a portion of their savings to purchase commercial life annuities in the open market, there is reason to doubt that they would for the annuity-puzzle reasons already mentioned. There is also reason to doubt that individuals would voluntarily purchase annuities even if states were to make them available within their state-sponsored plans.

Still, individuals might be more willing to annuitize if they could do so at a lower cost, with greater transparency, and with more investment choices; and that is exactly what assurance funds could provide. The trade-off for lower costs would be that assurance-fund payouts would not be guaranteed but would instead vary over time—with investment and mortality experience—in a way that would always ensure that the assurance fund is fully funded and that payouts would be made over the lifetimes of all participants. In short, lifetime income would be *assured* but not *insured*.

The Management and Operation of a State Assurance Fund

Each state's assurance-fund operation could look a lot like today's state-run 529 educational savings plans. In Oklahoma, for example, the state has contracted with a subsidiary of Teachers Insurance and Annuity Association (TIAA) to be the Oklahoma 529 College Savings Plan manager, and the plan offers participants a choice of nine different TIAA investment options that vary in their investment strategy and degree of risk (Oklahoma 529 College Savings Plan 2019). Of course, there is no reason why a state-sponsored pension could not separately contract for record-keeping and investment-fund management services (e.g. to select the best investment managers for each type of assurance fund).

Noting that a number of the Oklahoma 529 College Savings Plan funds are offered with fees of just 30 basis points, we anticipate that state-sponsored assurance funds could likewise be offered at a fee of as low as 30 basis points, consisting of around 10 basis points in fund management fees for assets managed passively and about 20 basis points for other administrative expenses (Forman and Sabin 2015).

Example

Suppose that a state opens a state-sponsored pension plan with the following features and options, which we simplify for the sake of brevity. Accounts are opened for new enrollees in the form of IRAs. Employers lacking qualified retirement plans would be required to offer these IRAs to their employees via payroll deduction. Any employees not covered by an employer-sponsored plan would be automatically enrolled in the state-sponsored pension.[9] Employee contributions are automatically invested in the state-sponsored pension's default investment option at a default contribution rate, although employees may opt out, elect a different investment option, or elect a different contribution rate at any time. For simplicity, assume that the state-sponsored pension offered three low-cost diversified investment options: a global equity fund, an investment-grade bond fund, and a set of diversified target-date funds (the default option). For clarity, let us refer to participant balances in these investments as 'regular' accounts, to differentiate them from balances they may hold in 'assurance-fund' accounts, discussed next.

To give participants the option to receive payouts in the form of a lifetime pension, the state could offer assurance funds as an additional investment option. Although contributions would be defaulted into a regular investment account, participants would have the option to instead direct any portion of their contributions into an assurance fund.[10] Similarly, they may transfer any portion of their regular account balances into an assurance fund at any time.

Contributions to assurance funds may be directed into any of the three low-cost investment options available in the regular investment accounts. In the simplest case, monthly payouts from the assurance fund would begin at age 65. Participants would have a choice about whether their payout stream would include a growth factor, i.e. whether their payouts would mimic a uniform level-payment annuity or an escalating annuity.

Some participants might want to invest in an assurance fund from the very start of their careers, so that they could begin receiving (and compounding) mortality credits earlier, and consequently, end up with larger retirement account balances. Others might instead prefer to wait until closer to retirement before deciding to invest in an assurance fund. This latter approach would sacrifice some mortality credits and account growth, but it would leave participants with the option to bequeath funds if they were to die before retirement.

A Simple Illustration

Suppose that a hypothetical worker elects to begin making retirement account contributions to the global equity fund starting on his 35th birthday, and this fund's expected return net of fees is seven percent per year. His salary at age 35 is $50,000 a year, and it increases at the rate of four percent each year. He contributes 10 percent of his salary each month.

Our hypothetical worker decides to put half of each month's contribution into a regular investment account and the other half into an assurance-fund account (i.e. 5% of his salary into each), directing both contributions into the same underlying global equity fund. If he dies before age 65, he would forfeit the balance in his assurance-fund account, while the balance in his regular investment account would go to his designated beneficiaries.

In this example, the assurance fund makes forfeiture redistributions based on the 2012 Individual Annuity Mortality (IAM) Basic Table (Society of Actuaries 2020). Mortality credits are allocated each year by multiplying the account balance of each member who survived the year by a 'mortality yield' that accounts for the fair redistribution of forfeited account balances from those who died during the year to those who survived the year.[11]

Table 10.1 shows how the balance of each of his two accounts would grow each year with the simplifying assumption that the rate of return on his investments is always seven percent each year and that members die and forfeit balances at exactly the rate predicted by the mortality table. Column 1 shows the worker's age, and column 2 shows his salary—starting at $50,000 when he is 35 years old and growing by four percent a year

TABLE 10.1 Account balances before retirement

Age	Salary ($)	Regular Investment Account			Assurance-Fund Account			
		Contri-bution ($)	Invest-ment Return ($)	Ending Bal-ance ($)	Contri-bution ($)	Invest-ment Return ($)	Mortality Credit ($)	Ending Bal-ance ($)
35	50,000	2,500	86	2,586	2,500	86	2	2,588
36	52,000	2,600	270	5,457	2,600	271	4	5,463
37	54,080	2,704	475	8,635	2,704	475	7	8,649
38	56,243	2,812	701	12,149	2,812	702	10	12,174
39	58,493	2,925	951	16,025	2,925	953	14	16,066
40	60,833	3,042	1,226	20,293	3,042	1,229	19	20,356
41	63,266	3,163	1,529	24,985	3,163	1,534	26	25,079
42	65,797	3,290	1,862	30,137	3,290	1,869	34	30,271
43	68,428	3,421	2,227	35,786	3,421	2,237	43	35,972
44	71,166	3,558	2,627	41,972	3,558	2,640	54	42,224
45	74,012	3,701	3,065	48,738	3,701	3,083	66	49,074
46	76,973	3,849	3,544	56,130	3,849	3,568	83	56,573
47	80,052	4,003	4,067	64,200	4,003	4,098	105	64,778
48	83,254	4,163	4,637	73,000	4,163	4,678	133	73,752
49	86,584	4,329	5,259	82,588	4,329	5,312	170	83,563
50	90,047	4,502	5,936	93,026	4,502	6,004	215	94,285
51	93,649	4,682	6,673	104,382	4,682	6,761	271	105,999
52	97,395	4,870	7,474	116,726	4,870	7,588	336	118,793
53	101,291	5,065	8,345	130,135	5,065	8,490	410	132,757
54	105,342	5,267	9,291	144,693	5,267	9,474	495	147,993
55	109,556	5,478	10,317	160,488	5,478	10,548	595	164,614
56	113,938	5,697	11,430	177,615	5,697	11,719	717	182,747
57	118,496	5,925	12,637	196,177	5,925	12,996	865	202,533
58	123,236	6,162	13,944	216,283	6,162	14,389	1,049	224,133
59	128,165	6,408	15,360	238,051	6,408	15,910	1,275	247,726
60	133,292	6,665	16,893	261,609	6,665	17,570	1,549	273,510
61	138,623	6,931	18,551	287,091	6,931	19,384	1,882	301,707
62	144,168	7,208	20,344	314,644	7,208	21,367	2,279	332,562
63	149,935	7,497	22,283	344,424	7,497	23,537	2,751	366,347
64	155,933	7,797	24,378	376,598	7,797	25,913	3,316	403,372
		140,212	236,386		140,212	244,385	18,775	

Note: For simplicity, this exhibit uses mortality rates without mortality improvements.
Source: Authors' calculations.

until it reaches $155,933 when he is 64. Columns 3 through 5 show how his regular investment account grows over the course of his working years. Column 3 shows his contribution amounts; column 4 shows the amount of his investment returns; and column 5 shows how the balance in his regular investment account would grow to $376,598 by the end of the year that he turns 64.[12]

Columns 6 through 9 show how the same contributions would grow in an assurance-fund account. Column 6 shows that his contributions to the assurance-fund account are the same as his contributions to his regular investment account (i.e. 5% of salary into each account). Column 8 shows his share of the mortality credits that surviving workers earn when other workers in the assurance fund die.[13] These mortality credits grow over time, not only because the account balance is growing, but also because the worker's death probability upon which the credits are based grows with age. Column 7 shows the higher investment returns that the assurance fund earns because those investment returns would be based on account balances that include those mortality credits. Finally, column 9 shows how the balance in our hypothetical worker's assurance-fund account would grow to $403,072 by the end of the year that he turns 64.

All in all, Table 10.1 shows that while an equal amount is contributed to each account each year, when our hypothetical worker reaches retirement at age 65, his regular investment account balance will be just $376,598, while his assurance-fund account balance will be $403,372 (7.1% higher) as a result of accumulating and reinvesting the mortality credits attributable to the deaths of workers who did not live to age 65.

Table 10.2 follows this worker's assurance-fund account after he retires at age 65, assuming that he elects a uniform (non-escalating) payout option. Of course, the payouts will stop when he dies, so the example illustrates the case of a long-lived participant who lives to age 120. The payouts are computed as a life annuity using the simple formula $s/\ddot{a}$, where s is his balance at the start of the year, and $\ddot{a}$ is his current 'annuity factor.' This annuity factor represents the expected present value of $1 paid at the start of this year and every subsequent year for the duration of his lifetime, with future payments discounted to the present using an assumed annual interest rate.[14] The assumed annual interest rate is computed as $(1 + r)/(1 + g) - 1$, where r is the expected rate of return on the investor's portfolio and g is the selected payout growth rate. In this example, r is seven percent and g is zero, so the assumed annual interest rate is seven percent. This calculation ensures that the present value of the future payouts will equal the present value of the account, and thereby be sustainable for as long as the investor lives.[15] If it happens that the investments earn exactly seven percent in every subsequent year and that members die and forfeit balances at exactly the rate predicted by the mortality table, the investor's payout will have the same value $s/\ddot{a}$ every year until it is finally exhausted at age 120.

Column 1 of Table 10.2 shows the age of our hypothetical retiree, and column 2 shows the balance in his account at the beginning of each year. Column 3 shows that, having elected to have the uniform payout option, he can expect to receive a level payout of $36,264 a year from age 65 until he dies at age 120. Column 4 shows his investment returns each year; column

TABLE 10.2 Assurance-fund account balance after retirement (uniform payout option)

Age	Beginning Balance ($)	Payout ($)	Investment Return ($)	Mortality Credit ($)	Ending Balance ($)
65	403,372	36,264	25,698	3,570	396,376
66	396,376	36,264	25,208	3,694	389,014
67	389,014	36,264	24,693	3,845	381,288
68	381,288	36,264	24,152	4,026	373,201
69	373,201	36,264	23,586	4,240	364,763
70	364,763	36,264	22,995	4,492	355,987
71	355,987	36,264	22,381	4,786	346,890
72	346,890	36,264	21,744	5,128	337,498
73	337,498	36,264	21,086	5,519	327,839
74	327,839	36,264	20,410	5,956	317,941
75	317,941	36,264	19,717	6,435	307,830
76	307,830	36,264	19,010	6,952	297,528
77	297,528	36,264	18,288	7,508	287,060
78	287,060	36,264	17,556	8,102	276,454
79	276,454	36,264	16,813	8,732	265,734
80	265,734	36,264	16,063	9,414	254,948
81	254,948	36,264	15,308	10,183	244,174
82	244,174	36,264	14,554	10,961	233,425
83	233,425	36,264	13,801	11,739	222,702
84	222,702	36,264	13,051	12,541	212,030
85	212,030	36,264	12,304	13,399	201,468
86	201,468	36,264	11,564	14,336	191,104
87	191,104	36,264	10,839	15,356	181,034
88	181,034	36,264	10,134	16,448	171,352
89	171,352	36,264	9,456	17,588	162,132
90	162,132	36,264	8,811	18,751	153,431
91	153,431	36,264	8,202	19,868	145,236
92	145,236	36,264	7,628	20,966	137,567
93	137,567	36,264	7,091	22,056	130,450
94	130,450	36,264	6,593	23,163	123,942
95	123,942	36,264	6,137	24,317	118,132
96	118,132	36,264	5,731	24,599	112,198
97	112,198	36,264	5,315	25,463	106,713
98	106,713	36,264	4,931	26,257	101,637
99	101,637	36,264	4,576	26,963	96,912
100	96,912	36,264	4,245	27,607	92,501
101	92,501	36,264	3,937	28,789	88,963
102	88,963	36,264	3,689	29,594	85,982
103	85,982	36,264	3,480	30,530	83,728
104	83,728	36,264	3,322	31,764	82,551
105	82,551	36,264	3,240	33,018	82,544
106	82,544	36,264	3,240	33,013	82,533
107	82,533	36,264	3,239	33,005	82,514

Continued

TABLE 10.2 *Continued*

Age	Beginning Balance ($)	Payout ($)	Investment Return ($)	Mortality Credit ($)	Ending Balance ($)
108	82,514	36,264	3,237	32,991	82,479
109	82,479	36,264	3,235	32,966	82,416
110	82,416	36,264	3,231	32,922	82,305
111	82,305	36,264	3,223	32,842	82,106
112	82,106	36,264	3,209	32,701	81,751
113	81,751	36,264	3,184	32,448	81,119
114	81,119	36,264	3,140	31,997	79,992
115	79,992	36,264	3,061	31,192	77,981
116	77,981	36,264	2,920	29,758	74,396
117	74,396	36,264	2,669	27,201	68,002
118	68,002	36,264	2,222	22,640	56,599
119	56,599	36,264	1,423	14,506	36,264
120	36,264	36,264	0	0	0
		2,030,783	578,571	1,048,840	

Note: For simplicity, this exhibit uses mortality rates without mortality improvements.
Source: Authors' calculations.

5 shows his mortality credits each year; and column 6 shows how the ending balance of his account will fall from $396,376 at the end of the year that he turns 65 to $36,264 at the end of the year that he turns 119 and to $0 at age 120. In passing, it is worth noting that mortality credit yields are relatively small early in a worker's career but tend to grow steadily with age to the modest level of nearly one percent per year at retirement, and eventually growing very large at advanced ages—to over 13 percent per year at age 90 and over 40 percent per year at age 100 (a bit less for women than for men, since women generally have lower death probabilities at each age).

Similarly, Table 10.3 shows what the payouts would be if our hypothetical retiree had instead elected to receive escalating payouts based on a 2.5 percent per year growth rate (modestly approximating an inflation-adjusted annuity). In this case, the assumed annual interest rate used to calculate the annuity factor is $(1 + r)/(1 + g)—1 = (1 + 0.07)/(1 + 0.025)—1 \approx$ 4.39 percent. As before, this calculation ensures that the present value of future payouts would equal the present value of the account—i.e. the payouts would be fully funded and sustainable for life. Column 3 of Table 10.3 shows how his payouts would increase by 2.5 percent a year from $29,195 at age 65 to $113,534 at age 120.

Table 10.4 illustrates the case in which a retiree starts with the same $403,372 balance at age 65 and tries to withdraw the same level of payouts as in column 3 of Table 10.2 (uniform payouts from an assurance-fund account), but this time makes those withdrawals *from a regular investment account*. With a regular investment account, withdrawals must stop when

TABLE 10.3 Assurance-fund account balance after retirement (2.5% per year escalating)

Age	Beginning Balance ($)	Payout ($)	Investment Return ($)	Mortality Credit ($)	Ending Balance ($)
65	403,372	29,195	26,192	3,639	404,008
66	404,008	29,925	26,186	3,838	404,107
67	404,107	30,673	26,140	4,071	403,644
68	403,644	31,440	26,054	4,343	402,601
69	402,601	32,226	25,926	4,661	400,963
70	400,963	33,032	25,755	5,031	398,717
71	398,717	33,858	25,540	5,462	395,862
72	395,862	34,704	25,281	5,963	392,402
73	392,402	35,572	24,978	6,537	388,346
74	388,346	36,461	24,632	7,188	383,705
75	383,705	37,372	24,243	7,912	378,488
76	378,488	38,307	23,813	8,709	372,703
77	372,703	39,264	23,341	9,582	366,361
78	366,361	40,246	22,828	10,535	359,478
79	359,478	41,252	22,276	11,568	352,070
80	352,070	42,283	21,685	12,710	344,181
81	344,181	43,341	21,059	14,008	335,908
82	335,908	44,424	20,404	15,367	327,255
83	327,255	45,535	19,720	16,774	318,214
84	318,214	46,673	19,008	18,266	308,815
85	308,815	47,840	18,268	19,894	299,138
86	299,138	49,036	17,507	21,703	289,311
87	289,311	50,262	16,733	23,707	279,490
88	279,490	51,518	15,958	25,900	269,830
89	269,830	52,806	15,192	28,257	260,472
90	260,472	54,126	14,444	30,741	251,531
91	251,531	55,480	13,724	33,245	243,020
92	243,020	56,867	13,031	35,816	235,000
93	235,000	58,288	12,370	38,475	227,556
94	227,556	59,745	11,747	41,268	220,826
95	220,826	61,239	11,171	44,260	215,018
96	215,018	62,770	10,657	45,746	208,652
97	208,652	64,339	10,102	48,392	202,806
98	202,806	65,948	9,580	51,009	197,447
99	197,447	67,596	9,090	53,556	192,497
100	192,497	69,286	8,625	56,085	187,920
101	187,920	71,019	8,183	59,845	184,930
102	184,930	72,794	7,850	62,973	182,958
103	182,958	74,614	7,584	66,531	182,459
104	182,459	76,479	7,419	70,924	184,322
105	184,322	78,391	7,415	75,564	188,911
106	188,911	80,351	7,599	77,439	193,598

Continued

TABLE 10.3 *Continued*

Age	Beginning Balance ($)	Payout ($)	Investment Return ($)	Mortality Credit ($)	Ending Balance ($)
107	193,598	82,360	7,787	79,350	198,375
108	198,375	84,419	7,977	81,289	203,222
109	203,222	86,529	8,168	83,241	208,102
110	208,102	88,692	8,359	85,179	212,947
111	212,947	90,910	8,543	87,053	217,632
112	217,632	93,182	8,711	88,774	221,936
113	221,936	95,512	8,850	90,182	225,455
114	225,455	97,900	8,929	90,989	227,474
115	227,474	100,347	8,899	90,683	226,709
116	226,709	102,856	8,670	88,348	220,871
117	220,871	105,427	8,081	82,349	205,873
118	205,873	108,063	6,847	69,771	174,429
119	174,429	110,765	4,456	45,414	113,534
120	113,534	113,534	0	0	0
		3,487,075	833,586	2,250,117	

Note: For simplicity, this exhibit uses mortality rates without mortality improvements.
Source: Authors' calculations.

the account balance goes to zero, which in this case occurs at age 84. Unfortunately, age 84 is only around the median age of death that a 65-year-old male retiree could expect—in other words, there is a substantial chance that he would outlive the assets in his regular investment account. Similarly, although not shown here, we found that if a retiree instead tried to withdraw the same level of payouts as in column 3 of Table 10.3 (escalating payouts from an assurance-fund account) from his regular investment account, that regular investment account would be depleted by age 85.

Of course, future investment returns will not be exactly seven percent each year, and future mortality experience will not follow the mortality table exactly. Thus, future payouts from an assurance-fund account would not actually be constant but rather would vary. For equity investments, this payout variability would be significant due to the high volatility associated with equity investments. For more conservative portfolios, payout variability would naturally be smaller. In the next section, we develop a model to simulate more realistically the effects of investment volatility and mortality variability on assurance-fund payout.

A More Realistic Illustration

To examine the potential range and volatility of investor payouts, we model a set of assurance funds using Monte Carlo simulations of investment returns

TABLE 10.4 Payout comparison to a regular investment account (uniform payout option)

Age	Beginning Balance ($)	Payout ($)	Investment Return ($)	Ending Balance ($)
65	403,372	36,264	25,698	392,806
66	392,806	36,264	24,958	381,500
67	381,500	36,264	24,166	369,402
68	369,402	36,264	23,320	356,458
69	356,458	36,264	22,414	342,607
70	342,607	36,264	21,444	327,787
71	327,787	36,264	20,407	311,930
72	311,930	36,264	19,297	294,963
73	294,963	36,264	18,109	276,808
74	276,808	36,264	16,838	257,382
75	257,382	36,264	15,478	236,596
76	236,596	36,264	14,023	214,355
77	214,355	36,264	12,466	190,558
78	190,558	36,264	10,801	165,094
79	165,094	36,264	9,018	137,848
80	137,848	36,264	7,111	108,695
81	108,695	36,264	5,070	77,501
82	77,501	36,264	2,887	44,124
83	44,124	36,264	550	8,410
84	8,410	8,410	0	0
		697,426	294,054	

Source: Authors' calculations.

and member deaths. Because our goal is to focus on payout volatility, we focus on members that are old enough to be receiving payouts (i.e. retirees).

We simulate an assurance-fund pool of 10,000 members. The size of the membership pool has a direct effect on the volatility of the mortality credits that members will receive. This volatility decreases as the size of the membership pool increases (or increases as the pool decreases), but mortality experience is usually quite close to expectations within a pool that has at least 5,000 members (Sabin and Forman 2016). This is simply the law of large numbers at work in diversifying the idiosyncratic mortality risk of the individuals in the pool. To aid in decomposing the contribution to payout volatility between investment return and mortality experience (as opposed to membership pool size), we hold the pool size steady by assuming that one new member joins each year for every member that died the previous year.

We assume that the assurance-fund pool is mature, meaning that it has been operating long enough to have many members who are old enough to be receiving payouts. At the time our simulation begins, some members are about to receive their first payout, while others have already been receiving payouts for many years. To model this maturity, we randomly assign each member an age, gender, investment portfolio, account balance, and age of death.

Ages are assigned in the range from 65 to 85, inclusive. Investment portfolios are assigned as a choice between equity and bond portfolios. The equity portfolio has an expected return of seven percent and volatility of 17 percent, and the bond portfolio has an expected return of three percent and volatility of four percent.[16] For simplicity, we assume no correlation between these portfolios. As a result, an allocation weighted, for example, 50 percent to the equity portfolio and 50 percent to the bond portfolio has an expected return of five percent and volatility of 8.73 percent.[17]

Account balances range from approximately $63,000 to $1,000,000 and are selected according to a log-uniform distribution that results in relatively smaller initial balances for most members.[18] Roughly one-third of initial balances are less than $158,000, and roughly two-thirds are less than $400,000. Only a small fraction of members have balances near $1,000,000.

We note that except for the size of the pool, none of the other parameter values discussed above will have a material effect on our results. This lack of material effects is a feature of actuarially fair tontine (or pooled annuity) designs: because the design is fair, payouts to any given member are largely unaffected by the ages, genders, investment amounts, and portfolio selections of the other members.

Times of death are modeled using the 2012 IAM mortality table—this time using projection scale G2 (Society of Actuaries 2020) to account for expected mortality improvement.[19] This table is also used to fairly redistribute forfeited account balances in the form of mortality credits from those who die to those who are still alive. The IAM mortality table with projection scale is a generational table, meaning that an individual's probability of death depends not only on age and gender, but also on year of birth. The table projects decreasing probability of death (i.e. a longer life) as the birth year increases.

Payouts are in the form of a life annuity that commences at age 65. We randomly assign a payout trajectory for each member, whether level/uniform or escalating at 2.5 percent per year.[20]

To fairly redistribute forfeitures when members die, we use the 'nominal-gain method' of tontine accounting described in Sabin and Forman (2016).[21] We performed 10,000 simulation runs, with each run spanning 56 years, which is long enough to ensure that everyone who is taking payouts at the start of the simulation will have reached the maximum age of mortality (i.e. age 120) by the end of the simulation. In each simulation run, random portfolio returns were generated for each of the 56 years and random years of death were generated for each member.

Payouts and Payout Volatility

Consider two 65-year-old men who each have $100,000 in their assurance-fund accounts at the start of the year and who each elect to receive uniform payouts in retirement. Edgar invests in the equity portfolio, and he receives an $8,646 payout at the start of the year.[22] Brian invests in the bond portfolio and receives a $5,970 payout at the start of the year (only about 69% of what Edgar receives). This difference is entirely attributable to the assumed annual interest rates used in their respective annuity factor calculations—seven percent for Edgar and three percent for Brian, matching the expected returns on their respective portfolios. As illustrated previously in Table 10.2, the expected payout in subsequent years for each investor will be the same as the payout in the initial year. These payouts will vary from year to year, but the expected value around which they vary will be uniform through time.

The volatility of assurance-fund payouts is primarily a function of two factors—the investment strategy (which affects investment return volatility) and the size of the membership pool (which affects mortality credit volatility). Assuming the membership pool is reasonably large, say at least 1,000 people, payout volatility will depend almost entirely on the investment strategy (Sabin and Forman 2016).

Mortality risk contribution

Recall that while risk pooling effectively diversifies idiosyncratic mortality/longevity risk, it does not eliminate it. Figure 10.1 illustrates the contribution to payout volatility that derives solely from undiversified idiosyncratic mortality risk. In other words, it illustrates what the range in payout levels would be if a member were to receive exactly the expected rate of return of his selected portfolio each year, with zero portfolio return volatility.[23]

Note that because the tontine is fair by design, the effect of mortality risk on a member's payouts will be the same regardless of which investment is selected: equity, bonds, cash, or any combination of these. For this reason, Figure 10.1 shows the *normalized* payout each year expressed as a percentage of the initial year payout, which will apply to both Edgar and Brian. In other words, Figure 10.1 shows the potential percentage change in payouts from that results from random variations in mortality rates among the membership from year to year.

Figure 10.1 shows the percentage change in payout values at the mean and at the 90th and 10th percentiles. The range of outcomes shown would be even narrower if the membership pool size were larger, because larger pools result in even greater diversification of the idiosyncratic risk.[24]

Notice that the mean of the payout simulations in each year is almost perfectly uniform. This is a feature of the fairness principle and conveys

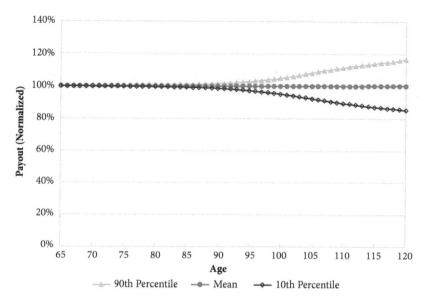

Figure 10.1 Range of yearly payouts by age (male) due to mortality credit volatility only

Source: Authors' calculations.

that our model is well-behaved. In addition, the deviation about the mean is largely symmetrical and growing with age—it is small and barely noticeable until about age 85 and then grows more noticeably after that. The reason for this is that the mortality credit is a function of the member's probability of death, which increases with age.[25] The range between the 10th and 90th percentile of outcomes is less than one percent at age 80, two percent at age 90, 10 percent at age 100, and 22 percent at age 110.

Note, however, that some of the year-to-year variation will 'cancel out' over time, because deaths will be somewhat higher than expected in some years and somewhat lower than expected in other years simply by random chance. The distribution of the cumulative average payout values will therefore be tighter than that of the year-to-year payout values.

Investment risk contribution

Next, we show the effect on payout variability when portfolio returns are also volatile, meaning the complete simulation that includes both sources of payout variability—the mortality credits and the investment returns.

Figure 10.2 shows the results for Brian with the bond portfolio. Payouts start at $5,970 at age 65 and gradually grow more volatile over time. By age

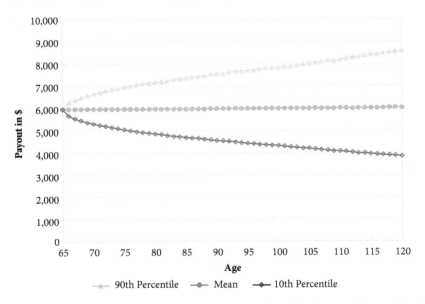

Figure 10.2 Range of yearly payouts by age (male) due to both mortality credit and investment volatility (bond portfolio with no payout growth rate)

Source: Authors' calculations.

90, there is a 10 percent chance that his payout that year would be less than $4,547 and a 10 percent chance that it would be more than $7,553.

Figure 10.3 shows the even larger volatility for Edgar with his equity portfolio. Payouts start at $8,646 at age 65 and grow more volatile over time. By age 90, there is a 10 percent chance that his payout that year would be less than $2,167 and a 10 percent chance that it would be more than $17,666. In both Figures 10.2 and 10.3, we see that the means of the payout simulations are almost perfectly uniform and that the deviation about those means (i.e. the payout volatility) is largely symmetrical. Again, this is expected of a fairly designed tontine.

The fact that Brian, the bond investor, receives only $5,970 in the first year, whereas Edgar, the equity investor, receives $8,646 might seem like a great reason to invest in equity. Perhaps so, but equity is a much riskier investment and thus there is a trade-off decision to be made between risk and reward. While Edgar is likely to continue receiving higher payouts than Brian throughout his retirement, there is a chance that he might not, and in the scenario of a severe bear market—which could occur at any time— his payouts could drop significantly below those of Brian. Naturally, those invested in a blended allocation of equity and bonds would receive initial payouts that are between those of an all-equity or all-bond investor, and the

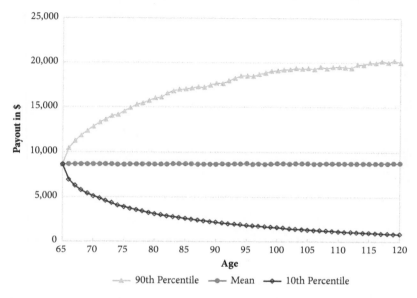

Figure 10.3 Range of yearly payouts by age (male) due to both mortality credit and investment volatility (equity portfolio with no payout growth rate)

Source: Authors' calculations.

volatility of their payouts would likewise be between those of an all-equity or all-bond investor.[26]

To reiterate, the potential for lower payouts is not unique to assurance funds. To keep payouts or withdrawals at high levels in the face of portfolio losses is an exercise fraught with peril. Assurance funds avoid such peril by automatically making the adjustments necessary (whether up or down) to remain fully funded, thereby maximizing payouts without risking ruin.

The Risk of Ruin

For those taking systematic withdrawals from a retirement portfolio, risk is commonly measured as the risk of ruin, referring to the risk that the participant outlives her retirement savings—as happened to the investor in Table 10.4. Assurance funds are designed to have a virtually zero risk of ruin before the maximum age of mortality (age 120 in our model). This is accomplished through strict adherence to the budget constraint, which ensures that the expected present value of the payouts is always equal to the present value of the fund's assets.

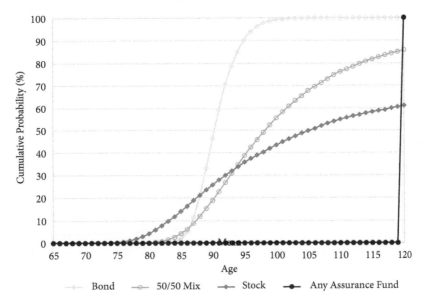

Figure 10.4 Cumulative probability of ruin for regular investment accounts under the 4 percent rule, compared to assurance-fund accounts
Source: Authors' calculations.

The risk of ruin is principally a function of an investor's age, spending rate, and investment returns. The so-called 'four percent rule' of Bengen (1994) has become a common rule of thumb in financial planning as the maximum 'safe' withdrawal rate for new retirees. The idea is that investors are likely to avoid ruin over a 30-year planning horizon when invested in a portfolio consisting of 50 percent equity and 50 percent bonds if they withdraw four percent of the portfolio in the first year of retirement and then adjust that amount for inflation in each subsequent year, which we assume to be 2.5 percent per year.

Figure 10.4 shows the risk of ruin for a regular investment account using this rule for three different investment portfolios used in our simulation. The portfolios are the equity portfolio, the bond portfolio, and a portfolio weighted 50 percent to equity and 50 percent to bonds. The plot shows the cumulative probability of ruin under each portfolio and compares these ruin probabilities with that of an assurance fund. For example, for a regular account with 100 percent invested in bonds, there is a 10 percent chance of running out of money at around age 86 and a 50 percent chance of running out of money at around age 90.

Using the returns in our model, the three portfolios held in a regular investment account all begin to exhibit a material risk of ruin by age 85 when following the four percent rule. More risky portfolios begin to face the risk of ruin sooner due to their higher volatility but also they have the potential to last longer due to their higher expected returns. A regular investment account invested in any of the three portfolios would have at least a 30 percent chance of ruin by age 93.

In contrast, assurance funds have zero chance of ruin before age 120 regardless of how they are invested, and they always make a full payout at age 120 with the remaining money left in the investor's account. Moreover, for *any* of these portfolios held in an assurance-fund account, an investor who elects to receive payouts with the 2.5 percent annual growth option will enjoy higher payouts *every year* than an investor would receive by applying the four percent rule and investing in the same portfolio in a regular investment account. The trade-off, of course, is that the assurance fund does not allow the investor to freely make any additional withdrawals or to leave any bequests at death.

Using Escalating Payouts to Reduce Downside Payout Risk

An examination of Figure 10.2 shows that even bond portfolios can result in meaningful payout volatility. The risk of falling payouts are concerning to many retirees, especially those who rely heavily on their DC plan savings to pay for living expenses in retirement.

When the payout growth rate used to compute an investor's payout is set equal to zero (as is the case with a uniform payout), there will be about a 50–50 chance that any future payout will be either above or below the initial payout received in the first year. This downside risk can be mitigated by instead selecting an escalating payout method. Doing so reduces the initial payout, but also reduces the risk that future payouts will fall below the level of prior payouts.

Figure 10.5 illustrates this by showing the payout on Brian's bond portfolio if he had instead selected his payout to include a 2.5 percent per year growth rate. The plot confirms that the payout does indeed increase by 2.5 percent per year, on average. In addition, the 10th percentile curve reveals that the risk that future payouts will drop below the initial payout is significantly reduced compared to the uniform payout option shown in Figure 10.2. The initial payout drops from $5,970 in the case of uniform payouts to $4,462 in the case of escalating payouts, but the growing payouts are expected to surpass the uniform payout level by age 77. Notably, even the 4.462 percent initial payout rate for the escalating payout assurance fund is greater than what an investor could get by applying the four percent rule to

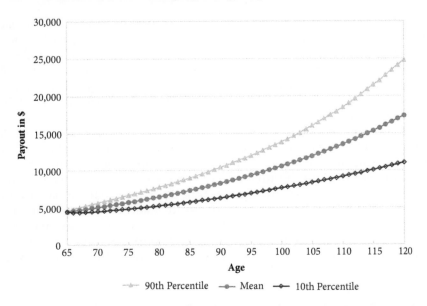

Figure 10.5 Range of yearly payouts by age (male) due to both mortality credit and investment volatility (bond portfolio with a 2.5% per year payout growth rate)

Source: Authors' calculations.

a regular investment account, and the assurance fund comes with no risk of ruin before age 120.

These beneficial effects of using a positive payout growth rate would also hold for assurance funds that use riskier investment portfolios. For example, Figure 10.6 shows the payout to a 65-year-old male using a portfolio allocated 50 percent to equity and 50 percent to bonds, using a 2.5 percent per year payout growth rate. In this case, the initial annual payout would be $5,655 (5.655%), considerably higher than what an investor could get from applying the four percent rule to a regular investment account—and, again, with no risk of ruin before age 120.

Of course, there is another very good reason that people should want growing payout trajectories—inflation. Accordingly, state-sponsored assurance funds may want to encourage the use of escalating payout options.

Note that using a positive payout growth rate by itself does not materially change the volatility of the payouts. It just shifts the payout distribution to one that is escalating rather than uniform, which has the welcome effect of reducing the chance that future payouts will fall below previous payouts.

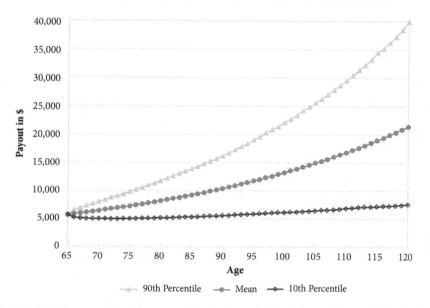

Figure 10.6 Range of yearly payouts by age (male) due to both mortality credit and investment volatility (50/50 equity/bond allocation with a 2.5% per year payout growth rate)

Source: Authors' calculations.

Managing Volatility

In the previous examples, the annual volatility of the payout stream as measured by the standard deviation of the payouts was 14.8 percent for the equity portfolio and 3.7 percent for the bond portfolio. What can be done for those who desire even less payout volatility?

For one thing, states that offer assurance funds might include a portfolio option that uses cash-flow matching techniques, such as with bond ladders. In addition, plan participants could smooth plan payouts by keeping a portion of their retirement assets in a regular investment account and taking additional withdrawals from that regular investment account as needed to smooth their overall consumption. In this way, the regular investment account would act as a type of reserve mechanism.

Bond ladders

Cash-flow matching techniques, such as with treasury bond ladders structured to produce a precise set of cash flows when held to maturity, could reduce payout volatility significantly. Although the market value of the bonds will vary as interest rates change over time, investor's cash flows will be unaffected. Furthermore, these cash flows would automatically adjust with inflation if the ladder was constructed using treasury inflation protected securities (TIPS).

It might seem a first glance that a laddering strategy would introduce reinvestment risk as the receipt of periodic mortality credits are reinvested into an investor's account. Yet, it turns out that this reinvestment has no effect on the payouts. The reason is that the reinvested mortality credits increase the par value of each bond in the ladder by a factor that depends only on the realized mortality credit yield and not on the current market value of the bonds. Thus, payouts are immunized from interest rate risk (see Fullmer and Sabin 2019b). Such strategies may prove popular among those with a strong preference for payout stability.

Side reserves

The whole idea of an assurance fund is to dispense with reserves in order to reduce costs, avoid counterparty risk, and maximize payouts. There is no reason, however, that an investor could not hold some assets in a regular investment account to dip into as needed or otherwise use for bequest motives. In fact, we expect that most assurance-fund investors would do this. An assurance fund combined with a regular investment account provides both a source of assured lifetime income and a flexible asset reserve that can be used to smooth consumption in years that the assurance-fund payouts fall, and to fund unexpected spending needs from time to time.

Systematic Mortality Risk

Our model incorporated idiosyncratic mortality risk, but not systematic mortality risk, which cannot be diversified away. This fact is highly significant to a DB plan sponsor or insurance company with liabilities that cover many persons. However, it is less significant to a single individual. To put it in perspective, an unexpected improvement in longevity might add a year or two or three to life expectancy over the course of a person's retirement years. This will matter to the person only if she is fortunate enough to live into the right hand tail of her age cohort. But even if she does, the effect of the systematic component is quite small compared to the idiosyncratic component. Absent any pooling, idiosyncratic longevity risk is remarkably high given that the remaining lifespan of a new retiree may be 10, 20, 30, 40 years or more. Thus, there is great benefit in cheaply diversifying this large idiosyncratic uncertainty away, and relatively little benefit in paying the more expensive cost to transfer the residual systematic risk to an insurer.

That said, the issue of systematic mortality risk is important, and we do not mean to marginalize it. Unexpected macro improvements (or declines) in longevity would surely result in a downward (or upward) force on assurance-fund payouts, and it is the members who bear this risk. An analytical discussion of systematic mortality risk is presented in Sabin and Forman (2016) and illustrated in the form of individual accounts (as would be the case of assurance funds) in Fullmer and Sabin (2019a). An interesting, and indeed useful, characteristic of assurance funds is that unexpected changes in macro longevity would be handled gradually and gracefully. The budget constraint forces the assurance fund to lower (or raise) payouts continually in response to actual member deaths from year to year. Should the membership systematically die more quickly or more slowly than expected, payout changes would begin immediately to reflect that change. Thus, payout changes due to systematic mortality risk will typically be small and gradual rather than large and lumpy.

An exception lies in the case of sharp spikes in mortality rates that can occur, for example, in a time of pandemic such as the outbreak in December 2019 of the severe acute respiratory syndrome coronavirus, SARS-CoV-2. If a pandemic were to cause the mortality rate within an assurance pool to increase unexpectedly, the mortality credits distributed to the surviving members would increase. As a result, payouts would also increase relative to what they would have been absent the pandemic. Essentially, a pandemic causes mortality credits—and thus payouts—to be pulled forward from future periods to the present. This unexpected 'payout bump' would likely be followed by a gradual payout dip in later years because those who died during the pandemic would, of course, not die later as they otherwise would have done. If, however, the higher mortality rates caused by the pandemic were more permanent (i.e. resulted in a permanent reduction in life expectancies), the fund's mortality tables would be adjusted accordingly, and payout rates would remain at the higher level. A cure for cancer, for example, would therefore have the opposite effect: by increasing life expectancies and reducing annual payouts.

People who prefer not to accept any amount of longevity risk could, of course, transfer that risk to an insurance company by purchasing a commercial life annuity rather than an assurance fund, although that risk transfer would naturally come at a cost. Because annuity providers bear systematic longevity risk, they are required to ensure their solvency by pricing in a suitable risk premium (NAIC 2013). Since assurance funds offer no such risk transfer or guarantee, no such risk premiums are charged. As a result, purchasers of commercial annuities sacrifice some amount of yield as the price for transferring the systematic component of longevity risk to the insurance company (Warshawsky 2012; Fullmer and Sabin 2019a). Assurance-fund members instead keep that yield for themselves.

Conclusion

Assurance funds can enhance DC plans by providing retirees with universal access to a pension-like lifetime income. This income would not be fixed, and it would not be guaranteed: it would be variable and nonguaranteed. Yet by adhering to a strict budget constraint, these plans and the income that they provide would always be fully funded and, therefore, fully sustainable.

Assurance funds are relatively simple. They payout out what they can— no more and no less—using simple, transparent formulas in a highly efficient way. Organized as either tontines or pooled annuities, payouts would be significantly higher, on average, than retirees could obtain from regular retirement savings accounts or comparable commercial life annuities. Moreover, if assurance-fund accounts were offered along with regular investment accounts, together they would provide investors with a sensible way to mitigate longevity risk, preserve liquidity, smooth consumption, and bequeath assets upon death.

State retirement savings programs could partner with various private-sector investment and record-keeping companies to add assurance funds to their investment platforms as a way to transform their programs from simple retirement savings plans into true lifetime pension plans. Costs could be quite low, and, since assurance funds make no guarantees, the sponsors would bear no fiduciary due diligence risks associated with selecting a guarantor. Assurance funds may also be of interest outside the US as an efficient, low-cost way to provide access to assured lifetime retirement income, perhaps especially in countries where a well-established insurance market does not currently exist.

Notes

1. Tontines are named after Lorenzo de Tonti, the 17th-century Italian who is credited with the idea (Milevsky 2015). Group self-annuitization (Piggott et al. 2005; Qiao and Sherris 2013) is a similar concept that could be used. Participating variable index-linked annuities (Maurer, Mitchell, et al. 2013; Maurer, Rogalla, and Siegelin 2013) could also be used—provided that the participation applies fully on both the upside and the downside. This would exclude 'one-way' participating annuities that offer upside participation with downside protection.

2. See Waring and Siegel (2018) for a discussion on the budget constraint as it relates to retirement spending. The budget constraint differentiates assurance funds from so-called 'collective defined contribution' (CDC) plans which may permit intergenerational wealth redistribution that can result in significant underfunding and unsustainability risks that we wish to avoid (see, e.g., Wilkenson 2018).

3. By this we mean efficient economically for individual retirement consumers; see the life cycle model in Yaari (1965), for example.

4. We use the terms 'member' and 'investor' somewhat interchangeably when referring to those that invest in an assurance fund. In general, we use the term investor
when referring to concepts that apply generally to any investor, and we use the
term member when referring to concepts that apply to risk pooling, risk sharing,
forfeitures, and other concepts that do not apply to regular investment accounts.

5. We use the term 'mutual fund' generically to include similar offerings such as collective investment trusts. Assurance funds might likewise be organized as either
funds or trusts.

6. See, for example, Warshawsky (2012) who notes that commercial life annuities
typically provide benefits that are worth just 88 percent of what an actuarially fair
annuity would provide. A comparison of expected assurance-fund performance
relative to fixed annuities is significantly more nuanced. The same rationale—
that assurance funds dispense with the risk costs required of commercial life
annuities—still applies, but we note that a theoretical comparison using historical fixed annuity prices in Canada by Milevsky et al. (2018) was not so clear-cut.
That study found that the comparison results depended significantly on the
assumptions used.

7. Similar arrangements go by other names, including participating annuities and
group self-annuitization schemes (Piggott et al. 2005; Qiao and Sherris 2013;
Maurer, Mitchell, et al. 2013; Maurer, Rogalla, and Siegelin 2013).

8. Moreover, these accounts could be used to automatically combine each worker's past pensions into a single account, which could help to reduce leakage and
preserve retirement savings for retirement purposes (Croce 2019; Retirement
Clearinghouse 2020).

9. Self-employed workers would also be allowed to participate in these state-
sponsored pensions, if they desired. For that matter, it might make sense to allow
anyone who can legally open or own an IRA to participate.

10. States might even automatically default a portion of each worker's contributions
into an assurance fund but allow the worker to opt out. We view this approach as
unlikely in the United States, where a default into any type of irrevocable, annuity-
like option would certainly be controversial. On the other hand, in countries
where government-mandated actions are more commonplace, it could be appropriate to automatically default a portion of each worker's contributions into an
assurance fund (either with or without an opt-out).

11. We illustrate yearly mortality rates and payout amounts here for brevity, but the
same principle applies when using monthly rates and payouts. Also, we are not
advocating that assurance funds should take gender into account but only noting
that they could. For more discussion of gender issues in annuities and pensions,
see Forman and Sabin (2015).

12. The monthly rate of return R_m is computed as $1.07^{(1/12)} - 1$. The monthly investment return is calculated as the beginning of period balance multiplied by R_m
plus the current month's contribution multiplied by $(1 + R_m)^{1/12} - 1$.

13. These mortality credits are calculated by taking the beginning of period balance
and adding the monthly investment return, then multiplying this sum by the
mortality credit yield.

14. The formula for the annuity factor at age x is $\ddot{a}_x = 1 + \sum_{t-1}^{\infty} v^t {}_t p_x$, where ${}_t p_x$ is
the probability of surviving to age $x + t$ given that the member is alive at age x,

and $v = 1/(1 + i)$ is the discount factor, with i the assumed interest rate (e.g. 7%). The value of $_tp_x$ is calculated from the mortality table. The IAM mortality table used here has a terminal age of 120, meaning there is zero probability of surviving to ages greater than 120, and so the sum in the formula has a finite number of terms. In practice, an assurance-fund provider could extend the table to even more advanced ages to accommodate the possibility of even longer lives.

15. At least until the maximum age of the mortality table, which is 120 in this case.

16. We assume that the returns on both portfolios are random and normally distributed. The reason is that we are not trying to model specific equity or bond portfolios, but rather to depict portfolios with higher/lower returns and higher/lower return volatility. In a later section, we will briefly discuss the potential of other investment strategies with different return characteristics.

17. The expected return on a blended portfolio is $w_e r_e + w_b r_b$, where w_e is the weight in the equity portfolio, r_e is the expected return of the equity portfolio, w_b is the weight in the bond portfolio, and r_b is the expected return of the bond portfolio. Because we assume no correlation between portfolios, the volatility is simply $\left(w_e^2 \sigma_e^2 + w_b^2 \sigma_b^2\right)^{1/2}$, where σ_e is the volatility of the equity portfolio and σ_b is the volatility of the bond portfolio.

18. Specifically, balances are assigned by the formula $10(1.2^{U+4.8})$, where U is a uniform random number in the range of zero to one.

19. With respect to the mortality improvement projection, the first year of the simulation is assumed to be 2020 and the last year of the simulation is 2075.

20. For level/uniform payouts, the assumed annual interest rate is seven percent for the equity portfolio and three percent for the bond portfolio. For escalating payouts, the assumed annual interest rate is $(1 + r)/(1 + g) - 1 = (1 + 0.07)/(1 + 0.025) - 1 \approx 4.39$ percent for the equity portfolio and $(1 + r)/(1 + g) - 1 = (1 + 0.03)/(1 + 0.025) - 1 \approx 0.49$ percent for the bond portfolio. The assumed annual interest rate for blended portfolios are computed similarly using the expected rate of return on the blended portfolio (refer to endnote 17) in the numerator of this calculation.

21. As explained in Sabin and Forman (2016), the nominal-gain method is not strictly fair in an actuarial sense, at least not exactly. The analysis is complicated, but for our purposes the bottom line is that its bias is negligible in an assurance-fund pool of the size described here (i.e. with 10,000 members). For all practical purposes, we can use the nominal-gain method and regard it as fair. We choose this method for its advantages of simplicity, transparency, and the fact that members will perceive it as being fair.

22. Note that Edgar's age 65 payout rate of 8.646 percent of the portfolio value in the first year is less than the 8.990 percent payout rate at the same age given in Table 10.2 (0.08990 = $36,264/$403,372). The reason is that Table 10.2 illustrated a simple example that assumed no mortality improvement, whereas our simulation model does assume mortality improvement.

23. At its simplest, imagine a fund that takes investor money and simply holds it, with zero return and zero volatility (in this case, a 65-year-old male investing $100,000 and selecting the uniform payout option would receive $4,183 in the first year and expect to continue receiving that amount every year thereafter).

24. For an analytical discussion of this effect, see Sabin and Forman (2016).
25. The expected mortality credit yield at age x is $q_x / (1-q_x)$, where q_x is the death probability at age x. Since q_x increases with age, so too does the expected mortality credit yield. This amplifies the effect of random mortality deviations on the actual mortality credit yield, resulting in increasing deviation of the percentile curves at higher ages.
26. Recall that Figures 10.2 and 10.3 (as well as Figures 10.1, 10.5, and 10.6) show the range in payouts from year to year, and in any particular simulation the payouts both rise and fall over the course of the payout years. These ups and downs 'average out' over time such that the range of the *average* payout received by a member over time will be narrower than the yearly values.

References

AARP Public Policy Institute (2020). *State Retirement Savings Resource Center*. Washington, DC: AARP Public Policy Institute. https://www.aarp.org/ppi/state-retirement-plans.html

American Academy of Actuaries (2015). 'Risky Business: Living Longer without Income for Life: Information for Current and Future Retirees,' *Issue Brief*. Washington, DC: American Academy of Actuaries. http://actuary.org/files/Retiree_PreRetirees_IB_102215.pdf

Aubry, J-P, C. V. Crawford, and K. Wandrei (2018). 'Stability in Overall Pension Plan Funding Masks a Growing Divide,' *State and Local Pension Plans Issue in Brief 62*. Boston College Center for Retirement Research: Chestnut Hill, MA. October: https://crr.bc.edu/wp-content/uploads/2018/10/slp_62.pdf

Benartzi, S., A. Previtero, and R. H. Thaler (2011). 'Annuitization Puzzles,' *Journal of Economic Perspectives*, 25(4): 143–164.

Bengen, W. P. (1994). 'Determining Withdrawal Rates Using Historical Data,' *Journal of Financial Planning*, 7(4): 14–24.

Board of Governors of the Federal Reserve System (2020). *Financial Accounts of the United States: Flow of Funds, Balance Sheets, and Integrated Macroeconomic Accounts: First Quarter 2020*. Washington, DC: Board of Governors of the Federal Reserve System.

Cooper, R. W. (1972). *An Historical Analysis of the Tontine Principle*. Philadelphia: Huebner Foundation/University of Pennsylvania.

Copeland, C. (2014). 'Employment-Based Retirement Plan Participation: Geographic Differences and Trends, 2013,' *EBRI Issue Brief 405*. Washington, DC: Employee Benefit Research Institute.

Croce, B. (2019). 'Auto Portability Program Gets Thumbs Up by Regulators,' *Pensions & Investments*. July 31. https://www.pionline.com/regulation/auto-portability-program-gets-thumbs-regulators

Donnelly, C. (2015). 'Actuarial Fairness and Solidarity in Pooled Annuity Funds,' *ASTIN Bulletin*, 45(1): 49–74.

Donnelly, C., M. Guillén, and J. P. Nielsen (2014). 'Bringing Cost Transparency to the Life Annuity Market,' *Insurance: Mathematics and Economics*, 56: 14–27.

Forman, J. B. (2020). 'Fully Funded Pensions,' *Marquette Law Review*, 103(4): 1205–1312.

Forman, J. B. and G. D. Mackenzie (2013). 'Optimal Rules for Defined Contribution Plans: What Can We Learn from the US and Australian Pension Systems?' *Tax Lawyer*, 66(3): 613–651.

Forman, J. B. and M. J. Sabin (2015). 'Tontine Pensions,' *University of Pennsylvania Law Review*, 163(33): 755–831.

Forman, J. B. and M. J. Sabin (2016). 'Survivor Funds,' *Pace Law Review*, 37(1): 204–291.

Fullmer, R. K. (2019). 'Tontines: A Practitioner's Guide to Mortality-Pooled Investments,' *CFA Institute Research Foundation Brief.* Charlottesville, VA: CFA Institute Research Foundation. https://www.cfainstitute.org/-/media/documents/article/rf-brief/fullmer-tontines-rf-brief.ashx

Fullmer, R. K. and M. J. Sabin (2019a). 'Individual Tontine Accounts,' *Journal of Accounting and Finance*, 19(8):
https://doi.org/10.33423/jaf.v19i8.2615

Fullmer, R. K. and M. J. Sabin (2019b). 'Tontine Bond Ladders.' https://dx.doi.org/10.2139/ssrn.3373251

Gale, W. and D. John (2018). 'State-sponsored Retirement Savings Plans: New Approaches to Boost Retirement Plan Coverage,' in O. S. Mitchell, R. L. Clark, and R. Maurer, eds., *How Persistent Low Returns Will Shape Saving and Retirement.* Oxford: Oxford University Press, pp. 173–193.

Goldsticker, R. (2007). 'A Mutual Fund to Yield Annuity-Like Benefits,' *Financial Analysts Journal*, 63(1): 63–67.

Holden, S. and D. Schrass (2019). 'The Role of IRAs in US Households' Saving for Retirement, 2019,' *Investment Company Institute Research Perspective*, 25(10): 1–40.

Lusardi, A. and O. S. Mitchell (2014). 'The Economic Importance of Financial Literacy: Theory and Evidence,' *Journal of Economic Literature*, 52(1): 5–44.

Mackenzie, G. A. (2010). *The Decline of the Traditional Pension: A Comparative Study of Threats to Retirement Security*, New York, NY: Cambridge University Press.

Maurer, R., O. S. Mitchell, R. Rogalla, and V. Kartashov (2013). 'Lifecycle Portfolio Choice With Systematic Longevity Risk and Variable Investment-Linked Deferred Annuities,' *Journal of Risk & Insurance*, 80(3): 649–676.

Maurer, R., R. Rogalla, and I. Siegelin (2013). 'Participating Payout Life Annuities: Lessons from Germany,' *ASTIN Bulletin*, 43(2): 159–187.

Milevsky, M. A. (2015). *King William's Tontine: Why the Retirement Annuity of the Future Should Resemble its Past.* New York, NY: Cambridge University Press.

Milevsky, M. A. and T. S. Salisbury (2015). 'Optimal Retirement Income Tontines,' *Insurance: Mathematics and Economics*, 64: 91–105.

Milevsky, M. A. and T. S. Salisbury (2016). 'Equitable Retirement Income Tontines: Mixing Cohorts without Discriminating,' *ASTIN Bulletin*, 46(3): 571–604.

Milevsky, M., T. S. Salisbury, G. Gonzalez, and H. Jankowski (2018). 'Annuities versus Tontines in the 21st Century: A Canadian Case Study,' Society of Actuaries. https://www.soa.

org/globalassets/assets/Files/resources/research-report/2018/annuities-vs-tontines.pdf

NAIC (National Association of Insurance Commissioners) (2013). 'NAIC Model Rule (Regulation) for Recognizing a New Annuity Mortality Table for Use in Determining Reserve Liabilities for Annuities,' National Association of Insurance Commissioners. http://www.naic.org/store/free/MDL-821.pdf

Newfield, P. (2014). 'The Tontine: An Improvement on the Conventional Annuity?' *Journal of Retirement,* 1(3): 37–48.

OECD (Organization for Economic Cooperation and Development) (2012). *OECD Pensions Outlook 2012.* Paris: OECD.

OECD (2015). 'Pension Policy Notes and Reviews: Colombia,' *Pension Policy Notes and Reviews.* Paris: OECD. https://www.oecd.org/pensions/policy-notes-and-reviews.htm

OECD (2019a). 'Country Profiles of Pensions Systems: Chile,' *Pensions at a Glance.* Paris: OECD. https://www.oecd.org/publications/oecd-pensions-at-a-glance-19991363.htm

OECD (2019b). *Pensions at a Glance 2019.* Paris: OECD.

Oklahoma 529 College Savings Plan (2019). 'Invest Today for a Brighter Future,' State of Oklahoma. https://www.ok4saving.org/documents/ok_enrollment.pdf

OregonSaves (2020). 'Work Hard: Save Easy,' OregonSaves. https://www.oregonsaves.com/

Pension Rights Center (2020). 'State-based Retirement Plans for the Private Sector,' Pension Rights Center, Washington, DC. http://www.pensionrights.org/issues/legislation/state-based-retirement-plans-private-sector

Piggott, J., E. A. Valdez, and B. Detzel (2005). 'The Simple Analytics of a Pooled Annuity Fund,' *Journal of Risk and Insurance,* 72(3): 497–520.

Qiao, C. and M. Sherris (2013). 'Managing Systematic Mortality Risk with Group Self-Pooling and Annuitization Schemes,' *Journal of Risk and Insurance,* 80(4): 949–974.

Retirement Clearinghouse (2020). 'Auto Portability: Increasing Retirement Security for Americans,' Retirement Clearinghouse. Charlotte, NC. https://rch1.com/auto-portability

Sabin, M. J. (2010). 'Fair Tontine Annuity.' http://ssrn.com/abstract=1579932

Sabin, M. J. and J. B. Forman (2016). 'The Analytics of a Single-Period Tontine.' https://ssrn.com/abstract=2874160

Society of Actuaries (2020). '2012 Individual Annuity Reserving Report & Table,' Society of Actuaries, Schaumburg, IL. https://www.soa.org/resources/experience-studies/2011/2012-ind-annuity-reserving-rpt/

Staff of the Joint Committee on Taxation (2016). *Present Law and Background Relating to Tax-Favored Retirement Saving and Certain Related Legislative Proposals: JCX-3-16.* Washington, DC: Joint Committee on Taxation.

Staff of the Joint Committee on Taxation (2019). *Present Law and Background Relating to Challenges in the Retirement System: JCX-20-19.* Washington, DC: Joint Committee on Taxation.

Stites, S. (2019). 'Thousands of Oregon Workers Now Saving for Retirement under New Program,' *Salem Reporter.* December 1. https://www.salemreporter.com/

posts/1562/thousands-of-oregon-workers-now-saving-for-retirement-under-new-program

US Department of Labor, Bureau of Labor Statistics (2019). 'National Compensation Survey: Employee Benefits in the United States—March 2019,' *Bulletin 2791.* Washington, DC: US Department of Labor.

US Department of Labor, Employee Benefits Security Administration (2013). *Target Date Retirement Funds: Tips for ERISA Plan Fiduciaries.* Washington, DC: US Department of Labor.

VanDerhei, J. (2019). 'What if OregonSaves Went National: A Look at the Impact on Retirement Income Adequacy,' *EBRI Issue Brief 494.* Washington, DC: Employee Benefit Research Institute. October 31: https://www.ebri.org/content/what-if-oregonsaves-went-national-a-look-at-the-impact-on-retirement-income-adequacy

Waring, M. B. and L. B. Siegel (2018). 'What Investment Risk Means to You: Strategic Asset Allocation, the Budget Constraint, and the Volatility of Spending During Retirement,' *The Journal of Retirement,* 6(2): 7–26.

Warshawsky, M. J. (2012). *Retirement Income: Risks and Strategies.* Cambridge, MA: MIT Press.

Wilkenson, L. (2018). 'What is CDC and How Might It Work in the UK?' *Research Report.* London: Pensions Policy Institute.

Yaari, M. E. (1965). 'Uncertain Lifetime, Life Insurance and the Theory of the Consumer,' *The Review of Economic Studies,* 32(2): 137–150.

Zelinsky, E. A. (2004). *The Origins of the Ownership Society: How the Defined Contribution Paradigm Changed America.* New York, NY: Oxford University Press.

Chapter 11

New Financial Instruments for Managing Longevity Risk

John Kiff

Lower expected rates of market returns and rising longevity risk make it challenging for employers to offer defined benefit (DB) pensions. In countries with large DB pension sectors (e.g. the United Kingdom and the United States), pension plan sponsors are increasingly transferring these obligations and the associated investment and longevity risk to life insurers (Figure 11.1). For life insurers, the longevity risk may provide a partial hedge for the mortality risk in their life insurance books. The geography of pension risk markets reflects the preponderance of private-sector DB plans in those countries (Figure 11.2).

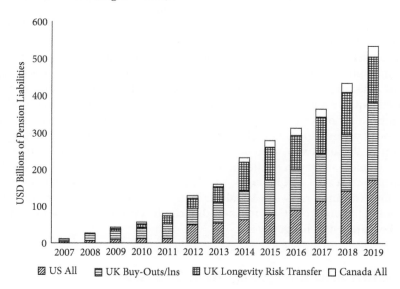

Figure 11.1 Cumulative pension risk transfer totals by country and product
Source: Kessler (2019).

John Kiff, *New Financial Instruments for Managing Longevity Risk.*
In: *New Models for Managing Longevity Risk.* Edited by Olivia S. Mitchell, Oxford University Press.
© Pension Research Council (2022). DOI: 10.1093/oso/9780192859808.003.0011

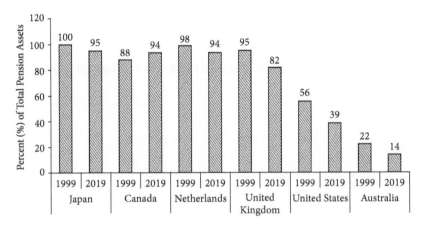

Figure 11.2 Assets held in defined benefit pension funds

Source: Willis Towers Watson (2020).

Ultimately, these markets are driven by the private-sector 'supply' of longevity risk. So, for example, we are not likely to see many of these transactions coming out of countries such as France, where the private-sector role in pension provision is minimal. The UK, on the other hand, has all the ingredients for a healthy demand for pension scheme longevity de-risking, as does the Netherlands. In both countries, there are still a great many DB pension schemes, and accounting rules and prudential regulations compel scheme sponsors to accurately measure and report their pension obligations. Also, the actuarial communities are actively seeking to disseminate more frequent and up-to-date longevity data and forward-looking models.

In what follows, we first explain the market for longevity risk by explaining the key transaction types: buy-outs, buy-ins, longevity swaps, and longevity bonds. We also explore some of the potential reasons why so little of this risk has made its way to capital markets for transferral. Second, we examine catastrophe (CAT) risk markets, which have been quite successful at transferring insurance risks to capital markets. The third section explores the potential lessons from CAT markets that can be applied to activating capital market interest in longevity risk.

Pension and Longevity Risk Transfer Markets

DB pension risks are transferred to insurers via buy-outs, buy-ins, and longevity swaps (IMF 2012; Joint Forum 2013). *Buy-outs* transfer all of a pension fund's liabilities in return for an up-front premium, which in some cases

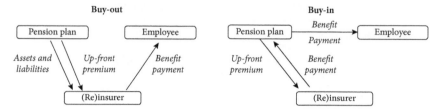

Figure 11.3 Structure of pension buy-out and buy-in transactions
Source: Joint Forum (2013).

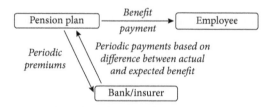

Figure 11.4 Structure of longevity swap transactions
Source: Joint Forum (2013).

is paid using an 'in-kind' transfer of the pension fund's assets (Daniel 2016). In a *buy-in*, the sponsor retains the pension plan's assets and liabilities, and receives periodic payments equal to those made to its members from an insurer in return for an up-front premium (Figure 11.3). Underfunded DB plans may prefer buy-ins to buy-outs, because buy-ins do not require that the funding gap be recognized as an accounting loss.

Longevity swaps transfer only longevity risk, and the premium is spread over the life of the contract based on the difference between the actual and the expected benefit payments (Figure 11.4). This approach is typically combined with a liability-driven investing (LDI) asset allocation approach that matches the expected cash-flow profile to that of the pension benefit payments, plus an inflation swap if the plan offers indexed benefits. Underfunded plans often implement LDI gradually to defer the cost of closing the funding gap (Citi 2016). Longevity swap counterparties are typically required to post collateral depending on whether the market value of the swap is positive or negative. Collateral plays a similar role in mitigating counterparty risk as the regulatory or solvency capital that (re)insurers are required to hold. Analysis by Biffis et al. (2016) found that the overall cost of such collateralization is comparable with that of interest rate swaps, but it does require that counterparties have on hand sufficient quantities of the required assets, usually liquid high-quality fixed-income securities, to meet collateral calls. The COVID-19 pandemic raised the possibility

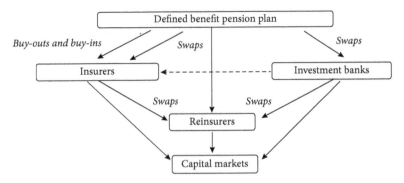

Figure 11.5 Structure of longevity transfers by defined benefit pension plans, by type of counterparty

Source: Joint Forum (2013).

that, although a pandemic might push down the value of liabilities to DB plan members, the short-term rise in mortality could trigger collateral calls (O'Farrell 2020).

Who uses which technique depends greatly on the type of counterparty. Insurers and reinsurers are associated with pension buy-ins and buy-outs, whereas longevity swap transactions are associated with investment banks and reinsurers. In most jurisdictions, banks are not allowed to issue or take on longevity risk in the form of annuities, buy-ins, or buy-outs, but they can take it indirectly via swap transactions (Figure 11.5).

The largest DB pension risk transfer (PRT) markets are in the UK and the US (Figures 11.6 and 11.7). In both cases, recent growth surges have been driven by the introduction of stricter pension disclosure standards, and stricter regulations that mandated risk-based guarantee schemes (2004 UK Pensions Act and 2006 US Pension Protection Act). Canada has also seen a steady and growing flow of buy-out transactions, and a large longevity swap (Figure 11.8).

PRT markets are supported by longevity risk transfer (LRT) markets in which (re)insurers transfer annuity-related risks to other (re)insurers. For example, Canada's Sun Life backed a C$5 billion longevity swap with Bell Canada Pension Plan with *longevity reinsurance* from a couple of Canadian branches/subsidiaries of foreign reinsurers. The size of the LRT market is difficult to track because it is more opaque than PRT markets, but since 2012 about half of all PRT transactions were probably backed by LRT trades. Many of these transactions cross borders, and fluid cross-border reinsurance markets are important to the functioning of any primary insurance markets (Swiss Re 2016). For example, since 2015, Dutch life insurer Aegon

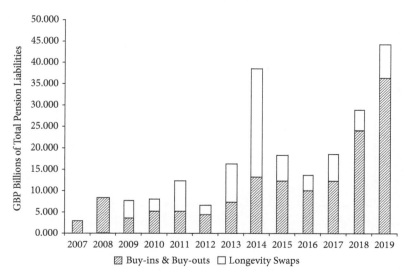

Figure 11.6 UK pension risk transfer transactions

Source: Hymans-Robertson (2009–2020).

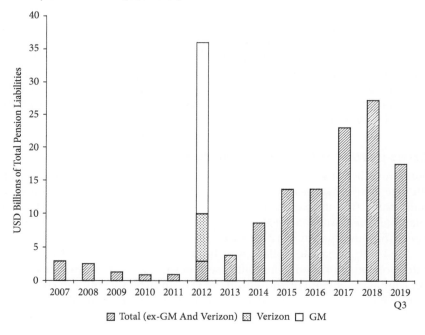

Figure 11.7 US pension buy-out and buy-in transactions

Source: Life Insurance Marketing and Research Association (2020, p.c.).

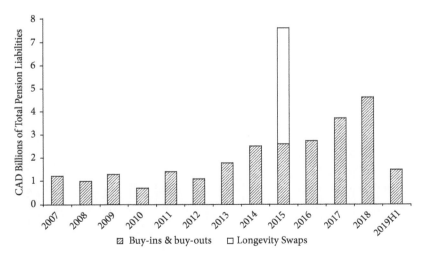

Figure 11.8 Canadian pension risk transfer transactions
Source: Willis Towers Watson (2014–2019) and Wolfe (2016).

has hedged the longevity risk associated with €18 billion of annuities with Canada Life Reinsurance (Aegon 2019).

Some cross-border LRT transactions may be motivated by regulatory arbitrage. For example, Solvency 2 insurance regulations may be incentivizing European (re)insurers to look to hedge their longevity risks with (re)insurers from foreign jurisdictions that have less stringent longevity risk capital charges and reserving requirements.

Cross-border reinsurance frictions

Some jurisdictions have imposed regulatory frictions on cross-border reinsurance. These can take the form of onerous or vague foreign (re)insurer registration requirements, or heavy collateralization requirements. For example, for Canadian (re)insurers to get capital credit through reinsurance from 'unregistered' (re)insurers, the reinsurance must be overcollateralized with Canadian dollar assets held in Canada (OSFI 2010). The US rules previously worked in a similar way, but since 2011, US (re)insurers can get capital relief from offshore-sourced reinsurance, without full collateralization if the reinsurer is rated at least BBB and from a qualified jurisdiction as determined by the National Association of Insurance Commissioners (NAIC).[1]

For European (re)insurers to get capital credit from offshore-sourced reinsurance, collateralization of covered liabilities and associated capital requirements may not be required if the reinsurer is rated at least BBB *or* from a jurisdiction deemed equivalent for reinsurance supervision.[2] Yet according to market sources, aside from the UK, country-specific implementation of the rules has been spotty (Pruitt et al. 2019). This should improve as the EU-US Covered Agreement is phased in, eliminating collateral and local presence requirements for qualified US reinsurers operating in the EU and UK insurance markets, and vice versa.[3]

Capital market transactions

A relatively untapped pool of potential longevity risk-takers may consist of asset managers, sovereign wealth funds, private equity funds, and hedge funds. Asset managers and sovereign wealth funds may be encouraged by the fact that longevity risk is likely to be largely uncorrelated to the other risk factors in their portfolios.[4] However, hedge funds may be put off by the long duration of the contracts (and the potential need to make collateral arrangements over this time frame), which may make them inappropriate for most hedge funds' investment styles.

Buyers of longevity risk may be discouraged by the illiquidity of instruments. Sellers of longevity risk would tend to seek customized hedge contracts to maximize effectiveness of risk transfer, yet many buyers of this risk would likely prefer standardized investments to maximize liquidity. This fundamental difference in perspective complicates the development of an active market. More standardized products would improve liquidity for risk buyers, but they would also increase basis risk for risk sellers, since standardization will likely increase the demographic differences between the actual pool of retirees and the reference pool on which payments are based.

In addition, buyers face the problem of asymmetric information. Given that a pension fund may be based on a better idea of how healthy its population of retirees is likely to be, the resulting asymmetric information may create a selection bias whereby only those pension funds with the longest-living populations would want to hedge the risk. The existence of such asymmetric information can lead to a breakdown of the market (see Mitchell and McCarthy 2002). Pricing contracts with asymmetric information is difficult, and so mispricing often occurs in the early stages of most markets when such asymmetries are most acute. Index-based transactions may lessen the problem of asymmetric information but they will increase basis risk.

Both buyers and sellers of longevity risk face counterparty risk. Counterparty risk arises because LRT deals tend to be long-term contracts where the counterparty may not (be able to) honor its financial commitments over time. It is usually dealt with by collateralization, which can involve significant costs because it requires that the proceeds be invested in high-quality liquid

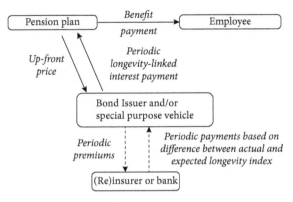

Figure 11.9 Structure of longevity bond transaction

Source: Joint Forum (2013).

securities that may be in short supply. This consideration favors longevity swaps, which require collateralizing only the difference between what each swap participant owes the other.[5]

Several unsuccessful attempts have been made to launch longevity bonds.[6] The payout on a longevity bond depends on the longevity experience of a given population, so the payment is related to the number of survivors in the population (Figure 11.9). In essence, it pays out a declining series of coupons as the proportion of survivors in the reference population declines (Blake and Burrows 2001). One disadvantage is that, unlike with a swap, the bond buyer makes a large upfront payment to the issuer, resulting in a counterparty risk exposure to the issuer. Such counterparty risk would be mitigated if the bonds were issued by a high-quality sovereign or supranational,[7] or by a special purpose vehicle that invested the proceeds in low-risk highly liquid fixed-income securities, from which the income covers the bond payouts. The issuer might also transfer some or all the longevity risk to a reinsurer, probably via a longevity swap contract.

Swaps may be more likely to activate broader capital market interest. For example, the 2012 €12 billion longevity swap between Dutch insurer Aegon and Deutsche Bank used standard International Swaps and Derivatives Association (ISDA) documentation and was targeted specifically at institutional investors (Whittaker 2012). It had a 20-year maturity with a close-out mechanism that determined the final payment, as opposed to the open-ended maturities of more traditional transactions. In addition, the longevity-indexed floating payments are floored and capped so that investors are not exposed to open-ended risk if longevity is either under- or overestimated. Finally, it used a longevity index based on publicly available data to drive cash flows, as opposed to the actual longevity experience of Aegon's annuity book.[8] Aegon followed up with a similar transaction in 2013, a €1.4 billion deal structured and syndicated by Société Générale (Osborn 2013). Nevertheless, there have apparently been no similar transactions since then.

Finally, both sides of the market are also affected by a lack of reliable and sufficiently granular information about longevity developments. Life tables are updated infrequently and are only available for relatively aggregated groups in the population. Several unsuccessful projects have attempted to solve this problem. In 2005, Credit Suisse introduced a US longevity index based on publicly available US government mortality tables but it quietly pulled it sometime later (Credit Suisse 2005). In 2007, Goldman Sachs introduced a mortality/longevity index (QxX) on the US insured population over the age of 65, aimed primarily at the life settlements market,[9] but it was shut down in late 2009 (Goldman Sachs 2007). In 2007, J. P. Morgan launched the LifeMetrics index of historical and current statistics on mortality rates and life expectancy, across genders, ages and nationalities (J. P. Morgan 2007). In 2010, J. P. Morgan transferred this operation over to the Life & Longevity Markets Association (LLMA) founded in 2010 to produce standardized index-based longevity swap curves and pricing models, but the LLMA closed down a few years later.[10] In 2007, Deutsche Bourse launched exchange-traded longevity swaps based on their XPect family of longevity indices supported by data from Club Vita, but these have also since closed (Sachsenweger and Rogge 2011). Nevertheless, Club Vita, founded in 2008, lives on and is producing Canadian, UK, and US VitaCurves. Because these are not publicly available, they have been of little use for pricing capital markets transactions.

Before examining more recent proposals for structuring LRT transactions, the next section looks at CAT risk transfer markets, from which useful lessons for LRT can be gleaned.

Catastrophe Risk Transfer Markets

(Re)insurers are using CAT risk transfer markets to finance their coverage of low-probability high-severity event risk in return for a pre-specified return.[11] These markets help (re)insurers diversify their sources of risk capital through highly collateralized transactions, while providing attractive yield to sophisticated investors (such as special purpose funds, hedge funds, pension funds, and family offices). Most market-based CAT risk protection is fully collateralized against peak exposures, and it is paid out more quickly than reinsurance liabilities (rarely redeemable on demand and where claims payments can be spread over many years). Most institutional investors active in this asset class probably do so via specialist funds,

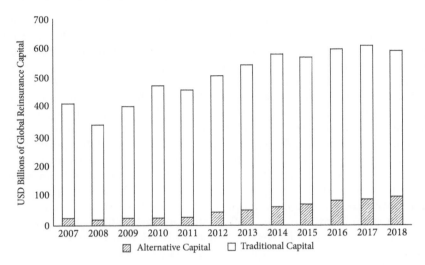

Figure 11.10 Global reinsurance capital

Source: Aon Capital (2019b).

of which there are more than 50 managing over $100 billion of investments (Evans 2020e).

Nonetheless, the market remains small relative to that of traditional reinsurance (Figure 11.10). At end of June 2019, outstanding CAT risk transfer instruments totaled $93 billion (about 15% of total global reinsurance capital) comprised of collateralized reinsurance ($49 billion), CAT bonds ($30 billion), and limited purpose reinsurance vehicles such as sidecars and industry loss warranties (ILWs) ($14 billion) (Aon 2019a, 2019b; Figure 11.11). Some of the growth may be related to Europe's Solvency II insurance regulation, which went into effect in 2016 and redefined how (re)insurers can use these instruments to hedge natural CAT risk (Braun and Weber 2017).

CAT bonds are like regular bonds, in that in exchange for an up-front investment, they pay interest until they are redeemed (Figures 11.12 and 11.13).[12] Embedded in these bonds is a call option that puts the principal payment of investors fully at risk. On the occurrence of a loss event, proceeds are released from the transaction to help the (re)insurer pay all claims arising from the event (i.e. 'creating insurance recoverable'); investors could lose their entire principal if the contingent event is sufficiently large. In return for the option, investors receive a premium to the investor based on the likelihood of such a loss event. If no loss event occurs during the term of the bond, the collateral is returned to investors based on

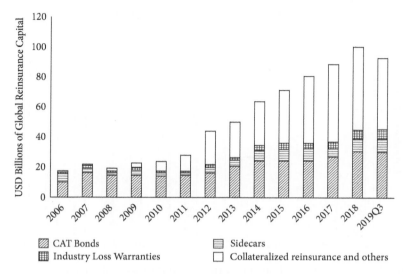

Figure 11.11 Alternative global reinsurance outstanding
Source: Aon Securities (2019a).

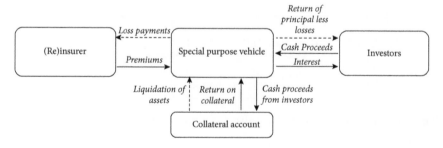

Figure 11.12 Structure of a catastrophe bond transaction
Source: Joint Forum (2013).

a release schedule that defines the time frame and threshold that must be met in order for the collateral release. If there is uncertainty as to whether there has been an event, part or all of the collateral can be 'trapped' until all facts have been clarified, and losses, if any, have been confirmed. For example, COVID-19 has introduced legal uncertainties around property (re)insurance coverage-related business interruption claims that could lead to collateral trapping in 2020 and beyond (Evans 2020c). All collateralized CAT risk transfer instruments are subject to trapped collateral risk.

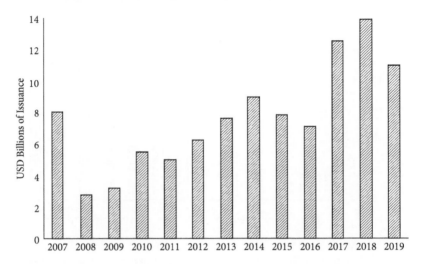

Figure 11.13 Catastrophe bond and insurance-linked securities issuance
Source: Evans (2020f).

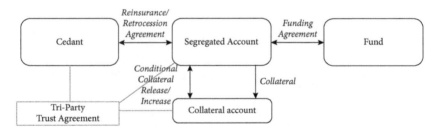

Figure 11.14 Structure of a collateralized reinsurance transaction
Source: Author.

Collateralized reinsurance is a contractual commitment in which a rein-surer assumes a portion of an insurer's risk in exchange for an agreed amount of premium (Figure 11.14). It can be structured on an excess-of-loss basis, by which losses are triggered if they exceed a pre-defined threshold, or on a proportional basis by which the reinsurer takes a pro-rata share of premiums and losses associated with a specific book of business. Collat-eralized reinsurance is much cheaper and more streamlined to structure than a CAT bond. A CAT bond issuer must pay for credit ratings, distri-bution costs, and legal costs; moreover, US SEC Rule 144A compliance requires extensive documentation and disclosure. Also, CAT bonds issued under Rule 144A can take an average of 10 weeks to close, versus four weeks

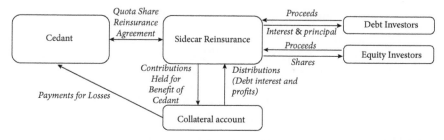

Figure 11.15 Structure of a sidecar transaction
Source: Author.

for a collateralized reinsurance deal. The latter may also dispense with the third-party risk assessment required for CAT bonds (Woodall 2013).

Sidecars are a limited-life special purpose vehicle funded by capital market participants and sponsored by a reinsurer from which it derives its business or quota share. The sidecar assumes a percentage of the ceding reinsurer's underwriting risk in exchange for a similar percentage of the associated premiums (Figure 11.15). The sidecar's capital is typically funded via equity and debt issuance the proceeds of which, along with premiums and investment income, are transferred to a collateral trust that fully collateralizes the underwritten risk. Because risk is shared via a quota share arrangement, information asymmetries between counterparties with regard to the sponsor's underwriting portfolio are reduced (Cummins and Barrieu 2013). Unlike other CAT risk transfer products, sidecars are often not restricted to covering losses from specifically named perils, so their performance tends to track the loss experiences of the (re)insurer and can often include a broader range of perils. Hence, sidecars could be more vulnerable, for example, to COVID-19-related claims burdens (Evans 2020d).

ILWs are dual-trigger reinsurance contracts that pay off when a specified industry-wide loss index exceeds a threshold and the issuing insurer's losses from the event equal or exceed a specified amount (Figure 11.16). The second trigger is usually quite low compared to the main trigger. The term is typically one year. ILWs may have binary triggers, where the full amount of the contract pays off once the two triggers are satisfied, or pro-rata triggers where the payoff depends upon how much the loss exceeds the warranty. Because the second trigger and the contingent payout is indemnity-based, ILWs are treated as reinsurance for regulatory purposes.

CAT products with indemnity triggers based on actual losses provide perfect coverage, which makes them a close substitute for a reinsurance contract. Yet loss recovery periods are longer, and investors cite potential

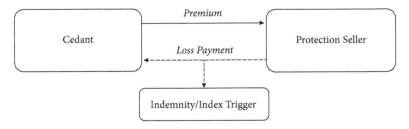

Figure 11.16 Structure of an industry loss warranty transaction
Source: Author.

moral hazards inherent in these structures. In this context, moral hazard refers to the risk that the reinsured counterparty might relax underwriting standards, including ongoing monitoring (where relevant), and/or may settle claims less stringently. Instead, investors tend to prefer index-based, modeled, and parametric indices. Parametric and index-based instruments determine the contingent payments on objective data that are correlated with issuer or insured party potential losses. Index-based contingent payments are based on generic industry-wide and/or geographic indices of insured losses correlated with the issuer's or insured party's potential losses.[13] Parametric instruments use scientific and statistical data related to the cause and magnitude of a catastrophe, such as wind speeds for hurricane-linked instruments. Index-linked instruments are simpler to structure and execute than parametric instruments, but they expose reinsured parties to the basis risk that the coverage may not exactly match actual losses.

The securitization of 'peak mortality' risks, primarily related to pandemic-type events, relies on parametric triggers. For example, the contingent payouts on the $521 million Swiss Re Vita III principal at risk notes issued in 2007 were based on indices of general population mortality rates in the covered countries. Losses to each of the note's nine tranches are triggered when the index exceeds their corresponding attachment point and reach 100 percent when the index reaches the exhaustion point (Moody's 2007).

Mortality bonds were last issued in 2017 when the World Bank issued $320 million of three-year pandemic bonds. Two classes of bonds were issued, $225 million of Class A bonds that cover flu and coronavirus, and $95 million of Class B bonds that cover filovirus, coronavirus, lassa fever, rift valley fever, and Crimean Congo hemorrhagic fever. The bonds provided parametric protection linked to the occurrence of specific pandemics, the trigger for both bonds being based on World Health Organization reported deaths and cases that hit the covered areas, which for some perils is global,

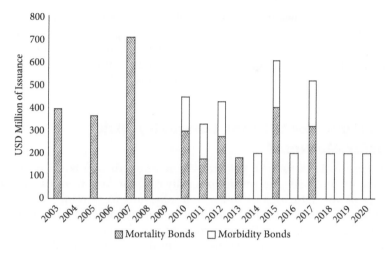

Figure 11.17 Extreme mortality/morbidity bond issuance
Source: Evans (2020f).

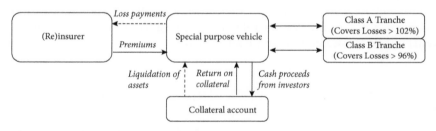

Figure 11.18 Structure of a morbidity bond
Source: Author.

others a subset of countries. In April 2020, the COVID-19 pandemic triggered payouts of $37.5 million on the Class A bonds and $95 million on the Class B bonds (Gross 2020).

Since 2010, Aetna has been issuing morbidity bonds that transfer risk of extreme claims for medical costs (Figure 11.17). For example, Aetna issued its 11th series of Vitality Re morbidity bonds in January 2020, a $200 million two-tranche deal, with $140 million of Class A and $60 million of Class B notes (Figure 11.18). For each annual risk period, the payout trigger is based on an index of Aetna's medical benefit claims ratio, the annual incurred benefits divided by the annual total premiums. If the index rises above a pre-defined attachment point level for either of the tranches, it will trigger a payment. The Class A notes cover Aetna for losses above an index of 102 percent (equivalent to a $1.02 billion loss level on the covered premia), and the Class B notes cover losses above 96 percent ($960 million). None of the Vitality Re ILS transactions have ever paid out for Aetna, even though the COVID-19 pandemic drove significant numbers to hospitals in the US and elevated health insurance claims levels (Evans 2020b).

What Hope for Vibrant Longevity Risk Transfer Markets?

If one were to look to CAT risk transfer markets for guidance on how to ignite capital markets' interest in longevity risk, the keys would seem to be short terms to maturity and full collateralization to minimize credit risk (Table 11.1). The theoretical literature seems to provide little guidance on other potential factors. Some models suggest that capital-markets-based insurance risk transfer is more viable for insurance risk portfolios in which potential losses are large and/or highly correlated, making retaining them expensive for (re)insurers to maintain prudent capital levels (Cummins and Trainar 2009). Yet most of the recent increase in CAT instrument issuance is due to collateralized reinsurance that protects smaller losses. Hence, large losses are still primarily either retained or transferred through traditional reinsurance (Subramanian and Wang 2018).

TABLE 11.1 Summary of active capital markets accessible catastrophe risk transfer vehicles

	CAT Bonds	Collateralized Reinsurance	Industry Loss Warranties	Sidecars
Credit risk	Minimal[a]	Minimal	Depends[b]	Depends[c]
Basis risk	Depends[d]	Minimal	Yes	Minimal
Moral hazard	Yes	Yes	No	Moderate
Transparency	High	Low	High	High
Typical term	3–5 years	1 year	1 year	1 year
Standardization	Moderate	Low	Moderate	Low
Liquidity	Moderate	Low	Low	Low
Outstanding (2019)	$30 billion	$49 billion	$14 billion	

Notes:
[a] CAT bond credit risk is usually minimal but depends on investment restrictions, swap counterparty arrangements, topping up rules, etc.
[b] Industry loss warranty credit risk depends on if the limit is collateralized.
[c] Sidecar credit risk depends on structure and collateral arrangements.
[d] CAT bond basis risk depends on whether it is indemnity-based (no basis risk) or not.
Source: Cummins and Weiss (2009), and author's assessments based on market surveillance and particularly the Artemis.bm website.

Hagendorff et al. (2014) found that access to insurance risk transfer markets should be easiest for (re)insurers with less risky portfolios. Investors will shy away from riskier portfolios because they do not have access to the private information that reinsurers have, so they must use publicly available information to assess portfolio risk. These investors will likely demand higher yields, making capital markets-based solutions less attractive than capital market-based solutions to such insurers. Yet Subramanian and Wang (2018) used a signaling model to show that (re)insurers riskier portfolios will be more likely to issue CAT bonds.

Product design could overcome information asymmetry problems. For example, according to Finken and Laux (2009), CAT risk transfer products with parametric or index triggers are insensitive to information asymmetry and may be attractive to low-risk insurers who suffer from adverse selection with reinsurance. Products with indemnity triggers may be unattractive to capital markets investors because they fear that low-risk insurers will opt for reinsurance, and only high-risk insurers will opt to tap capital markets. Low-risk insurers will only issue parametric or index triggered risk transfer products if the reinsurance premium exceeds the expected costs from the resulting basis risk.

As noted above, a few LRT transactions in the past did tap capital markets, but there has been no follow-up. A big challenge is resolving the tension between the long-term nature of longevity risk and investor preference for a short-term investment horizon (Blake et al. 2019). Cedents may also prefer shorter horizons due to the risk of the loss of capital relief if regulations change. Other challenges include finding, funding, and safekeeping prudent collateral. Bugler et al. (2020) proposed a sidecar structure for LRT (Figure 11.19). Langhorne Re was set up by Reinsurance Group of America (RGA) in 2018 to carry out such transactions, but it has yet to do any (Evans 2020a).

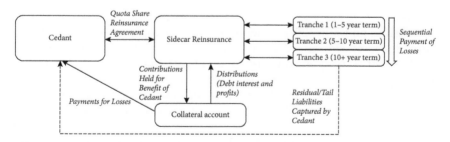

Figure 11.19 Structure of a long-term sidecar transaction
Source: Author.

Transferring risks in the financial markets depends on the ability to identify, measure, and isolate specific risk characteristics. In this regard, LRT markets may be held back by a lack of reliable and sufficiently granular information about longevity developments. Better longevity risk management and transfer would benefit from much more granular demographic data (including, for example, by postal code and cause of death), which can reduce basis risk and could generate indexes that would facilitate the design and trading of LRT instruments. Index-based transactions may also lessen the problem of asymmetric information.

A better marketplace would also be well-served by a common agreement between market participants on which mortality models to use for the design and pricing of each longevity-linked deal. A main reason why Aegon's deal with Société Générale went ahead in 2013 was that all parties agreed to use the same mortality model. Even if a particular model produced the wrong forecasts (which it is bound to do), if those forecasts were not systematically biased, then it becomes a potential candidate for use in this market. The Black and Scholes (1973) option pricing model and its variants are examples of such models operating in traditional financial markets. Ideally, such models are reasonably parsimonious and amenable to closed-form solutions, from which underlying parameters can be bootstrapped from market data.

We also recognize that there may a tension between investors' preference for index-based risk transfer, and cedents' for indemnity transactions. Yet Michaelson and Mulholland (2014) claim that hedge programs can be designed using customized population-wide index-based mortality data that minimize basis risk between the hedger's portfolio and the population referenced index. First, it involves customizing three elements of the hedge exposure: the cohorts (combinations of age and gender), relative cohort weighting over time ('exposure vector'), and 'experience ratio matrix' based on an experience study of the hedger's portfolio. Second, it involves designing an out-of-the-money spread option product structure with attachment and exhaustion points set to minimize the cost of capital for the cedent's capital relief taking into account market dynamics and investor preferences (see also Cairns and El Boukfaoui 2019).

MacMinn and Zhu (2018) have addressed the topic of optimal design at a broader level, showing that value-based hedging instruments dominate a full cash-flow hedging ones by generating a higher stock value to the company's shareholders. Cash-flow hedges consist of a series of payments that offset or stabilize the liability cash-flow of the cedent, such as buy-ins and buy-outs. Value-based hedges consist of one cash payoff contingent on a publicly observable longevity/mortality event. The key difference between the two is that, while the value-based hedge only benchmarks its payments based on the underlying systematic shocks, the cash-flow hedge also hedges unexplainable shifts in future mortality.

Nevertheless, MacMinn and Brockett (2017) note that hedging can make annuity portfolios more valuable and makes annuity holders better off, as it reduces the value of shareholders' effective put option on the cedent. So even if a hedge frees up reserves to invest in a positive net present value (NPV) project, it would only be worthwhile if the project NPVs exceed the firm's put value. The authors claimed that the failure of capital markets-based LRT could be as simple as this. Furthermore, Zelenko (2014) has blamed the failure of the Chilean longevity bond on another moral hazard problem: the perceived likelihood that the government would bail out (re)insurers and/or annuitants hit by systematic longevity risk events.

Conclusion

Today, LRT markets' 'buy side' remains largely comprised of (re)insurers, and there have been only sporadic efforts to tap capital markets. Although CAT risk transfer activity is also dominated by traditional reinsurance, there is active participation by institutional investors in alternative risk capital markets. The CAT risk transfer market analysis and academic literature summarized above suggests what some of the impediments and solutions may be.

A major constraint to new products is a dearth of granular longevity and demographic data. Governments are best placed to provide such data, perhaps through national statistical offices or government actuaries. Most important would be longevity information disaggregated by geographic area, gender, socioeconomic status, cause of death, and occupation. Governments could also usefully track the emergence and evolution of new diseases, especially those afflicting the elderly, medical advances, and life-style changes.

Ideally, LRT products would be based on common and publicly available data. In that regard, it is a shame that all efforts at building such databases and making them public have failed (e.g. LifeMetrics and XPect). Of course, there may a tension with cedents' preference for indemnity transactions to minimize basis risk, but there are some promising ways to bridge this gap (Michaelson and Mulholland 2014; Cairns and El Boukfaoui 2019). For instance, Blake et al. (2014) have advocated government-issued longevity bonds that would provide benchmarks and liquidity to the market, in the same way that government-issued inflation-linked bonds helped capital markets thrive. Although governments are already heavily exposed to longevity risk, they argue that there would be no increase in aggregate longevity risk if such issuance were coupled with the indexation of retirement ages to longevity increases. In practice, however, such indexation has proven to be politically very difficult.

There also needs to be agreement between market participants on mortality models, ideally models that are reasonably parsimonious and amenable to closed-form solutions from which underlying parameters can be bootstrapped from market data. Standardized data and models could also open the door to investors who prefer shorter terms to maturity. Taking a cue from CAT risk transfer markets, the sweet spot could be three to five years, since as MacMinn and Zhu (2018) showed, value-based products with shorter terms could be more attractive to cedents than cash-flow based risk transfer. Biffis and Blake (2014) have also proposed that an optimal format would entail a tranched principal-at-risk instrument very much like a CAT bond.

Of course, it may be that activating investor interest in LRT markets is an intractable problem, as suggested by MacMinn and Brockett (2017): what is good for annuitants may not be best for cedents, on account of the loss of the balance sheet put option. Moreover, markets may be held back by the moral hazard problem related to the perceived likelihood that the government would bail out (re)insurers and/or annuitants hit by systematic longevity risk events Zelenko (2014). The next decade will provide new insights.

Acknowledgements

The views expressed herein are those of the author and do not necessarily represent the views of the International Monetary Fund (IMF), its Executive Board, or IMF management.

Endnotes

1. Although the new rules were introduced in 2011, it was not until January 1, 2019, that all US states adopted them. Under these rules, the collateralization requirement is 10 percent for AA-rated reinsurers, 20 percent for those rated A+ and A, 50 percent at A−, and 75 percent at BBB (NYDFS 2020). Bermuda, France, Germany, Ireland, Japan, Switzerland, and the UK are NAIC-qualified jurisdictions (NAIC 2019).
2. The European Commission has granted Australia, Bermuda, Brazil, Canada, Japan, Mexico, Switzerland, and the US equivalence for reinsurance, excepting Bermudan captives and special purpose insurers (EIOPA 2020).
3. The EU-US Covered Agreement (and the parallel US-UK Covered Agreement) entered into force on April 4, 2018, but the reinsurance collateral reduction elements are not required to be fully implemented until September 22, 2022.
4. The value of LRT instruments is correlated with interest rate levels via their role in the present value discounting of future payouts, so the lack-of-correlation rationale may be less than expected.
5. Biffis et al. (2016) show that longevity swap collateral costs can be quite reasonable, especially when counterparty default risk and collateral rules are symmetric.

6. There was the Swiss Re-issued 2010 Kortis Bond, which was touted as a longevity bond but was actually more of a longevity basis bond. The bond's payout was based on the divergence in mortality rates between the UK and the US, where Swiss Re reinsured pensions and annuities in both countries (Hunt and Blake 2015). It was touted to be the 'next big thing,' but there have been no similar offerings since.

7. The AAA-rated European Investment Bank tried to issue a longevity bond in 2004, but it was cancelled due to lack of interest on both the buy and sell side (Biffis and Blake 2009). The AAA-rated World Bank tried a similar product in 2010, but it also failed (Zelenko 2014).

8. The Aegon-Deutsche Bank transaction references Dutch population mortality data published by the Dutch National Office for Statistics. See Sagoo and Douglas (2012) for more details.

9. A life settlement occurs when the owner of a life insurance policy sells the policy for an amount below the face value of the policy. The purchaser becomes responsible for making premium payments in return for collecting death benefits.

10. The LLMA was a nonprofit group made up of several investment banks, insurers, and reinsurers interested in facilitating the structuring of LRT deals (Evans 2011).

11. Reinsurers provide insurance for insurers and reinsurance for reinsurers ('retrocession'). Reinsurance gives (re)insurers capital relief and expanded underwriting capacity with opportunities for regulatory arbitrage (IAIS 2012).

12. The proceeds from these bonds fully collateralize the transfer of insurance exposures (up to the aggregate contractual policy limit) from or more ceding (re)insurance companies.

13. A frequently used set of indices for US-based perils is that compiled by Property Claims Services (Insurance Services Office, Inc. 2020).

References

Aegon (2019). 'Aegon Reinsures Longevity Exposure in the Netherlands,' Press Release, Netherlands, December 19.

Aon (2019a). 'Insurance-Linked Securities Annual Report.' http:// thoughtleadership.aonbenfield.com/pages/Home.aspx?ReportCategory =Insurance-Linked%20Securities

Aon (2019b). 'Reinsurance Market Outlook.' http://thoughtleadership.aonbenfield. com/pages/Home.aspx?ReportCategory=Reinsurance%20Market%20Outlook

Biffis, E. and D. Blake (2009). 'Mortality-Linked Securities and Derivatives,' Cass Business School Pensions Institute Working Paper PI 0901, London: Cass Business School Pensions Institute. http://www.pensions-institute.org/wp-content/ uploads/2019/workingpapers/wp0901.pdf

Biffis, E. and D. Blake (2014). 'Keeping Some Skin in the Game: How to Start a Capital Market in Longevity Risk Transfers,' *North American Actuarial Journal*, 18(1): 14–21.

Biffis, E., D. Blake, L. Pitotti, and A. Sun (2016). 'The Cost of Counterparty Risk and Collateralization in Longevity Swaps,' *Journal of Risk & Insurance*, 83(2): 387–419.

Black, F. and M. Scholes (1973). 'The Pricing of Options and Corporate Liabilities,' *Journal of Political Economy*, 81: 637–654.

Blake, D., T. Boardman, and A. Cairns (2014). 'Sharing Longevity Risk: Why Governments Should Issue Longevity Bonds,' *North American Actuarial Journal*, 18(1): 258–277.

Blake, D. and W. Burrows (2001). 'Survivor Bonds: Helping to Hedge Mortality Risk,' *Journal of Risk and Insurance*, 68(2): 339–348.

Blake, D., A. J. G. Cairns, K. Dowd, and A. R. Kessler (2019). 'Still Living with Mortality: The Longevity Risk Transfer Market after One Decade,' *British Actuarial Journal*, 24: 1–80.

Braun, A. and J. Weber (2017). 'Evolution or Revolution? How Solvency II Will Change the Balance Between Reinsurance and ILS,' *NAIC Journal of Insurance Regulation*, 36: 4.

Bugler, N., K. Maclean, V. Nicenko, and P. Tedesco (2020). 'Reinsurance Sidecars: The Next Stage in the Development of the Longevity Risk Transfer Market,' *North American Actuarial Journal*, 25(1): S25-39.

Cairns, A. J. G. and G. El Boukfaoui (2019). 'Basis Risk in Index-Based Longevity Hedges: A Guide for Longevity Hedgers,' *North American Actuarial Journal*, 25(1): S98-118.

Citi (2016). 'The Coming Pension Crisis,' *Global Perspectives and Solutions*, March.

Credit Suisse (2005). 'Credit Suisse First Boston Introduces Credit Suisse Longevity Index,' *Business Wire*, December 12.

Cummins, J. D. and P. Barrieu (2013). 'Innovations in Insurance Markets: Hybrid and Securitized Risk-Transfer Solutions,' In G. Dionne, ed., *Handbook of Insurance*. New York: Springer, pp. 547–602.

Cummins, J. D. and P. Trainar (2009). 'Securitization, Insurance, and Reinsurance,' *Journal of Risk and Insurance*, 76(3): 463–492.

Cummins, J. D. and M. A. Weiss. (2009). 'Convergence of Insurance and Financial Markets: Hybrid and Securitized Risk-Transfer Solutions,' *Journal of Risk and Insurance*, 76(3): 493–545.

Daniel, W. (2016). 'Supplanting Cash in Annuity Buyouts: Asset-in-Kind Transfers Move Toward Mainstream,' in B.R. Bruce, ed., *Pension & Longevity Risk Transfer for Institutional Investors*. London: Institutional Investor Journals, pp. 14–17.

EIOPA (European Insurance and Occupational Pensions Authority) (2020). 'Equivalence.' https://www.eiopa.europa.eu/browse/international-relations/equivalence_en

Evans, S. (2011). 'Life and Longevity Markets Association Takes Ownership of J. P. Morgan's LifeMetrics Index,' *Artemis.bm*, April 27. https://www.artemis.bm/news/life-and-longevity-markets-association-takes-ownership-of-j-p-morgans-lifemetrics-index/

Evans, S. (2020a). 'First Langhorne Re Transaction Still Elusive for RGA, but Pipeline Building,' *Artemis.bm*, January 30. https://www.artemis.bm/news/first-langhorne-re-transaction-still-elusive-for-rga-but-pipeline-building/

Evans, S. (2020b). 'Aetna's Claim Ratio Well-Below Vitality Re ILS Trigger in Q1 despite COVID-19,' *Artemis.bm*, June 20. https://www.artemis.bm/news/aetnas-claim-ratio-well-below-vitality-re-ils-trigger-in-q1-despite-covid–19/

Evans, S. (2020c). 'Varying Pandemic ILS Impacts, Trapped Capital May be Held for Years: A.M. Best,' *Artemis.bm*, May 11. https://www.artemis.bm/news/varying-pandemic-ils-impacts-trapped-capital-may-be-held-for-years-a-m-best/

Evans, S. (2020d). 'Sidecars & Quota Shares May Face Highest COVID-19 Claims: A.M. Best,' *Artemis.bm*, May 15.

Evans, S. (2020e). 'Insurance Linked Securities Investment Managers & Funds Directory,' *Artemis.bm*. https://www.artemis.bm/news/sidecars-quota-shares-may-face-highest-covid-19-claims-a-m-best/

Evans, S. (2020f). 'Catastrophe Bond & ILS Market Statistics and Data,' *Artemis.bm*, June 20. https://www.artemis.bm/dashboard/cat-bond-ils-market-statistics/

Finken, S. N. and C. Laux (2009). 'Catastrophe Bonds and Reinsurance: The Competitive Effect of Information-Insensitive Triggers,' *Journal of Risk and Insurance*, 76: 3.

Goldman Sachs (2007). 'Goldman Sachs Launches Tradeable Index for Longevity and Mortality Risks,' *Business Wire*, December 14.

Gross, A. (2020). 'World Bank Pandemic Bonds to Pay $133m to Poorest Virus-Hit Nations,' *Financial Times*, April 19.

Hagendorff, B., J. Hagendorff, K. Keasey, and A. Gonzalez (2014). 'The Risk Implications of Insurance Securitization: The Case of Catastrophe Bonds,' *Journal of Corporate Finance*, 25: 387–402.

Hunt, A. and D. Blake (2015). 'Modelling Longevity Bonds: Analysing the Swiss Re Kortis Bond,' *Insurance: Mathematics and Economics*, 63(C): 12–29.

Hymans-Robertson (2009–2020). 'Buy-outs, Buy-ins and Longevity Hedging,' *Quarterly and Semi-Annual Reports*. https://www.hymans.co.uk/insights/research-and-publications

IAIS (International Association of Insurance Supervisors) (2012). 'Reinsurance and Financial Stability,' July 19. https://www.iaisweb.org/file/34046/reinsurance-and-financial-stability

IMF (International Monetary Fund) (2012). 'The Financial Impact of Longevity Risk,' *Global Financial Stability Report*, World Economic and Financial Surveys. Washington, DC: IMF, chapter 4, April, pp. 1-31.

Insurance Services Office , Inc.(2020). 'PCS: ISO's Property Claim Services (PCS) Unit Is an Internationally Recognized Authority on Insured Property Losses from Events,' https://pcs.iso.com/

Joint Forum (2013). 'Longevity Risk Transfer Markets: Market Structure, Growth Drivers and Impediments, and Potential Risks,' Bank for International Settlements, Basel, December.

J. P. Morgan (2007). 'J. P. Morgan Launches Longevity Index,' *Business Wire*, March 13.

Kessler, A. (2019). 'New Solutions to an Age-Old Problem: Innovative Strategies for Managing Pension and Longevity Risk,' *North American Actuarial Journal*, 25(1): 1–18.

Life Insurance Marketing and Research Association (2020). Personal communication. On file with author.

MacMinn, R. and P. Brockett (2017). 'On the Failure (Success) of the Markets for Longevity Risk Transfer,' *Journal of Risk and Insurance*, 84(S1): 299–317.

MacMinn, R. and N. Zhu (2018). 'Hedging Longevity Risk: Does the Structure of the Financial Instrument Matter?' Unpublished manuscript.

Michaelson, A. and J. Mulholland (2014). 'Strategy for Increasing the Global Capacity for Longevity Risk Transfer: Developing Transactions That Attract Capital Markets Investors,' *The Journal of Alternative Investments*, 17(1): 18–27.

Mitchell, O. and D. McCarthy (2002). 'Annuities for an Ageing World,' NBER Working Paper No. 9092. Cambridge, MA: National Bureau of Economic Research.

Moody's (2007). 'Vita Capital III,' Moody's Investors Services, April 9.

NAIC (National Association of Insurance Commissioners) (2019). 'NAIC List of Qualified Jurisdictions.' https://content.naic.org/sites/default/files/inline-files/committees_e_reinsurance_qualified_jurisdictions_list_1.pdf

NYDFS (New York State Department of Financial Services) (2020). 'Certified Reinsurer Information.' https://www.dfs.ny.gov/apps_and_licensing/insurance_companies/certified_reinsurer_information

O'Farrell, S. (2020). 'Longevity Swap Investors Warned over Collateral Calls,' *Pensions Expert*, April 28.

Osborn, T. (2013). 'SG CIB Completes Longevity Trade for Aegon.' *Risk.net*: December 5. https://www.risk.net/derivatives/2317036/sg-cib-completes-longevity-trade-aegon.

OSFI (Office of the Superintendent of Financial Institutions Canada) (2010). 'Guidance for Reinsurance Security Agreements,' December. https://www.osfi-bsif.gc.ca/Eng/fi-if/rai-eri/sp-ps/Pages/rsa.aspx (updated December 23, 2015).

Pruitt, J. S., H. Laing, C .R. Shoss, and D. Moreira (2019). 'Covered Agreement: An Overview,' Eversheds Sutherland Legal Alert, August 20. https://us.eversheds-sutherland.com/mobile/NewsCommentary/Legal-Alerts/196936/Covered-AgreementAn-overview

Sachsenweger, S. and H. Rogge (2011). 'Index-Based Longevity Risk Transfer to Capital Markets,' Deutsche Börse Market Data, September 8.

Sagoo, P. and R. Douglas (2012). 'Recent Innovations in Longevity Risk Management: A New Generation of Tools Emerges,' Eighth International Longevity Risk and Capital Markets Solutions Conference, September 8.

Subramanian, A. and J. Wang (2018). 'Reinsurance versus Securitization of Catastrophe Risk,' *Insurance: Mathematics and Economics*, 82: 55–72.

Swiss Re (2016). 'The Benefit of Global Diversification: How Reinsurers Create Value and manage Risk,' October.

Whittaker, T. (2012). 'Aegon €12 Billion Longevity Swap Shows Appetite of Capital Market for Diversifying Assets,' *Risk.net*, February 27.

Willis Towers Watson (2020). 'Global Pension Assets Study 2020.'

Willis Towers Watson (2014–2019). 'Group Annuity Market Pulse.'

Wolfe, H. (2016). 'The Insider's Guide to the Canadian Annuity Market,' Sun Life Assurance Company of Canada.

Woodall, L. (2013). 'ILS Investors Fuel Collateralised Reinsurance Growth,' *Risk.net*, July 12.

Zelenko, I. (2014). 'Longevity Risk and the Stability of Retirement Systems: The Chilean Longevity Bond Case,' *Journal of Alternative Investments*, 17(1): 35–54.

Chapter 12

Property Tax Deferral

Can a Public-Private Partnership Help Provide Lifetime Income?

Alicia H. Munnell, Wenliang Hou, and Abigail N. Walters

In many states, qualified senior homeowners can defer their property taxes for as long as they stay in their home. By reducing taxes upfront, such programs free up money that can be used for other purposes, providing a stream of income for life that is very similar to having an annuity. The deferred amounts are repaid with interest when the person sells the home or dies, so the programs have no long-run cost for states or localities. Despite these advantages, eligibility is limited and take-up is low. A proposed redesign of the tax deferral program in Massachusetts would (1) open up the program by removing income limits; (2) simplify sign-up; and (3) have the state—rather than the localities—finance the program. This proposal raises issues both with respect to the potential demand for the option and with the potential role for a public-private partnership to finance the start-up costs when loans far exceed repayments. This chapter provides a case for property tax deferral, proposes some design elements, estimates potential costs, and calls for additional ideas to explore how such a broad-based program might work.

In what follows, we first describe the nation's retirement income challenge and the particular problem for states with high housing costs, using Massachusetts as an example. Next we describe the major existing programs for homeowner tax relief in Massachusetts: two that cost the government, and one that allows low-income homeowners to help themselves through limited property tax deferral. Our third section describes the proposal for a new state-wide program of property tax deferral that would be open to all homeowners. A fourth section addresses likely utilization, including an assessment of whether people stay in their homes long enough to make property tax deferral a reasonable option. The fifth section discusses possible roles for the public and private sectors in the financing of such a program, particularly in covering any shortfalls in the early years. The sixth section discusses the impact of a property tax deferral on homeowners by

Alicia H. Munnell et al., *Property Tax Deferral*. In: *New Models for Managing Longevity Risk.*
Edited by Olivia S. Mitchell, Oxford University Press.
© Pension Research Council (2022). DOI: 10.1093/oso/9780192859808.003.0012

comparing outcomes under such a program with those available through reverse mortgages. Our final section concludes that a comprehensive property tax deferral program would provide retirees an efficient way to access their home equity and secure their retirement.

The Retirement Income Challenge

Many retirees are unlikely to have sufficient income to maintain their standard of living once they stop working. The National Retirement Risk Index (NRRI), which relies on data from the Federal Reserve's Survey of Consumer Finances (SCF), compares projected replacement rates—benefits as a percentage of pre-retirement earnings—to target replacement rates that permit households to enjoy the same consumption before and after retirement.[1] The current NRRI estimate shows that about half of today's working-age households are at risk—the risk is larger for the bottom third of households but it is also substantial for those in the middle and top of the income distribution range (Figure 12.1). Therefore, the problem is widespread.

The reasons for this shortfall are twofold: (1) Baby Boomers and generations that follow are going to need more retirement resources; and (2) traditional sources of retirement income are providing less support than in the past.

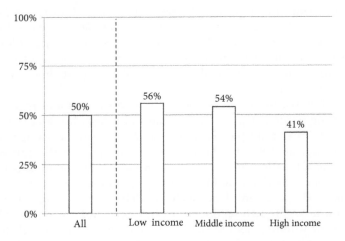

Figure 12.1 Percentage of households 'at risk' at age 65 by income group, 2016
Note: Households are defined as 'at risk' if they are unable to maintain their pre-retirement standard of living in retirement.
Source: Munnell et al. (2018).

On the needs side, the drivers are longer life expectancies coupled with relatively early retirement ages, rising health care costs, and very low interest rates. These factors combined mean that people are going to need to accumulate substantially more retirement resources now than in the past. On the income side, social security will provide less relative to pre-retirement earnings because of the rise in the full retirement age from 65 to 67. In addition, higher Medicare premiums and the taxation of social security benefits for more households will lower *net* benefits. Furthermore, the program faces a 75-year deficit, and additional benefit cuts could be part of a package to restore balance.

The other major source of retirement income, the private retirement system, is not working well for much of the population. Due to the lack of universal coverage, many households end up with no source of retirement income other than social security. And for those households that do have a retirement plan, balances are often modest. In 2016, the typical working household with a 401(k) plan approaching retirement (ages 55–64) had only $135,000 in combined 401(k)/IRA assets (Munnell and Chen 2017). That may sound like a lot to some, but it could provide only $600 per month in retirement income.

However bleak the outlook for the nation as a whole, the situation in high-property-tax states is more serious. The Gerontology Institute at the University of Massachusetts-Boston calculates—for each state—the Elder Economic Insecurity Rate, which is the percentage of single individuals and couples with income below the level required to cover basic living expenses. The most recent report shows that, of the ten states with the highest Elder Economic Insecurity Rate, seven have high levels of property tax (Figure 12.2). The high property taxes mean that high-income states such as Massachusetts, New York, New Jersey, and California have about the same percentage of elderly at risk as low-income states such as Mississippi, Maine, and Louisiana. Policymakers in a number of states have recognized the problem created by high housing costs and have attempted to provide some relief.

Existing Provisions for Property Tax

Twenty-four states currently offer some seniors the ability to defer all of their property taxes until their home is sold or they are deceased.[2] Eligibility depends on age, residence, income (in most instances), and (in some instances) property value. Program parameters are usually set at the state level, but municipalities generally administer the programs and can often adjust their eligibility criteria and interest rates. Typically, to be eligible, homeowners must be age 65 or older and have an annual household income under $20,000. The typical interest rate charged on property tax deferrals

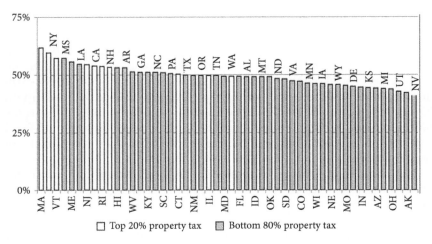

Figure 12.2 Percentage of state single population age 65+ below the Elder Index by property tax level, 2019

Notes: The Elder Index measures the cost of living for older adults by county and state; households that fall below the Index lack sufficient income to meet their basic needs. The property tax level is for homeowners age 65+.

Sources: US Census Bureau, American Community Survey (2018); and Mutchler et al. (2019).

is about six percent. Yet these key program parameters vary widely across states and municipalities. In nine states—Arizona, California, Colorado, Idaho, Illinois, Minnesota, Oregon, Washington, and Wisconsin—the state finances the program, sending money to the local governments to offset lost revenue.

Massachusetts provides an example of how states attempt to alleviate the burden of homeownership for older residents. The state currently has three programs for property tax relief.[3] Two are transfer, or welfare, programs. The Circuit Breaker Tax Credit, administered at the state level, provides a credit against the state income tax to taxpayers age 65+ who own or rent residential property in Massachusetts. The credit equals the amount by which real estate tax payments and half of water and sewer bills exceed 10 percent of the taxpayer's income.[4] The maximum credit is $1,130. The amount of the credit is subject to limitations based on the taxpayer's total income and the assessed value of the real estate (Table 12.1). This program costs the state about $80 million per year. The second program is Senior Property Tax Exemptions, administered at the local level; it provides a $500 exemption on the property tax bill for those age 70+ who meet specific ownership, residency, income, and asset requirements. Cities and towns which bear the cost of this exemption can increase the exempt amount to $1,000 and reduce the

TABLE 12.1 Massachusetts property tax relief provisions for seniors, 2019

Parameter	Provision Circuit breaker	Exemptions	Deferral
Age	65+	70+[a]	65+
Income limit	$60,000 single $75,000 head of household	$13,000 single $15,000 married[b]	$20,000 single or married[c]
$90,000 joint filers			
Asset limit	$808,000 assessed property value	$28,000 single[d] $30,000 married	None
Exemption	Tax credit up to $1,130	$500[e]	Deferral up to 50 percent of fair cash value [f]
Interest rate	N/A	N/A	8 percent
Payment due	N/A	N/A	When homeowner sells property or dies

Notes: [a] Locality may reduce to age 65.
[b] Locality may raise to $20,000 for single or $30,000 for married.
[c] Locality may raise to $60,000. Localities may petition the state to raise the level even higher (above the Circuit Breaker limit for single head of households).
[d] Locality may raise up to $40,000 for single and up to $55,000 for married.
[e] Locality may raise to $1,000.
[f] Homeowners with a mortgage must get permission from their lender to participate in the program.
Sources: Massachusetts Department of Revenue (2019a); and Massachusetts Acts of 2016 (2016).

age to 65. In 2019, cities and towns granted about $10 million in property tax exemptions

The third program is the Senior Property Tax Deferral program, which allows local governments to permit some seniors to defer payment of their property taxes and to recoup those taxes plus interest when the homeowner sells the house or dies. The state sets the program parameters but allows localities some flexibility. For example, the state's maximum gross income for participants is $20,000, but local governments can raise that limit to $60,000 (the Circuit Breaker limit for a single non-head of household).[5] Similarly, the state sets a maximum interest rate of eight percent, but localities can adopt a lower rate. The total value of liens against the property cannot exceed 50 percent of the assessed market value.[6] Once the homeowner sells the home or dies, deferred taxes and accumulated interest must be paid back within six months, during which time interest accrues at a rate of 16 percent.[7]

Figure 12.3 shows that participation in all three programs is limited. In the case of the Circuit Breaker Tax Credit and the Senior Property Tax

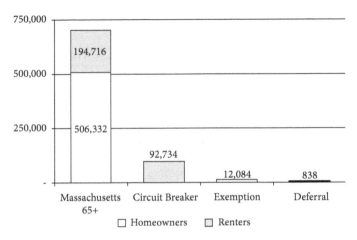

Figure 12.3 Massachusetts property tax payers age 65+ and participants in senior tax relief programs, financial year 2019

Notes: Circuit Breaker figure is for financial year 2017 participants. Exemption and deferral data are for financial year 2019 participants.

Sources: US Census Bureau, American Community Survey (2018); Massachusetts Department of Revenue (2019b); and Massachusetts Department of Revenue, Division of Local Services (2019).

Exemptions, participation clearly reflects income restrictions for eligibility. In the case of the local property tax deferral program, other factors appear to be at play as well. First, many homeowners are not aware of the program (since, given the potential financial burden, only wealthy communities tend to publicize their programs) and many confuse it with other tax credit and exemption programs. Second, homeowners who are eligible and aware may not know how to apply for them; are concerned about a stigma attached to an income-tested program; view the interest rate as too high (especially during the pay-back period); or hesitate to place a lien on their home. A new state-wide Property Tax Deferral Program could address many of these shortcomings.

A Proposal for a New State-wide Property Tax Deferral Program

The proposed program would not be based on income but rather would be open to all homeowners in Massachusetts age 65+. Deferrals would be based on the first $1,000,000 of assessed value on a primary residence; this amount would be adjusted each year to keep pace with inflation. The rationales for this approach are fivefold. First, the problem of inadequate retirement income is not limited to low-income homeowners; the NRRI shows that many homeowners in the top and middle thirds of the income distribution also will be at risk in retirement. Second, the program is self-financing: homeowners repay the deferred property tax with interest when they move or die. Third, universal eligibility would eliminate any stigma associated with the program and enhance its acceptability. Fourth, the absence of income limits simplifies the administration of the program and avoids people being denied access should they make a large 401(k) withdrawal in a given year. Finally, history suggests that programs for poor people often turn out to be poor programs, so universal participation enhances the chances for the program's success.

The program would function as follows (see Appendix A for further details):

- Individuals age 65+ with a primary residence in Massachusetts would be able to defer their property taxes until the sum of deferrals, accumulated interest, and mortgages reached 60 percent of the first million dollars of assessed value.
- Participation in the program would be triggered by simply checking a box on the city or town's first-quarter property tax bill (see Appendix B for a sample tax bill).
- The city or town would continue to have an automatic lien on the home for the unpaid municipal property taxes; this lien would still be senior to other liens such as mortgages.[8]
- When the city or town forwards the tax bill to the state, the state would send the city or town an amount equal to the deferred taxes.
- The interest rate each year would be set at the state's borrowing cost plus a buffer to cover administrative costs and defaults.
- Once notified that the homeowner has moved or died, the city or town would collect the deferred taxes plus interest upon the sale of the property and remit this amount to the state.
- The deferred taxes and interest would be due within one year, after which the interest rate penalty would begin.

This new program would achieve several important goals. First, an average older homeowner in Massachusetts (without a mortgage) would be able to defer about $5,000 a year in property taxes (see Appendix C). This amount substantially exceeds the funds provided though the state's existing tax deferral, exemption, and credit programs, which could be phased out gradually for homeowners (retaining the Circuit Breaker for renters) as part of this initiative. The homeowner could choose to defer for a single year to cover, say, the cost of a new roof, or to defer on an annual basis to supplement social security and any other retirement income—although such flexibility raises some administrative issues.[9]

Second, property tax deferral would help seniors to age in their own homes. Survey after survey finds that people strongly prefer to stay in their own communities (AARP 2014; Age Wave 2015; Hodgson 2022; Chapter 6, this volume). Moreover, enabling those with dementia to be cared for in their own home by a combination of family and outside support could help control future Medicaid costs. Aging in place also allows homeowners to enjoy the benefit of any appreciation in the market value of their homes. Reducing the costs associated with homeownership would increase the ability of older homeowners to achieve these outcomes.

Third, the program would alleviate the burden on Massachusetts' local governments. Under current provisions, widespread use of a tax deferral program would have a significant short-term impact on local budgets. The proposed program removes this burden by having the state advance to cities and towns the deferral amount and receive the money it is owed when houses are sold.

In 2019, Massachusetts legislators introduced two significant bills to enhance the ability of senior homeowners to defer their property taxes. The first bill—H.3617 'An Act relative to senior property tax deferral'—would immediately improve the existing income-tested program by reducing residency tenure requirements, increasing income eligibility to the level of the Circuit Breaker Tax Credit, reducing the default interest rate, and delaying the interest rate penalty to a year after the homeowner's death (General Court of the Commonwealth of Massachusetts 2020). The second bill—S.1693 'A Resolve providing for an investigation and study by a special commission relative to a senior state property tax deferral program'—proposed a three-year pilot to test a universal state-run program open to all households ages 65 and over, modeled after the proposal described above (General Court of the Commonwealth of Massachusetts (2020a). Under this new program, local governments would still administer the program, while the state would handle the finances. A pilot program would help answer key questions like what percentage of people are likely to participate, how much start-up funding is needed, and the program's effect on the economic security of homeowners. The following sections describe what is known currently about each of these questions.

Program Participation

The extent to which homeowners participate in a property tax deferral program depends, in part, on the stability of housing patterns: that is, does it make sense for people to tap their home equity to cover expenses in retirement, or will they need the full equity for a subsequent move? Participation also depends on how well the program is publicized and understood by potential participants, and on the ease of the application process.

The stability of housing patterns

A potential reason for homeowners' reluctance to borrow against their houses is the concern that, if they did decide to move, they would have to pay back the loan with interest and could be left with inadequate resources at a vulnerable time in their lives.

A recent study examined the stability of homeownership precisely to assess whether borrowing against home equity is a reasonable option (Munnell et al. 2020), using data from the 1992–2016 waves of the Health and Retirement Study (HRS). To describe the typical housing trajectories of people in their 50s until death required the creation of a synthetic cohort, 'splicing' together two cohorts to create a complete picture of late-life housing trajectories. Sequence analysis was used to group together common residential patterns among homeowners who do move. The analysis uncovered four groups (Figure 12.4).

The first two groups could be characterized as 'never movers' and 'stable movers.' Group 1 (53%) includes those who never move from the original home they owned in their early 50s. Group 2 (17%) moves around retirement into a new owner-occupied home and then generally stays in that new home until death. Both of these groups end up with substantially

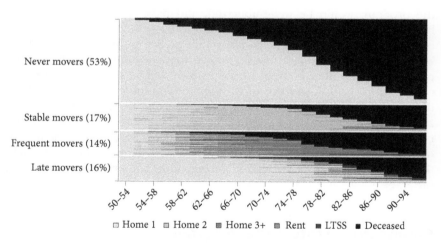

Figure 12.4 Sequence groups for homeowning households in the synthetic cohort, 1992–2016

Source: Munnell et al. (2020).

more housing wealth than the movers the last time they are observed. The movers consist of two distinct groups—'frequent movers' (Group 3) and 'late movers' (Group 4). The 'frequent movers' (14%) end up with less combined housing and financial wealth than any other group at the end of the observation period. The 'late movers' (16%) stay in their original homes until their 80s and then move into either a rental or a long-term services and support (LTSS) facility, likely due to a health impairment.

The overall conclusion is that most homeowners—the exception being the 'frequent movers'—experience enough residential stability to tap home equity through property tax deferrals. The question then is whether they would choose to participate.

Participation rates in existing programs

To date, property tax deferral programs appear to be used infrequently. As noted above, one practical hurdle is awareness of their existence: the programs are generally administered locally and have limited budgets for outreach.[10] In addition, the actual process of applying poses a barrier, as potential participants must often mail or deliver tax returns, deeds, and birth certificates with application forms. Despite these hurdles, over 10 percent of eligible homeowners in Oregon participated in its property tax deferral program from the mid-1980s to mid-1990s—a period of rising property tax rates and high interest rates for consumer loans.[11]

One could expect participation in an improved Massachusetts program to exceed that of Oregon, since the property tax burden is substantial, the program would be well-publicized, and participation would require homeowners simply to check a box on their tax bills. In that environment, one would expect that participation would be driven by need. The NRRI, based on data from the 2016 SCF, predicts that—without using their home equity—61 percent of homeowners age 55–59 will be at risk in retirement, compared to just 33 percent of this group if home equity is used. A little over half of these homeowners report a strong bequest motive (34%) and are probably unlikely to participate in the program. But those with no bequest motive (11%) may well be willing to defer taxes, and perhaps half of those with a weak bequest motive (17%) as well. These assumptions yield the estimate of roughly a 20 percent participation rate with a well-publicized program.

Financing a State-wide Program

The proposed property tax deferral program would be revenue neutral at the household level; the state provides the cities and towns the money up front and recoups the outlay with interest when the home is sold. Two

TABLE 12.2 Home value remaining and survival probability at selected ages for a household starting deferrals at age 65

Age	Home value used plus interest (%)	Home value remaining (%)	Survival probability (%)
95	37	63	29
100	45	55	8
105	52	48	1

Note: The calculations assume no mortgage on the property and use the same assumptions as the model (see Appendix D).
Source: Authors' calculations.

buffers in the proposal would reduce risks to the sponsor. First, a surcharge of 50 basis points could be added to the interest rate to cover administrative costs. Second, deferrals would be capped to protect the sponsor against a decline in home value below the amount owed due to a failure to maintain the home or a more general decline in housing prices.

While stopping deferrals once a homeowner owes more than a set percentage of the home's assessed value in deferred taxes, interest, and mortgage protects the sponsor, it could force some homeowners to start paying taxes again after years of deferrals. Thus, setting the appropriate cap involves striking a balance between protecting the sponsor and protecting homeowners. A cap at 60 percent appears to balance these interests. To reach this cap, a 65-year-old homeowner without a mortgage could defer taxes every year for over 40 years—a deferral period that few homeowners would require (Table 12.2). From the sponsor's perspective, this cap would leave at least 40 percent of the first million dollars of home value as a buffer to ensure that proceeds from selling the house would be sufficient to repay the deferred taxes plus interest.[12] In a similar vein, the cap would limit the risk to the sponsor of falling property values, as the dollar amount of the cap would fluctuate with changes in the assessed value.

While a cap and a buffer on the interest rate should protect the sponsor from losses, the program start-up would involve an extended period when deferred property tax payments would exceed the amounts recouped from the sale of houses due to a move or the death of the homeowner. The financial shortfall would need to be covered either by the state or through some arrangement with the private sector.

To get a sense of the pattern of the shortfall during the start-up and to understand the factors that could affect its size, consider a world where the amount of property taxes collected did not increase and the population of homeowners over 65 remained constant. In this simple model, the amount required to finance a property tax deferral program would be highest in the first year of the program, declining each year thereafter as people exited the

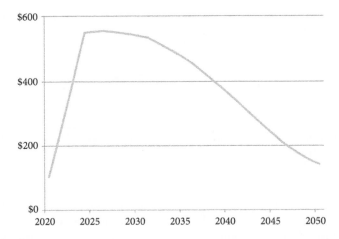

Figure 12.5 Annual net property tax deferral program cost, millions of 2019 dollars, 2020–2050

Source: Authors' projections of proposed Massachusetts program.

program and paid back the taxes they had deferred. The total outstanding amount therefore would grow quickly at first before stabilizing as taxes paid back began to equal new deferrals.

In reality, home prices do increase, the population over age 65 is growing, and interest and administrative expenses accrue each year. So instead of reaching a steady state, the revolving debt account would grow. The cost projections presented below take all these factors into account. In addition, the assumption is that the 20 percent of homeowners age 65+ who are estimated to participate in the program would defer taxes every year until the last homeowner died. The results of the model show that—with a five-year phase-in—the program would require about $100 million in new loans in the first year, with the amount rising to $555 million in 2026 before declining (see Figure 12.5). The question is how to finance these shortfalls, particularly during the start-up period.

A public approach

In our view, the most efficient approach would be for the state of Massachusetts to cover the costs through borrowing. That is, when an age 65+ household in Natick, MA, checks the box on its property tax bill indicating a decision to defer its $5,000 in property taxes, Natick would automatically have a lien against the home for the deferred taxes. Natick would notify the state and the state would then forward $5,000 to Natick. The state would then need some way to cover the $5,000 expenditure and associated interest costs in its budget.

Since general obligation bonds are typically utilized only for capital expenditures, and the terms of the bonds are typically tied to the projects that are being funded, the most logical vehicle would be debt based on anticipated revenues. This approach could involve Revenue Anticipation Notes (RANs) or Tax Anticipation Notes (TANs), which are general obligations of the state but are repaid with the revenues or taxes collected at some point in the future. Traditionally, these notes are shorter term obligations (almost like commercial paper), typically repaid within the same fiscal year. But experts suggest that the proposed legislation could extend that term. For example, in the early 1990s, the state issued a seven-year general obligation debt to fund the deficit, in anticipation of revenues to be collected in the future. Regardless of the specific approach taken, homeowners would only be charged the low interest rate that states would have paid on the debt, which would have been exempt from federal and state personal income tax.

The bond deal would be much easier to structure if interest were paid to the bond holders each year. One option is for the state to front the interest out of its budget each year and get repaid when the property is sold. Some experts are skeptical, however, as to whether the state would be willing to take on this responsibility—even though the interest would amount to only a tiny fraction of the budget. A second option is for the homeowner to pay the interest and administrative surcharge each year instead of including these costs in the deferred amount. While the latter approach would simplify the bond deal and substantially reduce borrowing amounts, it would also complicate the program and perhaps dissuade homeowners from participating. Of course, the alternative is not to pay the interest each year but rather to issue zero-coupon bonds, which is a way to finance the interest through borrowing. But zero-coupon bonds are more expensive and rarely used by state governments. In any event, financing the accruing interest would need to be addressed.

For calculating the cost of the program, we have assumed that the interest on the deferred taxes is financed by borrowing. The borrowed amounts would add to Massachusetts' outstanding debt, which currently equals about 14 percent of gross state product (GSP). At its peak, program borrowing would increase Massachusetts' debt outstanding from 14 percent to 15.1 percent of GSP (Figure 12.6).[13] Thereafter, the program's impact would decline steadily. The key question for the state is whether the additional borrowing would affect its credit rating. One would think that since the deferred taxes are secured by liens on the properties, rating agencies would conclude that the financial strength of the state had not been compromised.

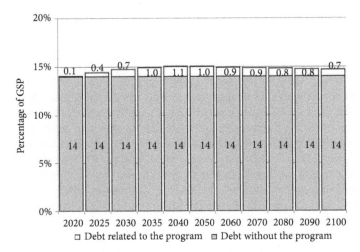

Figure 12.6 Massachusetts debt relative to gross state product with and without the program, assuming 20 percent participation rate, 2020–2100

Sources: Commonwealth of Massachusetts (2002–2019); Federal Reserve Bank of St. Louis (2018); and authors' projections.

In the end, the state must decide if it is willing to take on the financing of a broad-based property tax deferral program. If the state is reluctant to do so, the obvious question is whether private sources of funding would be available.

Relying on the private sector

It is possible that a private-sector company might be interested in funding a property tax deferral program, providing it generated a meaningful volume of transactions. One approach might involve a private financial intermediary working directly with cities and towns. That is, when a 65-year-old Natick homeowner checks the box that he or she would like to defer $5,000 of property taxes, the private company would give the town of Natick $5,000 and then take an assignment of the deferred tax amounts and the related lien on the homeowner's house. The company would repeat this process with other Massachusetts cities and towns. The attractiveness of such a proposition would depend in the first instance on the interest rate the company could charge the homeowner. But even with an interest rate noticeably above that charged by the state, the company might have to wait 30 years or more to get back its $5,000 plus interest. To get an immediate payment, the company could potentially package together a batch of these loans, securitize them, and sell the securitization instruments on the open market. The success of such transactions depends on how receptive investors are to the new security.

The costs of a private company dealing with 300+ cities and towns in Massachusetts at a local level could be prohibitively expensive. Alternatively, the private financial intermediary could work directly with the state, whereby the state would aggregate all the property tax deferrals and related tax liens. It would then sell these claims to the private financial intermediary, which would securitize them and sell the securities. This approach would require less private-sector involvement, but the state would have to charge a rate higher than its general obligation borrowing rate to compensate the financial intermediary for liquidating these claims earlier in the process.

One option might be to have the state's portion of the program overseen by the Massachusetts Housing Finance Agency (MassHousing).[14] This state agency offers numerous programs to facilitate homeownership, so a property tax deferral program might be a logical addition to its portfolio. The agency has the ability to issue tax-exempt debt, and it also issues mortgage debt which it then securitizes. Given its focus and expertise, MassHousing might be able to facilitate the private financing of a state property tax deferral program.

These two approaches represent different options for how involved a private company could be in managing the program. In the first instance, the private financial intermediary could take on the task of providing educational materials for local officials. In the second instance, the company could work directly with the state or MassHousing to structure and manage the program. A question of sequencing also arises. The government could get the program up and running by issuing government debt and then, if reluctant to increase its indebtedness further, invite a private financial intermediary to purchase and securitize these claims.

The involvement of the private sector requires a clear trade-off. The costs to the homeowner would be higher with private-sector involvement, but a less expensive publicly financed program is of no use to anyone if it is never enacted.

Effects on Homeowners

Tapping home equity would provide a way for many resource-strapped seniors to make ends meet or to maintain their pre-retirement standard of living. In fact, for many households, particularly those with less wealth, their home equity is larger than their financial assets. They could access their equity most directly by selling the house and purchasing a smaller, less expensive house for their retirement. Such a shift would not only produce a cash bundle but also it might reduce the expenses associated with homeownership. The problem is that most retirees are attached to their homes and want to age in place. For retirees who want to stay put, the only alternative is to borrow against their home. This borrowing could be done through a state property tax deferral program or a reverse mortgage.

Property tax deferrals and reverse mortgages are similar in three ways: (1) they require homeowners to occupy the home as their primary residence;[15] (2) they allow older homeowners to tap their home equity while remaining in their home; and (3) they are repaid when the borrowers sell the home, no longer occupy it as a primary residence, or die. However, these approaches also differ along three dimensions: complexity, cost, and access to funds.

Complexity

Relative to reverse mortgages, property tax deferrals are a simple way to tap home equity. Essentially all reverse mortgages are government insured Home Equity Conversion Mortgages (HECMs), available to homeowners age 62+. The application process is daunting, and borrowers need to meet many requirements before they can be approved for a reverse mortgage. They need to:

- certify that at least one of the owners is over age 62;
- own the property free and clear or have paid down a considerable amount;
- verify their income, assets, monthly living expenses, and credit history;
- have a history of timely payment for real estate taxes and hazard and flood insurance;
- have no delinquency on any federal debt;
- ensure that the property meets all of the Federal Housing Authority's standards and flood requirements; and
- participate in a consumer information session given by a Department of Housing and Urban Development (HUD)-approved HECM counselor.

In comparison, homeowners applying for a property tax deferral would only need to certify that:

- at least one of the owners is over age 65; and
- they owe less than 60 percent of the property's assessed value in deferred taxes, accrued interest, and mortgages.

While mandatory counseling sessions would not be required for property tax deferral, a major educational initiative by cities and towns would be needed to ensure that applicants fully understood that deferring taxes— in the absence of appreciation in house prices—reduces the amount that could be left to their heirs. But property tax deferral—checking a box on the property tax bill—is an infinitely easier way to access home equity than taking out a reverse mortgage.

Costs

Two types of costs can be involved in accessing home equity: up-front costs to gain access to the product and interest costs associated with the loan (to be repaid, in both cases, when the homeowner moves or dies).

Reverse mortgages have both up-front costs and an interest charge on funds borrowed. In the case of a $500,000 house, the upfront cost would total about $19,000—a $6,000 origination fee, a $10,000 insurance premium, and $2,500 in other closing costs.[16] In terms of costs of borrowed funds, the interest rate is set at 2.5 percentage points over London Interbank Offered Rate (LIBOR), which in January 2020 was 2 percent.[17] Another 0.5 percentage point is added to the rate for ongoing insurance costs to bring the total to 5 percent.

In contrast, borrowing through a property tax deferral program would involve no up-front costs and most likely a lower interest rate. If, as discussed above, the government funded the program by issuing longer term TANs or RANs, the interest rate plus buffer could be as low as 2.5 percent as of January 2020.[18] In short, the costs for a homeowner to tap home equity would be substantially lower through property tax deferral than taking out a reverse mortgage.

Access to funds

Access to funds has two dimensions: the amount that can be borrowed against the house and flexibility in accessing those funds.

In terms of the maximum amount the homeowner can borrow, a comparison between reverse mortgages and property tax deferrals requires some assumptions. The amount available via a reverse mortgage depends on the age of the youngest borrower or eligible non-borrowing spouse; the current interest rate; and the lesser of the appraised value, the HECM Federal Housing Administration (FHA) mortgage limit of $765,000, or the sale price. Reverse mortgage borrowers can choose equal monthly payments, a line of credit, a combination of monthly payments and a line of credit, or a single disbursement lump sum. Typically, HECM loans are set up as a line of credit (Pinnacle Actuarial Resources 2019). Let us assume for purposes of comparison, however, that homeowners want their money up front. In early 2020, the 65-year-old owner of a $500,000 house could receive $230,000 through a reverse mortgage.[19] If the owner accessed that money and used the 4 percent rule of thumb (the withdrawal rate that should allow the home-owner not to exhaust the principal), the $230,000 would provide $9,200 in additional annual income for as long as the homeowner was alive.[20]

For the same $500,000 house, property tax deferral would reduce the average homeowner's expenses—and thereby increase income available for items—by $5,000 annually. Thus, the reverse mortgage offers the home-owner the ability to borrow more against home equity than a property tax deferral program. This relationship holds until the house value exceeds the FHA limit of $765,000, after which the gap between the two sources nar-rows a bit as property tax deferral (as proposed) would be applied to the first $1,000,000 of assessed value. In no case, however, could a property tax defer-ral program offer a homeowner hundreds of thousands of dollars up front.

On the flexibility side, both approaches offer the homeowner some lee-way. One advantage of property tax deferral is that homeowners can choose to use the program to cover only unusual expenditures, such as a new roof, or to use it year after year to supplement their other sources of retirement income—although, as noted above, this option raises some administrative issues. Reverse mortgages also offer flexibility in that borrowers can (and do) take their money as a line of credit. Under the HECM program, any unused balance of the line of credit grows over time at the same interest rate used for the loan. So, borrowers selecting this option see an increase over time in the amount available to them. The downside of not borrowing all the money available through the line of credit is that the homeowner will have paid substantially more in up-front costs than necessary.

The bottom line from the perspective of the householder is that the prop-erty tax is far less complicated and less costly than a reverse mortgage, but for most homeowners the reverse mortgage offers the opportunity to access more home equity. Of course, accessing more home equity is not costless; the more that must be repaid with interest at moving or death, the less is left for homeowners or their heirs.

Conclusion

Many retirees will have insufficient money from conventional retirement programs to maintain their standards of living when they stop working. To help support themselves, they will need to tap into their home equity, which is the major asset for most middle-income households. But tapping home equity is difficult. Most people are reluctant to downsize and, even when they do, they rarely reduce their housing expenses. Reverse mortgages are an option, but most households are put off by the enormity of the decision, the complexity of the product, and the high up-front costs.

A state-wide property tax deferral program overcomes the hurdles to accessing home equity. Property tax deferral does not provide access to as much home equity as a reverse mortgage, but the offsetting advantage is that some of the house value after the repayment of the loan and interest will be available for a bequest.

At the household level, the proposed program is revenue neutral: all taxes owed by a participating household are paid back, with interest sufficient to cover the cost of borrowing and to cover administrative expenses. Nevertheless, because loans are made well in advance of repayments, the sponsor of the plan must cover start-up costs. If the state government simply borrowed money to cover the annual outlays, Massachusetts' ratio of debt to GSP would rise from 14 percent to 15.1 percent. The alternative is to involve the private sector. This decision would raise the costs to homeowners, but nevertheless may be a necessary step to get a broad-based program up and running.

Appendix A

Outline of Proposed Massachusetts Property Tax Deferral Program

Individuals age 65 or older who have owned a home in MA and occupied it as their principal residence for at least five years would be eligible to defer their property taxes.

The state's new property tax deferral program procedure would work as follows:

(1) The first-quarter property tax bill for all cities and towns will include a check-box where homeowners certify their eligibility for the program and indicate their desire to participate on an annual basis.

(2) Under Chapter 60 Section 37 of the Massachusetts General Laws, unpaid municipal property taxes are automatically secured by a lien on the home. The city or town would continue to retain the lien for deferred taxes and interest; and this lien would still be prior to other liens, such as mortgages.[21]

(3) For those choosing to participate, the city or town will forward a copy of the property tax bill to the Massachusetts Department of Revenue.

(4) The Massachusetts Department of Revenue will send the town an amount equal to the deferred taxes.

(5) The legislation would provide that the state will be repaid the principal plus interest when the homeowner sells the home or dies. In the case of property owned jointly, the state will be repaid when the surviving owner sells or dies. The deferral amount can also be repaid earlier at the homeowner's discretion.

(6) The homeowner can defer property taxes until the sum of deferrals, accumulated interest, and mortgages reaches 60 percent of the first million dollars of assessed value.

(7) The interest rate each year will be set at the state's borrowing cost plus a buffer of 50 basis points to cover administrative costs and defaults.

(8) The state will borrow the funds each year to transfer an amount equal to the deferred taxes for that year to the city or town.

(9) Once notified that the home has been sold, the city or town will collect the deferred taxes plus interest and remit this amount to the state.

(10) The deferred taxes and interest would be due within one year, after which the interest rate penalty would begin.

Appendix B

Sample property tax bill

COMMONWEALTH OF MASSACHUSETTS
CITY OF BOSTON
OFFICE OF THE COLLECTOR-TREASURER
ONE CITY HALL SQUARE, BOSTON, MA 02201

FY 2020
CITY OF BOSTON
REAL ESTATE TAX

Office of the Assessor   617-635-4287

Office of the Collector   617-635-4131

Office Hours: Monday - Friday 9:00 AM – 5:00 PM

JANE DOE
123 MAIN STREET
BOSTON MA 02201

PAYMENTS CAN BE MADE ONLINE AT:
www.boston.gov/taxpayments
credit/debit card payments are subject to fees

If you are using a payment service to pay this bill, you MUST indicate the **TAXYEAR** and **BILL NUMBER** on the check.

MAKE CHECKS PAYABLE TO:
THE CITY OF BOSTON

MAIL CHECKS TO:
BOX 55808
BOSTON, MA 02205

Do not send cash

TAXPAYER'S COPY
1st Quarter

WARD	PARCEL NO.	BILL NUMBER	BANK NO.
1	12345-123	123456	123

LOCATION			AREA
123 MAIN STREET			

Tax Rate	RESIDENTIAL	OPEN SPACE	COMMERCIAL	INDUSTRIAL
Per $1,000	10.00	10.00	25.00	25.00

CLASS	DESCRIPTION	ASSESSED OWNER
CD	Building	JANE DOE

IMPORTANT: SEE REVERSE SIDE FOR IMPORTANT INFORMATION

TOTAL FULL VALUATION	500,000
RESIDENTIAL EXEMPTION	.00
TOTAL TAXABLE VALUATION	.00
PRELIMINARY OVERDUE	.00
SPECIAL ASSESSMENTS	.00
CODE VIOLATIONS	.00
TOTAL TAX & SPEC. ASSMNT. DUE	.00
PERSONAL EXEMPTIONS	.00
PAYMENTS TO DATE/CREDITS	.00
NET TAX & SPEC. ASSMNT. DUE	.00
TAX PAYMENTS DUE BY 08/01/2020	1,250.00
TAXES DEFERRED	.00
FEES	.00
INTEREST	.00

TOTAL DUE	
Pay by 08/01/2020	$1,250.00

You may be eligible to defer your tax payment on the assessed value of your property up to $1 million.

You are eligible to defer paying your property taxes if you are over the age of 65, own and occupy your home solely for residential purposes, and the sum of your deferrals, accumulated interest, and mortgages are less than 60 percent of the total full valuation of your house.

If you defer paying your property taxes, deferred taxes will accrue 2.5 percent interest each year. But you will not have to pay back the taxes or interest until you sell your home or you and your spouse pass away and leave the house to an heir.

To defer your taxes this year, check the box under your total due.

OR defer paying this amount by checking the following box:

I wish to defer my taxes for this quarter and the rest of this fiscal year. I certify that I am eligible and that the sum of my deferrals, accumulated interest, and mortgages are less than 60 percent of the total full valuation of my house as stated above.

☐

Appendix C

Effect of Property Tax Deferral Program on Homeowners in Massachusetts

On average, homeowners age 65+ in Massachusetts will be able to defer about $5,000 per year in tax expenditures through the proposed program. This average deferral amount varies by county, from a low of $3,614 in Bristol County to a high of $5,963 in Middlesex County.

TABLE C1. Average property value and tax for households age 65+, 2017

County	Property value ($)	Property tax ($)	Median income (before taxes) ($)
State-wide average	475,754	4,745	63,050
Barnstable	562,732	4,068	62,460
Berkshire	326,970	3,378	45,500
Bristol	332,937	3,614	58,000
Dukes	652,153	3,525	58,000
Essex	469,248	5,138	67,070
Franklin	315,913	4,707	69,700
Hampden	240,417	3,862	53,700
Hampshire	294,059	4,325	66,200
Middlesex	654,093	5,963	71,090
Nantucket	652,153	3,525	58,000
Norfolk	590,009	5,644	74,200
Plymouth	404,798	4,539	62,100
Suffolk	702,768	3,898	71,900
Worcester	357,330	4,847	59,250

Note: American Community Survey (ACS) Public Use Microdata Sample (PUMS) is used to calculate county-level statistics; PUMS is a subsample of the full ACS (IPUMS) sample.
Source: US Census Bureau, American Community Survey (2018).

Appendix D

Modeling assumptions and sources for state-wide Massachusetts deferral program

TABLE D1. Modeling assumptions and sources for statewide Massachusetts deferral program

Variable	Assumption	Sources
Economic Variables		
Housing price appreciation	0.5 percent real	*All-Transactions House Price Index for the United States* (1980–2018).
State ACS borrowing cost	1.2 percent real	a
Demographic Variables		
Homeowners age 65+ in Massachusetts	506,332	US Census Bureau (2018) *American Community Survey*
Average Massachusetts home value	$475,754	US Census Bureau (2018) *American Community Survey*
Average Massachusetts property tax rate	1 percent	US Census Bureau (2018) *American Community Survey*
Mortality	Age-based period life table	SSA Period Life Table 2019)
Population growth	Based on UMass (2019–2035); and SSA (2035–2100).	University of Massachusetts Donahue Institute (2015); 2019 *SS Trustees Report*
Program Variables		
Borrowing cap	60 percent of home value assuming no mortgage	Program assumption
Interest charged to household	State borrowing cost +50 basis points for administration	Program assumption
When deferral and interest paid back for married households	When last member of a couple dies	Assumption for estimate
Participation rate	20 percent	NRRI[b]
Phase-in period for the program	5 years	Program assumption

Notes: [a] Massachusetts assumed borrowing rate is based on a 10-year general obligation bond rate, which historically tracks closely to the 10-year treasury bond rate. The 10-year treasury yield over the past two decades averaged 1.2 percent in real terms. Financial institutions such as J. P. Morgan use the same long-run projection for 10-year treasury bonds. See Electronic Municipal Market Access (2005-2019) and J. P. Morgan (2019).
[b] Share of NRRI homeowning households ages 55–59 who are at risk of being unable to maintain pre-retirement standard of living with no bequest motive plus half of at risk households with a moderate bequest motive

Acknowledgements

The authors thank Joseph Craven (former Deputy Treasurer of the Massachusetts' Pension Investment Division and former Managing Director of Retirement Policy at BlackRock) for his detailed review of the draft and his extremely helpful comments. His insights were an invaluable addition to the chapter.

Notes

1. For details on the NRRI methodology, see Munnell et al. (2018).
2. For detailed information on each state's program, see Lincoln Institute of Land Policy (2019).
3. In addition, qualified senior homeowners can work off *up to* $1,500 on their property tax bill by volunteering for their city or town. The city or town administers the program, keeping track of hours worked, and credits for each hour worked an amount not to exceed the minimum wage ($12.75). Each city or town can change the income limits and benefit amounts up to the maximum. The tax work-off credit cannot exceed the total tax due after any other exemptions. An approved representative may do the volunteer work for people physically unable to provide such services. See Massachusetts Acts of 2016 (2016).
4. Renters are also eligible for the Circuit Breaker Credit, if one-quarter of their annual rent exceeds 10 percent of their income.
5. In Massachusetts, localities may petition the state for permission to set the income limit even higher than the Circuit Breaker limit for single head of households. For instance, Newton set their income requirement at $86,000, well above the $60,000 Circuit Breaker limit.
6. Any mortgage lender must agree that the locality's interest in the property would take priority over all other interests (Massachusetts Acts of 2016).
7. After six months, the treasurer may petition to foreclose the lien on the property.
8. The legislation enacting the deferral program will need to provide that the lien continues during the deferral period. Under existing law, the lien disappears if foreclosure proceedings are not commenced within a specific period after the tax is due.
9. The ability to turn the deferral on and off would have to be carefully delineated. At a minimum, the election should properly be done on an annual—as opposed to quarterly—basis. In addition, for the homeowner who defers in 2020, but pays full taxes in 2021, does the 2021 payment go to pay off the 2020 deferral or to cover the current year only? A simpler, but less flexible, approach would have the election carry forward unless the homeowner revokes the deferral and repays the deferral in full.
10. For example, a 1998 AARP report found that just 20 percent of people who were eligible for property tax relief programs knew they existed. But even of those who knew of the programs, just 1.4 percent participated.
11. This estimate was derived using Oregon Legislative Revenue Office (2001); Oregon Department of Revenue (2009); and authors' calculations from US Census Bureau, American Community Survey (1960–2008).

12. Almost 60 percent of Massachusetts homeowners age 65+ own their home free and clear (US Census Bureau, American Community Survey, 2018).

13. The projection assumes a population growth pattern that follows the University of Massachusetts Donahue Institute (2015) for the short term and the SSA Trustees Report (2019) for the long term; a home appreciation rate of 0.5 percent in real terms; a 1.2 percent state borrowing rate in real terms; a 14 percent debt to GSP ratio (a stable ratio from 2011 to 2018) in the absence of the program, and a 2.1 percent growth rate for GSP. See Appendix D for details on model assumptions.

14. For information on the agency's role in encouraging homeownership, see Massachusetts Department of Housing (2020).

15. Ensuring that the property is owner-occupied raises an administrative issue for property tax deferral programs. Even though prohibited, a 65-year-old could defer property taxes and then rent out the home. Cities and towns do not currently provide any oversight in this area. On the other hand, MassHousing does have this obligation for some of its programs, which offers another reason for considering embedding the program within the agency.

16. In this example, the origination fee used is the maximum allowed (the greater of $2,500 or 2% of the first $200,000 of the home's value plus 1% of the amount over $200,000); the insurance premium is calculated as 2 percent of the home value for all borrowers (based on data since late 2017); and the estimate for other closing costs (which include appraisal and legal fees) relies on the calculator from the National Reverse Mortgage Lenders Association (NRMLA 2020).

17. The interest rate in this example is an adjustable rate, like most reverse mortgage loans taken out by homeowners. The lender's margin of 2.5 percent comes from NRMLA. For historical statistics, such as adjustable rates and fixed rates on all HECM originations, see the monthly publications by HUD. Interest rates may have declined as a result of the COVID-19 pandemic, but this chapter relies on rates from a less atypical period.

18. The estimate used here reflects the most recent data available. Given the COVID-19 pandemic, the rate may have declined since January 2020.

19. HECM principal limit factors (PLFs) provide the percentage of the maximum claim amount (MCA) allowable in total cash draws, given the age of the borrower(s) and the 'expected' interest rate of the loan. Based on the HECM PLF tables (effective October 2, 2017), the factor for a homeowner at age 65 with the assumed interest rate (one-year LIBOR rate plus lender's margin only) is 0.459, which yields $230,000 for a $500,000 house.

20. Regarding the 4 percent rule, some investment experts have suggested it is outdated and that individuals would be safer using a lower withdrawal given the prolonged environment of low returns on fixed-income portfolios. Alternatively, if instead of using any such rule of thumb the homeowner purchased an annuity, the annual income would be greater—$14,450 for a single life and $12,200 if the homeowner selected a joint and survivor product. But few people actually purchase annuities. The annuity amount is calculated using market quotes as of January 22, 2020, from WebAnnuities Insurance Agency, Inc. for a 65-year-old male in Massachusetts.

21. The legislation enacting the deferral program will need to provide that the lien continues during the deferral period. Under existing law, the lien disappears if foreclosure proceedings are not commenced within a specific period after the tax is due.

References

AARP Public Policy Institute (1998). 'Awareness and Popularity of Property Tax Relief Programs,' Report No. 9803, Washington, DC.

AARP Public Policy Institute (2014). 'What is Livable? Community Preferences of Older Adults,' Report No. 2014-01, Washington, DC.

Age Wave (2015). 'Home in Retirement: More Freedom, New Choices,' Emeryville, CA.

Commonwealth of Massachusetts (2002–2019). *Comprehensive Annual Financial Reports, Fiscal Years 2001–2018.* Boston, MA: Commonwealth of Massachusetts.

Electronic Municipal Market Access (2005–2019). 'Massachusetts General Obligation Bond Rates.' https://emma.msrb.org/IssuerHomePage/State?state=MA

Federal Reserve Bank of St. Louis (1980–2018). 'All-Transactions House Price Index for the United States.' St. Louis, MO: US Bureau of Economic Analysis.

Federal Reserve Bank of St. Louis (2018). 'Total Gross Domestic Product for Massachusetts.' St. Louis, MO: US Bureau of Economic Analysis.

General Court of the Commonwealth of Massachusetts (2020). *An Act Relative to Senior Property Tax Deferral.* H.3617. Boston, MA: The 191st General Court of the Commonwealth of Massachusetts.

General Court of the Commonwealth of Massachusetts (2020a). *Resolve Providing for an Investigation and Study by a Special Commission Relative to A Senior State Property Tax Deferral Program.* S.1693. Boston, MA: The 191st General Court of the Commonwealth of Massachusetts.

Hodgson, N. (2022). 'Aging-in-Place: The Role of Public/Private Partnerships.' In O.S. Mitchell, ed., *New Models for Managing Longevity Risk: Public/Private Partnerships.* Oxford, UK: Oxford University Press, pp. 91–104.

J. P. Morgan Asset Management (2019). 'Long-Term Capital Market Assumptions Executive Summary,' New York, NY.

Lincoln Institute of Land Policy (2019). 'Residential Property Tax Relief Programs.' Cambridge, MA. https://www.lincolninst.edu/research-data/data-toolkits/significant-features-property-tax/access-property-tax-database/residential-property-tax-relief-programs

Massachusetts Acts of 2016 (2016). 'Chapter 59, Section 5: Property; Exemptions,' The 190th General Court of the Commonwealth of Massachusetts, Boston, MA.

Massachusetts Department of Revenue, Division of Local Services (2019). 'Municipal Databank/Local Aid Section: Exemptions Granted and Dollars Abated,' Boston, MA. https://dlsgateway.dor.state.ma.us/DLSReports/DLSReportViewer.aspx?ReportName=ExemptionsGrantedandDollarsAbated&ReportTitle=Exemptions%20Granted%20and%20Dollars%20Abated

Massachusetts Department of Revenue, Division of Local Services (2019a). 'Real Estate Tax Credit for Persons Age 65 and Older,' Boston, MA. http://www.

mass.gov/dor/individuals/filing-and-payment-information/guide-to-personal-income-tax/credits/real-estate-tax-credit.html

Massachusetts Department of Revenue, Division of Local Services (2019b). 'Senior Circuit Breaker Credit Usage Report by Community,' Boston, MA. https://www.mass.gov/service-details/local-options-relating-to-property-taxation-cpa-meals-and-room-occupancy

MassHousing (Massachusetts Housing Finance Agency) (2020). 'Home Ownership,' Boston, MA. https://www.masshousing.com/en/home-ownership

Munnell, A. H. and A. Chen (2017). '401(k)/IRA Holdings in 2016: An Update from the SCF,' *Issue in Brief 17–18*. Chestnut Hill, MA: Center for Retirement Research at Boston College.

Munnell, A. H., W. Hou, and G. T. Sanzenbacher. (2018). 'National Retirement Risk Index Shows Modest Improvement in 2016,' *Issue in Brief 18-1*. Chestnut Hill, MA: Center for Retirement Research at Boston College.

Munnell, A. H., A. N. Walters, A. Belbase, and W. Hou. (2020). 'Are Homeownership Patterns Stable Enough to Tap Home Equity?' Chestnut Hill, MA: Center for Retirement Research at Boston College.

Mutchler, J. E., Y. Li, and P. Xu. (2019). 'Living Below the Line: Economic Insecurity and Older Americans' Insecurity in the States: 2019,' Working Paper 2019-11, University of Massachusetts Boston, Center for Social and Demographic Research on Aging, Boston, MA.

Oregon Department of Revenue (2009). 'Property Tax Deferral Programs Annual Report,' 150-490-475, Salem, OR.

Oregon Legislative Revenue Office (2001). 'Oregon's Senior Population Growth and Property Tax Relief Programs,' Report No. 7-01, Salem, OR.

Pinnacle Actuarial Resources (2019). 'Fiscal Year 2019 Independent Actuarial Review of the Mutual Mortgage Insurance Fund: Economic Net Worth from Home Equity Conversion Mortgage Insurance-In-Force,' Bloomington, IL.

University of Massachusetts Donahue Institute (2015). 'Long-term Population Projections for Massachusetts Regions and Municipalities,' Amherst, MA.

US Census Bureau (1960–2008, 2018). *American Community Survey*. Washington, DC.

WebAnnuities Insurance Agency, Inc. (US) (1996–2020). 'Immediate Annuities.' https://www.immediateannuities.com/

Chapter 13

The Market for Reverse Mortgages among Older Americans

Christopher Mayer and Stephanie Moulton

Reverse mortgages have long been viewed with skepticism by some retirees, financial planners, and financial institutions. Potential concerns are many, including high costs, dicey sales practices, and the potential for retirees to lose their home if things go badly. Interestingly, the same concerns about reverse mortgages or similar products ('equity release' options) seem to persist in many countries with very different institutions and financial systems.

Yet the need to access additional retirement assets like home equity has never been stronger. Academics and researchers lament the lack of adequate retirement savings and growing debt among older Americans. Media headlines such as 'Over 60 with Decades Left on the Mortgage: The New Retirement Math' in the *Wall Street Journal* (Rexrode 2020) are common. Recent studies by the Urban Institute, the Federal Reserve Bank of New York, and a number of academics point to the increase in the number of American householders entering retirement age with a mortgage and growing average mortgage balances, both in real dollars and as a share of home equity.[1] For example, the proportion of older adults entering retirement with mortgage debt has more than doubled from 20 percent in 1992, to more than 40 percent in 2016.[2] This is occurring even as ever fewer households have a traditional pension and retirees have shrinking 401(k) and other retirement savings. The economic and financial shrinkage associated with COVID-19 will only make this problem worse.

Yet the growth in housing debt in the US can also be seen in a different light—as evidence that older householders are effectively consuming home equity in retirement. Many older householders use traditional mortgage instruments like a Home Equity Line of Credit (HELOC), second lien, or cash-out refinancing to draw down home equity during retirement years.[3] Similarly, by leaving existing debt in place for longer, retirees are missing out on the increase in home equity that used to take place in previous generations, effectively further reducing savings.

Christopher Mayer and Stephanie Moulton, *The Market for Reverse Mortgages among Older Americans.*
In: *New Models for Managing Longevity Risk.* Edited by Olivia S. Mitchell, Oxford University Press.
© Pension Research Council (2022). DOI: 10.1093/oso/9780192859808.003.0013

Of course, the problem with using traditional mortgage debt to fund retirement is that such debt must be paid back just as many householders are retiring and facing sharp drops in their income. Research by Englehardt and Eriksen (2019) shows that elderly homeowners with a mortgage face housing expense burdens that mirror those of renters, with a growing share of retirees spending 30 to 50 percent or more of their income on housing expenses. One in four older adults engages in expensive credit card behaviors, including paying only the minimum balance, paying over the limit fees, and using credit cards for cash advance (Lusardi et al. 2020). Rates of personal bankruptcy are increasing more quickly for older adults than any other age group in the US (Fisher 2019; Li and White 2020). It is perhaps not surprising that a higher level of debt—particularly non-housing consumer debt—is associated with increased stress among older adults (Haurin et al. 2019). While many workers report an offsetting desire to retire later, data shows that few elderly people retire as late as they had planned to at younger ages.[4]

For most retirees, home equity is the largest single asset they bring into retirement, even after subtracting mortgage debt. Nearly 80 percent of adults age 65+ own their homes, and most do still own those free and clear. Using data from the 2016 Survey of Consumer Finances, Moulton and Haurin (2019) estimated that the median homeowner age 62 and older held more wealth in the form of home equity than in financial assets: $139,000 in home equity, compared to $101,800 in financial assets.

Finding a way to responsibly use home equity would seem to be a priority. Yet it has also been an elusive goal. One exception is in the United Kingdom, where equity release options have been growing rapidly in recent years. By one estimate, about one-in-three mortgages taken out by borrowers over age 55 is an equity release product. Relative to the population of retirees, the effective market in the UK is nearly five times the size of that in the US. Similarly, Canada has seen a sharp rise in the use of reverse mortgages. One reason for the growth in equity release products in the UK is that mortgage originators are asked to ensure older borrowers are able to afford mortgage payments using retirement income, not just current income at the time of the mortgage. This has pushed mortgage originators to raise the option of equity release products with older borrowers, and it is likely an important factor behind their increasing use. Furthermore, UK financial planners do not face some of the regulatory restrictions in place in the US and often discuss equity release and other options to use home equity. Also, unlike in the US, they can also earn a commission from the sale of such products.

In this chapter we explore the US reverse mortgage market and the reasons behind its apparent failure to help fund retirement. We do so while also exploring how older borrowers use home equity and various types of mortgages to finance their retirement. To do this, we access data from the 2018

260 New Models for Managing Longevity Risk

Home Mortgage Disclosure Act (HMDA), which, for the first time, includes significantly expanded data such as the type of mortgage available, age of borrowers, interest rate and costs for each loan, and the lender. Lenders must also provide information on rejected applicants. We can separately identify reverse mortgages and compare them to other types of cash-out borrowing. We also explore other types of mortgages taken out by seniors, including traditional refinancing and purchase mortgages.

The results show that Americans age 62+ access a wide variety of sources to borrow against their principal residence. In 2018, only 33,000 originated reverse mortgages were reported in HMDA, versus 609,000 originated equity extraction loans such as HELOCs, cash-out refinancing, first liens not for refinance or purchase, and second liens, all of which require traditional mortgage payments, typically for 15 to 30 years. An additional 688,000 older Americans originated a mortgage for home purchase or a refinancing, many of which will require payments beyond age 90. Our analysis focuses on the Home Equity Conversion Mortgage (HECM) program, a US government-insured reverse mortgage that represents 94 percent of all reported reverse mortgage originations.

After documenting the extent to which home equity borrowing is important for many retirees, we examine the barriers to accessing home equity for older adults and find that denial due to excessive debt payments is a bigger problem for the elderly than for younger potential borrowers. Our data show that more than 50 percent of older adults denied HELOC or second liens in 2018 were denied because they could not afford the monthly mortgage payment, compared to 41 percent who were denied for credit reasons. An estimated 70 percent of older adults denied HELOC and second liens had debt to income (DTI) ratios in excess of 41 percent. By contrast, for homeowners under the age of 46, only 35 percent were denied a HELOC or second lien due to affordability (nearly half being denied due to a poor credit history). At an age where retirement (and thus a loss of income) is increasingly likely, the large amount of existing debt appears to be a problem for a large number of older homeowners.

Given that high debt payments are a barrier to affordability for the elderly, we consider reasons that no-payment loans like a reverse mortgage represent such as small share of total borrowing. For example, simulations show that between 26 and 36 percent of rejected HELOC and second lien applicants likely could have accessed a reverse mortgage (n = 54,000 to 74,000). Similarly, between 28 and 40 percent of approved HELOC and second lien borrowers could have used a reverse mortgage (n = 77,000 to 108,000). Maybe not surprising, given the large amount of borrowing among many older applicants, the principal reason that reverse mortgages couldn't help more HELOC and second lien applicants is that they would not qualify for a reverse mortgage because they need to borrow *too much* money. Initial loan to value ratios (LTVs) for reverse mortgages are much lower than for traditional mortgages because of the negative amortization of the balance when a borrower is not making mortgage payments.

Next, we explore various reasons why reverse mortgages may not be used more frequently. Our analysis considers four potential reasons that older borrowers already considering home equity borrowing do not choose a reverse mortgage, including product reputation, higher costs, bequest motives, and regulatory barriers. We also discuss other motives for not using home equity among those who don't explore a new mortgage, including precautionary savings and the more general puzzle of why many retirees fail to spend down other assets in retirement (Poterba et al. 2011, for example). We conclude that while high product costs may be a barrier for some potential borrowers, the poor product reputation and regulatory barriers also play an important role, particularly in discouraging the participation of mainstream financial institutions which might be able to bring distribution efficiencies, lower costs, and retirement advice that incorporates home equity into financial plans.

The Market for Reverse Mortgages and Equity Release Products
Equity release options in the US and abroad

A reverse mortgage is a loan that allows an older borrower to borrow against the value of the home without required payments. In most countries including the US, a borrower can take some up-front cash and the balance of the loan either as a line of credit (LOC or 'drawdown') or with fixed monthly payments (tenure payments). A recent survey of selected global equity release originators by Ernst & Young Global Limited (EY 2020) summarizes products available across the world. According to the survey, most borrowers take a combination of a fixed up-front payment plus a LOC when the LOC is available. The LOC allows borrowers to access additional funds as they desire, similar to a HELOC. In the US, borrowers can make optional payments and can deduct the portion of the payment that is applied to the interest in the same way as a traditional (forward) mortgage. Since the loan balance is expected to grow over time as interest accrues, the origination LTV ratio of a reverse mortgage is typically much lower than for a traditional mortgage, and the product is restricted to older borrowers who have a shorter expected time in the property. Common minimum age ranges between 55 (UK and Canada) and 62 (most often in the US) or 65 (Germany). The amount of proceeds available typically rises for older borrowers.

A reverse mortgage is not the only product that allows borrowers to use home equity in retirement. It fits inside a larger category of 'equity release' products. In some countries, particularly Italy, Germany, and France, there is an active market in home reversions (or viagers), in which the owner 'sells' some or all of the future sale proceeds of the home in return for an up-front lump sum or annuity payment and the right to live in the home as long as he or she lives.

Equity release products have a number of insurance features that should be appealing for retirees and allow them to hedge risks that might otherwise materially impact their financial position in retirement. This is because the lender/purchaser is giving up-front cash in return for an uncertain future payoff from the sale of the home. In the vast majority of countries (exceptions include Spain and Germany), the borrower or his or her estate is never liable for more than the home is worth. Thus, if the borrower lives longer than expected or home prices fall, the lender/purchaser bears the risk that the present value of eventual proceeds will be below the amount of money advanced to the borrower at the underwritten cost of capital. Few other products exist that allow a homeowner to otherwise hedge home price and longevity risk.

Who can benefit from home equity release?

The most obvious candidates for using home equity in retirement are those for whom few other options exist. For example, Cocco and Lopes (2019) have simulations that suggest that reverse mortgage demand should be the highest among those with low levels of nonhousing wealth relative to home equity, who have a weak bequest motive, and who have high levels of other pre-existing debt. The importance of pre-existing debt is consistent with prior empirical research finding that a large proportion of reverse mortgage borrowers use reverse mortgages to pay off debt.

Some studies look to calculate the share of borrowers with a relatively large amount of home equity relative to total assets or income, finding an appreciable minority of seniors have little income or financial assets and a comparably large amount of home equity. For example, Goodman et al. (2017) estimated that as many as 2.5 million to 4.5 million senior households (10% to 17% of the 26 million senior homeowners) could benefit from a vehicle to tap into home equity, including a reverse mortgage. Mayer (2017) showed that almost one-quarter of senior households have at least $50,000 in home equity and less than $50,000 in financial assets in 2012. Moulton and Haurin (2019) estimated that nearly one in five of older homeowners held less than $10,000 in financial assets, but had at least $40,000 in home equity. As we show below, originations of reverse mortgages represent a relatively small share of such potential demand.

An alternative approach to access home equity is through home sale, however most older adults express strong attachment to their homes.

In a 2018 survey, 76 percent of respondents age 50+ indicated a desire to remain in their current home as long as possible (Binette and Vasold 2018). These preferences are consistent with data: for example, from 2012 to 2014, only 1.8 percent of homeowners age 65+ extracted equity by selling their homes (Goodman et al. 2017). Of older adults who sold their homes between 1998 and 2014, only about one in four purchased a home of lesser value, allowing for liquidation of home equity (Begley and Chan 2019). Those who did sell their homes tended to have higher incomes and more nonhousing financial wealth (Englehardt and Eriksen 2019).

An important reason that homeowners do not sell their homes is that their retirement consumption is tied to the home's value, and owning a home provides a hedge against outliving their assets. That is, the home is not simply a financial asset that can be tapped at will, it is also an asset that pays a 'dividend' in the form of imputed rent. Thus, selling the home creates a challenge: how to invest the proceeds from a sale to ensure sufficient returns to pay rent over the remaining lifetime. Seniors who rent bear the risk of running out of money if they live a long time or financial returns are not what they expect. This might explain why homeownership rates across most developed countries peak at age 65–74 (around 75% to 90%), regardless of the mortgage finance or pension systems (Goodman and Mayer 2018).

Accordingly, there appears to be an appreciable number of older borrowers who fit into categories that might benefit from taking an equity release product like a reverse mortgage. Some are the traditional 'house rich, cash poor' households or those who want to eliminate mortgage payments. Others might want to access liquidity from home equity rather than selling financial assets, effectively ending up with a portfolio that becomes increasingly concentrated in home equity with age.

Market size and growth of equity release in the US, the UK, and Canada

In the aggregate, the total value of home equity for seniors is quite large. In the US, home equity seniors age 62 had a total of $7.54 trillion in Q1 2020 (NRMLA 2020). Home equity for seniors in large European countries exceeded €8 trillion in 2013 according to Haurin and Moulton (2017). By comparison, the aggregate value of equity release products is much smaller.

While aggregate data on equity release products in many countries is difficult to obtain, we can summarize the reverse mortgage market in the US and compare it to two growing markets including those of Canada and the UK.[5] The number of reverse mortgages in the US is small and sensitive to market and policy dynamics affecting who can borrow and the proceeds available. In the UK and Canada, equity release markets are much larger as a share of the elderly population.

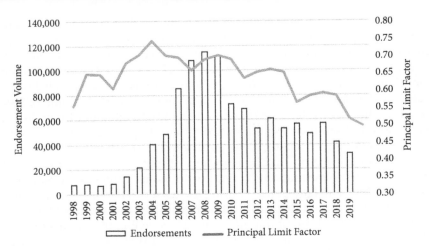

Figure 13.1 Home Equity Conversion Mortgage endorsements by calendar year, median principal limit factor (loan to value)

Source: Authors' calculations.

For the US, we examine the market for HECM reverse mortgages, or loans insured by the Federal Housing Administration (FHA), an agency of the US Department of Housing and Urban Development (HUD). While there is also a small private-label reverse mortgage program, over this period, it is estimated that 96 to 100 percent of all reverse mortgages were HECMs, and systematic data were not available prior to 2018.[6]

Figure 13.1 charts the volume of HECM reverse mortgages since the program became permanent in 1998. As is apparent, the growth in the number of reverse mortgages (LHS axis, white bars) in the US has been hump shaped and has suffered an appreciable decline in the last decade. Right before and after the global financial crisis of 2008, reverse mortgage production peaked at nearly 115,000 reverse mortgages, accounting for under 0.5 percent of older homeowners. With about 10,000 people turning 65 every day in the US, the share taking out a reverse mortgage is still well under one percent of the eligible population during most years of the sample. The growth during the financial crisis is not surprising; seniors who watched their stock portfolios collapse seemed ever more willing to turn to their homes to help finance retirement, even as home prices were falling. As well, there was a large increase in traditional mortgage debt during the mid-2000s, leaving many older borrowers with relatively big mortgage payments that they could eliminate with a reverse mortgage.

After the 2008 peak, reverse mortgage originations plummeted for more than a decade, with tighter underwriting, lower borrowing proceeds, and the exit of many brand name originators. Until 2014, the FHA did not require financial underwriting for borrowers. While there are no required mortgage payments for a reverse mortgage, borrowers must still pay property taxes and insurance (T&I) to be in compliance, and an appreciable number of borrowers from 2009 to 2012 took out full draws and were left with no money to cover these costs. This led to a sharp increase in defaults and FHA-required foreclosures on borrowers unable to make homeowner's property T&I payments, with attendant poor publicity. With these and other challenges, larger financial institutions such as Wells Fargo, Bank of America, and MetLife exited the reverse mortgage business.

The increase in defaults and foreclosures and sharp decline in home values led the FHA to reassess its underwriting and curtail available proceeds for borrowers as a share of home value. The maximum amount of proceeds for an HECM is called the 'principal limit' (PL) or the share of home value that can be used as a borrowing base. To protect itself, the FHA lowered the principal limit factor (PLF)—the proportion of home equity that can be borrowed; similar to an LTV—substantially between 2012 and 2017. While the average home value for HECM borrowers (called maximum claim amount, or MCA) grew 30 percent between 2009 and 2019, the PL did not grow at all.[7] In addition, in 2015, the FHA limited the amount of money that a borrower could get to 60 percent of the PLF, unless the borrower had a mortgage or other required property or federal tax liens with an amount above the 60 percent limit, in which case the borrower could cover these 'mandatory obligations' plus an additional 10 percent (capped at 100% of the PL). The effective reduction in proceeds available to borrowers, combined with the exit of brand name financial institutions, led to a sharp decline in the number of HECM mortgages originated.

By comparison, originations of equity release products in Canada and the UK followed a very different pattern, more than doubling since 2013. In the UK, equity release offerings increased from £1 billion in 2013 to £3 billion in 2017, with a further 32 percent growth to more than £4 billion by 2019.[8] Furthermore, equity release mortgages represent an estimated 36 percent of all mortgages for borrowers over age 55 in 2018, doubling their share from the previous decade. A total of 46,000 equity release plans were originated in 2018 versus fewer than 42,000 in the US, despite the US having almost five times the number of retirees. While total volume in 2019 was flat with 2,018, the membership in the Equity Release Council almost doubled and, prior to COVID-19, the industry expected continued growth in 2020.

In Canada, HomeEquity Bank, the sole seller of reverse mortgages until recently, reported a record CA$820 million up from CA$309 million five years earlier. As in the UK, mortgages are available for borrowers age 55 and above, although the bulk of originations are for those over age 65. In both the UK and Canada, lenders advertise widely in the media. In the UK, equity release products are offered by some of the largest life insurance companies.

Home Equity and the Market for Reverse Mortgages
Reverse mortgage originations in the US

The current number of outstanding reverse mortgages in the US is small, estimated to be below two percent of older homeowners.[9] In general, it is difficult to measure the home equity market for older adults. Surveys such as the Health and Retirement Study (HRS) lack details about mortgage types and terms, and they rely on self-reported data on loan balances. These data are good for tracking trends in the stock of mortgage debt held by older homeowners, but they are less useful for examining new originations and, in particular, the share of reverse mortgages versus other mortgage products. Researchers also use consumer credit panel datasets to track trends in home equity borrowing among older adults over time (Moulton et al. 2019; Brown et. al. 2020). However, credit data do not include borrower-specific information on home values and do not include important information about loan terms and costs. Further, reverse mortgages are not reported in credit data because they do not require borrowers to make payments.

Below, we examine data on the vast majority of new mortgages originated in the US using the 2018 HMDA Loan Application Register (LAR). Under HMDA, lenders are required to collect and report specific information about mortgage applications acted upon and loans purchased during the prior calendar year. Beginning in 2018, new reporting requirements came into effect that required most lenders to report on mortgages structured as open-ended lines of credit, such as HELOCs and reverse mortgages that were previously only voluntarily reported (CFPB 2019).[10] Importantly, the 2018 HMDA data include new information on both federally insured HECMs and proprietary reverse mortgages, as well as the age of borrowers, so we can compare various types of borrowing used by seniors.

The 2018 HMDA data allows us to compare the characteristics of applicants and borrowers of reverse mortgages to the characteristics of mortgage applicants and borrowers for other types of loans. The goal is twofold: first, to understand the characteristics of reverse mortgage borrowers; and second, to compare reverse mortgage borrowers to applicants for all other mortgage debt taken out by potential borrowers age 62 and older who might otherwise have been eligible for a reverse mortgage.[11]

Data description

We begin by restricting the HMDA database to those observations where the applicant or co-applicant is age 62+, as we wish to focus on older adults who would otherwise be eligible for a reverse mortgage. To avoid double counting, we exclude loans that were simply purchased by another institution during the reporting period. We further restrict the sample to loans for single family, owner-occupied properties, excluding investment properties and second homes. These restrictions result in a sample of 2,510,080 loan applications, of which 1,329,505 resulted in loan originations during the 2018 period.

Table 13.1 provides a breakdown of observations by loan type and loan outcome. We separate loan observations into seven different mortgage types. The first three mortgage types are reverse mortgages, including 'traditional HECMs,' HECMs used to purchase a property ('HECMs for Purchase'), and non-HECM proprietary reverse mortgages ('Other Reverse Mortgages'). Prior to the 2008 housing crisis, there was a nascent market for proprietary reverse mortgages, but this market more or less disappeared after 2008. In the last few years, a small proprietary reverse mortgage market has developed, but it became more substantial in 2018 when several lenders began offering the product. Proprietary reverse mortgages are mostly concentrated among higher value homes that exceed the property value limits for an HECM[12] or for condominiums that do not qualify for the FHA's HECM program.

The other four categories represent different types of traditional (or forward) mortgages; that is, mortgages that require a monthly payment and must be paid off over a fixed term. Two categories offer the borrower the option to take out cash. The first category includes home equity lines of credit and loans. HELOCs include new loans structured as an LOC, where the borrower typically makes interest-only payments at an adjustable rate on borrowings up to an approved credit limit for 10 years, followed by a payback period, usually 15 years, where the borrower must pay back the outstanding amount. The cost of originating a HELOC is quite low and HELOC borrowers tend to have very good credit scores. 'Second liens' are loans that are defined as second liens excluding lines of credit and loans with a purpose of refinancing. These loans typically have a fixed rate and payoff period and are often given to borrowers with riskier credit histories and have higher-than-average interest rates. The second category of equity extraction loans includes first mortgages. 'Cash-out refinancing' is defined to include loans originated for the purpose of cash-out refinancing that are not structured as a LOC and are typically paid back over 15–30 years. 'First liens not for purchase' are closed liens in first position that are not for the purpose of refinancing or for home purchase.

The remaining two types of mortgages do not involve the borrower obtaining additional cash. 'Refinance no cash' loans include both closed and open lines of credit for the stated purpose of refinancing without cash-out, excluding loans for the purchase of a home. Finally, 'purchase

Table 13.1 Mortgage applications reported in 2018 Home Mortgage Disclosure Act for applicants or co-applicants age 62+

	HECM traditional	HECM for purchase	Other reverse mortgage	HELOC or second	Cash-out first lien	Refinance no cash	Purchase mortgage	Total
Application Status								
Originated	0.562	0.776	0.646	0.487	0.465	0.502	0.661	0.530
Number of originated loans	28,946	1,952	1,952	274,388	334,791	268,210	419,266	1,330,342
Denied	0.167	0.075	0.128	0.365	0.245	0.237	0.118	0.236
Withdrawn or incomplete	0.271	0.15	0.18	0.148	0.29	0.261	0.221	0.234
N	51,493	2,517	3,021	563,653	720,251	534,572	634,573	2,510,080
Reason for Denial								
Credit history	0.088	0.074	0.062	0.407	0.296	0.273	0.322	0.33
Debt to income ratio	0.05	0.048	0.026	0.506	0.303	0.388	0.376	0.397

Collateral	0.394	0.207	0.474	0.186	0.186	0.172	0.124	0.178
Insufficient cash	0.262	0.112	0.171	0.012	0.022	0.026	0.077	0.03
Credit application incomplete	0.218	0.362	0.073	0.037	0.173	0.13	0.109	0.109
Other reasons	0.157	0.223	0.334	0.164	0.173	0.191	0.227	0.18
N	8,574	8188	8386	205,922	176,391	126,737	75,189	593,387

Note: Sample is restricted to loans for single family, owner-occupied properties where the applicant or co-applicant is age 62 or older, excluding investment properties and second homes.

Source: Authors' calculations from 2018 HMDA data, excluding purchased loans.

mortgages' are closed-end loans with the stated purpose of home purchase. In both cases, the bulk of such mortgages involved fixed rates (although some are also hybrid adjustable-rate mortgages, or ARMs) and a payback period that is usually 30 years, although some traditional mortgages may have a shorter 15-year payback period.

Of the modes of extracting home equity, HELOC and second liens are slightly more common in 2008 than cash-out refinancing or first liens not for purchase. Both options are quite a bit more prevalent than HECMs.

Reasons for loan denial: Older versus younger borrowers

Table 13.1 also compares the proportion of applications denied or approved by the lender, as well as those considered incomplete or withdrawn by the applicant. Rates of denial were highest for HELOCs and second liens, with more than one-third of older applicants in 2018 being denied. About one-fourth of cash-out refinancing and first lien mortgages were denied. Notably, having a weak credit history or high DTI ratio were the top reasons for denial among these applicants, with more than half of HELOC denials being due to an inability to afford the monthly payments (e.g. high DTI). By contrast, reverse mortgage applications were less likely to be denied, with primary reasons for denial being related to the collateral value of the property or insufficient cash to cover required costs.

These differences in reasons for loan denial make sense, given that reverse mortgages carry different criteria for underwriting than forward mortgages. There is no required monthly repayment of a reverse mortgage, and thus there is no additional DTI burden from a reverse mortgage. Beginning in 2015, HECM borrowers must demonstrate the ability to pay ongoing property T&I payments or have sufficient home equity to set aside funds to pay these expenses in an escrow-type account at the time of loan closing (Moulton and Haurin 2019). The primary barrier to obtaining a reverse mortgage is not poor credit history or lack of income, but lack of sufficient home equity (Moulton et al. 2017). Any existing mortgage debt on a home at the time of application for a reverse mortgage must be paid off with the proceeds of the reverse mortgage or in cash at closing.

To give additional perspectives on the reasons that seniors are turned down for mortgage credit, Figure 13.2 compares reasons for denial of mortgage applications by applicant age, including applicants age 45 and younger, age 46 to 61, and age 62 and older. Here, it is clear that inability to afford the monthly payment is a more substantial barrier to originating a mortgage for older adults than it is for younger cohorts. For example, more than 50 percent of older adults denied HELOC and second loans were denied them due to inability to afford monthly payments, compared with only 35 percent of those age 45 and younger. For younger applicants,

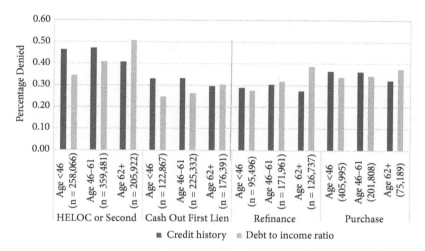

Figure 13.2 Denied Home Mortgage Disclosure Act applications by age, loan type, and reason for denial, 2018

Source: Author's calculations from 2018 HMDA data.

a poor credit history is a more common reason for denial across all loan types.

We next consider the proportion of mortgage applicants with DTI ratios greater than 41 percent, which is a typical maximum DTI for underwriting. Figure 13.3 compares older and younger applicants by loan type, including both those with originated loans and those with loans that were denied. The proportion of older applicants with high DTI ratios is striking—70 percent of older applicants denied HELOC or second liens had DTIs greater than 41 percent. Across all loan types, a higher share of older applicants—both originated and denied—have high DTIs compared to younger applicants. High debt incurred at younger ages appears to be an appreciable barrier to additional borrowing or consumer home equity at older ages. At an age where income will eventually fall as applicants start to retire, debt burdens remain quite high.

Characteristics of older borrowers

Table 13.2 summarizes the loan and borrower characteristics for originated reverse mortgage loans, reported in the 2018 HMDA data, compared to loan and borrower characteristics for traditional mortgage originations to borrowers age 62+ in the 2018 HMDA data. These data include information for 30,898 HECM loan originations, of which 28,946 were structured as traditional HECMs and 1,952 as HECMs to purchase a home.[13] An

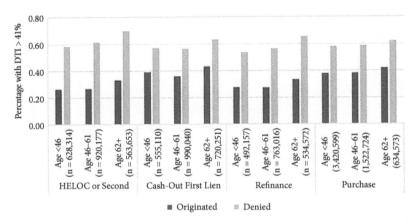

Figure 13.3 Denied Home Mortgage Disclosure Act applications by age and loan type, % with debt to income ratio > 41 percent, 2018

Source: Author's calculations from 2018 HMDA data.

additional 1952 non-HECM proprietary reverse mortgages are reported in the 2018 HMDA data.

The loan amount reported in the HMDA data for a reverse mortgage is the initial principal limit (IPL), or the maximum amount of home equity available to a borrower based on the borrower's age, expected interest rate, and home value. For HECMs, HUD establishes a PLF, which is the maximum LTV ratio at origination. The PLF is multiplied by the value of the property or the limit set by the FHA, whichever is lower, to determine the IPL.[14] In 2018, the property value limit was $679,650. Borrowers with homes worth more than this limit may have access to a larger share of their home equity from a proprietary reverse mortgage.

The average loan amounts for traditional HECMs ($165,751) and HECMs for purchase ($174,918) are much lower than the average loan amount of $703,735 for proprietary reverse mortgages. This is not surprising, given that the average property value of proprietary reverse mortgage borrowers in 2018 was $1.66 million, compared with an average home value of $358,011 for traditional HECMs and $362,701 for HECMs used to purchase a home. The average HECM borrower had a slightly higher LTV of 0.48, compared to 0.44 for proprietary reverse mortgage borrowers. In 2018, the average interest rate for HECM borrowers was about two percentage points lower than the rate for proprietary reverse mortgage borrowers.

With regard to demographic characteristics, traditional HECM borrowers were more likely to be Black or Hispanic, compared to HECM for purchase or other proprietary reverse mortgage borrowers. They were also

TABLE 13.2 Summary characteristics reported in 2018 Home Mortgage Disclosure Act (means)

	HECM traditional	HECM for purchase	Other reverse mortgage	HELOC or second	Cash-out first lien	Refinance no cash	Purchase mortgage
Loan amount (IPL for reverse mortgage)	165,751	174,918	703,735	108,915	206,545	179,065	228,399
Property value	358,011	362,701	1,655,046	433,561	393,734	426,760	342,161
Combined loan to value ratio	0.478	0.486	0.437	0.55	0.63	0.565	0.78
Loan to value ratio for this loan	0.479	0.486	0.437	0.304	0.625	0.509	0.774
Interest rate	4.789	4.603	6.513	5.93	5.07	5.335	5.346
Interest rate spread	.	.	.	0.398	0.634	0.236	0.624
Total loan costs	.	.	.	322	4,762	3,335	4,513

Continued

TABLE 13.2 *Continued*

	HECM traditional	HECM for purchase	Other reverse mortgage	HELOC or second	Cash-out first lien	Refinance no cash	Purchase mortgage
Percent reporting total loan costs (%)	·	·	·	7.1	93.2	57.4	91.8
Origination charges	·	·	·	77	2,276	1,708	1,529
Discount points if non-zero	·	·	·	246	2,361	2,189	1,509
Percent reporting non-zero discount points (%)	·	·	·	0.4	52.8	38.2	31.7
Lender credits if non-zero	·	·	·	386	738	835	821
Percent reporting lender credits (%)	·	·	·	27.7	34.7	38.4	38.3
Loan term (months)	·	·	·	304	305	298	340

Percent with loan term 360+ months (%)	100.0			59.0	70.5	57.9	88.3
FHA or VA (%)	100.0	100.0	0.0	0.1	25.9	9.5	25.4
Black or Hispanic (%)	15.0	10.2	10.2	10.5	15.8	12.7	15.3
Missing race and ethnicity (%)	5.3	2.9	5.4	7.6	13.3	9.4	8.2
Borrower gender: single female (%)	39.6	33.1	40.8	22.1	22.8	22.4	23.5
Borrower gender: single male (%)	23.7	16.4	37.4	19.1	22.7	20.2	22.3
Borrower gender: joint female and male (%)	35.8	48.9	20.1	53.1	44.8	50.4	48.2

Continued

TABLE 13.2 *Continued*

	HECM traditional	HECM for purchase	Other reverse mortgage	HELOC or second	Cash-out first lien	Refinance no cash	Purchase mortgage
Borrower gender: missing (%)	1.0	1.6	1.6	5.7	9.6	7.1	6.0
Percent with co-applicant (%)	38.8	54.8	42.4	59.7	53.6	57.9	58.9
DTI<36% (%)	.	.	.	46.3	35.7	47.1	36.2
DTI 36–41%	.	.	.	20.5	21.2	19.2	21.6
DTI >41% (%)	.	.	.	33.2	43.1	33.7	42.1
Income used for underwriting	29.352	42.268	42.021	118.844	119.332	127.145	173.91
Census tract % minority	34.16	25.803	35.768	24.407	30.886	26.432	27.085
MSA median family income	74,384	71,966	93,472	76,089	74,257	75,282	71,573
Census tract income to MSA income (%)	107.391	115.877	158.244	120.203	112.34	117.008	113.559
Observations	28,946	1,952	1,952	274,388	334,791	268,210	419,266

Notes: The summary statistics are based on lender reported values, where values not reported are treated as missing. An exception is the loan amount (IPL) and LTV, where we estimate an age and interest rate adjusted PLF and replace values where the loan amount/MCA is not within 0.10 of the PLF, this resulting in replacement of 26 percent of the values. The sample sizes are smaller for particular variables with missing data or outliers.
Source: Authors' calculations from 2018 HMDA data, excluding purchased loans.

more likely to be single, to have a lower income to underwrite the loan, and be located in a lower income census tract—although still slightly above the median income for the Metropolitan Statistical Area (MSA). Compared to either type of HECM borrower, proprietary reverse mortgage borrowers tend to be older and from higher income census tracts as a percentage of the MSA median income.

Next we compare reverse mortgage borrowers to those who take other types of mortgages. The average property value of $433,561 for HELOCs and second liens and $393,734 for cash-out refinancing or new first liens not for purchase is higher than the average traditional HECM property value of $358,011. The average loan amount for HELOC and second lien borrowers of $108,918 is smaller than the average loan amount of HECM borrowers. It is important to note that an appreciable share of the HELOC and second loan borrowers held existing first mortgages, as the combined LTV for all mortgages on the property of 0.55 is considerably higher than the LTV of 0.30 for the HELOC or second loan by itself.

The average interest rate of HELOC and second loans of 5.93 percent is a bit *higher* than the 4.8 percent interest rate on HECM loans, which becomes 5.3 percent when we add the 0.5 percent mortgage insurance premium (MIP) that must also be paid on an FHA-insured HECM. This insurance fee also exists for traditional FHA loans, where the MIP is also unreported, but also for traditional Fannie Mae and Freddie Mac loans with an LTV above 80 percent where there is a required private mortgage insurance (PMI) policy. Loan costs are not reported in HMDA for reverse mortgages or HELOCs, but they are reported for closed-end forward mortgages, with average up-front costs of about $4,500 for cash-out refinancing and purchase mortgages, or about 2 percent of loan proceeds.

Notably, the average combined LTV for the cash-out loan types ranges between 55 (HELOC and second loans) and 63 percent (cash-out refinancing and nonpurchase first mortgages). This is striking, given the size of mortgage debt owed over a repayment period of 25 to 30 years, extending into borrowers' 90s and beyond. Such borrowers are taking on mortgage payments as a share of home value that are nearly as large as much younger borrowers who have a much longer expected working period.

Consistent with the perception of having strong credit requirements, HELOC borrowers also appear to have higher income characteristics than do reverse mortgage or other cash-out borrowers. HECM borrowers live in lower income census tracts (107% of MSA median) versus cash-out refinancing or nonpurchase first liens (112%) or HELOCs and second liens (120%). HELOC and second lien borrowers are less likely to be Black or Hispanic (10.5%) than cash-out first lien borrowers (15.8%), who are closer to the traditional HECM minority share of 15 percent. Strikingly,

HECM borrowers are almost twice as likely to be single female (40%) versus approximately 22 percent of HELOC and second lien borrowers.

When we examine traditional purchase or refinance mortgages, HECM borrowers have a similar share to Black or Hispanic borrowers (13–15%) and also almost double the share of single female borrowers. Furthermore, those in neighborhoods for refinancing and purchase mortgages have higher incomes relative to their MSA compared to HECM census tracts.

HECM simulations using 2018 HMDA data

Next, we leverage the HMDA data to estimate a series of counterfactual simulations to determine whether applicants in the HMDA data could have obtained HECMs instead of the mortgages actually chosen. The simulations focus on the size of the loan requested without taking credit into account. In part, this is because we do not observe borrower credit indicators across all loan types. Nevertheless, relatively few HECM borrowers are rejected due to low credit for two reasons. First, since HECMs do not have required principal and interest payments, borrowers must only show the ability to pay property T&I, a much lower income standard. Second, HECM borrowers with a poor credit history or low income can always choose to take a lower IPL and set aside borrowing proceeds to pay future T&I.[15] Thus, HECM borrowers can have a poor credit history or low income and still qualify for the loan.

To examine eligibility for an HECM, we determine the amount of money a borrower could qualify for using the initial PLF tables from the HECM program in 2018. Inputs to the IPL tables include the age of the youngest borrower and the property value, estimates of which are reported in HMDA. For the expected interest rate on an HECM loan, another input required for the PLF table, we use two different values as described below. We compare the loan size requested through a forward mortgage with what we estimate the borrower could have obtained with an HECM.

We run the simulation with two different sets of assumptions regarding the HECM expected interest rate and loan costs. The first scenario is a conservative estimate, with the maximum permissible loan origination fee and an expected interest rate of 4.75 percent (the median rate in 2018). The second scenario relaxes some of these assumptions, waiving the lender origination fee and using an expected interest rate of three percent.

The lower interest rate in the second scenario is important, as borrowers are able to obtain the maximum possible proceeds in the PLF table by gaining access to a lower interest rate loan. In practice, borrowers who shop around are often able to obtain more preferable terms on an HECM, including lower rates and thus higher loan proceeds. Also, lenders are often willing to offer borrowers a lower interest rate on their HECMs if the borrowers take more proceeds. This is especially true where the lower rate allows a borrower to obtain an HECM when, at a higher rate, that borrower would not obtain sufficient proceeds to pay off a previous lien. The second scenario would be particularly relevant in times when the 10-year treasury rate falls below that in 2019, when rates peaked above three percent, compared to average rates that were 0.5 to 1 percent lower in the other years between 2016 and 2019. In 2020, with COVID-19 and recent Fed moves, many reverse mortgages are being originated at or near the three percent rate that obtains a maximum PLF. Recent experience along with the data in this chapter suggest that demand for reverse mortgages may be quite sensitive to interest rates due to the much larger proceeds available in lower interest rate economic environments.

We conduct the simulations for both originated forward mortgages and for applications for forward mortgages that were denied—the latter being a group of older adults with an expressed preference for borrowing from home equity who were unable to do so through the mortgage type selected. The results for originated forward mortgages and for denied applications can be seen in Table 13.3.

To illustrate our approach, consider the case of HELOC and second lien originations in Table 13.3. Based on the age of the youngest borrower and an expected interest rate of 4.75 percent, the estimated average PLF is 0.457 percent (top section of Table 13.3). Multiplying this factor by the borrower's property value or the loan limit of $679,650 (whichever is less) results in an average maximum HECM loan amount (IPL) of $158,258. Note that reducing the expected interest rate to 3 percent (bottom section of Table 13.3) increases the PLF by nearly 10 percentage points, raising the maximum loan amount to $192,299.

We then calculate the borrower-specific up-front costs associated with an HECM, comprised of lender origination fees, an up-front MIP charged by HUD, and standard closing costs (e.g. appraisal and closing fees). For the simulation at the top of Table 13.3, we assume that the maximum origination fee is assessed by a lender at an average of $4,711 for HELOC and second lien borrowers in our sample.[16] We waive the origination fee in the bottom of Table 13.3, as this fee is assessed at a lender's discretion and lenders might choose not to charge it for borrowers who take large proceeds and also comparison shop on prices. The up-front MIP is currently set by HUD at two percent of the home value, amounting to $6,951 for the average HELOC or second lien borrower in our sample. We also include an estimated $2,500 for standard closing costs,[17] resulting in total estimated up-front costs of $14,162 for the average HELOC borrower (top section), or $9,451 with the origination fee waived (bottom section).

It is important to note that the MIP for an HECM buys some protections not available for other types of mortgages, especially HELOCs. All HECMs

TABLE 13.3 Counterfactual simulations, Home Equity Conversion Mortgage feasibility by loan type, 2018 Home Mortgage Disclosure Act applicants age 62+

	Originated				Denied			
	HELOC or second	Cash-out first lien	Refinance no cash	Purchase mortgage	HELOC or second	Cash-out first lien	Refinance no cash	Purchase mortgage
Simulation 1: 4.75 Interest Rate and Origination Fee								
Estimated HECM PLF	0.457	0.457	0.457	0.443	0.459	0.462	0.461	0.438
Estimated HECM IPL	158,258	144,783	148,158	127,795	156,563	130,180	144,288	92,721
Estimated HECM origination fee	4,711	4,533	4,498	4,338	4,586	4,177	4,322	3,314
Estimated HECM initial mortgage insurance premium	6,951	6,371	6,510	5,801	6,834	5,644	6,268	4,260
Estimated HECM total up-front costs	14,162	13,405	13,508	12,639	13,920	12,321	13,090	10,074
Existing mortgage debt to be paid off with HECM	112,196	14,379	36,936	22,018	122,386	8,735	40,108	19,223

Estimated total loan amount with HECM	236,684	237,411	231,172	268,110	240,377	228,244	245,778	255,167
Estimated HECM loan to value or MCA	0.643	0.715	0.665	0.859	0.68	0.798	0.748	0.952
Could obtain HECM	0.282	0.161	0.252	0.064	0.259	0.112	0.177	0.029
HECM PLF less estimated HECM	−0.186	−0.259	−0.208	−0.416	−0.221	−0.335	−0.287	−0.514
HECM LTV Shortfall for HECM	−0.324	−0.335	−0.327	−0.453	−0.36	−0.397	−0.38	−0.533

Simulation 2: 3.0 Interest Rate and No Origination Fee

Estimated HECM PLF	0.555	0.555	0.555	0.542	0.557	0.56	0.559	0.538
Estimated HECM IPL	192,299	175,992	180,052	156,499	190,044	157,779	174,970	113,917

Continued

TABLE 13.3 *Continued*

	Originated				Denied			
	HELOC or second	Cash-out first lien	Refinance no cash	Purchase mortgage	HELOC or second	Cash-out first lien	Refinance no cash	Purchase mortgage
Estimated HECM initial mortgage insurance premium	6,951	6,371	6,510	5,801	6,834	5,644	6,268	4,260
Estimated HECM total up-front costs	9,451	8,871	9,010	8,301	9,334	8,144	8,768	6,760
Existing mortgage debt to be paid off with HECM	112,196	14,379	36,936	22,018	122,386	8,735	40,108	19,223
Estimated total loan amount with HECM	231,969	232,877	226,666	263,717	235,761	224,038	241,414	251,354
Estimated HECM loan to value or MCA	0.627	0.699	0.649	0.843	0.664	0.781	0.732	0.935
Could obtain HECM	0.395	0.268	0.38	0.12	0.356	0.189	0.282	0.058
HECM PLF less estimated HECM LTV	-0.072	-0.144	-0.094	-0.301	-0.107	-0.221	-0.173	-0.397
Shortfall for HECM	-0.26	-0.261	-0.267	-0.362	-0.292	-0.313	-0.313	-0.43
N	274,388	334,791	268,210	419,266	205,922	176,391	126,737	75,189

Source: Authors' calculations from 2018 HMDA data.

are non-recourse, which means that borrowers, their heirs, and lenders are not responsible for anything owed on the HECM balance beyond the value of the home. By contrast, for HELOCs, borrowers in most states bear personal liability for any negative equity. Personal liability is a feature of almost all second liens and some first lien mortgages, depending on the state. Also, HELOCs are subject to being suspended in an environment of falling home prices, whereas the HECM LOC will not be cut if home prices decline (although the LOC can be suspended if a borrower fails to meet other reverse mortgage obligations such as making timely payment of property T&I, adequately maintaining the home, and living in the home as their primary residence).

To estimate the total loan amount from the HECM, we add together the borrower's requested loan amount for the forward mortgage, any existing mortgage debt held by the borrower in addition to the new loan being requested (e.g. the balance on a first mortgage for borrowers requesting a second lien or HELOC), and the estimated HECM closing costs. We then divide this amount by the borrower's property value or the MCA (whichever is lower) to get the estimated LTV if the borrower were to obtain an HECM. If the estimated LTV is less than the estimated PLF, the borrower could obtain an HECM. For HELOC and second lien borrowers, the ratio averages 0.643 (top panel) or 0.627 percent (bottom panel), which exceeds the estimated maximum PLF by an average of 0.186 (top panel) or 0.072 percent (bottom panel). At an expected interest rate of 4.75 percent and with the full origination fee, we estimate that 28 percent of HELOC and second lien borrowers could have obtained an HECM. At an expected rate of three percent with no origination fee, this proportion increases to about 40 percent of HELOC and second lien originations.

Across all loan types, we estimate that about 17 to 27 percent of older adults originating mortgages in 2018 could have obtained an HECM for the same loan amount obtained through a forward mortgage, corresponding to a total of 225,000 to 350,000 older adults. A key reason that a majority of borrowers may be choosing a traditional mortgage is simply that they are borrowing too much money to choose an HECM. In other words, the large required debt means that an HECM was not an option for at least three-quarters of older mortgage borrowers in 2018.

Equally interesting is that roughly the same proportion of *rejected borrowers* may have qualified for an HECM as for actual borrowers. The simulations in the right hand columns of Table 13.3 indicate that 17 to 25 percent of denied forward mortgage borrowers would have sufficient home equity to originate an HECM at their requested loan amount, corresponding to 98,000 to 147,000 older adults. For the rejected borrowers, an HECM would have made the difference between getting and not getting a mortgage, while at the same time eliminating the required mortgage payment.

Next, we examine the characteristics of forward mortgage applicants who originated or were rejected for loans, but who had sufficient home equity to obtain an HECM for the requested loan amount at an expected interest rate of 3 percent and no origination fee.[18] Table 13.4 reports summary statistics for originated loans (left hand columns) and rejected borrowers (right hand columns). Both groups had lower LTVs than average for the loan type, which is not surprising given that the HECM LTVs are lower than those of other mortgages that require principal and interest payments.

Nonetheless, an HECM could have helped many of the borrowers and rejected applicants. For rejected borrowers, nearly half were denied the loan because the resulting DTI ratio from having a monthly mortgage payment would have been too high. Based on HMDA characteristics, 56 to 66 percent of the rejected applicants would have a DTI of 41 percent or more if they obtained a forward mortgage. Even among those who took out a new mortgage, 28 to 32 percent had DTIs greater than 41 percent, leverage ratios that are very high for borrowers at retirement age and likely to have reductions in income as they get older and possibly become unable to work. Aside from having very high DTI ratios, rejected applicants were also older, more likely to be Black or Hispanic, and from lower income census tracts compared to the full population of forward mortgage borrowers.

Summary of Findings

In conclusion, five key findings are worth noting: (1) Older (forward) mortgage borrowers tend to be taking on quite a bit of debt, with an average LTV of 55 (HELOC or second liens) to 78 percent (purchase mortgages). (2) Mortgage rates are similar for HECMs relative to other cash-out refinancing and traditional mortgage types, almost all averaging 4.8 to 5.9 percent, although reverse mortgages are much more likely to be adjustable versus fixed rate. (3) Reverse mortgage borrowers are almost twice as likely to be single women (40%) compared to other older mortgage borrowers, have a similar share of minority borrowers, and live in slightly higher income communities relative to the MSA median. (4) Only 17 to 27 percent of actual and rejected borrowers would have qualified for an HECM, depending on the interest rate and closing costs of the HECM, though this would represent 301,000 to 460,000 borrowers, it is still nine to 14 times the size of the actual HECM market. Even the number of rejected traditional mortgage borrowers who might have obtained an HECM was 2.6 to 3.9 times the actual number of reverse mortgage borrowers. (5) A large share of actual and rejected borrowers had very high DTI ratios, with 71 percent of rejected borrowers and 40 percent of actual borrowers having a DTI over 36 percent. An HECM could have substantially lowered debt payments for this group.

TABLE 13.4 Summary characteristics of 2018 Home Mortgage Disclosure Act applicants, would qualify for Home Equity Conversion Mortgage at 3.0 rate

	Originated				Denied			
	HELOC or second	Cash-out first lien	Refinance no cash	Purchase mort-gage	HELOC or second	Cash-out first lien	Refinance no cash	Purchase mortgage
Estimated HECM Loan Characteristics								
Estimated HECM total up-front costs	14,367	14,367	14,043	14,614	9,443	9,056	9,705	9,292
Mortgage debt to be laid off with HECM	28,151	2,886	9,426	1,199	29,820	2,840	12,106	2,074
Estimated loan amount with HECM	121,877	137,240	126,119	146,099	116,158	127,654	136,829	140,483
Estimated HECM loan to value or MCA	0.352	0.393	0.378	0.416	0.341	0.394	0.391	0.419

Continued

TABLE 13-4 *Continued*

	Originated				Denied			
	HELOC or second	Cash-out first lien	Refinance no cash	Purchase mortgage	HELOC or second	Cash-out first lien	Refinance no cash	Purchase mortgage
Reasons for Denial								
Reason for denial: credit history					0.453	0.31	0.279	0.18
Reason for denial: debt to income					0.489	0.33	0.448	0.391
Select HMDA Characteristics								
Loan amount (or IPL for reverse mortgage)	84,159	124,789	107,360	135,290	76,895	115,757	115,018	129,116
Property value	392,938	387,937	378,220	366,373	411,596	362,212	414,666	367,910
Combined loan to value ratio	0.303	0.346	0.33	0.375	0.291	0.345	0.341	0.373
Loan to value ratio for this loan	0.243	0.345	0.313	0.379	0.229	0.345	0.321	0.377

Interest rate	4.933	4.596	4.402	4.548	.	.	.	.
Interest rate spread	0.212	0.593	0.157	0.361	.	.	.	.
Total loan costs	266	2,916	2,151	3,259	.	.	.	
Percent reporting total loan costs	0.048	0.954	0.488	0.973	0	0	0	0
Black or Hispanic	0.101	0.141	0.099	0.079	0.262	0.219	0.192	0.143
Borrower gender: single female	0.273	0.294	0.264	0.262	0.366	0.323	0.339	0.307

Continued

TABLE 13-4 Continued

	Originated				Denied			
	HELOC or second	Cash-out first lien	Refinance no cash	Purchase mortgage	HELOC or second	Cash-out first lien	Refinance no cash	Purchase mortgage
Borrower gender: single male	0.186	0.201	0.178	0.146	0.289	0.319	0.273	0.214
Borrower gender: joint female and male	0.489	0.424	0.499	0.537	0.299	0.268	0.313	0.389
DTI <36%	0.528	0.476	0.545	0.536	0.259	0.318	0.26	0.308
DTI 36-41%	0.178	0.201	0.167	0.183	0.08	0.116	0.087	0.106
DTI >41%	0.294	0.323	0.288	0.281	0.66	0.566	0.653	0.586
Income used for underwriting	85.339	95.983	81.46	172.578	63.702	57.666	58.215	65.481
Census tract % minority	24.953	30.44	24.762	22.963	37.041	35.772	33.29	24.814
MSA median family income	76,359	75,855	76,507	73,423	75,945	73,784	77,235	66,359
Census tract income to MSA income %	118.7	114.5	118.2	121.3	110.9	107.6	113.2	105.7
Observations	106,016	84,555	93,595	46,277	66,973	29,539	30,927	2,869

Source: Authors' calculations from 2018 HMDA data.

What about older borrowers with an existing mortgage?

In other work, Moulton and Haurin (2019) examined the potential size of the HECM market among older Americans with a mortgage. They found that in 2016, at least half of existing older homeowners with a mortgage would have been able to take out an HECM: at least five million households in total. This much larger group was still making mortgage payments, although only a minority appeared to have a DTI as high as the new mortgage borrowers in our sample above.

Why Older People Do Not Use Reverse Mortgages

The large proportion of older adults for whom home equity is their primary source of wealth, combined with growing levels of consumer and mortgage debt held by older adults—and resulting increases in their DTI burden—presents a puzzle: why do older adults in the US not turn to reverse mortgages more often? In this section, we consider several reasons why this may be the case, including why people may be reluctant to spend down home equity generally in retirement as well as reasons specific to the institutional features of the American reverse mortgage market.

Reluctance to consume home equity in retirement

It is well-established that people tend to not spend down their wealth in retirement as would be predicted by a simple life cycle hypothesis (Modigliani and Brumberg 1954; De Nardi, French, and Jones 2010, 2016; Lockwood 2018). Housing wealth is no exception, and in fact it tends to be the last asset consumed, typically only near the end of life following a major health event or the death of a spouse (Venti and Wise 1990, 2004; Poterba et al. 2011, 2017; Mayer 2017; Englehardt and Eriksen 2019). Financial wealth is more liquid and accessible than housing wealth, without the transaction costs of selling the home or taking out a loan. There are also numerous financial and tax incentives to spend down financial wealth before housing wealth, including housing wealth being treated more favorably by tax policy when left as a bequest.

The economics literature generally suggests two interrelated reasons for holding on to wealth in retirement: (1) precautionary savings for uncertain health costs, including long-term care; and (2) Importantly, these motivations do not necessarily preclude borrowing from home equity in retirement. For example, retaining home equity as precautionary savings for major health expenses suggests that homeowners anticipate being able to liquidate home equity when a health shock occurs. Nevertheless, such motivations may help explain the timing and nature of home equity consumption in retirement.

Health costs in retirement can be considerable. While the majority of older adults receive Medicare, nearly 20 percent of health expenditures are paid for as out-of-pocket costs (De Nardi, French, Jones, and McCauley 2016). Recent estimates indicate that the average 65-year-old man or woman needs $72,000 or $93,000 (respectively) to have a 50 percent chance of being able to cover necessary health expenses in retirement; for those who experience major health shocks, this could exceed $350,000 (Fronstin and VanDerhei 2017). Further, more than half of older adults will require long-term care in a nursing home or at home prior to death (Favreault and Dey 2015; Hurd et al. 2013, with average lifetime costs of $133,700 in 2015 dollars (Favreault and Dey 2015).

Despite these risks, few households purchase long-term care insurance; instead viewing home equity as a precautionary saving to cover such costs if they do arise (Costa-Font et al. 2018; Davidoff 2010). Indeed, evidence indicates that home equity is one of the main resources used to pay for long-term care in the US (Costa-Font et al. 2018), with Medicaid covering costs for 60 percent of nursing home residents (Borella et al. 2018). Medicaid policy further incentivizes older homeowners to hold assets in the form of home equity rather than as liquid wealth. To qualify for Medicaid, households must spend down their financial assets to a minimum set by states, typically around $2,000, but home equity is typically exempt from eligibility thresholds (Ricks 2018). Therefore, older adults with a high probability of needing long-term care (and potentially having to rely on Medicaid to pay for such services) may have a strategic incentive to spend down or transfer financial wealth, and to save remaining wealth in the form of home equity.

In line with a precautionary savings motive, recent studies document a decline in home equity after a health shock (Gilligan et al. 2018; Gupta et al. 2018; Poterba et al. 2018), with home equity being second only to formal health insurance for financing health-related consumption after a health shock in later life (Dalton and LaFave 2017). The ability to access home equity is also linked to better health outcomes. In an analysis of cancer patients, Gupta et al. (2018) found that cancer patients who borrowed from their home equity were 23 percent were more likely to perform necessary treatments and had lower rates of mortality than those who did not borrow from home equity.

In addition, a desire to leave a bequest to heirs may prevent spending from home equity in retirement; in fact, this need not be a separate motivation and can actually reinforce precautionary savings. For example, adults who intend to leave a bequest but are uncertain of their future health risks may prefer to self-insure through precautionary savings rather than purchase long-term care insurance or spend down their financial assets to qualify for Medicaid (Lockwood 2018).

Whether intended or unintended, a large proportion of older adults do leave home equity to their heirs when they die: bequests from home equity totaled an estimated $90 to $100 billion per year from 1992 to 2014 (Englehardt and Erikson 2019). Several economists have estimated structural models to parse out the importance of an intentional bequest motive, relative to other factors that might lead older adults to retain wealth in retirement (De Nardi, French, and Jones 2010, 2016; Ameriks et al. 2011; De Nardi, French, Jones, and McCauley 2016; Lockwood 2018; Nakajima and Telyukova 2020). These models generally indicate that, while bequests are certainly an important factor in explaining wealth holding, they do not explain everything. For instance, Nakajima and Telyukova (2020) estimated that bequest motives explained about 7 to 28 percent of median net worth in retirement, depending on the individual's age—well below the amount of home equity left to heirs at death.

Structural models estimating demand for reverse mortgages predict higher home equity use for those with weaker bequest motives, elders who have low levels of financial wealth relative to housing wealth, and for those with relatively high levels of pre-existing debt (Nakajima and Telyukova 2017; Cocco and Lopes 2019). Health expenditures are complicated: on the one hand, those with high uncertainty regarding future health costs are predicted to retain home equity as precautionary savings. On the other hand, those with high health expenditures due to underlying health conditions or the onset of a health shock may have a higher demand for borrowing through a reverse mortgage to help pay for health-related expenses (Nakajima and Telyukova 2017).

Despite a general tendency to hold more wealth than would be predicted following a life cycle model, as demonstrated above, older adults can and do extract equity in retirement—they just more commonly use other debt instruments rather than reverse mortgages to do so. As we discussed earlier, this is not the case in some countries like the UK or Canada, where equity release products are much more widely used by older borrowers. Furthermore, these countries saw sharp rises in the use of equity release through 2019, a pattern similar to the large growth of reverse mortgages in the US through 2009; nevertheless, the growth in Canada and the UK occurred during an economic boom, versus during a downturn in the US. The uneven economic pattern combined with sharp increases and decreases in equity release usage over a few years is inconsistent with a bequest motive or precautionary savings as the main explanation for why US retirees do not choose equity release more often. This raises questions about the institutional features of reverse mortgages and the market in the US that may be impeding their use.

Institutional features of reverse mortgages in the US

One longstanding claim is that high costs limit demand for reverse mortgages; in particular, there are substantial costs associated with taking out these loans (Lucas 2015; Nakajima and Telyukova 2017). Traditional reverse mortgages do carry up-front costs that are larger than up-front costs associated with other home equity borrowing options. For HECMs, this is primarily due to the up-front MIP charged by HUD, which is currently set at 2 percent of the value of the home.[19] Yet it is not clear that the MIP is excessive, or that it is driving down demand for HECMs.

In an analysis of reverse mortgage costs, Davidoff (2012) found that the ability of a borrower to walk away from negative equity (the 'put option' embedded in the HECM) was worth more than the cost of the mortgage insurance, if borrowers used the product to the maximum. It could be that borrowers do not value the embedded put option, as they typically do not extract all remaining equity and default on the loan when house prices fall (Davidoff and Wetzel 2014). If this were the case, then one would expect demand to rise if the MIP were reduced or eliminated. Yet from 2010 through 2013, there was little demand for a 'Saver' version of the HECM product with a negligible up-front MIP. This does not imply that high up-front costs might not be part of the equation for low demand, but it certainly does not seem to be the driving factor. In a survey of older homeowners who considered but did not originate a reverse mortgage, 26 percent indicated high costs being a factor behind their decision: the same proportion that indicated a desire to leave their home as a bequest as a reason for not taking a reverse mortgage (Moulton et al. 2017).

Another possibility is that the interest rate charged to borrowers is too high, with the spread between the cost of credit to the lender ranging between one and three percent (Lucas 2015). But as noted in the previous section, interest rates on reverse mortgages, including the ongoing MIP, were quite similar to those on other more commonly used traditional mortgage products, including HELOCs, cash-out or straight refinancings, and purchase mortgages. Also, borrowers in traditional mortgages paid closing costs that ranged from zero (HELOC) to two percent (cash-out refinancing) of total proceeds. Reverse mortgage origination costs are much higher, especially because they include an up-front MIP charged by the FHA equal to two percent of the MCA (home value) plus an origination fee that is capped at $2,500 to $6,000, depending on home value.

To do an apples-to-apples comparison of the impact of higher up-front charges on the total cost of the mortgage, we added the up-front cost to the mortgage balance and then computed the increase in the imputed interest rate required to pay those costs over the life of the loan (assumed to be 12 years). A similar calculation is often presented to borrowers at closing, called the TALC (total annual loan cost). While HMDA does not report the actual value of the closing costs and the origination fee charged, we ran two scenarios, one with a higher rate (4.75%) plus maximum charges for the origination fee, and a second scenario with a lower rate (3.0%) and no origination fee. In both cases, the mortgage borrower would also pay a 0.5 percent annual MIP. In the case of the high-rate loan, the cost increased from 5.3 to 6.6 percent, an increase of 1.3 percentage points. For the low-cost loan, the rate increased from about 3.5 to 4.1 percent, about 0.6 percentage points per year.

By comparison, in the UK, where in 2019 equity release mortgages represented about 36 percent of total mortgage originations for borrowers age 55+, the quoted mortgage rate was 5.21 percent versus a rate of 2.66 percent on a 75 percent LTV 10-year fixed rate mortgage, an annual spread of almost 2.6 percent (before considering any difference in origination costs for an equity release mortgage). From 2017 to 2019, that spread was nearly constant, even as the equity release market grew 32 percent. So higher costs of equity release, at least in the UK, were not an appreciable impairment to much faster growth than in the US.

Aside from the costs of reverse mortgages, other barriers to demand include lack of accurate information about how reverse mortgages work, combined with generally negative product perceptions. In a survey of a random sample of older adults in the US population, Davidoff et al. (2017) found older adults were generally aware of reverse mortgages but had inaccurate information about how they worked. For example, only 56 percent answered correctly that the borrower can stay in the home if the loan balance exceeds the value of the home. Their results also indicated a significant and positive relationship between having accurate knowledge of the product and the stated intention to use a reverse mortgage in the future.

According to a Fannie Mae National Housing Survey (2016), 49 percent of homeowners age 55+ were familiar with reverse mortgages, and only six percent of homeowners indicated preferring reverse mortgages to extract equity. Twenty percent of the homeowners who were familiar with reverse mortgages reported that the risk of being scammed was their biggest concern about reverse mortgages.

Further, lending to an aging population where death is often the way that the mortgage resolves, creates the potential for headline risk, exacerbating negative public perceptions and discouraging larger institutional actors from participating in the market. A 2018 industry survey of lending institutions indicated that reputational risk was the leading reason that certain banks did not originate reverse mortgages (Cameron 2018). Headline risks can be lowered by reducing the threat of evicting a borrower while alive, such as for failure to pay property taxes (preventative servicing), maintaining good communication with heirs, etc.

Of course, there is also one other appreciable common factor in the UK growth after 2012 and in the US up to 2011: the impact of large brand name financial institutions selling reverse mortgages. In the US, during the growth and in peak years, banks such as Wells Fargo, Bank of America, and BNY Mellon, as well as the insurance company MetLife, were in the reverse mortgage business. In the UK, large, brand name insurers and asset managers such as Aviva, Legal and General, and Canada Life, sell equity release products. In addition, in the UK, financial planners may also sell (and earn commissions from) reverse mortgages as long as they have an appropriate license, which American financial planners almost never obtain. In the US, the exit from the market of brand name financial services firms was followed by an appreciable decline in originations of the HECM product.

Conclusion

This chapter has examined the usage of reverse mortgages among mortgage borrowers age 62+, as well as looking at reasons for applicants, of the same age, being rejected for new mortgage credit. We find that 17 to 27 percent of actual and rejected borrowers would likely have qualified for an HECM, depending on the interest rate and closing costs. This group of 301,000 to 460,000 borrowers is nine to 14 times the size of the actual HECM market. These potential borrowers chose another product (or were rejected from their preferred product) despite having very high DTI ratios of 36 to more than 50 percent in the case of half or more of the sample. Among seniors with an existing mortgage, at least five million could have used a reverse mortgage to eliminate mortgage payments.

The existence of a large number of seniors with an existing mortgage or taking out new mortgages with quite high LTVs (an average of 55 to 78% combined LTV, depending on the product) suggests that many seniors do, in fact, utilize home equity in order to fund their retirement. However, they choose products that require monthly payments that last decades into retirement and rise as a share of (falling) income as they get older. Of course, the puzzle remains for home equity as for other savings, as to why seniors enter retirement with fewer assets than the life cycle model would predict and spend less in retirement than the model implies would be optimal.

We consider a number of possible explanations for why American seniors do not use reverse mortgages to spend home equity and instead rely on loans with high required monthly payments, reasons which include precautionary savings for health shocks, bequest motives, high costs of reverse mortgages, and the lack of brand name institutions in the reverse mortgage business. We show that equity release products have exhibited enormous growth in the last decade in Canada and the UK, the latter of which has an active market that includes large insurance companies. In the US, the reverse mortgage market hit its peak at a time when brand name financial institutions sold the product to the public. Thus, it appears that institutional barriers that discourage entry by brand name companies may be an important factor limiting the distribution of reverse mortgages in the US.

Of course, this then raises the question as to why these companies do not enter the reverse mortgage business. One possibility is the negative reputation of reverse mortgages, which may discourage companies sensitive to their brands. Policies by the US government in the HECM program that require foreclosures as a way to resolve the failure to pay T&I suggest the potential for appreciable headline risk. By comparison, in the UK, foreclosures to resolve T&I defaults are nearly non-existent. In the US, regulation also restricts financial planners or insurers from selling reverse mortgages without obtaining a mortgage origination license. Such licensing is time consuming, expensive, and has potential legal risks associated with cross-selling different products. In the future, the continued rise of fee-based planners who are paid for advice rather than product sales could spur planners to consider home equity as part of the planning process. Finally, the adoption of a fiduciary or 'best interest' standard might also move planners to consider housing in the planning process.

Acknowledgements

Mayer is also CEO of Longbridge Financial, a reverse mortgage lender. The authors wish to thank Michael McCully for helpful comments and data.

Endnotes

1. See, for example, Goodman et al. (2017); Lusardi et al. (2017, 2020); Mayer (2017); and Brown et al. (2020).
2. Authors' calculations using the 1992–2016 Survey of Consumer Finances in 2016 dollars (Goodman et al. 2017).
3. See Goodman et al. (2017) and Haurin et al. (2019).
4. In one survey (EBRI 2019), eight in 10 workers reported that they expected to work in retirement, but only 28 percent of retirees actually work for pay.
5. While we do not have formal data, equity release issuance in Australia has declined in recent years as some larger banks exited the market. Germany, Ireland, Italy, Portugal, and Spain have small markets with fewer than five lenders. Norway has between five and 10 lenders (EY 2020).
6. We report some data on private-label reverse mortgages in the empirical work that follows for 2018.
7. The MCA is subject to a cap, which was $679,650 in 2018, but lower in previous years.
8. Data on the UK from Equity Release Council, 2018 and 2019 market reports.
9. Approximately 600,000 HECMs are outstanding today out of a pool of approximately 26 million elderly homeowners age 65+. Factoring in those age 62–64 probably lowers the number by about 10 percent.

10. These new reporting requirements were added by the Consumer Financial Protection Bureau through a 2015 HMDA rule that amended Regulation C (HMDA's implementing legislation). The new reporting requirements first went into effect with the 2018 HMDA data release. Not all lenders are required to report under HMDA, with exemptions for smaller institutions and those originating a small number of loans in the prior two years (CFPB 2019).

11. A small number of proprietary reverse mortgages are offered to borrowers age 60+, but these private-label products were quite rare in 2018 and available in only a handful of states.

12. An estimated eight percent of all homes in 2019 according authors calculations using data from Zillow.

13. While the FHA data indicate that 41,690 HECM loans were endorsed by HUD in 2018, the number originated in 2018 is smaller (endorsements typically occur one to two months after closing). Based on a one-month lag between loan closing and endorsement, we estimate that about 37,000 HECM loans closed during the 2018 calendar year. The 2018 HMDA data thus represents about 85 percent of HECM loans closed.

14. To correct for HMDA reporting errors, we merged in the PLF from HUD data using the borrower's age and interest rate in HMDA. If the lender reported loan amount (property value or loan limit) was 0.1 percentage points smaller or larger than the PLF, we replaced the lender reported loan amount with an estimated IPL using the HUD PLF. This resulted in the replacement of about 26 percent of reported HECM loan amounts in the 2018 HMDA data. Most of the replaced loan amounts were much smaller than the IPL, and likely reflected misreporting of the loan amount as the initial draw amount rather than the IPL.

15. This is called a Life Expectancy Set Aside (LESA) and is used by between five and 10 percent of HECM borrowers.

16. HUD sets the maximum lender origination fee to be two percent of the first $200,000 of property value or $2,500 (whichever is greater), plus one percent of additional property value above $200,000, with a maximum of $6,000.

17. Closing costs vary widely by state and mortgage amount and can be higher in states with a mortgage recording tax, for example, in Florida.

18. The characteristics are quite similar for those who would have qualified at the 3 and 4.75 percent rate groups, so we presented the former group to economize on tables. Results are available for the 4.75 percent group upon request.

19. The lender origination fee of $2,500 to $6,000 is another potential up-front cost. However, this is negotiable, and can be reduced or eliminated depending on the market and the circumstances of the borrower.

References

Ameriks, J., A. Caplin, S. Laufer, and S. Van Nieuwerburgh. (2011). 'The Joy of Giving or Assisted Living? Using Strategic Surveys to Separate Public Care Aversion from Bequest Motives,' Journal of Finance, 66: 519–561.

Begley, J. and S. Chan (2019). 'Understanding Older Adult Mobility Decisions: The Role of Children,' Working Paper. New York, NY: NYU Furman Center for Real Estate and Urban Policy.

Binette, J. and K. Vasold (2018). *Home and Community Preferences: A National Survey of Adults Age 18-Plus.* Washington, DC: AARP. August: https://doi.org/10.26419/res.00231.001

Borella, M., M. De Nardi, and E. French (2018). 'Who Receives Medicaid in Old Age? Rules and Reality,' *Fiscal Studies*, 39(1): 65–93.

Brown, M., D. Lee, J. Scally, and W. van der Klaauw (2020). 'The Graying of American Debt,' in O. S. Mitchell and A. Lusardi, eds., *Remaking Retirement: Debt in an Aging Economy*. Oxford: Oxford University Press, pp. 35–59.

Cameron, J. (2018). 'Moving Forward in Reverse,' Stratmor Group Insight Report, February. https://www.stratmorgroup.com/insights_article/moving-forward-in-reverse/

CFPB (Consumer Financial Protection Bureau) (2019). 'Introducing New and Revised Data Points in HMDA,' OIG, Washington, DC, August 30. https://www.consumerfinance.gov/data-research/research-reports/introducing-new-revised-data-points-hmda/

Cocco, J. F. and P. Lopes (2019). 'Aging in Place, Housing Maintenance, and Reverse Mortgages,' *The Review of Economic Studies*, 87(4): 1799–1836. https://doi.org/10.1093/restud/rdz047

Costa-Font, J., R. G. Frank, and K. Swartz (2018). 'Access to Long Term Care after a Wealth Shock: Evidence from the Housing Bubble and Burst,' NBER Working Paper No. 23781. Cambridge, MA: National Bureau of Economic Research.

Dalton, M. and D. LaFave (2017). 'Mitigating the Consequences of a Health Condition: The Role of Intra-and Interhousehold Assistance,' *Journal of Health Economics*, 53: 38–52.

Davidoff, T. (2010). 'Home Equity Commitment and Long-term Care Insurance Demand,' *Journal of Public Economics*, 94(1): 44–49.

Davidoff, T. (2012). 'Can 'High Costs' Justify Weak Demand for the Home Equity Conversion Mortgage?' *The Review of Financial Studies*, 28(8): 2364-98.

Davidoff, T., P. Gerhard, and T. Post (2017). 'Reverse Mortgages: What Homeowners (Don't) Know and How it Matters,' *Journal of Economic Behavior and Organization*, 133: 151–171.

Davidoff, T. and J. Wetzel (2014). 'Do Reverse Mortgage Borrowers Use Credit Ruthlessly?' University of British Columbia Working Paper (July 22). https://papers.ssrn.com/sol3/papers.cfm?abstract_id=2279930

De Nardi, M., E. French, and J. B. Jones (2010). 'Why Do the Elderly Save? The Role of Medical Expenses,' *Journal of Political Economy*, 118: 38–75.

De Nardi, M., E. French, and J.B. Jones (2016). 'Savings after Retirement: A Survey,' *Annual Review of Economics*, 8: 177–204.

De Nardi, M., E. French, J.B. Jones, and J. McCauley. (2016). 'Medical Spending of the US Elderly,' *Fiscal Studies*, 37(3–4): 717–747.

EBRI (Employee Benefit Research Institute) (2019). *2019 Retirement Confidence Survey Summary Report*. Washington, DC: EBRI.

Englehardt, G. and M. Eriksen (2019). 'Homeownership in Old Age and at the End of Life,' Presented at the Symposium for Housing Tenure and Financial Security, Fannie Mae and the Joint Center for Housing Studies, Harvard University, Cambridge, MA, March.

EY (Ernst & Young Global Limited) (2020). *2020 Global Equity Release Roundtable Survey*. London: Ernst & Young Global Limited.

Fannie Mae (2016). 'Older Homeowners: Accessing Home Equity in Retirement,' National Housing Survey, Topic Analysis, Q2. http://www.fanniemae.com/resources/file/research/housingsurvey/pdf/Q2-2016-accessing-home-equity-in-retirement.pdf

Favreault, M. and J. Dey (2015). 'Long-Term Services and Supports for Older Americans: Risks and Financing Research Brief, Office of the Assistant Secretary for Planning and Evaluation, US Department of Health and Human Services, Washington, DC. https://aspe.hhs.gov/basic-report/ong-term-services-and-supports-older-americans-risksand-financing-research-brief

Fisher, J. D. (2019). 'Who Files for Personal Bankruptcy in the United States?' *The Journal of Consumer Affairs*, 53(4): 2003-26.

Fronstin, P. and J. Van Derhei (2017). 'Savings Medicare Beneficiaries Need for Health Expenses: Some Couples Could Need as Much as $350,000,' *EBRI Notes*, 38: 1

Gilligan, A. M., D. S. Alberts, D. J. Roe, and G. H. Skrepnek (2018). 'Death or Debt? National Estimates of Financial Toxicity in Persons with Newly-diagnosed Cancer,' *The American Journal of Medicine*, 131(10): 1187–1195.

Goodman, L., K. Kaul, and J. Zhu (2017). 'What the 2016 Survey of Consumer Finances Tells Us about Senior Homeowners,' Urban Institute Research Report, November. https://www.urban.org/sites/default/files/publication/94526/what-the-2016-survey-of-consumer-finances-tells-us-about-senior-homeowners.pdf

Goodman, L. and C. Mayer (2018). 'Homeownership and the American Dream,' *Journal of Economic Perspectives*, 32(1) Winter: 31–58.

Gupta, A., E. R. Morrison, C. R. Fedorenko, and S. D. Ramsey (2018). 'Home Equity Mitigates the Financial and Mortality Consequences of Health Shocks: Evidence from Cancer Diagnosis.' Working Paper: New York University, Stern School of Business.

Haurin, D., C. Loibl, and S. Moulton (2019). 'Debt Stress and Mortgage Borrowing in Older Age: Implications for Economic Security in Retirement,' Working Paper prepared for the Retirement Disability Research Consortium. Madison: University of Wisconsin.

Haurin, D. R. and S. Moulton (2017). 'International Perspectives on Homeownership and Home Equity Extraction by Senior Households,' Ohio State University Working Paper, June 5: https://ssrn.com/abstract=2985917

Hurd, M., P.-C. Michaud, and S. Rohwedder (2013). 'The Lifetime Risk of Nursing Home Use.' *National Bureau of Economic Research*. Microsoft Word - Lifetime NH_Hurd_Michaud_Rohwedder.docx (nber.org)

Li, W. and M. White (2020). 'Financial Distress among the Elderly: Bankruptcy Reform and the Financial Crisis.' In O. S. Mitchell and A. Lusardi, eds, *Remaking Retirement: Debt in an Aging Economy*. Oxford: Oxford University Press, pp. 89–105.

Lockwood, L. M. (2018). 'Incidental Bequests and the Choice to Self-insure Late-life Risks,' *American Economic Review*, 108(9): 2513–2550.

Lucas, D. (2015). 'Hacking Reverse Mortgages,' MIT Center for Financial Policy Working Paper. Cambridge, MA: Massachusetts Institute of Technology. http://gcfp.mit.edu/wp-content/uploads/2013/08/ReverseMortgagesV10.pdf

Lusardi, A., O. S. Mitchell, and N. Oggero (2017). 'Debt and Financial Vulnerability on the Verge of Retirement,' NBER Working Paper No. w23664. Cambridge, MA: National Bureau of Economic Research.

Lusardi, A., O.S. Mitchell, and N. Oggero (2020). 'Debt Close to Retirement and its Implications for Retirement Wellbeing,' in O. S. Mitchell and A. Lusardi, eds., *Remaking Retirement: Debt in an Aging Economy*. Oxford: Oxford University Press, pp. 15–34.

Mayer, C. (2017). 'Housing, Mortgages, and Retirement,' in L. Fennell and B. Keys, eds., *Evidence and Innovation in Housing Law and Policy*. New York: Cambridge University Press, pp. 203-30.

Modigliani, F. and R. H. Brumberg (1954). 'Utility Analysis and the Consumption Function: An Interpretation of Cross-section Data,' Iin K. Kurihara, ed., *Post-Keynesian Economics*. New Brunswick, NJ: Rutgers University Press, pp. 388–436.

Moulton, S., S. Dodini, D. R. Haurin, and M. D. Schmeiser (2019). 'Seniors' Home Equity Extraction: Credit Constraints and Borrowing Channels,' Ohio State University Working Paper, June 25. https://papers.ssrn.com/sol3/papers.cfm?abstract_id=2727204

Moulton, S. and D. Haurin (2019). 'Unlocking Housing Wealth for Older Americans: Strategies to Improve Reverse Mortgages,' Brookings Economic Studies Working Paper, October. https://www.brookings.edu/wp-content/uploads/2019/10/ES_20191016_MoultonHaurin_ReverseMortgages.pdf

Moulton, S., C. Loibl, and Haurin, D. (2017). 'Reverse Mortgage Motivations and Outcomes: Insights from Survey Data.' *CityScape*, 19(1), 73-98.

Nakajima, M. and I. A. Telyukova (2017). 'Reverse Mortgage Loans: A Quantitative Analysis,' *The Journal of Finance*, 72(2): 911–950.

Nakajima, M. and I. A. Telyukova (2020) 'Home Equity in Retirement,' *International Economic Review*, 61(2): 573-616.

NRMLA (National Reverse Mortgage Lenders Association) (2020). 'Senior Housing Wealth Reaches Record $7.23 Trillion,' April 3. https://www.nrmlaonline.org/about/press-releases/senior-housing-wealth-reaches-record-7-23-trillion

Poterba, J. and S. Venti (2017). 'Financial Well-being in Late Life: Understanding the Impact of Adverse Health Shocks and Spousal Deaths,' Prepared for the 19th Annual Joint Meeting of the Retirement Research Consortium, August 3–4. Washington, DC. http://crr.bc.edu/wp-content/uploads/2017/08/4a.-James-Poterba.pdf

Poterba, J., S. Venti, and D. Wise (2011). 'The Composition and Drawdown of Wealth in Retirement,' *Journal of Economic Perspectives*, 25(4) Fall: 95–118.

Poterba, J., S. Venti, and D. Wise (2017). 'What Determines End-of-life Assets: A Retrospective View,' in D. Wise, ed., *Insights in the Economics of Aging*. Chicago, IL: University of Chicago Press, pp. 127–157.

Poterba, J., S. Venti, and D. Wise (2018). 'Longitudinal Determinants of End-of-life Wealth Inequality,' *Journal of Public Economics*, 162: 78–88.

Rexrode, C. (2020). 'Over 60 with Decades Left on the Mortgage: The New Retirement Math,' *Wall Street Journal*, April 11. https://www.wsj.com/articles/over-60-with-decades-left-on-the-mortgage-the-new-retirement-math–11586556588

Ricks, J. S. (2018). 'Homeowner Behavior, Health Status, and Medicaid Payment Eligibility: Evidence from the Deficit Reduction Act of 2005.' *Journal of Policy Analysis and Management*, 37(4) 732–54.

Venti, S. and D. Wise (1990). 'But They Don't Want to Reduce Housing Equity,' in D. Wise, ed., *Issues in the Economics of Aging*. Chicago, IL: University of Chicago Press, pp. 13–29.

Venti, S. and D. Wise (2004). 'Aging and Housing Equity: Another Look,' in D. Wise, ed., *Perspectives on the Economics of Aging*. Chicago. IL: University of Chicago Press, pp. 127–181.

The Pension Research Council

The Pension Research Council is a research center at the Wharton School of the University of Pennsylvania committed to generating knowledge and debate on key policy issues affecting pensions and other employee benefits. For over 60 years, the Council has sponsored high-level analysis of private and public retirement security and related benefit plans around the world. Research projects are motivated by the need to address the long-term issues that underlie contemporary concerns about retirement system structures and resiliency. Members seek to broaden understanding of the complex economic, financial, social, actuarial, and legal foundations for and impacts of privately and publicly provided benefits. The Pension Research Council is a nonprofit organization, and contributions to it are tax-deductible. For more information about the Pension Research Council please visit http://www.pensionresearchcouncil.org.

The Boettner Center for Pensions and Retirement Research

Founded at the Wharton School to support scholarly research, teaching, and outreach on global aging, retirement, and public and private pensions, the Center is named after Joseph E. Boettner. Funding to the University of Pennsylvania was provided through the generosity of the Boettner family, whose intent was to spur financial well-being at older ages through work on how aging influences financial security and life satisfaction. The Center disseminates research and evaluation on challenges and opportunities associated with global aging and retirement, how to strengthen retirement income systems, saving and investment behavior of the young and the old, interactions between physical and mental health, and successful retirement. For more information, see http://www.pensionresearchcouncil.org/boettner/.

Executive Director

Olivia S. Mitchell, International Foundation of Employee Benefit Plans, Professor of Business Economics/Public Policy and Insurance/Risk Management, The Wharton School, University of Pennsylvania.

Advisory Board

Joel Dickson, The Vanguard Group, Malvern, PA
Peter A. Fisher, Cortus Advisors, Boston, MA
P. Brett Hammond, Capital Group, Los Angeles, CA
J. Mark Iwry, Brookings Institution, Washington, DC
Melissa Kahn, State Street Global Advisors, Washington, DC
Emily Kessler, Society of Actuaries, Schaumburg, IL
Surya P. Kolluri, Bank of America, Boston, MA
David I. Laibson, Department of Economics, Harvard University, Cambridge, MA
Annamaria Lusardi, School of Business, The George Washington University, Washington, DC
Jeannine Markoe Raymond, National Association of State Retirement Administrators, Washington, DC
Raimond Maurer, Finance Department, Goethe University, Frankfurt, Germany
Alicia H. Munnell, Caroll School of Management, Boston College, Chestnut Hill, MA
Michael Orszag, Willis Towers Watson, London, United Kingdom
Anna M. Rappaport, Anna Rappaport Consulting, Chicago, IL
Catherine Reilly, Smart Pension, Cambridge, MA
David P. Richardson, TIAA Institute, Charlotte, NC
John Sabelhaus, Washington Center for Equitable Growth, Washington, DC
Richard C. Shea, Covington & Burling, LLP, Washington, DC
Kent Smetters, Department of Business Economics and Public Policy, The Wharton School, University of Pennsylvania, Philadelphia, PA
Jack L. VanDerhei, Employee Benefit Research Institute, Washington, DC
Stephen P. Zeldes, Graduate School of Business, Columbia University, New York, NY

Members of the Pension Research Council

AARP
Almanac Reality Investors
Bank of America
Capital Group
Federal Reserve Employee Benefits System
FINRA Investor Education Foundation
International Foundation of Employee Benefit Plans
Investment Company Institute
J. P. Morgan Asset Management
Prudential Financial
Smart USA
State Street Global Advisors
T. Rowe Price
TIAA Institute
Willis Towers Watson
The Vanguard Group

Recent Pension Research Council Publications

Remaking Retirement: Debt in an Aging Economy. Olivia S. Mitchell and Annamaria Lusardi, eds. 2020. (ISBN 978-0-19-886752-4.)

The Disruptive Impact of FinTech on Retirement Systems. Julie Agnew and Olivia S. Mitchell, eds. 2019. (ISBN 978-0-19-884555-9.)

How Persistent Low Returns Will Shape Saving and Retirement. Olivia S. Mitchell, Robert Clark, and Raimond Maurer, eds. 2018. (ISBN 978-0-19-882744-3.)

Financial Decision Making and Retirement Security in an Aging World. Olivia S. Mitchell, P. Brett Hammond, and Stephen Utkus, eds. 2017. (ISBN 978-0-19-880803-9.)

Retirement System Risk Management: Implications of the New Regulatory Order. Olivia S. Mitchell, Raimond Maurer, and J. Michael Orszag, eds. 2016. (ISBN 978-0-19-878737-2.)

Reimagining Pensions: The Next 40 Years. Olivia S. Mitchell and Richard C. Shea, eds. 2016. (ISBN 978-0-19-875544-9.)

Recreating Sustainable Retirement. Olivia S. Mitchell, Raimond Maurer, and P. Brett Hammond, eds. 2014. (ISBN 0-19-871924-3.)

The Market for Retirement Financial Advice. Olivia S. Mitchell and Kent Smetters, eds. 2013. (ISBN 0-19-968377-2.)

Reshaping Retirement Security: Lessons from the Global Financial Crisis. Raimond Maurer, Olivia S. Mitchell, and Mark Warshawsky, eds. 2012. (ISBN 0-19-966069-7.)

Financial Literacy. Olivia S. Mitchell and Annamaria Lusardi, eds. 2011. (ISBN 0-19-969681-9.)

Securing Lifelong Retirement Income. Olivia S. Mitchell, John Piggott, and Noriyuki Takayama, eds. 2011. (ISBN 0-19-959484-9.)

Reorienting Retirement Risk Management. Robert L. Clark and Olivia S. Mitchell, eds. 2010. (ISBN 0-19-959260-9.)

Fundamentals of Private Pensions. Dan M. McGill, Kyle N. Brown, John J. Haley, Sylvester Schieber, and Mark J. Warshawsky. 9th Ed. 2010. (ISBN 0-19-954451-6.)

The Future of Public Employees Retirement Systems. Olivia S. Mitchell and Gary Anderson, eds. 2009. (ISBN 0-19-957334-9.)

Recalibrating Retirement Spending and Saving. John Ameriks and Olivia S. Mitchell, eds. 2008. (ISBN 0-19-954910-8.)

Lessons from Pension Reform in the Americas. Stephen J. Kay and Tapen Sinha, eds. 2008. (ISBN 0-19-922680-6.)

Redefining Retirement: How Will Boomers Fare? Brigitte Madrian, Olivia S. Mitchell, and Beth J. Soldo, eds. 2007. (ISBN 0-19-923077-3.)

Restructuring Retirement Risks. David Blitzstein, Olivia S. Mitchell, and Steven P. Utkus, eds. 2006. (ISBN 0-19-920465-9.)

Reinventing the Retirement Paradigm. Robert L. Clark and Olivia S. Mitchell, eds. 2005. (ISBN 0-19-928460-1.)

Pension Design and Structure: New Lessons from Behavioral Finance. Olivia S. Mitchell and Steven P. Utkus, eds. 2004. (ISBN 0-19-927339-1.)

The Pension Challenge: Risk Transfers and Retirement Income Security. Olivia S. Mitchell and Kent Smetters, eds. 2003. (ISBN 0-19-926691-3.)

A History of Public Sector Pensions in the United States. Robert L. Clark, Lee A. Craig, and Jack W. Wilson, eds. 2003. (ISBN 0-8122-3714-5.)

Benefits for the Workplace of the Future. Olivia S. Mitchell, David Blitzstein, Michael Gordon, and Judith Mazo, eds. 2003. (ISBN 0-8122-3708-0.)

Innovations in Retirement Financing. Olivia S. Mitchell, Zvi Bodie, P. Brett Hammond, and Stephen Zeldes, eds. 2002. (ISBN 0-8122-3641-6.)

To Retire or Not: Retirement Policy and Practice in Higher Education. Robert L. Clark and P. Brett Hammond, eds. 2001. (ISBN 0-8122-3572-X.)

Pensions in the Public Sector. Olivia S. Mitchell and Edwin Hustead, eds. 2001. (ISBN 0-8122-3578-9.)

Available from the Pension Research Council web site: http://www.pensionresearchcouncil.org/

Index

For the benefit of digital users, indexed terms that span two pages (e.g., 52–53) may, on occasion, appear on only one of those pages.